THE ACCIDENTAL INVASION OF BAGHDAD ZOO

Copyright © 2021 Brendan Whittington-Jones

All rights reserved

The events portrayed in this book are as I remembered them. Any similarity to real persons, living or dead, is coincidental if those persons are offended.

No part of this book may be reproduced, or stored in a retrieval system, or transmitted in any form or by any means, electronic, mechanical, photocopying, recording, or otherwise, without express written permission of the author.

ISBN: 9798597354132

Cover design and illustration by: Robert Durrant

Printed in the United States of America

CONTENTS

Title Page
Copyright
Preface   1
PART 1: Embracing chaos and other ill-advised project management strategies   5
Chapter 1   6
Chapter 2   17
Chapter 3   65
Chapter 4   94
Chapter 5   127
Chapter 6   153
Chapter 7   185
Chapter 8   203
PART 2: Tea and death in Margaritaville   233
Chapter 9   234
Chapter 10   250

Chapter 11	257
Chapter 12	296
Chapter 13	323
PART 3: Fear, guilt, hope and duct-taping lions	365
Chapter 14	366
Chapter 15	379
Chapter 16	412
Epilogue – Beyond 2004	421
Gratitude	435
References	437

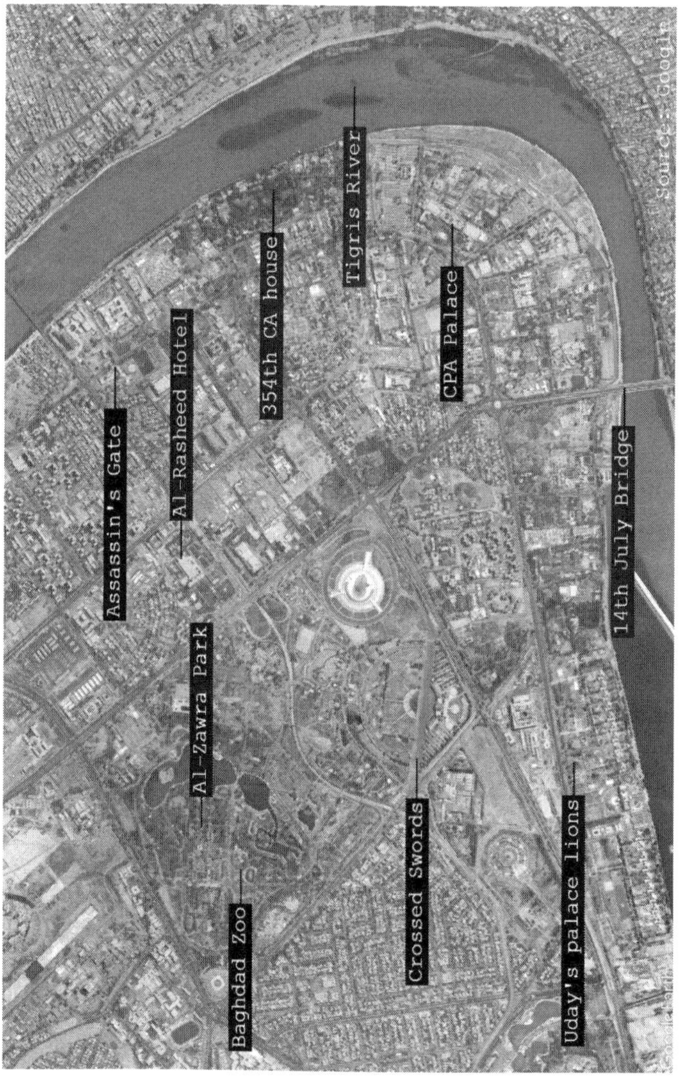
Assassin's Gate
Al-Rasheed Hotel
354th CA house
Tigris River
CPA Palace
14th July Bridge
Al-Zawra Park
Crossed Swords
Uday's palace lions
Baghdad Zoo
Source - Google

A Saddam Hussein motif with a post-invasion update.
(Photo: F. Almurrani)

A destroyed Iraqi tank confirms the reports of one-sided battles of armour.

PREFACE

In March 2003 United States president George W. Bush publicly announced the beginning of Operation Iraqi Freedom. Superpower war was unleashed on Iraq. Within the contrived, new nerve centre of one of the world's most televised military invasions, the Green Zone, stood a small, battered zoo. One might sensibly assume that would have nothing to do with a game reserve in Zululand, South Africa.

This book is an account of seizing an invented opportunity, and the many subsequent decisions that should probably be considered ill-advised. Lawrence Anthony, my boss, dismissed *sensible* as the burden of the middle-class, and accompanying bureaucracy as the shackles of the uninspired. In response, he launched into multiple ambitious and well-intentioned projects. Rarely it seemed did he anticipate the actual versus intended outcome. I'm paraphrasing slightly but "Do you think we should go to Baghdad and try to find a zoo?" was meant to be interpreted as "I'm going to Baghdad to find a zoo, are you coming?" How does one respond to that? Little did we know the U.S. Army would unintentionally invade Baghdad's public zoo just days later.

It has been over 17 years since I first arrived in Baghdad. In that time passed I have read or heard numerous accounts or sentiments of incidences that occurred at the zoo between early 2003 and mid-2004, often by people who were not there. Some are accurate. Some intersect the truth. All are recollections of shorter periods than covered by this book. Few accounts reached into the powerfully loyal quasi-tribal sense we felt while being bound together by a zoo most of us had never previously heard of.

I have three motivations for writing this book. The first two are self-centred. It often feels surreal to be inextricably linked with this adventure and given my Iraqi wife's mutterings about what I already forget, it seems likely one day I'll need a reference of a journey once taken to Iraq. Then there is a nagging personal urge to disentangle truths from the more creative reports and assumptions of these events. Thirdly, and most significantly, this is a tool to draw attention to animals in catastrophic situations and the many humans who sacrifice much and work tirelessly to aid these animals.

This book does not intend to advocate for zoos or to rally against zoos, or spark an activist social media blitz. If we incarcerate animals for our gratification, we have no excuse but to treat them with reverence and afford them a lifestyle their wild cousins would envy if they could. This narrative is about recognising and trying to solve problems. It is about navigating ignorance and pre-conceived ideas and finding joy, comfort, despair and small triumphs when ordinary people connect despite the dominant rhetoric. Human and animal lives and emotions frequently intertwine in times of political and natural disasters. They likely always will. I believe this story needs recollection with a depth of detail that enables people who perceive solutions in conflict to be simple, or quick to achieve, to grasp how dynamic and complicated even modest change can be to implement. Allies, humility, stubbornness and humour are essential. Rules or standard operating procedures in a peaceful, bureaucratic context may be useless in conflict locations. Sometimes that is the attractiveness of the chaos.

Nobody that arrived to assist the Baghdad Zoo, Iraqi or not, ever claimed to be experts at resolving all that we encountered. Our help was unsolicited. Our vastly different backgrounds added richness to the common threads of trying to do good, survive and absorb the cultural shocks we were steeped in. It created an intensely addictive sense of purpose. We worked to develop solutions when it was easy only to see problems and so much progress relied on improvisation and the combined skills of whoever was available at the time. Availability and willingness trumped technical expertise. It was invigorating to be mostly free of the mind-numbing drain and irritations of ordinary bureaucratic life that usually leaves us wanting something more exciting or meaningful. We were occasionally undeniably stupid, fortunate and ignorant, yet sometimes that helped us. Hindsight taught me that. We were forced by circumstances to learn and adapt.

In a war setting, it seemed perception amplified sentiment; cooperation felt more generous, and any small slight appeared spiked with malice. Every mind-boggling habitat in our new world had a smell that is still seared into the memory and unlocks immediate, curiously happy flashbacks – diesel fumes, burning rubbish or in the case of the zoo, brush fire and farmyard. That we outsiders survived is another reason I feel this story left an indelibly positive memory on us – and a residual craving for more.

We were blessed that somehow in the freaky, serendipitous universe many paths crossed in the chaos on the western bank of the Tigris River. It was where my perception of reality took a royal beating while still occasionally delirious from the shared happiness of conjured up common purpose and too much sugar-saturated tea. This story played out in the shadow of a war where a terrifying despot was smashed out the global political game at the instruction of his excitable arch-enemy on the eastern bank of Washington's Potomac River.

I write with my own biases, but I have attempted to be thorough in excising the layered reflections and errors of recollection so many years after the events. What I have written here is as I saw it, with insight from other weirdos who were also seduced by the opportunity. Numerous other cooperative sources from those days, and photographs, also helped to piece together context.

Some names of individuals have been changed or redacted to minimise aggravation or risk. If you consider all the rude words unnecessary, I am sure my mother will agree with you.

PART 1: EMBRACING CHAOS AND OTHER ILL-ADVISED PROJECT MANAGEMENT STRATEGIES

CHAPTER 1

The rental car entered the fringes of Baghdad, a sprawling war zone city of over five million inhabitants. The Kuwaiti driver steered it to the side of a road and asked for directions to the zoo, as one does. Traffic was unexpectedly manic. Hadn't there just been an invasion? It appeared life in Baghdad was continuing in its typically intense, gridlocked manner. The two passengers, another Kuwaiti and a South African, sat apprehensively, anticipating what the next minutes may hold for them. With hasty, general directions sourced they navigated their way to the edge of a lush, heavily fortified sector which the U.S. authorities had designated the Green Zone; the palace-dominated, 10km^2 neighbourhood nestled adjacent to the western fringes of a colonic twist in the Tigris River. It was the conspicuously imperial setting for the mammoth crossed swords so characteristically representing Baghdad in international media broadcasts. The Green Zone incorporated the ruling Baath Arab Socialist Party headquarters, newly garrisoned U.S. troops, an array of vast, domineering government buildings, dense stands of apartment blocks and hundreds of large houses and luxurious river-facing villas. West of the crossed-swords parade ground lay the expansive Al-Zawra Park, the tree and canal dominated setting (about half the size of New York's Central Park) enveloping Lawrence's target, the Baghdad Zoo. Not even Comical Ali, Saddam Hussein's creative Information Minister, could have articulated the lunacy of the events unfolding in Lawrence's head.

Body armour-laden soldiers of the U.S. Army 3rd Infantry Division (ID) roasted in their filthy, sweaty crusts at their checkpoints. The thick, Kevlar helmets and dark, reflective sunglasses added to the impression of the soldiers as canvas-wrapped Stormtroopers. The setting was brutish, angular and intentionally intimidating. Callously threatening 27-ton Bradley fighting vehicles, defensive HESCO barriers (a wire mesh and geotextile frame filled with sand), concertina razor wire, and readied automatic weapons were their office stationery. Belt-fed light machine guns mounted on the inverted V of their bi-pods waited for the trigger-squeeze that would clatter out death. Camouflage netting provided the only respite from the baking sun. Lawrence's first attempt at engaging in a discussion did not get him closer than it took to hear his introduction dismantled by a belligerent, verbal tirade. Threats were to "back the fuck off!" or be killed. It was not a civilian habitat. They scrambled back, U-turned the car and left. The soldiers were tense, tired and primed to defend their gains. Understandably so. It was only a week earlier that *Reuters* had reported an Iraqi counteroffensive by busses and tanks loaded with 500 elite Republican Guard soldiers, Fedayeen militia and Baath Party loyalists in the centre of Baghdad. Assaults by U.S. forces, armour, artillery and prowling aircraft reportedly killed fifty Iraqi troops in intense running battles. A U.S. Army tank had also fired an explosive round that smashed into the balcony of the 14th floor of the Palestine Hotel, killing two foreign journalists. The Guardian newspaper article by Jeffery and Deans (8 April 2003) captured the setting leading into the week of Lawrence's arrival –

"On the eastern edge of the city, U.S. Marines spent the night scouring foxholes, trenches and what appeared to be bunkers dug under roads to make sure the area was free of Iraqi soldiers. U.S. Central Command in Qatar today revealed it bombed an upmarket residential area of Baghdad yesterday where President Saddam and his aides were believed to be meeting. At least three buildings were destroyed in the attack on the district of

al-Mansour in western Baghdad, which blasted an 18-metre-deep crater, ripped orange trees from their roots and left a heap of concrete, mangled iron rods and shredded furniture and clothes."

They attempted another approach route. Nervous tension pulsed through Lawrence and the Kuwaitis with each corner turned and each new road. Another checkpoint choked the way ahead. The soldiers were partly distracted, occupied with scrutinising credentials of several opportunistic journalists hoping to gain access to the secure zone. Lawrence seized what he perceived as an opening, despite the rapidly configured, suspicious hostility towards his sweating, hairy mass of inquisitive South African claiming to be looking for the zoo. His outrageous request and official documentation triggered radio calls. He waited. He wasn't told to "fuck off". That was progress. Small steps. Sweat leaked in the unrelenting heat. He drew deeply on cigarettes; calmed by the ritual. Half an hour ground past. While persistence was Lawrence's strong point, patience was not. What were the alternative options to get to the zoo?

A Lieutenant arrived. Szydlik. At the time, they had no way of realising the enduring significance of that encounter. It was a crucial breakthrough. Lieutenant Szydlik was not interested in wasting time. He did not have any to lose anyway. He was pragmatic. Lawrence offered a solution, a partial easing of Szydlik's swarming burden of responsibilities. In the harassing meleé of ground assaults and armoured battles against Fedayeen militia in the park, the U.S. Army units had suddenly acquired an abandoned, festering wound of a zoo. How the hell were they meant to deal with that while they were still fighting a war? They knew nothing about running zoos. In the dust and heat and chaos of this foreign city, a South African with two Kuwaitis offering help was a surreal but welcome twist. Lawrence was inside. They were finally, officially on the zoo side of another nerve-wracking checkpoint.

The stout, clanking M113 armoured personnel carrier (APC) with its mounted .50 calibre Browning machine gun led the incongruous looking Toyota rental car into the battered Al-Zawra Park. There was an absurdity in the starkly utilitarian, camouflaged hulk of the military APC leading the undoubtedly underwhelming but eager saviour through the chaos. The caterpillar tank tracks of the APC rumbled and ground along on the tarmac roads winding through to the gates of the 15-hectare zoo that would later capture the imagination of world news.

Among the abandoned cafes, train tracks, monuments and playgrounds of the densely treed park lay a wasteland of desiccated grass and weeds, ammunition boxes, dying flowers, random leftovers from obliterated cars, truck wheel axels, assaulted irrigation piping and shards of trees. Anti-aircraft and artillery weaponry stood defeated. Rubble from detonated buildings lay sprayed out across the remains of lawns. Tank tracks had crumpled the paving. The pedal boats of the stagnating artificial lake and canal network had become transport for enterprising thieves who laid waste to the park's infrastructure and the zoo's menagerie. The human plague emerged like clusters of bipedal locusts with screwdrivers; a degenerate reaction to the crumbling of law and order had hatched out and then rampaged across parts of the city. Hospitals, museums, universities, galleries, and government offices were ransacked, vandalised and in some cases set alight. Images filled the international media of burning buildings as mobs scattered in all directions with chairs, vases, paintings and wooden carts laden with war spoils. More destructive to the park than the war, the insatiable looters were scorned as "Ali Babas", despised by many Baghdadis who saw no dignity and freedom in that voracious behaviour. It was raw, destructive and totally unleashed.

Donald Rumsfeld attempted to sugar-coat the madness flippantly by claiming "freedom's messy". Although the roads to the park had checkpoints, its partially wrecked boundary wall and fence were haemorrhaging looters in and plunder out. Al-Zawra Park and the Baghdad Zoo were stripped of every movable object and almost any creature that did not have the claws or teeth to discourage handling. Parrots, ibexes, light fittings, monkeys, giraffes, buckets, water pumps, door handles and air conditioners were all stolen to be eaten or re-sold. Frustrated U.S. soldiers patrolling the area tried to maintain a semblance of order but had no official mandate to do so. Their impotence in the face of the destruction incensed them. They did not have the resources to cover every sector at the same time. Threats were empty. At worst the looters would get a few hours of detention locked in a zoo cage. The thieves knew it. It was no deterrence. Saddam was gone. It was a free-for-all.

Among the degeneration, there was a residual elegance of design at the zoo. An enormous white stone arch at the zoo entrance opened out to a brick-paved avenue flanked by towering palm trees. Between the palm trees stood terribly small, but neatly arranged cages emptied of their birds. Former lawns were dried mud and tufts of dead grass. On the left of the entrance stood the white stone administration building, superficially tidy, but effectively a pillaged husk courtesy of looters. Dr Hussam, the zoo's forlorn deputy director, walked across to greet Szydlik and his strange and unfamiliar, non-military entourage.

Dr Hussam, bearing a striking physical resemblance to a moustachioed Peter Sellers, had courageously returned to the zoo at the first opportunity after the battles had ceased. His entry point into the park was over a mutilated, burnt-out truck and rubble that was bulldozed into a berm to block a broken section of park gates. His neatly pressed office shirt had become dishevelled and sweat-soaked by efforts to get the water supply functioning again. He found animals starving, dramatically dehydrated and surrounded by faeces and filth. Cut electricity supply and the thief-damaged pump systems for the park and zoo meant that even with functional piping there would be no water flowing from taps. When it was possible between duties, soldiers had also tried to get buckets of murky water from the canals to the animals. That was all happening between patrols and holding territory in a war zone. One evening the soldiers had to contend with six lions escaping into the zoo grounds when a stray incoming mortar round destroyed part of the predators' enclosure boundary wall. Extraordinarily, and to their immense credit, the soldiers used Humvees to herd three lions back into the enclosure. Three lions that avoided coercion were shot dead. It was a risk-management judgement. It was not a situation soldiers trained to handle. A small crater in a road was what remained of a donkey hit by an incoming explosive round. Dead animals were fed to living carnivores. The soldiers had sourced meagre but crucial supplies of packaged meat and vegetables which they stored at a nearby abandoned palace. It was keeping the few remaining lions, tigers, bears, boars, dogs, badgers, vultures and a wolf alive. From over 650 animals the zoo was stripped to less than 40. It was quickly depleted to 12 by more looting raids.

A skeleton crew of two devoted Iraqi staff had returned to the zoo to assist the battling, worn-out Hussam with whatever they could. None of them knew what the invasion of their country and city would mean for them. Could Saddam really be gone; simply like that? After years of being dominated and controlled, there was ominous insecurity and anger and despair at the rampaging. There was no plan and no declaration of what was next. Thieves still freely roamed the city's previously secure facilities. The zoo's staff had been forced to abandon their animals before the beginning of the battle. Those that returned did so to a broken imitation of the facility they had left two weeks prior. It had been a substandard facility before the war started (when compared to modern iconic, well-funded zoological gardens), neglected by the government, and isolated from the international community through sanctions and draconian isolationist policies of Saddam's regime.

There were still some staff who cared deeply for their animals, no matter how little management insight, husbandry training or access to funds they had.

The cluster of U.S. soldiers, Iraqis, Kuwaitis and a South African gathered in the oppressively hot shade of the dusty palm trees. Through Szydlik and the Kuwaitis, Lawrence navigated the introductions, cordial pleasantries and explanations of who he was. It was a jumble of gestures, pidgin-type English and Arabic. He wanted Hussam to believe there was international empathy for the desperately shocked state of the zoo. Outside help had arrived. The first gesture of goodwill was to present the token emergency supplies driven through the melee from Kuwait. They offloaded the boxes of medicines before Hussam guided Lawrence on a walk-through tour of the monumental task at hand.

Among the filth, the stench was a wretched blend of putrefying excrement and breath-sucking ammonia. The energy of desperation of the few remaining creatures had withered to emergency bodily functions. They survived at the cusp of death through the little help Hussam and the soldiers could provide. Animal enclosures had not been cleaned for weeks; maybe months. Desiccated, white urine crusts interconnected, fringing the orange stains on the floor tiles. Lumps and smudges of black, sun-baked faeces nourished the heaving masses of black flies. The walls and bars exploded into feverish swirls of humming as swarms of the scavengers launched. It was their world of opportunism; animal ooze from carcasses, eyes, wounds and anuses. Remnants of dead animals, repurposed to save others, reinforced the sense of despair as rancid flesh enriched the nauseating odour. As grizzly as it was, it validated Lawrence's internal call for action.

With the invasion of Baghdad imminent, the Fedayeen militia had threatened to shoot the remaining animal keepers if they did not abandon their animals and leave the zoo. Lawrence considered shooting dead the remaining animals. He thought it would be the humane approach to end the suffering, but within the despair was an opportunity. He had left the comparative comfort of Thula Thula to provide relief and aid. Quickly leaving Baghdad was not considered as an option. It would almost certainly guarantee animals languishing in squalor until the liberation of a miserable, starving death. The plans started fizzing in his thoughts. Small bites. He assured Dr Hussam any returning staff would be paid in U.S. dollars. The small matter of sourcing enough of those dollars would need to be overcome. He did not tell Dr Hussam that. With the infrastructure broken a labour force was critical to moving water and the paltry food rations to where they were desperately needed. The survival of the animals was the first burning goal. The accumulated filth of the weeks required scraping, scouring and sluicing away.

With the shock of the zoo still raw in their minds, Lawrence and the two Kuwaitis followed the road-grating APC back through the debris of the park, around the clusters of razor wire and barricades to the grounds of the imposing, dusty beige behemoth of the Al-Rasheed Hotel. The walls along the road leading to the hotel were pockmark-scarred from shrapnel and bullets. Lamp posts stood decorated with bands of holes where bullets had torn through the metal. Paving was dotted with shallow, isolated baseball-sized holes from exploded anti-personnel mortar rounds. It was another step into the rabbit hole of the surreal that Lawrence found himself in.

The Al-Rasheed was the 1980's-chic hotel formerly favoured by spies, leather-jacketed henchmen of the regime and Baghdad families in search of a restaurant treat. It was the hotel into which an Iranian air force pilot attempted to crash after his Phantom fighter jet was hit by a Surface-to-Air missile when overhead Baghdad. It was the hotel from which CNN's Peter Arnett had broadcast live television footage of the First Gulf War bombing of Baghdad in 1991 (my family had watched that from our lounge in Cape Town). A battered elegance still clung on despite the 3rd ID's rapid transformation of the hotel into a makeshift barracks. Soldiers of the 15th Infantry Regiment, 3rd Battalion were the new tenants. Although the hospitality was commendable, it was apparent that the recently assaulted interior would no longer pass traditional housekeeping muster. Within hours Lawrence became resident on the 7th floor of the hotel among a crew of compellingly unconventional Department of Defence film contractors. Within the first week, he was drinking cold beers with hospitable South African security contractors in a palace seized by U.S. forces. The intoxicating fusion of ex-special forces soldiers and war zone veterans of ages from teenager to grizzly lifer swathed Lawrence in a world of banter and storytelling - a seemingly fictional universe apart from life at Thula Thula. That he was in their territory to save a zoo was another layer of compelling, inescapable absurdity. He was surviving on the curious luckydip delights of ubiquitous U.S. Army ration packs (Meals Ready to Eat – MREs) and had been introduced to retired Lieutenant General Garner who headed up the Office of Reconstruction and Humanitarian Assistance (ORHA). Garner was the highest-ranking U.S. *civilian* in Baghdad.

Lawrence's rented satellite phone, which was hastily arranged weeks before at Johannesburg airport, was being used to invest in the economy of favours, with troops keen to make calls back to family and girlfriends. The continuous noise and energy of war effort was the soundtrack. Tanks would clank and grind along hard roads. Apache, Blackhawk or Kiowa helicopters drifted and weaved overhead Baghdad in aerial surveillance pairs. The repetitive, chopping purr of the blades would fade or flare up. When nightfall shrouded the city, the rattles of gunfire seemed to spark additional, protracted exchanges in the dark streets beyond the comparative safety of the hotel. Tracer bullets would flicker and arc into nowhere. The statue of Saddam Hussein may have been pulled off its plinth in Firdos Square, and crowds may have spontaneously celebrated the arrival of armoured convoys pressing down highways into suburbs, but Baghdad was by no means a pacified city. Seemingly innocuous, temporary lulls would be interrupted by a sudden eruption of a localised skirmish. Illuminating flares sparked up from between city buildings to hang momentarily high in the blackness, indicating attacked or attacking military patrols needing urgent firepower backup. Darkness and the murmur of the night would return until the next outburst.

During the ensuing days, Lawrence found himself and the Kuwaitis, with the assistance of a growing crew of returning Baghdad Zoo staff, running ostriches past perplexed checkpoint soldiers, down the road from palaces to the zoo. How else did one relocate such enormous birds from their abandoned holding pens when there were no trucks to help? The team had also encountered young lions, dogs and cheetahs in palace garden menageries. They had to fashion a makeshift plan to lure the lions, dogs and cheetahs into individual transport cages to be moved to the zoo. It was considered logistically pragmatic to care for all the animals in a single location. Baghdad Zoo became that focal point. The exertion was non-stop. Plans and decisions were made on the fly to try to create order in the chaos. In the overbearing heat, water was being ferried from canal to animal mouth by buckets stolen from the Al-Rasheed, which were then taken by looters, and replaced by more buckets from the hotel. Dr Hussam's wish list extended to a car battery to start a portable water pump and an electricity generator.

The recently returned and initially insular Zoo Director, Dr Abbas attempted to make emotional sense of his wrecked zoo, and a shocking new world dominated by the American military. Resourceful zoo staff armed with the power of a few dollars delivered two donkeys and the somewhat deranged, alcohol-powered former zoo butcher, Kadhim. The brutal business of slaughter with an axe kept the zoos predators alive for a couple more days. The staff saw the predators representing the dignity of the zoo. The predators had to survive. Donkeys were considered expendable, ill-fated beasts of burden to their last breath.

In the 3rd ID's Captain Burris, Lawrence had befriended a crucial contact. Captain Burris was the unyielding officer in charge of troops at the Al-Rasheed, and sympathetic to the zoo cause. Antiseptic detergent and necessary food supplies like rice were sourced from the hotel basement and hastily ferried to the zoo in a Humvee to make a start on enclosure cleaning and to feed the contingent of hungry staff who had been stealing the food sourced for the animals. By Lawrence's reckoning, the supplies were "borrowed from Mr Hussein under the understanding that if he ever comes back and asks for it, we will return it." Theft of animals by looters was still a persistent problem. In one evening, replacement padlocks (for those that had previously been broken by looters) were cut, and four peacocks were stolen.

Foreign media quickly discovered the bizarrely compelling story of a conspicuous, white South African from a game reserve called Thula Thula among staff at the Baghdad Zoo. It was a platform for Lawrence to eagerly engage the world, or whoever would listen. False rumours of a possible punitive Kuwaiti invasion of Iraq caused heated arguments among zoo staff and the Kuwaitis, and the prospect of an explosive confrontation was looming. The two Kuwaitis returned to their home with the rental car. It left Lawrence entirely reliant on U.S. Army assistance, perverse optimism and an ability to "make a plan" in his new realm. Courtesy of the ever-accommodating 3rd ID warriors, the unforgivingly Spartan and baking hot interior of an APC was his unique morning taxi ride experience to the zoo.

It had been a strange fortnight.

CHAPTER 2

Lawrence's greying, ginger beard bristled wildly after it endured a contemplative scratch. "Shit Brendan do you know how insane that'll be? Jeez boy! That'll be something hey! You think it'll happen?" His gravelly voice paused. Fifty-two restless years had not jaded or weathered his ambition to leave a positive legacy; however that might manifest itself. He was determined to create change, frequently urging "we need to be cause, not the effect." If anything, the passing years accelerated his urgency to seize opportunities, often simultaneously, irrespective of how untidy action looked from the outside. Despite his imposing size and unleashed facial hair, he was unable to hide the impish grin as he drew deeply on his cigarette. He nudged his spectacles up towards his unruly eyebrows with his index finger and took another slow, determined drag. We stared at nothing in particular, soaking up the dizzying, distracting air of anticipation, thinking of the storm that was about to engulf us.

Beyond the stately Marula tree and the neglected shell of the concrete swimming pool at the end of the garden, zebras on the opposing hill ambled lethargically out from beneath the shade of thorn trees. The belly-deep grass scarcely concealed the late births of the season. Above us, Vervet monkeys scrambled and chased each other over the thatched roofs like diminutive silver ninjas, victoriously clutching fistfuls of the dog's food after another successful raid. In early April 2003, the lingering summer still defied the imminent autumn in Zululand. Late afternoon brought welcome relief from the oppressively moist heat as the sun appeared to lazily sink towards the horizon. The smell of frying chicken drifted out the open doorway from the kitchen inside. I sat quietly on the waist-high stone wall of the farmhouse veranda until Lawrence decided a drive into the game reserve would be a better way to distract us from our nervous energy.

When you're a bit bored with the daily scramble of keeping a game reserve financially and almost functionally operational, what is one to do? Maybe, just maybe, there was a zoo in Iraq that would need our help. Of course. With CNN or SKY News rolling almost perpetually on the television at the house, we had watched scratchy live satellite feeds as embedded reporters in Iraq divulged the latest grand military manoeuvres and enticingly one-sided engagements with great gusto and a little panic. It was war but on television! It was riveting to us. Emerald green night-vision footage showed artillery and laser-like tracer fire. We lived desert dust, tanks, palm trees, canals, precision bombing, mayhem and razor-like incisions towards the heart of Iraq by the U.S. led troops; from the sanitised distance of another continent. Finding a zoo in Baghdad was an idea born by Lawrence's younger son, Dylan, a few days earlier. It was as a quip rather than a final suggestion.

We were happily ignorant. Our reference to internation war was stories, media and movies. We hadn't personally smelled it or felt it. We had no idea of the torment, exhaustion, bone-deep discomfort, adrenaline-spiking fear and the daily reality of those delivering or facing the fury of this onslaught. We didn't know the endorphin-pumping thrill of surviving combat action or the excruciating waiting and tedious boredom between it. We didn't realise the helpless anxiety of hiding in a cramped underground bomb shelter. We didn't know what it was like to have the concussive blast wave of bombs blow out our house windows. We didn't know what it was like to genuinely anticipate death for weeks on end. We didn't talk about it. We didn't particularly care about Iraq or Iraqis more than other strangers. Their problems were abstract to us. We were engrossed at a primitive level at the tangle of politics and destruction.

The compelling energy generated around the idea of doing something exhilarating but potentially idiotic often has a way of allowing one to conveniently mould the truth into a deliciously addictive cocktail. We wanted a taste. Our taste. We wanted to own the sensation not hear about it second-hand. Curiosity faded thoughts of ghastly consequences. We didn't pretend to understand any of the deep-seated, obscenely complicated politics at play. We couldn't recognise spoken Arabic, and we definitely couldn't list five Arabic names. We didn't even know about the Iraqi national preoccupation with cultivating such ubiquitously masculine moustaches that they will stir the envy of Tom Selleck. Yet we thought we knew enough and had our opinions about that faraway land.

This is what we *knew*; more or less. Saddam Hussein was the archetypal tyrant with delusional perceptions of divine dominion he enforced with his family and sycophants by terror and sadism. His colourful, grandiose dress sense for every occasion was tailored to match his Scarface persona, accompanied of course by an impressively majestic moustache. To the media, he projected a playful father-like demeanour in the style of the other psychopathic, self-deluded humanitarians like Joseph Stalin and His Excellency President for Life, Field Marshal Alhaji Dr Idi Amin Dada, VC, DSO, MC, CBE. He was depicted in western media exclusively as a savage gangster with a vicious family and an inability to play nicely with his neighbours in the sandpit. To be fair the track record of neighbourly invasions and mass executions (multiple estimates place this figure in the hundreds of thousands) by his regime and brutality towards those he didn't like, spoke volumes about his aversion to negotiation. Some political commentators had said this was the only way to rule Iraq.

Reports of infrastructural development, social progress and educational reform naturally paled in comparison to the barbarism. The brutal Baathist machinery of state was still seething at the outside world meddling in Iraq's domestic raping and pillaging of its new "19th Province" – as Kuwait was referred too. Instead of licking their wounds and filing the failed adventure in their catalogue of *1991 - An Annus horribilis*, they concocted a new horror from within their shamanic cigar smoke. After international coalition forces pushed the Iraqi army back into Iraq, emboldened, agitated anti-Saddam factions had detonated into wild armed rebellions. There was no contrition, no acceptance of guilt, no attempts at reconciliation by the government. That was not their style. Saddam loyalists responded ferociously to defend the regime. Helicopter gunships unleashed body-shredding vengeance as they flayed the resistance. There were mass executions, a genocide to halt the sedition, and even the added inventiveness of utterly catastrophic ecocide. To crush the defiant Marsh Arabs, a unique culture that had occupied the Mesopotamian wetlands for thousands of years, the Iraqi government annihilated most of their abundant, ecologically complex habitat. Historically the marshes extended over approximately 20 000km^2, an area roughly the size of Slovenia, fed by both the Tigris and Euphrates Rivers. The saturated ecosystem was systematically carved up and drained by spectacular engineering works, and then burned. By 2003 it was estimated 90% of that land was a desert.

Yet in parts of the Arab world Saddam was (and still is) revered as the bulwark against Israel, who, we were assured by more political commentators, had stolen Palestine. So in the intractable blur of diplomatic complexity, we blithely assumed Iraq was a singularly minded, warmongering society, all towing the Baath Party line, all complicit. We trustingly, mostly believed the caricatures of all Iraqi women as oppressed in black abayas, of the religious obsessions (the wrong ones of course), and Chemical Ali's obscene penchant for gassing Kurds and gloating about it. Tariq Aziz's (Iraq's Deputy Prime Minister) military outfits, impressive moustache and thick-rimmed spectacles combination screamed dictatorship chic. Camels navigating endless sands added more imagined absurdity. Iraq was at the core of George Bush's proclaimed Axis of Evil. Hell yeah!

Freedom was the gift that needed to be delivered by the *coalition of the willing*. It was difficult not to laugh at the unwilling French being charged with such disloyalty (for disagreeing with the proposal of the coalition invasion) and being punished by having their namesake French Fries changed to Freedom Fries in some U.S. government cafeterias. Iraq needed to be relieved of their indisputable caches of Weapons of Mass Destruction (WMD). Bush, Cheney, Rumsfeld, Rice and Powell told us.

The reality was transformed into detached, desensitised entertainment no matter how hard the reporters tried to give us a feeling of what was happening on the ground. In the more conservative U.S. media, the war was portrayed as a simplistic exaggeration of the good guys kicking the crap out of the bad guys. Iraqi's were frequently either the enemy or uncouth peasants, sometimes both. We did not think we were flippant about the context, but we chose not to ask questions with potentially very uncomfortable answers. We also wondered what happened to wildlife during wars. Still, we watched enthralled from the game reserve, thousands of kilometres away in Zululand.

Prompted by Dylan's comment, we thought back to the events surrounding an international relief effort led for Kabul Zoo as foreign troops attempted to rinse Afghanistan of its Taliban rulers and Al Qaeda after 2001's 9/11 attack. It seemed a distinct possibility (when assumptions in our thoughts evolved into facts) that there would also be a zoo in Baghdad even though the omniscient internet we searched did not appear to know it at the time. A few beers later at Thula Thula game reserve's elegant lodge bar, with its setting of the electric-blue pool overlooking cropped lawns, grazing nyala and enormous, ghostly-pale figs lining the Enseleni River, it was certain. U.S. invasion = war zone = buggered zoo = adventure in a location history was spotlighting. On the balance of emotion, it felt more exciting to be going than to be staying. Emotion and animal welfare outweighed any rational concept of altruism, legacy or genuine risk. We were sure there must be a zoo, and we were going to find it. Of course! Why wouldn't there be?

Sure of ourselves now, we drove back the two kilometres to the office telephone. We contacted Henry Richmond on one of the Hawaiian Islands, with the help of a slightly perplexed international telephone operator. Apparently, Richmond is not an uncommon name, and Hawaii has more than one island. That was a quick geography lesson. A former commercial attaché to the United States Embassy in Durban, Henry and his wife had become regular, popular, guests at Thula Thula. We knew that he had retired, but thought he would still be the one American we knew who would not only entertain this slightly unusual idea but who would actually have the contacts to be able to facilitate the paperwork. Did we need paperwork? What did it require to get into a war zone to find a zoo? We didn't know. We presumed a letter with a signature and stamp from the government of the military with the most ferocious firepower would always help. We decided unequivocally to get into Baghdad Zoo for a month or two, resolve the immediate crisis we were convinced existed, and then hand it over to "real zoo people" like the team that were helping Kabul Zoo.

Within days of frantic letter typing, faxing, e-mailing and numerous phone calls, Lawrence had an invitation to Kuwait. We did not have any zoo experience, money, insurance or an evacuation plan. Those seemed like inconvenient details. We were convinced surviving the eclectic challenges of start-up years of a manic, financially strained game reserve in Zululand was enough basic grounding for whatever we would encounter. Lawrence always advocated the philosophies of "find out what is needed and wanted and do it" and "break big problems down to smaller, manageable components". That logic seemed reasonable enough in the unknown circumstances. Above all, we had further convinced ourselves we needed to do it.

As much as we believed the animals needed help, there was also an undeniably selfish foundation to the decision. Both Lawrence and I felt it, were driven by it and conceded to it. It was an opportunistic, compelling adventure in the making. Simple. We craved the excitement. I had resigned from Thula Thula the previous year but had never left. A part of me wanted to explore more of the world. Still, I did not want to disconnect from the intense emotional energy spent over three years of working with colleagues to forge a new conservation and tourism identity for Thula Thula. A part of me also feared the potentially unfulfilling life of drudgery outside the game reserve.

Lawrence's foundation was unrelenting stubbornness. Using an abundance of charisma and enthusiasm, he could creatively screen inconvenient truths. He deployed his calculating gift of talking his way into (and out of) unlikely situations while projecting a deceptively naive, joviality. The U.S. officials had no idea what hit them. And Lawrence didn't waste time. He convinced them that if there were a zoo, it would need our help. By the 16th of April 2003, Lawrence was in Kuwait City. There he had the ear of the experienced U.S. diplomat Tim Carney (whose previous postings included Saigon, Phnom Penh and Mogadishu). Carney was the choice of Paul Wolfowitz, the U.S. Deputy Secretary of Defence, to enhance the post-war governance team in Baghdad. Lawrence embedded himself into an influential network; the South African ambassador to Kuwait, Martin Slabber, and genial military officials from the newly established Humanitarian Operations Centre (HOC), the American Lieutenant Colonel, Jim Fikes and the British Major, Adrian Oldfield. The HOC aimed to deliver humanitarian aid to the people of Iraq but also served as a central point of coordination with international relief agencies and the Office of Reconstruction and Humanitarian Assistance (ORHA). ORHA was rapidly assembled under retired Lieutenant General Jay Garner to lead the U.S. post-war reconstruction mission in Iraq until the country was to be handed over to Iraqi civilian governors. It was there, in Kuwait, that Lawrence was linked to Colonel McConnell who had arrived from Baghdad to source supplies for Baghdad Zoo. It existed! It was real, and conditions were dire!

That did not mean a resolution to activate a response was quickly at hand. Instead, there was to be seemingly interminable logistical and diplomatic dancing until Lawrence was furnished with a letter from the Kuwaiti Ministry of Agriculture to accompany his U.S. coalition documentation; to enter Iraq. It had felt like an endless wait when, in reality, it had been merely a couple of days. In their own unique and essential ways, those characters all aided, advised (usually against Lawrence entering Iraq) and contributed to Lawrence making it to Baghdad. For Lawrence, a conspicuous ginger-bearded foreigner with no experience in the Middle East, there was then also the small matter of renting a car, filling it with potentially beneficial medical and food supplies and trusting two staff from the Kuwait Zoo to accompany him on a road trip into a war zone. That would include talking his way through the border and U.S. military checkpoints – as one does - and driving 650km north to Baghdad, past grinding military convoys, charred vehicle wrecks, annihilated Iraqi tanks, and through intimidatingly alien ancient towns. It was gambling with lives through a dramatic war zone, with a pair of gentlemen that barely spoke any English and who, as Kuwaitis, would not be particularly welcome by some people if their nationality was discovered in Iraq. The malicious legacy of the First Gulf War still lingered.

◆ ◆ ◆

The brown box tape was peeled from reel after reel to stick in overlapping strips across the insides of the house windows. The brown stars would hopefully prevent the glass shattering completely or blasting into the house when the bombing started. Some windows were reinforced with towels taped over them, partly for protection against the glass fragments, but also to provide a barrier against the orange, powdery sandstorms that penetrated any gaps. It was a regular Baghdadi middle-class home preparing for another war. The bombing of Baghdad during 1991's Operation Desert Storm was vivid in the memory. In March 2003 the expensive and intricate Isfahan and Kashan Persian carpets were still on the floors to insulate against the last days of winter. In Baghdad, the shift from winter to scorching summer appears to materialise overnight.

Breakables, expensive crystal glasses and decorative figurines were carefully wrapped in newspaper, cloths or pashminas. Packaged into sponge-filled boxes, they were stored in a room where they were more likely to survive undamaged. The preparations had begun weeks earlier. Money in U.S. dollars was drawn from the banks. Iraqi dinars were purchased at street-side exchanges. Some of it was stored with jewellery and passports in a getaway bag should the point of abandoning the house be forced on the occupants. The extended process of stocking up with supplies meant a house full of tinned and dried foods, meat and fish being salted, eggs, more eggs, long-lasting vegetables like cauliflowers and aubergines; and more damn aubergines. An inverter had been installed to ensure at least one fridge could be run off a car battery when the electricity invariably failed. Hurricane lamps and fuel, oil lamps and candles were stockpiled. A borehole well was drilled in the manicured garden to ensure access to water should it be needed.

From early 2003 the likelihood of another war in Iraq was looking increasingly ominous. In their experience as residents of Baghdad, when the U.S. said that they would attack, and when they would attack, they did exactly that. They had done so both in 1991 and 1998's 4-day bombing campaign, Operation Desert Fox. From the time of the 2001 9/11 attacks in New York, it seemed many Iraqis believed their country would get the blame and they would face the retribution, despite the talk of Osama bin Laden being the mastermind. The Iraqi media propaganda was defiant against the threats and access in Iraq to the international news was, as always, restricted and censored. Talk of Saddam's extensive stock of operational Weapons of Mass Destruction began to surface in the international media. It was being used by the United States government as a means to justify an invasion of Iraq at the United Nations, among allied nations and consumers of the international media.

In Baghdad, rumours and conspiracy theories found fertile soil among residents. It was common knowledge that Saddam's Baathist Regime had previously stockpiled and utilised chemical weapons. As far back as the Reagan administration, the U.S. authorities knew of Saddam's stockpile – it was a cruel irony that Donald Rumsfeld had been one of the conduits to supply Saddam with some of those weapons and now was using a reworked logic to attack Iraq. The Iraqi military had poison-gassed Iranian troops in the Iraq-Iran war of the 1980s and later slaughtered Kurdish civilians in much the same way in retribution for Kurdish support for Iran. After the 1991 Gulf War, international weapons inspectors under United Nations mandate had overseen the large-scale destruction of much of Iraq's chemical weapon stockpile. At times the lengths inspectors would have to go to inspect facilities appeared farcical as Iraqi authorities choreographed political roadblocks, media bombast and infernal bureaucracy to thwart inspection teams. How functional any further development programs or stockpiles of chemical or biological agents were seemed open to severe speculation. Some Iraqi citizens believed weapons probably were not accessible even if they still existed. It had been over a decade since they were last used. The world had been watching Iraq intently. Jokes were made about how deep the tunnels were that perhaps hid the weapons; if they existed. In the atmosphere of repression, suspicion and informants, talk about the government was never in public, and only with trusted friends. The imminent risk of detention and cruel torture was too high. Iraq was still a country of government-ordered abductions, appallingly graphic stories of inflicted pain, and where families were occasionally required to pay (and even rarely reported receiving receipts) for bullets used to execute loved ones.

The U.S. led coalition attack was scheduled for late March 2003. Farah was a slim, rebellious, vibrant 26-year-old veterinarian in Baghdad. A year earlier, her small veterinary practice had been appropriated by Iraqi authorities due to its strategically valuable location across the road from the Russian Embassy. As a recent graduate who had poured emotion, hope and ambition into the endeavour, the theft of her clinic without compensation had been a bitter blow. The cruel experience had put her off the idea of wanting another business or a clinic. She was over it. Like her friends, she was keen to leave Iraq, travel, and experience some freedom from her existing life situation. They all knew a U.S. attack was likely. In that prospect, there was hope that all the awfulness with Saddam and his government and the potential bombing would at some point end, and she could leave.

She spent her days at home in the suburb of Mansour, driving her two younger brothers to school and her mother to work at the university veterinary department. Her father worked in veterinary pharmaceutical supplies. At night she gathered with friends, either at their homes or the local Orfali art gallery cafeteria, to drink coffee, attend piano concerts and play the guitar. Widad Al Orfali, the elegant and sophisticated gallery owner, was a mentor to aspiring artists and mother to all those who gathered; chastising bad manners such as elbows on the table. They enjoyed every day like it was their last.

Most of Farah's friends were Muslim, but the sectarian issue of Sunni and Shia was not a concern. Her family was of Mandean background. First names may have given an indication of the sect, but among her friends and acquaintances, they did not ask or push to know who was what. Friends were simply friends. It was a concept considerably more straightforward than making Iraqi tea. Among the families in the neighbourhoods, the sect was a nonissue. They had grown up with large sociable families, birthday parties, picnics and ambitions. It was a country where education was valued, compulsory and free for both girls and boys, where women and men could be engineers and doctors and architects. Baath Party membership and bribery definitely helped smooth some people's access to university and job opportunities, but the foreign media's obsession with portraying the government as the sole reflection of the country's people was jaundiced and simplistic.

Life went on. School. Markets. Work. During that time, some families, friends and relatives engineered ways to leave Iraq. Television showed American sitcoms. Pirated DVDs of international movies were abundant; from horror to porn to comedy. Most music genres were readily available on the black market. Farah and her friends did not go to the zoo. Its reputation was poor, a dirty mess not worth the effort to visit. Until the expansive Al-Zawra Park was shut for renovations in late 2002, families would picnic there and on the nearby, crossed swords parade ground lawns. Or they would flock to the rickety amusement park near the zoo. Adjacent to the zoo was a favourite restaurant under the dome of the 54m tall viewing tower that protruded out from the trees like a massive decorative mushroom. The panoramic views of the surrounding flat neighbourhoods were unrivalled for a public space in the city. Mostly, despite the egotistical agendas and merciless machinations of the megalomaniacs in charge of the country, there was much going on that many conservative societies in the world would consider rather dull and normal; albeit with more cardamom.

Closer to "shock and awe" day Farah was worried about how to keep her family's dogs settled during the next bombing; especially her epileptic German Shepherd. There did not seem to be visible, overt military preparations on a grand scale – although perhaps it was a matter of perspective. Residents of Washington D.C. may well have been alarmed if they saw the same changes around them. People in Baghdad would talk about, for example, how Al-Zawra Park seemed to have been fortified against attack overnight. Military vehicles were parked under overpasses or in the suburbs. Oil wells and tyres were set alight across the city in a futile attempt to obscure the modern guidance technologies the coalition forces possessed for precision bombing. The acrid black smoke filled the Baghdad air, laundry and the curtains.

The bombing started at midnight. It always started at night. Missile airstrikes from jets and Tomahawk cruise missiles slammed into targets around the city. Krump! Boom! Through the first few nights of bombing, utilities survived in working order. Electricity. Water. Phones. Infrastructure was functional. Citizens did not know what would happen next. More areas and more utilities were hammered, with explosions flaring and expanding shock waves pulsing through concrete and trees. More of the extended family started to gather in Farah's family's house. Cousins, aunts, uncles, grandmothers and children. Clustering under a table during bombardment wasn't only the realm of children. Card games and cooking were seemingly endless pursuits for distraction. Communal stress would feed reactive bouts of musical jam sessions and a joy to still be alive. What would be their fate in the face or aftermath of the invasion? The question always hung in the air.

Her youngest brother, born during the bombing of Baghdad in 1991, was too young to remember the experience of war. He would huddle up with Farah and his woolly dog, Snoopy, to sleep. The wooden headboard of her bed would rock to the concussion of the explosions when bombs hit. The pounding was expected. When the bombing was distant, the gnawing awareness of impending drama, pain or gruesome physical threat only simmered. Like a typical pre-war morning, the family would wake up, eat breakfast and carry out the routine tasks before heading to the grocery stores, although some like the bakery were only open at limited times. Initially, it was safe enough to drive around during the day to check on friends and see what had been hit by missiles overnight. Life grew more restricted. Schools closed. Work closed. There was a greater need for petrol (gasoline) for generators. Days passed by with chatting and backgammon. The bombing was usually nightly but not always. On the afternoon of the 7th of April, Farah sat on the bed with her father. A flash of orange shockingly whipped past the bedroom window. Split seconds later the missile crashed with devastating impact into a house being targeted near the Al Sa'ah restaurant less than two kilometres away.

There would be the talk of where coalition troops were reported. Basra, Fallujah...? As the U.S. military closed in on Baghdad, clusters of Iraqi soldiers deserted posts in gut-wrenching fear of what may happen if they had to fight. They knew they would likely be slaughtered. It was about survival; especially for those who had no loyalty to the regime. Farah's friend, a conscript, arrived at their house dishevelled, in half a mud and dirt-covered army uniform desperate to exchange his weapon for civilian clothes. The unit commander had run away, and many of his compatriots had stripped down to tracksuits beneath their uniforms before also making a break for it. He had not been as well prepared. Farah's mother refused the weapon but made him breakfast and tea, got him fresh clothes and sent him on his way. He was trying to get to his mother and sisters in another neighbourhood. It was a situation of real people in real shit.

As the rumour mill churned, Farah and her family still didn't know precisely where the invading U.S. troops were. They had heard forces were in Baqubah, 50km northeast of Baghdad; and then the next day heard troops were in Baghdad. Later that day during a trip with her father to the local cooking herbs shop they were surprised to see

U.S. soldiers for the first time. A small group in desert camouflage with M16 rifles were gathered at the little roasted nuts and coffee shop next door. Some soldiers lounged on the pavement near their Humvees as others sampled the products at the store like tourists. Within a day they started seeing mammoth-sized, clanking tanks grinding along their main roads, and tank crews waving to welcoming residents. The base, resonant pounding of airstrikes had stopped. As Humvee convoys cruised along the streets of their suburb, past their house, there seemed a palpable lull. The suburbs like Mansour felt like they had rapidly normalised to some degree.

On the 9th of April, the footage of Saddam's domineering statue being pulled down in Firdos Square was broadcast globally and on Iraqi television. As U.S. Marines noosed and then dragged the giant figure from its pedestal, the legs snapped, tumbling the effigy before an eager mob waiting to thrash it with sandals. The dictator's illusion of supremacy had proven ephemeral, even if his stamp on the psyche was to endure. Throughout the invasion, a few television channels still functioned when there was electricity. Farah watched with her family. There was little emotion except from her mother who cried, not for Saddam, but for Iraq. The frightening question of "What now?" loomed ominously.

As a sense of normality appeared to return, friends started gathering at houses and socialising again. A group of U.S. Special Forces soldiers had commandeered a home nearby to that of a close friend of Farah and her brother. Over the following days, as the friend, his family and the soldiers with their Humvees unavoidably encountered each other more regularly; the traditional Iraqi hospitality took over. The soldiers would visit the friend's house frequently for teas and coffees and meals. When Farah and her brother visited, they were immediately part of the gathering. It would turn into morning coffees all day long.

Then one day Farah saw a sketchy, weak-signalled foreign channel on the television. The big, bearded, Thula

Thula cap-wearing foreigner was just intriguing enough for her to pay attention. She could barely make out that it was an insert about the Baghdad Zoo and that Lawrence Anthony was appealing for help. Farah saw her opportunity. It was an impulsive response that grabbed her. She quickly mentally pieced together a potential plan to meet Lawrence - using the influence of her newly acquired Special Forces acquaintances. By then, they knew Farah's veterinary background, and they knew she was passionate and resourceful. She knew how to play the charmer.

They bit. The operators quickly facilitated permission from their commander, and the momentum of action was rolling. She was soon in a Humvee, scouting past the crossed swords parade ground, searching for a route to the zoo. It was a brief, peculiar introduction. Special Forces soldiers dominated the space near the zoo building while a petite, energetic and compelling Iraqi girl with brightly coloured hair, dressed in short pants and smoking a cigarette, was introduced to the physically imposing but convivial, dishevelled South African. She had shown enough initiative to get to the zoo. That was a great start. "You like dogs, and you're a vet, you speak English. You can come every day" was Lawrence's response. It would be a matter of days before the Special Forces contact furnished Farah with a Civilian Employee Pass as "*Baghdad Zoo – Irag Humane Society Coordinator*" to pass through the checkpoints into the *American* sector. She started at the zoo on the 11th of May 2003. It was Farah's peculiarly stylish arrival at the zoo that would for months disconcert the Iraqi management staff who suspected she was appointed by the U.S. military to work there.

◆ ◆ ◆

For nearly two decades before the 2003 invasion of Iraq, the U.S. Army recruiting slogan was "Be All You Can Be". It is unlikely it was ever envisaged that one of its part-time officers, a father with a month-old daughter, a Master's degree in Education and nearing another in Archaeology and Heritage, would be attempting to resolve the predicament of abandoned lion cubs and dogs in a palace belonging to the son of a Middle Eastern dictator, during a war. Captain William Sumner's early attempts in the mission to conform to the military's textbook tactical doctrine was perhaps one of the only concessions to planned, conventional war-fighting practice that he had experienced in the previous weeks. As for the rest of the mission, that seemed characteristically thin on detail and gratuitously reliant on improvisation. His commanding officer, Colonel Sollenberger, issued the formal instruction to "go out and do good things." An indulgent sense of adventure permeated days that were thrilling, miserable, chaotic and punctuated with brutal realisations of mortality. Blazing heat, palaces, sweat-soaked body armour (always), menageries, rotting corpses, burning corpses, scorched vehicles, explosions, gunfire, acrid plumes of black smoke, palm trees, dust, and flies intermingled with navigational fuck-ups. These sensory jolts all collided in a foreign land, confused by an utterly foreign guttural language, where invading soldiers could not tell if they were loved or hated or only a freak show. "That it sucked was part of the experience. It was the Army. It was what it was meant to be."

In 2002, with the disclosure of his wife's pregnancy, William's impending deployment to Afghanistan was deferred. His grandfather had been in the military. His father had been in the military. He was a legitimate history nerd with an insatiable curiosity. He wanted his war. Pragmatism was the result of frustration at the opportunity missed, offset by optimism and the keen excitement to be a father. America's leadership had lined up Saddam Hussein for a beating. The cogs of the industrial war machine continued to grind.

Within days of his first daughter's birth, William was disembarking with battalions of troops and armour from the cavernous diaphragm of a Boeing 747. Beyond the massive beige tents and guy-ropes, trucks and Humvees, layered cargo pallets and gravel, the ubiquitous shades of beige, flat sands stretched out to a distant blur of nothing. At Camp Arifjan he was closer to the idyllically warm waters of the Arabian Gulf and the Saudi Arabian border, than to Iraq, and nearly 10 500km from his family in Germantown, Maryland. On good days in Kuwait, they were basted in the warm, claustrophobically moist air. Other days there was no escape from tasting, breathing and wearing the grit and haze of dust and sand swirling in waves of wind. The sun never appeared to set, but instead dissolved into the layers of orange haze on the horizon.

As the only soldier in the 354th Civil Affairs Brigade with archaeological experience, William had been designated the Arts, Monuments and Archives officer. Pre-deployment planning had meant scrounging and scouring all resources available, like university records, to try to catalogue what they were expecting to find and secure in Baghdad. No-shoot lists were created to try to inform the battle planning and limit the destruction of antiquities. The planning and grit-chewing continued in Kuwait as the immense coalition force, dominated by the U.S. troops and weaponry, crossed the border and pushed its invading forces deeper into Iraq. Casualty rates on both sides of the war multiplied, although the coalition deaths paled in comparison to the devastation absorbed by the Iraqis. As ferocious battles ensued, Abrams tanks and Bradley Fighting Vehicles backed by ruthless air superiority incised into Baghdad. Foreign forces started to dominate the landscape. The authority of Saddam's repressive regime was fragmented and scattered, unleashing a torrent of spontaneous pillaging of the capital city by rebellious, un-yoked citizens.

Reports of the plundering of the treasures of the National Museum of Iraq in Baghdad quickly filtered through the chain of command to William. He was ordered to head to Baghdad with a cobbled-together public health team. That was a fighting force of William, his commanding colonel, three reservist medical doctors (in their civilian lives), one young enlisted driver, five 9mm pistols and one rifle in two un-armoured Humvees with canvas tarpaulin roofs. The hastily added flapping orange patch on the roof of their vehicle (that was still painted in the camouflage intended for European forest manoeuvres) would hopefully indicate to target-seeking aircraft they were "friendly" forces. Their navigational supplies were a paper map and William's personal Magellan GPS he had packed back in Maryland. In 2003, Civil Affairs units were still the alienated step-child of the military, under-funded and under-equipped.

With confidence, optimism and the enthusiastic anticipation of seeing war first-hand, so often attributed to those who haven't seen the ghastly side of war, they headed sort-of in the direction of Baghdad. It was only about 650km to navigate. For William, it was the culmination of years of ambition; he wanted to test himself and his training during the war but also recognised the rare privilege of his intended destination to feed his passion for archaeology. As invasion reinforcements streamed north through the desert highways and side-roads in snaking, wheezing columns of supply trucks, Humvees and armour, they passed the debris of war left by the overwhelming firepower of the coalition forces. The team's convoy of two would join grander, more imposing convoys before over-taking and then occasionally finding themselves lost down dirt tracks, or unmarked roads. Major highways were easily navigable because of the standard Arabic and English text road signs, but on minor routes, the exclusively Arabic script was of no reference help. As they avoided congestion or detours and strayed from main highways, they passed desolate, forsaken villages with excited, running children. Adult men dressed in rags or tatty dishdashas, with heads wrapped in patterned *yashmaghs* (the traditional headscarf), stood motionless and staring. Women enveloped from head-to-toe in black abayas would glare too, occasionally while holding an impassive, gazing toddler. Who was friend or enemy – what rash decision would end in trauma, death or maiming? The overwhelming poverty was evident. When the soldiers stopped, the oppressive heat roasted them as eager black flies descended to feast on the salty, wet sweat-stained skin, clothing and body armour. The exotic, moist tastes in the Meals Ready to Eat ration packs were another playground for the hyperactive, tenacious insects.

Halfway through the journey, lost and concerned as the evening loomed, they fortuitously encountered an outpost of U.S. Army engineers. It was the respite from stress, driving and tedium they needed before finally finding the navigational relief of the historic Euphrates River. The river's iconic status was of little immediate concern; its value lay in that it flowed from the north of the country to the south. They loosely followed the route of the river among the intertwined myriad agricultural plots and tracks on the vast expanses of flat floodplains until heading northeast towards Baghdad. The outskirts of the city were a dense network of mud berms and chaotic pockets of palm trees, plantations, reeds, lush agriculture, derelict dusty fields, drainage canals and ditches, long beige walls, and burnt-out vehicles. Deliberately, cautiously they navigated along the highways and lanes to the south-west of the vast expanse (nearly 60km^2) of Baghdad International Airport and its adjoining palace and artificial-lake complexes. To the east of the palaces lay the densely populated grid of neighbourhoods, best avoided by two un-armoured Humvees.

As they entered the grounds of the airport, the battle scarring on buildings became increasingly noticeable. Smashed windows, crumpled walls, plaster spattered by shrapnel and bullets stood among the debris of rubble. It was there they encountered Iraqi corpses splayed out in the dirt and grass and bushes and besides the roads. The rigidity of rigour mortis had slackened as the muscles decayed. Bloat, putrefaction and flies had contorted bodies that had days earlier attempted to resist the invasion. The odour of the fetid corpses hung and seeped in the warm air. Maggots crawled over the green-tinged flesh. Some bodies were in pieces of military uniform, and some were not. U.S. soldiers had been tasked to clear the bodies. For the occupants of the vehicle, it seemed more expected and surreal than perhaps was initially anticipated. William had previously worked in a medical facility where wheeling the occasional corpse from one room to another was a routine, emotionally disconnected task.

The first assignment was to find an empty, mostly in-tact building they could commandeer, and then liaise with the joint command to understand and navigate their role and logistical options in the massive, rapidly evolving military expedition. The airport was the staging point for military activities leading into the heart of the city. Despite the increasing and overwhelming U.S. military presence in the immediate area of the airport, it wasn't immune from the looting. Securing such a vast perimeter as platoons, battalions, brigades and divisions of elements of the different armed forces tried to grasp the scale, logistics and sequential complexity of the task was always likely to cause confusion. Between changeovers of responsibility, when replacements or reinforcements left gaps undefended, looters swarmed in to plunder the opulent palaces and annexes; sometimes before and sometimes after soldiers had secured their own souvenirs. William was among those to witness a zoo facility at a palace being raided. In the chaos, a cougar had escaped. It may have been a bobcat. It didn't matter. In the war zone, such a predator could as easily escape and evade capture as be shot. What would be, would be. Geese, swans, pelicans and gazelles were stolen. For the soldiers, the priority was not securing the animals. It was suppressing the threat posed by civilian looters inside the supposedly secure perimeter of U.S. control. As the U.S. forces gained greater, coordinated control over the area, the avenues for looters to exploit were locked down.

More of William's colleagues arrived, and they

began to operate missions separately from the public health team. The team started to coordinate with other squads and platoons and drive forays into Baghdad, down the airport highway onto the Qadisaya expressway and into the area of palaces, monuments and government buildings that would later become known as the Green Zone. For William, he was now finally travelling in small convoys with some reasonable ability to fight their way out of confrontation, with the roof-mounted Squad Automatic Weapon (SAW) light machine gun. Roof-mounted, in that case, meant a soldier was standing on the back of the vehicle with his weapon resting on the roof tarpaulin. Avoiding death by friendly-fire was, however, still a matter of shape assessment and common sense. One road led them unexpectedly towards a U.S. tank blocking an avenue – the Humvees backed up and turned away to avoid being obliterated in an instinctive, reactive act of blue-on-blue. William was trying to liaise with the museum and understand the baseline state of antiquities theft, damage or safe-keeping following the looting. That was his job. Yet there was so much more to mentally process. After the comparative tranquillity of the journey from Kuwait to Baghdad, the heat and intensity of the ventures beyond the airport rapidly defrosted any extraneous illusions of invincibility. The city's developed infrastructure made for ease of movement, and ease of lethal resistance. Snipers cracked out rifle rounds at the vehicles; still un-armoured Humvees. The series of overpasses to be driven under on the airport highway were devastatingly opportunistic ambush locations where grenades would be dropped onto passing military vehicles or gunmen would unleash sporadic sprays of automatic weapon fire. The radio communications network between vehicles and temporary base-stations was almost non-existent. That exacerbated the confusion, dramatically impacting the response reactions of Quick Reaction Forces; whose responsibility it was to deliver devastating firepower to extract troops in firefights or caught in ambushes.

On one occasion the small convoy William was

in encountered an ambushed Humvee torn up by intense eruptions of gunfire. Blood smears and spatter coated the inside of the Humvee and streaked the door. In a chaotic howling and firing, one of the ambushers was shot off the overpass while soldiers attempted to drag one of the ambushed soldiers, a doctor, from the exposed position. The doctor had been shot through the lung and was bleeding profusely. Another soldier in the vehicle had been shot through the leg. When attempts to find him failed, they realised he had dragged himself from the scene. They eventually located and stabilised him. William recognised the shot up soldiers in the bloodied view. They were the doctors he had driven with from Kuwait to Baghdad. Moments earlier, before they had come across the ambush, they had passed children playing football in the street, a good-natured, disarmingly ordinary scene from any typical day. It was William's first experience seeing such graphic violence at close range.

Mortality was questioned. The risk of becoming a casualty was immediately real, tangible and likely. Yet when it was unknown soldiers, there was still oddly a converse implication of disconnection. Any remaining gap was smashed closed when days later another assaulted vehicle was a cocoon of death for soldiers he had known. He had spoken to one of them in the preceding days. A grenade had been dropped into the vehicle. One soldier was mangled flesh. Another was scorched. Reality hit. It was all William could think about for the following hours, but the fact was also that nothing could be done about it. They had jobs to do – responsibilities to fulfil.

The rest of William's Civil Affairs colleagues arrived from Kuwait and quickly commandeered a villa in a luxurious neighbourhood adjacent to the palace that would become the foreigner-dominated ganglion of the Green Zone and coalition administration. Despite the efforts to engage the converging Army parties who had been designated to mitigate the perceived disaster at the Iraqi National Museum, William wasn't enjoying much traction. It had rapidly detonated into a political storm. Exaggerated media and military reports of extensive devastation, the smashing of glass cases and the theft of antiquities (few people knew that the resourceful Iraqi curators had pre-empted much of the carnage and securely hidden many of the precious artefacts) coupled with the apparent international outcry. Retribution and accusatory finger-pointing had handed Lieutenant Colonel Schwartz from the 1-64 Task Force, an unwinnable battle. Out of immense frustration, the senior officer yelled at William, who quickly realised the situation was not one he would have any jurisdiction or influence over. He asked if there was any other way he could be of assistance. "Yeah, we got a little zoo to deal with!" was the curt response. So William clambered back into his Humvee with his weapons and armour and passion for archaeology and headed to the zoo with an Associated Press photographer, Maya Alleruzzo.

It was the same scene of devastation Lawrence had recounted. William had no experience working at zoos, but given the complete mess, that actually seemed irrelevant. He met an Iraqi veterinarian, Dr Hussam, and in days later, Dr Abbas. They seemed to appreciate his "bushy" moustache. In the confusion and chaos of those initial days, William heard about a South African civilian who also arrived at the zoo. William had not met him, and between personnel movements in and out of the zoo and park grounds, the omnipresent chaos of looting, and trying to make sense of reports of animals in private collections in palace gardens, he was still trying to work out the details of the best approach. Suddenly he had gone from the Captain that was the Civil Affairs "antiquities guy" to the Civil Affairs "zoo guy". For good measure, he was also given temporary responsibility for a wildlife reserve near Ar-Rutba (400km west of Baghdad), where gazelles had been abandoned and were reportedly being slaughtered for food. He had no resources to deal with that situation.

Any effort, anywhere, was going to be about improvisation of logistics; about borrowing, trading and stealing. Effectiveness would be measured by restoring order, keeping the remaining animals alive and stopping more being stolen. That was how William found himself attempting to resolve the predicament of abandoned lion cubs and dogs in the gardens of a palace belonging to the son of a Middle Eastern dictator, during a war. When he returned to make final plans to move the young lions, he heard that the South African, Lawrence, had already moved them to the Baghdad Zoo. William returned to the zoo and finally encountered the large, sweating, ginger-bearded, Lawrence. The situation of food supplies had reached desperation. Despite only 12 of the initial estimated 500 animals at the Baghdad Zoo remaining, they had now acquired additional animals from palace collections. Sourcing sufficient volumes of meat was an almost impossible task. Lawrence's meagre cash supply was depleted, and buying meat was still incredibly difficult given the sporadic battles in the city blocking access to any market or source of donkey meat. Paltry collections of scrounged vegetables and donations of rice were barely enough to hold off the animals' impending starvation. It was then, in a case of spectacular final-bell timing that a mixed blessing, Hilde, from the animal welfare charity CFTW, arrived with a truckload of packaged buffalo meat. The lions, tigers, bears and vultures would survive another few days.

◆ ◆ ◆

The telephone was ringing. Francoise the elegant, astute, blonde and imposing French matriarch of Thula Thula (and Lawrence's wife) answered. "He's found the zoo" she blurted out in richly accented, excited tones. It had only been about a week since we had last seen him at the game reserve. "He says it's bloody hot, the animals are a mess and the place is being stolen around them". The satellite phone was paying its dues and broke the news we had all been itching to hear.

"Howzit boy, you'll love it here. It's mad. Soldiers are everywhere. Did you hear that? These bloody helicopters are flying overhead. Jeez, it's hot! And the flies! Brendan, you've never seen anything like it. Flies like you can't see the wall they're so thick. And these guys, the looters, they call them Ali Babas. I swear they come out of the sand and steal and disappear again. It's unbelievable! Like something out of Mad Max. They're bloody everywhere carrying animals, computers whatever. You lock animals up overnight, and the next morning the lock's broken and animals are gone. The animals are buggered. Tigers, bears, lions. Some lions escaped the other day, and the soldiers had to shoot the ones they couldn't round up again. I'm staying at the Al-Rasheed Hotel with some soldiers. Great guys. They bring me here in one of these armoured personnel carriers in the morning. It's insane, they think I'm bloody mad, and there's no way they'll let me come here on my own. They come to pick me up in the afternoon again. They're relieved someone is somehow here to help them with this zoo. They're trying to fight a bloody war, and there's a zoo with starving animals in the middle. Get to Kuwait and find Colonel Fikes at ORHA. I'm in room 715 at the Al-Rasheed Hotel in Baghdad. Get here when you can."

Breaking the news to my parents was a challenge that had been causing me more angst than the idea of entering Iraq. I figured if I could convince myself it was reasonably safe, it would be an easier sell. I knew that was an unjust burden I should not place on them given how remarkably supportive and understanding they had been my entire life. My parents managed to contain their undoubted disbelief and anxiety quite well, but understandably, were still not thrilled.

The connecting flight timing meant a 13-hour layover in Dubai airport. Flush with $100 Lawrence's mother had given me (after she paid for the travel tickets), I celebrated my first entry into the exotic Middle East with a last gasp of televised cricket and a small flurry of Guinness pints at the Irish pub. It made the nap on the carpeted floor between a row of chairs and the travellator feel more dignified. The wall-tile motif of galloping Arabian horses seemed to feed the regionally romantic, iconic stereotype in my head, more so than the flamboyance of the excessively lit polystyrene palm trees. The flight over the ocean and drab dust was uneventful until we started circling over Kuwait City airport. Between listening to Arabic instructions on how to handle customs, the translated phrase "and we remind you it is illegal to possess alcohol in Kuwait" spun my thoughts into a little naive startle. I realised I was not quite as cunning as I had thought when I packed three bottles of South African red wine into my luggage. Mild panic flustered me. What a potentially humiliating end to the great adventure. A grand evasive plan sprung to mind. Deny everything.

Passport control was a breeze. With luggage in hand, I jubilantly thought I had won my cunning little battle of wits. I had beaten the system, a notable rarity in my life. I confidently followed the exiting passengers walking past the first security guard with my grubby red backpack and Lawrence's leather bag containing the immoral bottles. "Easy as that," I thought smugly. The sight of x-ray machines between us and the exit door lurched my stomach into a wretched, anxiety knot. I had never seen luggage being screened before an airport exit. It struck me as inconveniently excessive. Obviously, there was no place to indicate that in customer satisfaction reviews. I confess I rather quickly mentally conceded that I was to be singled out. I immediately felt like I was radiating guilt and like all eyes in the immediate vicinity were obviously on me. All I had to work with was denial or honesty. Neither seemed a novel or great strategy in a high-security airport. The bags whisked along far too quickly for my liking, through the rubber flaps, and into the belly of the machine that would decide my fate. The man ahead of me was already having the soles of his shoes cut open by the security guards. Of course, the panic stirred. Bloody hell. Shoe-cutting as the go-to response to suspicion!

"Sir do you have any illegal substances in your bag?"

"Not that I know of" I piped up knowing I was sinking.

"My boss's wife packed this bag for my boss, who's in Baghdad trying to fix the zoo. Seriously, I didn't pack the bag. Maybe she put something in the bag for him because he's in Baghdad trying to fix the zoo. I'm going to meet him at the zoo. In Baghdad."

Say "Baghdad" a lot I thought. It wasn't composed or classically articulate, but I was instinctively plunging headfirst into denial at packing a bag, at an international airport in the Middle East. "Keep blaming", I thought. My feet felt sluggish, and I felt immediately warmer as I basked in my culpability.

A sharp burst of irate Arabic erupted from the passenger whose next shoe was being sliced apart on the counter next to us. A security guard opened the zipper of my bag, slid his hand in amongst the clothes and quite clearly had reached the objects of interest. His eyes rolled up to stare at mine. I felt hot guilt rise up. As I stood there, a skinny, pink-skinned ginger in a khaki Thula Thula reserve uniform with maroon coloured epaulettes (which I had believed may somehow give me an official look), I bordered on confession. Raised in comfortable suburbia, I was acutely aware of my lack of street-savvy. "Seriously if there is anything there then I guess I'm stuffed, but I don't know what's in there. My boss's wife packed it. He's in Baghdad. At the zoo. I'm going to Iraq tomorrow." I believe I saw a slight glint of pleasure in the officer's penetrating brown eyes as I squirmed. "It's ok, it's fruit juice" he declared in heavily accented English with just enough authority and volume for those around him to hear. "Carry on. Good luck with the zoo." His mouth creased to a stifled smile.

The white dishdasha-robed taxi drivers clearly saw "prey" etched on my forehead as I exited the arrivals terminal. With one grabbing at my luggage and another at my arm, it was slightly tricky to explain the destination which I thought would be quite a significant factor in the equation. Obviously, I was wrong again. The accepted norm quickly became apparent. Grab the foreigner. Stuff him on the back seat of the car like a kidnap victim. Fight the other drivers for the luggage while arguing and gesticulating. Throw that prize in the trunk and slam it shut before anyone else can whip out the cargo. Then ask "so where you go now?" "ORHA. The Office for Reconstruction and Humanitarian Assistance." It was a mystery to the driver. ORHA rolled out his mouth over and over like a confusing mantra as he consulted his fellow taxi drivers who by now had settled down to wild gestures and several interpretations of what ORHA could mean.

With the navigational puzzle loosely and then miraculously definitively solved, the destination was found. The heat and glare off the white walls of the former primary school were stunning. I squinted and sweated as I shuffled with my luggage up to the security booth. Explaining I had arrived see Colonel Jim Fikes, the surly security guards opened the boom and pointed me down the parking lot. An English accent piped up from a man who ambled along beside me.

"How much you pay for the taxi?"
"8 Dinars."
"You should've paid 6. You were screwed over. Welcome"

Fikes rose from his chair in the makeshift plywood cubicle. The surrounding cubicles and passages were filled with military figures hustling to and fro. Small in stature with a crisply manicured moustache and dressed in desert camouflage U.S. Army fatigues, Fikes's outwardly friendly welcome was a relief to my slightly overwhelmed brain. It felt like the ball of chance was rolling, and there was no turning back to my comfort zone. Lawrence had managed to get a message through to Fikes once he had heard I had left Thula Thula. It was a relief to me that I was at least in the system, whatever that was. I was set up with a stretcher cot in an empty, spotlessly clean classroom. It was time to explore. I was conveniently armed with a little rubber bouncing ball for company, the perfect toy for mindless entertainment in empty classrooms and hallways, as I set out to find people and figure out what ORHA was.

A queue of westerners dressed in pale khaki chinos and a variety of pastel-coloured cotton shirts with sweaty armpits, trying to look casual in an official sort of way, snaked out a room and into the hallway. Plastic dinner trays! Their bearers projected the insipid expression of administrative drones, empowered by the lanyard, being served a safe alternative to the aberrant, wildly exotic local or sub-continental flavours. Stouter individuals were in desert camouflage military attire. Looking conspicuous in my khaki game ranger outfit and epaulettes, I became self-conscious when I realised I did not have any official badges dangling from my neck. I joined the queue in the hope of hustling a free meal. I thought I was more cunning than I actually was. Working on the premise that if you act as if you should be there, people often don't ask any questions, I loaded my tray up with food. Nobody cared I was there.

"So whadda ya here for?" came the twang as I sat at a table with what I assumed were three soldiers based on the camouflage fatigues. "Going to help fix the Baghdad Zoo", I replied. Hearing it come out my mouth, I was struck by how odd that idea must sound to young military men and women from faraway states of North America sitting in a canteen in Kuwait City. The blank stares also hit the point home.

"Huh?" one mumbled through the mouthful of lettuce leaves, noticeably confused by the concept and the accent. "Ja I'm heading to the zoo in Baghdad. Sounds like it needs some work", I continued, growing in confidence once I noticed what a novelty the line of conversation was. Novelty meant a talking point, and once we got talking, it was clear these Marine reservists were not the gung-ho, *Conan the Barbarian* types we had always been led to believe every Marine is by Hollywood. Slightly unfit and recently having been called up for deployment, I understood they were fortuitously still enjoying the comfort of a building with functional amenities while their colleagues sweated their backsides off in the miserable heat and dust of the desert outside of the capital city. We quickly became companions in boredom, surfed the satellite's European porn adverts on the communal television when no commanding officers were around, ate together and talked about U.S. politics. There were numerous theories and gossip of what was happening north of the border in Iraq. An attempt by the reservists to get me onto a U.S. Marines humanitarian mission to deliver food packages and bottled water to Basra was greeted with a crooked eye by the commanding officer as we sat in the Ben & Jerry's ice cream shop a few blocks from the ORHA. It was a no-go for me.

    I was waiting in ORHA for one reason. Kuwaiti customs refused to release a tranquilliser dart gun donated to the project by CFTW because of the potential danger such an unusual device may pose. The caution was obviously merited when considering national security and its likely impact on the multinational military invasion. Without the dart gun which had become a vital and much-anticipated piece of equipment for the Baghdad Zoo, Fikes was not going to bother finding me a flight to Baghdad. He knew it was essential equipment and that I would be the quickest, most direct means to get the dart gun to the zoo. It meant more hours of bouncing the rubber ball aimlessly, repeatedly hurling it down empty hallways, waiting for it to hit a target and bounce back. When that didn't suffice as entertainment, and the Marines were working, I was sitting in the searing desert sun on the roof, among the satellite dishes and white water tanks of the building, staring into the utterly alien aesthetic of the surrounding city. White stone-facade mansions covered in brash Arabian trimmings reflected light and heat among immaculately maintained roads, verges and mosque minarets. A never-ending source of large, glinting 4x4 vehicles driving past hinted at a casual opulence in the neighbourhood. By day two, it quickly became clear I needed a new hobby. I was bursting at the seams to get to Baghdad. It was all so close, yet it was waiting, wait, wait some more. Hang on. Yes. No. Wait. U.S. President George W. Bush had already declared "Major combat operations in Iraq have ended" and that "in the Battle of Iraq the United States and her allies have prevailed." Time was ticking. I genuinely felt like I was missing the action – the impatience of youth.

After breakfast, I discovered the daily briefing. A large room was filled with neatly groomed humanitarian NGO representatives of all descriptions. A tendency for cargo pants seemed to reflect their on-the-ground credentials. It was like a slick new ecosystem into which international agencies could neatly project their worldly experience, industriousness and agendas. It was an opportunity for the many stakeholders to represent their humanitarian planning and delivery prowess to their peers. It was professional, targeted and those in their respective fields undoubtedly believed in the process and the mechanisms of trying to resolve the myriad complex logistical crises and suppurating social wounds that were being picked open by the invasion. It was a world so sanitised and apparently efficient that it all seemed so quickly solvable; provided there were no ungrateful, agitated, militant, tardy, unskilled, angry, maimed, criminal, suspicious, power-jockeying or corrupt humans to deal with. Baghdad and Iraq already seemed to be improving according to the numbers and projections. It kept the swarm of bureaucrats, disaster management strategists and idealists excitedly scribbling notes. My cynicism of smart clothes representing smart results simmered.

Finally! On day three, the 12th of May, Colonel Fikes handed me the meter-long box containing the dart gun, and a smaller box containing darts and immobilising drugs. "Customs doesn't know. You needed it. Now you've got it. Get out of here. The car will take you to the airport. We've heard there is a flight to Baghdad in two hours. Good luck. I might see you there. Send my regards to Lawrence." With the bags and boxes loaded into the hastily arranged transport at the ORHA, Fikes's right-hand man drove quickly to the U.S. military-controlled section of a nearby airport.

The display of aircraft lined up in precise rows on the edge of the runway was a visual feast of the awesome firepower at the disposal of the U.S. military. Matt black Apache attack helicopters, and dirty grey Cobra helicopters, those sinister, angular predators, accompanied endless, grey F-15 Eagle jets. I tried not to look like an excited child in a sweet shop as I processed the abstract television perspective transforming into my new reality. Everyone was going somewhere looking like they had a purpose. This seemed to be the military way. Look busy even if you're maybe not. The glass door led from the exotic world of an airbase supporting a war to a room scattered with bored soldiers in assorted states of dishevelment lounging on the awkward plastic benches, moaning about baseball matches lost and delayed flights.

"The flight to Baghdad's cancelled" shouted the harassed Specialist from behind the makeshift check-in counter. He looked as enthusiastic as staff at a British Airways missing-baggage office. "Aaah gaaaddammitt man!" came several frustrated gripes out of the lethargic passengers to anywhere except that waiting room. My car had left, and I had no contact details for anyone who could collect me once that flight was cancelled. I had not considered that it would be an option I had to prepare for.

"Hey, I'm trying to get to the zoo in Baghdad. Yes, seriously. I need to get on the next flight" I shouted over the noise of machinery and baggage hauliers behind the designated flight list coordinator. "Flight is cancelled go wait with the others!" He paused briefly. The cogs in his head ground slowly. He stared. "You say a zoo? Fuck man. You kidding me? Well, leave your kit here. If anything comes up, I'll let you know". There was that novelty opening a door again.

Hours passed, and the anticipation, anxiety, heat and lack of food had tempered my energy. The musty aroma of the unwashed, of sweating feet and body funk saturated my nostrils. I learnt that bored soldiers stuck in stuffy waiting rooms fart, moan and swear a lot. I sat and stared and drifted into my imagination. Hurry up and wait was tediously playing itself out.

"Flights on! Who's going to Baghdad?" shouted the by now clearly frustrated Specialist, hoping to get the moaning mob out of his responsibility. "Zoo guy you're up".

"A zoo? In Baghdad? Really?" the 6.4ft, balding British Army Colonel in the queue leading onto the tarmac queried. I put out a speculative sales pitch about the zoo as we walked out of the room towards the choreographed loading activity around our giant taxi. I reasoned the more people that knew about the zoo, the higher the likelihood someone may be a useful contact at some point. Issued with yellow, peanut-sized foam-rubber earplugs by the loadmaster we strolled up the ramp into the gut of the gungrey, U.S. Air Force C-130 transport plane. The thunderous rumbling of the engines faded as I squished the plugs in. The sparse cargo netting seats were folded off the sidewalls of the fuselage. We jammed together like expectant battery chickens, with me looking a little out of place in my now grimy Zululand game ranger outfit. The loadmaster in his tan coloured jumpsuit issued incomprehensible instructions, waving his arms and shouting as if someone could hear him. I assumed the soldiers all knew what he was talking about and figured I would follow them in case there was a problem. I must have looked confused since the man next to me bellowed through the earplugs "he says if you see a fire to let him know!"

"Ah, yes! Of course" I loudly replied as I gave him the thumbs up. "Wouldn't think about keeping that little bit of news to myself" I mumbled. How anyone could see much out the murky little portholes remained a mystery to me. The cargo palettes with the luggage were loaded into the hold with us, and the door hydraulics sealed us into the metal storeroom. Kuwait City was left behind in its barren sandbox.

With my mind drifting in thoughts, stuttering sleep and the occasional jolting through turbulence the 2-hour flight into Iraq felt shorter than expected. Before long we were tucked into a steep descent towards what was, until the U.S. Army's 3rd ID's arrival on 3 April 2003, known as Saddam International Airport. The pilot's presumed rationale of *the quicker you get the hell out of the air, the less chance of being shot at* was being actioned. The faded beige scars of dust-covered runways lay amongst the parched turf and sand below.

Touchdown. Relief. The adrenaline started leaking into my body. Bombing damage to some of the runways meant a long, convoluted taxi route past the derelict main airport building. Its cheerless Iraqi Airways jets stood as reminders that not long before, the airport had served passengers heading out on eagerly anticipated holidays (although even those had been severely curtailed after the flying restrictions imposed following the 1991 invasion of Kuwait). The C-130 slowed to a halt next to a grizzled, battle-wounded, dusty square building. That damn, all-smothering, choking dust was apparently everywhere. The hydraulic ramp slowly opened. Palettes were whisked out with orderly efficiency. We exited to what felt like the furnace breath of a mythical beast being whipped past us by the propellers as they eased in pitch. The enveloping ambient blaze reflecting off every surface was so novel, so acute, that it briefly knocked out a gasp from my lungs as my brain scrambled frantically to adjust to the malicious intensity. My body sensed it was being dehydrated and squeezed by the depth and severity of the heat. The glare felt like it would dry out eyeballs immediately if one blink were missed. I didn't know it was still three months until mid-summer.

"Get the bags, get the boxes and get the hell into that building for some shade," I thought. I shuffled alongside the

British colonel in the hope that I could hitch a ride into town, to somewhere. I had no clue where the Al-Rasheed Hotel was, or the zoo, or even where the city actually was. I posed the question. "Not sure when my ride is coming, or where they are going. Will find out when they get here" he stated as he walked away with a look of sudden discomfort merited by being asked to take a civilian youngster to a zoo in a war zone during working hours.

I lumbered with my bags and equipment through the duct-taped entrance into the dusty chaos of the small building. The windows were either smashed or taped together. Coloured wires dangled out the ceiling like entrails. Presumably, there had been some sort of battle or blast near the building. Bits of cardboard boxes had been fashioned into makeshift doors, and a motley crew of grimy U.S. Army soldiers of all shapes and descriptions were scattered over the floor. This was not the refined warrior crew I was mistakenly expecting. Some lay or sat on stretchers listening to CDs through headphones. Others sat with disembowelled meal ration packs and empty water bottles spread around them while a handful sucked confidently on cigars. A gap-toothed, shaven-headed Specialist was propped up behind some wooden planks that looked somewhat like a desk. It became my information kiosk. Specialist seemed a bit of an exaggerated rank.

"So how do I get into Baghdad?" I queried. I should have expected it. My fault.

"You are in Baghdad" he mumbled.

"I'm looking for the zoo". I should have expected it.

"A zoo? In Baghdad?"

"Where is the Al-Rasheed Hotel?" I should have expected it.

"Huh?"

I moved the target. A disgruntled lady in uniform palmed me off onto a more efficient looking individual in fresher combat gear. I was surprised that he immediately agreed to let me ride with him if transport ever arrived. They had already been waiting for most of the day. Fortunately, within half an hour, a khaki-straw coloured Land Rover pulled up in a haze of dust. It presented an opportunity to once again harass the British colonel who had politely been trying to avoid eye contact with me. With the situation explained to the refreshingly accommodating driver, it was a stroke of luck the British were heading to the conference centre buildings opposite the Al-Rasheed Hotel. We loaded up and navigated our way through the maze of palm trees, powdery tracks, military transport trucks and desert colour U.S. Army Humvees to an impromptu checkpoint on the edge of a runway. The checkpoint soldier leaned towards the window. "Ordnance. Wait here."

"Fire in the hole! Fire in the hole! Fire in the hole!" yelled his animated colleague as we all watched a distant tract of bare earth. An orange-yellow flash flared silently out the sand as smoke and dust erupted in expanding plumes. A second or two later the thunderous clap and rumble swept over us. The Land Rover rocked lightly. We were waved onwards.

I tried to absorb what was happening. It seemed too surreal for my brain to comprehend. This was Baghdad. The place we had been watching on the news only a few days earlier. It was nothing like the press had portrayed. Or maybe it was, but I had never really paid too much attention to the details until then. I had expected something like the desolate, flat sandy edges of Kuwait City. Where was the endless bare dust, camels and the unhealthy dose of destruction supposedly everywhere? The buildings should have been piles of rubble, and the stench of filth and decay should have lingered in the air. That is what struck me about Luanda, Angola, a few years earlier during a university visit, in a temporary hiatus in the country's 27-year civil war. I had no idea of the reality of Baghdad. Yes, there was dust everywhere, but the highway leading from the airport was lined with thin groves of mature date palm trees up to the edges of the pale, flat-roofed houses about 50m from the road. There were visible signs of previous battle but not of wholesale destruction. The columns of resolute, iconic palm trees had immediately fed the clichéd, expected Middle Eastern setting. Perhaps that was eerier. It was not clear where the danger lay and where it was disguised. The areas on the edge of the road were unkempt but growing. Deep tank track furrows crisscrossed the chewed up sandy soil between the trees. Isolated trees were knocked over, I presumed from an explosion or from having come off second best against a tank. Some trees had fibrous gouges and wounds from the past weeks' antisocial activities. A few had scorch marks on them. A mangled, burnt shell of a civilian car lay on the edge of the road. A few thin columns of black smoke wisped into the painfully bright sky in the distance. We passed intermittent traffic, almost all military of some sort of description; mainly Humvees loaded with soldiers staring blankly out the doorless frames, weapons pointed at the road. Some Humvees had a soldier slotted into the hard-top roof like a birthday candle with a mounted machine gun attached. The highway was, well, was a highway. There were overhead bridges. It appeared normal and similar to home in many ways.

The talk in the vehicle was of military business, politics and how they had heard there was some other South African at the zoo. On the short drive to our destination, I drifted in and out of conversation preferring to look through the dusty windscreen absorbing the geometry of the tan-coloured, stucco-cloaked square houses and the Islamic domes of a mosque or palace. A palace! Sure. Why not? That was very far from my usual daily reference. There were repetitive, random signs of a battle. What types of civilian vehicles were parked next to houses? The lack of contrasting colours was conspicuous. There was so much beige, except the orange flashes of a taxi and the green of the palm fronds. More good roads lined with palm trees. Muddy coloured houses. White houses. Overpasses. Was that a tank? Where the hell is this desert the news always showed? Fuck I can't believe this is Baghdad! Thoughts raced in my head. An Apache helicopter throbbed past overhead, then another.

The road ahead was partially blocked by a weave of chest-high, sand-filled barriers. Razor wire, traffic cones and more barriers guided us towards the mouth of the checkpoint. Soldiers were milling around among the structures, overlooked by the ominous presence of an Abrams tank. The barrel aimed down the road at oncoming traffic. That was us. A camouflage netting covered more soldiers with barrels of weapons aimed towards us. We slowed. A courteous wave from our driver, a flash of the identification passes from the military men in the Land Rover and the red and white boom raised to let us through.

Enormous swords arched out from the palm trees. The Baghdad landmark of two sets of colossal swords crossed over either end of a military parade ground was more impressive than I could have conceived without seeing them in person. I guessed about forty or fifty metres at the apex. Between the tree trunks and dusty columns of street lamp posts that flashed past I could make out the back of the parade ground and floodlight towers, razor wire coiled out between desert coloured transport trucks, Humvees, tents, water and fuel bowser trucks. Beyond the second set of swords, a massive chunky upturned dish of sorts dwarfed the trucks parked next to it. A narrowing spiral of glossy green, white, black and red tiles rose up next to the dish like an inverted, exotic lollypop. The entire gigantic arrangement was fringed with white-pointed slopes aimed at the ground like a collar of sharpened daisy petals.

The scale of all these structures seemed huge and made as little sense to me as Tate gallery displays. "The Tomb of the Unknown Soldier. This is all the Green Zone. Supposed to be safer. The rest of Baghdad is the Red Zone. The hotel's around the corner" said the voice that broke my concentration. Square, officious looking buildings rose out from behind dusty walls. The tops of tanks with angled, khaki turrets and death delivering 120mm cannon barrels and .50 calibre machine guns lurked amongst the dishevelled gardens and green hedges. A metal statue, once a symbol of power, of a now headless Saddam riding a horse, lay stiff and undignified, tipped on the side of its pedestal at the entrance to the building. Another statue of Saddam still stood defiantly erect on a low roof of the building, right arm raised straight, clutching a rifle. Below it, a collective of chunky modernist bronze frieze artworks of industrial activity, oil wells included, stretched out across the wall.

It was my first viewing of the bullet and shrapnel damage sprayed along the perimeter walls of the hotel grounds. A lethargic soldier pulled aside the checkpoint razor wire at the gate, and we drove past the piles of sandbags, round the peculiarly distorted statue of a maiden escaping a jar in the dry fountain, to the collection of black and silver SUVs at the hotel entrance. "Good luck with the zoo, mate" the driver chirped as they drove off.

I stood at the entrance to the tall, dusty-beige rectangle with its rows of mini blast walls sloping symmetrically out from each floor like concrete Venetian blinds. A collection of hulking tanks, Humvees and armoured vehicles in the visitor parking bays made me more aware I was dressed in my, by then, slightly foul game ranger outfit. With a collection of bags and boxes, I blended into the surroundings like a kleptomaniac backpacker lost at a Veterans Day parade.

I stepped over the outline of the chipped out mosaic of U.S. President George Bush senior's face which used to greet the soles of visitors shoes through prior years. It seemed like strangely petty symbolism for mature adults to design such a feature – but what did I know? The hotel opened up into the expansive entrance foyer followed by the main reception foyer. Tired eighties-style décor was mixed in with leather couches, pot plants, massive cracked and smashed plate glass windows, dust, the familiar reek of sweat and stale cigarette smoke all embellished with a touch of teenager-bedroom chaos. Soldiers slouched in various states of collapse, lethargically digging into MRE ration bags and swapping the inner treasures and evils. They laughed at the rhetoric of partisan commentators of FOX News on a rigged up television. If these commentators, with the diplomacy skills of wolverines on heat, were anything to base American public opinion on, it appeared Iraq was due to be turned into a desolate parking lot with a few handheld pumps to steal oil with. Behind the former reception counter, some more soldiers stood in grimy, sweaty uniforms with cups of coffee discussing the day's events or whatever else passed the time before the next patrol.

"Sorry, you guys know where room 715 is? I've got some stuff for the zoo" I enquired trying not to look like a tourist with the appearance of a UPS delivery boy.

"Yeah, yeah the South African zoo guy. He ain't in. Should be back later. Go round the corner and up the stairs."

The crumpled elevator door next to the stairs exposed a cavity with a tangle of cables; apparently the result of an over-zealous engineer's generosity with the explosive. The lingering dust in the air and the wretched smell of clogged toilets drained my remaining energy as I choked my way up the dark stairwell for seven floors. The clutch of bags felt heavier than ever. My throat was dry, and my lungs ached. I wished I had water to drink. I had some adapting to do. The elevator lobby of the 7th floor opened to a corridor of dirty brown carpets. That same decorator that has taken so much care to colour code the brown tones with appropriate odours in the hotel foyer had apparently made it that far too. 720 was the first room I saw. The door was slightly ajar. I pushed my way through and dropped the boxes and bags. A puff of dust rose from the carpet to remind me I was still in Baghdad. The room was covered in a fine layer of dust as if it was the place vacuum cleaners went to explode.

The view from the windows was thrilling and absorbing. Before me lay a vast expanse of Baghdad. A few prominent landmarks stood clear of the palm and eucalyptus trees saturating what I was to later find out was Al-Zawra Park, the suburbs of Kindi, Mansour and beyond.

Palaces, gargantuan uncompleted mosques and abandoned cranes were unmistakable. More palm trees. More blocky, beige, flat-roofed houses. Out to the left, the oil refinery coughed out a thin, erratic plume of black smoke. Straight ahead stretched the mammoth, arching swords and the parade ground. Further towards the horizon stood the iconic silhouette of the mangled, bombed-out shell of the telecommunications exchange and tower. Below on the road, beyond the hotel lawns and the lonely tennis court, a barricade of HESCO barriers, sandbags and armour created a choke point. Tanks parked next to camouflage-netted machine gun placements and overheating soldiers at the checkpoint. The hotel swimming pool diving boards stood watch over the exposed bare concrete and remaining murky green scum of the deep end. Swimming pools. Poor things. Always the unwilling barometer for progress or regression. "Like a bloody Arabian Disneyland," I thought as I stared out, captivated. Over half an hour passed before I left the window to explore my new home. I started to check out all the unlocked rooms along the corridor, all of which looked similar with their worn leather chairs, blue and white beds, the essential layer of dust and a welcoming turd in the toilet. It was later explained that without running water, the game was to find a new toilet with a flush left in it and feed it like a bee would its expectant brood. Judging by the sweet reek permeating through the building, this game had naturally extended well beyond the 7th floor. I was apparently late for the start.

   That view from 720's window drew me back again. I sat on the window sill and gawked at the landscape, wondering what lay ahead. It was immediately clear to me I was not leaving after a month as anticipated, but I had no idea I was already knee-deep into one of the most intimidating and refreshing years of my life.

   Lawrence's coarse laugh rose out from the temporary quiet below. He was walking past a cluster of soldiers, headed for the outside shower next to the neglected swimming pool. It was the only working water point at the hotel. Apart from showers, it was used to fill buckets that were carried to rooms to flush toilets for those who had given up trying to find a fresh target in the porcelain game. I definitely had not expected that my first sighting of Lawrence would be him stripping naked outside in the wide open. I exited out of the foyer stairwell as a fresher Lawrence entered through the side doors of the foyer.

"Rollence!" (we'd always joked how many of the Zulu staff at the game reserve had struggled to pronounce the 'l's' and 'r's' in his name the correct way around).

"Brendan! Howzit boy?"

I couldn't believe how much weight he had already lost. His excess shirt fabric creased and draped over his shoulders and chest. He couldn't believe I was finally there. He beamed a smile like an excited child, plainly thriving in the chaotic, novel surrounds. The snap of familiarity, even if out of context, brought an immediate, tangible release of physical and mental tension in me. We headed straight towards the foyer's improvised café at the former telex/cashier counter. The weathered Sergeant Diehl had brewed up a fresh pot of the most coveted coffee in the building, an inescapable lure for some of the tank crews from the 3rd ID. The alternative was lurking around the furniture, bored, tired and wanting to be somewhere else. From the thrill of punching through and tearing up defences and dominating ground, now they were comparatively sedentary – navigating the dreariness of routine patrols and defending checkpoints. These were some of the soldiers that had conducted the armoured *thunder runs* into central Baghdad from the airport. They had delivered coordinated, incisive strikes, destroying key targets and human cannon fodder along their routes into and out of the city, again and again. The crews had repelled repeated assaults by buses, pickups, taxis and civilian cars bristling with the disorganised fury of fanatical Fedayeen militia, Iraqi foot soldiers and Syrian jihadis armed with AK-47's and rocket-propelled grenades (RPG). Suicide bombers and pickups mounted with an assortment of improvised weaponry had been launched against the 3rd ID's heavy armour that received and mostly withstood unrestrained pummelling. The ragged Iraqi defenders of Highway 8 (connecting Baghdad to Kuwait), in particular, had been scythed down or obliterated by these young American men and their colleagues. In some cases, telling civilians from combatants had been impossible, and death was still usually the outcome (later reports would suggest some civilians genuinely had no idea they would likely encounter an American tank when they left home). Despite the brevity of the battles and disparity in war-making firepower, U.S soldiers had also been impaled, disfigured, burnt, maimed or torn apart in the raging assaults. Where Iraqi tanks, artillery and transport trucks hid from the aerial attacks of A10 Warthog jets, by being parked under bridges and highway overpasses, they had been left erupting and burning furiously in the wake of the rolling American Abrams tanks and Bradley Fighting Vehicle attacks. These were also the troops rumbling menacingly through Baghdad as Minister of Information, Comical Ali, goaded the invaders and misled his believers as he colourfully asserted that there were "no American troops in Baghdad", and that "Americans are committing suicide by the hundreds at the city's gates". It was not long before the city fell to the tactics, intensity and sustained firepower of those supposedly non-existent troops. As an utterly surreal and unanticipated sub-plot, the soldiers had become allies of the zoo cause. Lawrence had made sure of that. Their lives over the previous few months had seared in memories which put the state of affairs into perspective for us. It was their war; it was not ours. Lawrence had earned their respect by his effective persistence and wit at the zoo during previous weeks. Even though I still felt like a tourist in their world of manliness, by being associated with Lawrence, I could bask a little in the sweaty, unpretentious magnetism of the camaraderie. "It's like the fuckers are bringing knives to a gunfight" came the comments when recalling the mismatched arsenals. Recollections of "pink misting" (effectively vaporising a human) seemed shared. Before arrival in Baghdad, unsuspecting walking, living Iraqi conscripts were erased at distances of several kilometres, at night. On one occasion, it was so dark a soldier in the exposed terrain didn't see his nearby colleague "get smoked." Or it happened at point-blank range, instinctively, when the tank crew didn't have the time to change from firing depleted uranium rounds to conventional munitions. Coaxial machine guns added to the violent separation of flesh from the body. There was no sense at all that it was a callous boast. It was simple, vicious reality. It was almost so abnormal it was abstract. Encounters felt weirdly unreal at the same time as being viscerally real. I was led to understand it is like a computer game with all this destruction being executed impersonally on a computer screen using unrivalled night vision or thermal imaging technology. Most enjoyed it, and some seemed captivated by a sense of patriotic duty. Perhaps not as glossy recruitment adverts would frame it but still a sense that it was America's duty to restore some "order". 9/11 had been a motivator of sorts but not the defining overwhelming stimulus. It helped to be on the winning side. That was acknowledged. Some inherently knew the tension, fear, thrill, battle memories and camaraderie were a fleeting segment of their lives. There was tangible, openly expressed relief from the soldiers that their immediate comrades, their friends in the war had survived the fight into Baghdad. It was relief that they didn't have to process mental scar tissue of inescapable, connected death. They had heard of casualties, but those weren't from their immediate surrounds. Some of their parents had not been so fortunate, intractably burdened by *their* war in Vietnam. Despite the cocoon the armour temporarily provided, it wasn't all sanitary disconnection from the dreadful. Some chuckled while recalling the mock revulsion of their colleague who had drawn the short straw to "peel the dead Hadji" out of a burnt-out truck cab near to the temporary camp at the Tomb of the Unknown Soldier. The rotting stench of putrid charred flesh needed to be buried. The stink stuck. I couldn't help reflect on the outrageously weird shift in my reality. Most striking, and perhaps disturbing of all, was that these guys seemed like us in so many ways. My expectations of weary, withdrawn soldiers tired of war or brashly, hilarious characters had been drawn from media and imagination. They were all personable, physically unimposing, mostly charming and immediately likeable. Career soldiers mixed with youngsters with university ambitions. A soldier discussed his recent reading of James Michener's "The Covenant" set in South Africa. Familiar ease and comfort quickly infused my perception of the beaten-up hotel foyer as we talked on, despite me experiencing nothing of their recent combatant world. Novelty laced with recognisable normality generated refreshing energy of anticipation and blind faith that I wouldn't get physically or psychologically mashed in Iraq.

Lawrence, in his unique style, had created a wildly exaggerated illusion I was some sort of a Steve Irwin-like, crocodile wrestling lion-heart. I had no convincing ammunition to prolong that. In one unintentional snort-laugh at a question about grappling buffalo, I dismantled the rugged illusion and reinforced my placid, grass-mowing, suburban heritage. They quickly noticed I was the antithesis of the shredded, weather-beaten marauder he had created. Having shaved about two days earlier, and despite being 26, I still looked like a shiny, jovial 18-year-old compared to Lawrence and the worn personnel surrounding us. With the introductions completed and the new realities of my résumé affirmed, the coffee was sunk, and we headed upstairs to our adoptive home.

Alistair, Bob and Peter were the self-proclaimed landlords of the Al-Rasheed's 7th floor. They were part of the team contracted by the U.S. Department of Defence to investigate, film, photograph and catalogue the explicit realities of Saddam's Iraq. Everything from appalling mental asylums, currency swapping in the streets, tea cafes and the excavation of putrid mass graves fell under their lens. They exuded a compelling blend of adventurer charisma and upbeat confidence borne of analytical brains and youthful energy subjected to volleys of wars and global travel. Conversations could flick from intellectual to cynical, to hilarious and riotous on the back of a single comment. They were veteran British and South African fixers and operators with backgrounds in elite military units, ground-breaking war journalism, a few fringe hobbies like antique weapons collection and impromptu war zone hospitality. Their collective abilities to scrounge supplies, souvenirs and cold beers was a revelation I quickly admired. It was a captivating introduction into a largely unseen world of expatriate entrepreneurs who apparently coexist in an evolving symbiotic relationship with modern warfare. Collectively they never ceased working. There was always a mission to plan, a topic to document, film to edit or catalogue. Outrageous anecdotes were the norm. Of course, Peter had interviewed Osama bin Laden and set up a guest house in Kabul the year before arriving in Baghdad. Of course, others had been security consultants or filmed series of the *Amazing Race* and *Survivor*. That seemed appropriately ordinary in the setting. Boxes of mixed rations lay among bottles of water, camera equipment, silver cutlery, a couple of guns and a homely pot plant. Lawrence had become a fixture on their social scene as the day's zoo madness was discussed with vigour. After chilled Bavaria beer, an introductory lesson on how to operate the modern wonder of the U.S. Army MRE ration's heating pad, and talk of the days past, my brain was finally calling for a timeout. I needed a place to fall over and sleep. Being a colleague of Lawrence, the zoo connection and being South African got me Room 713. It was prime real estate within the inner territory of the D.O.D. crews' mini-empire and spared the wrath of the common soldier's faecal touch. Its door had been locked to avoid rogue defecators. The room was to become my sanctuary of calm for the ensuing months. The intermittent clattering of machine-gun fire carried on somewhere out in the dark streets as my head sunk into the dusty pillow. It was Baghdad. It felt a bit insane and ballsy to be there for a zoo, and it was fucking exhilarating. The whole situation and the purpose of mission felt so captivating, so all-consuming on the senses that there wasn't room for doubts to surface about the point of going or the impact we would make.

CHAPTER 3

Lawrence and I stood in the shade of a tree outside the hotel gates discussing the contrived absurdity of our surrounds and the zoo initiative. The early morning heat was quickly gaining in oppressive intensity. I inspected the clusters of bullet holes ripped through the nearby lamp posts. Soldiers, wrapped up in bulky body armour, sat awkwardly on chairs behind the razor wire at the gates, staring out towards the road. The sticky residue of a removed corpse still stained the concrete pavement slabs next to us in a profile that was undoubtedly human. Apart from that, there was an unexpected serenity in the stillness. Then the deafening half roar, half whine, of the 1500 horsepower gas turbine Abrams tank engines firing up in the adjacent tree-lined parking lot reverberated through our bodies. The ground rumbled as if it had indigestion. The tracks of the 60-ton beasts rattled and clanked as they manoeuvred their massive, squat, angular, armour-plated hulls out the hotel entrance checkpoint, past us hitchhikers and on their way to patrol the city streets. The helmeted young battle veteran standing in the turret raised a thumb in greeting. As the clatter faded, the orange and white Chevrolet Caprice with the word "ZOO" emblazoned in black tape on the hood drove up to us.

Stephan Bognar, a field agent for the NGO WildAid, stepped out the passenger side, immaculately dressed in combat trousers, a white t-shirt and black baseball cap. His tri-athlete physique and groomed features stood out from the less urbane surrounds. His welcome was overwhelmingly charming, and his vibrant character immediately apparent. In time he would be my reference into the world of the everlasting expatriate; caught in that compelling space of conservation ambition and philanthropic aid in remote areas, reflectively thinking of *normal* life back home. A Canadian, he was based in Cambodia working on rural development projects. While on assignment in Israel he was issued with new instructions to get to Baghdad Zoo. He seemed infinitely resourceful as he described the ease of travelling to neighbouring Jordan and then securing a taxi to Baghdad – as one does during a war. He had moved by road under the shield of the imposingly built, broad-bellied, boldly moustachioed, street-savvy taxi driver Mohammed Ali. Ali, by a twist of circumstances and the arrival of a polite Canadian with U.S. Dollars, quickly became embedded as Baghdad Zoo's fixer, our bodyguard, lion tamer, personal deal negotiator, and white-knuckle urban rally driver extraordinaire. Stephan was based at the Al Fanar Hotel on Abu Nawas Street across the Tigris River from the Green Zone. The journey from Amman to Baghdad had evolved into a daily taxi routine with Ali ferrying Stephan to collect and return Lawrence to the Al-Rasheed. Ali's taxi had replaced Lawrence's morning APC runs. Arriving a few weeks after Lawrence and William, Stephan's injection of fresh energy and desperately needed funds was a vital reprieve for the zoo's troubled recovery that coincided with Hilde's CFTW meat delivery. Until that point, Lawrence had been using up his small pot of personal funds to bargain food for the animals, lure back any hesitant workers and acquire the most basic equipment for the zoo.

Stephan, despite his surprisingly glamorous appearance, worked tirelessly. His ability to put in the heavy, sweat-soaked labour or wield chunks of a bloody carcass for the lions and still look immaculate, led us to believe he was covered in Teflon. No filth stuck to him. However, charm and dashing looks did not always fight in his favour, particularly when his boldness and frustration overcame good sense on the day he was denied access to the Green Zone. He reportedly suggested the checkpoint soldier shove his military radio up his arse like a dildo. Through some delicate behind-the-scenes negotiating from Lawrence with his Al-Rasheed contacts, Stephan avoided incarceration in the hotel tennis court, as was the plan of the infuriated Captain Burris. Stephan's flamboyant, energetic personality combined with a stubbornness of principle and unquestionable courage. These character traits powered a desire to broach any conversational topics, no matter how apparently bizarre or sexually creative. Add in the repercussions of extreme heat and a remarkably fragile digestive system, and there were few dull moments when he was nearby.

Since Al-Zawra Park was within the perimeter of the Green Zone, it was possible to cross the road in front of the hotel, wave politely to soldiers while weaving between checkpoint barricades and traffic cones, and enter the park. We headed past an assortment of old military aircraft mounted alongside the park road, over small concrete canals fed from the Tigris River, between coils of razor wire and past an abandoned pink and cream restaurant being used as sleeping quarters by an engineering unit. The somewhat incompatible plinth-mounted white statue of an elegantly dressed, but heavily set couple seated on a bench had been given a decorative update of old rounded Iraqi soldier helmets. Oddly enough, it made them look like Laurel and Hardy sitting in front of an Armoured Personnel Carrier. The anti-aircraft guns, burnt-out Iraqi military vehicles, Surface-to-Air Missile launchers, ripped and twisted irrigation pipes and cracked walls folded over piles of battered bricks still showed the brutal reality of recent months. "You see that building over there?" said Lawrence. "The crumpled one. Apparently, there was a massive cache of weapons and ammo for the Fedayeen militia in it. AK's, RPGs, 9mms and loads more. The U.S. Army engineers were trying to blow it up and came under heavy fire. They only partially destroyed it so apparently there's still a pile of the stuff in there under the rubble".

The zoo entrance took me by surprise. It was remarkable, principally because it was totally unexpected. I expected a ramshackle hovel. The enormous flat-topped arch with a white brick façade stood imposingly over two intricate green steel gates, each with a golden, lion head emblem. It was quite elegant and grand for an establishment that was by all accounts quite the opposite. The A4 paper with the no entry sign stuck on the gate for the attention of any would-be looters was more like what I had expected. It implied politely in English that *Ali babas* should turn around and piss off rather than try to steal more critters and fittings from the zoo. It seemed appropriate, if unrealistically optimistic. A column of dusty, olive green patterned Humvees was neatly parked nose-to-tail along the side of the central road leading under the arch into the zoo grounds.

William Sumner greeted us warmly as he sweated away beneath the heavily adorned camouflage webbing and body armour. Naturally, as seemed befitting of genuine cultural immersion, he too wore a luxuriant, neatly cropped moustache. Its refined style reflected mastery of the scissor and comb trim, a subtle reflection on the 354th Civil Affairs Brigade Captain's attention to detail; or so I thought. With a smoke grenade dangling from his chest, strategically placed pens, a Sterling sub-machine gun slung under his arm and refined manners, he impressed as every bit the polished fixer Lawrence had described him as. Talk of the next rescue quickly ensued between William, Stephan and Lawrence as I was anxious to get around the zoo to see what all the fuss was about.

It was a few minutes earlier that the somewhat theatrical Hilde arrived to say her goodbyes. Her first entry at the zoo had been as remarkable as any of the other foreigners, but her volatile force of personality had unexpectedly created some disrupting social politics. Her arrival with critically needed meat supplies for the zoo had been a crucial intervention at a desperate time, and the CFTW sponsorship of the precious dart gun was to prove invaluable in the ensuing months. I had only heard snippets of tales recounting that she also brought an intense animal welfare commitment flavoured with an abrasive, distinctly emotional character and a remarkable affinity for television cameras.

She was leaving Iraq that morning and quickly choked up with tears while talking to Lawrence, Stephan and William in her curiously high-pitched and distinctive, clipped German-English accent. Her short experience had clearly been emotional. I shuffled around awkwardly, not knowing how to handle the unexpectedly demonstrative introduction. It was an intensity of passion that caught me off guard as I was still grappling with remembering people's names. She certainly cornered my attention as she moved into my personal space, handed me a pair of small scissors and sobbed out the unforgettable, richly accented "and you Brendan, pleaze don't forget to trim the wolfz earz" before wiping the dribbling tears off her cheek. "Sorry. Um, did you say to trim the wolf's ears?" I asked slightly baffled at what I perceived as a madcap request in the context. Was that meant to be a privileged responsibility? I looked at Lawrence, raised an eyebrow and turned to nod slowly at Hilde. "Riiight, yes, ok, I'll be sure to do that," I said hoping a television camera would miraculously appear and break her potent concentration. Standing there with the delicate scissors was not the Screaming-Eagle grand entrance to the zoo restoration I had envisaged, but hairstylist to a wolf still seemed a workable compromise. Fortunately, cameras did appear, and both Hilde and Stephan headed off smartly, jostling for position to describe the zoo's tenuous state to whoever would listen. Introductions to the zoo director, Dr Abbas, and Lawrence's reliable ally, Dr Hussam, followed.

Lawrence, as a boost to Dr Hussam's morale and for my context, explained Dr Hussam's initial heroics in returning to the zoo with unshakable determination to reverse its dreadful state. Both he and Dr Abbas welcomed me warmly with handshakes and broad smiles. Again the facial grooming was compelling to me. I could not help but notice. Both sported such wonderfully ample moustaches that I was quickly starting to wonder if all these cultural attachments would spark nationalistic grooming envy between American soldiers and Iraqis. Then came Akram, Sa'ad, Ahmed (the gunslinger moustache), Jaboory, Kadhim - and the entirely unfamiliar names started swimming in my memory as an unpronounceable soup. I figured I could decipher and learn names later as long as I remained polite. Given the apparently dire state of the zoo, there was still enough joviality and curiosity that made one want to help without reservation. A white Volkswagen Passat slipped in amongst the Humvees almost unnoticed. A petite, young Iraqi lady in tight, flared-jeans, a collared shirt, gold jewellery and rose-tinted shades climbed out and walked quietly past us towards the office entrance. "That's Farah. She's a vet, speaks good English and I reckon we can start up an animal welfare society with her. I think you'll like her" Lawrence chirped up with a barely disguised grin.

Discussions about sourcing food for the animals and the evacuation of animals from the vile Luna Park zoo the following day continued inside the minimalist office. Luna Park was an atrocious facility across the city. A rescue mission coordinated the previous week had already relocated some of its starving animals to Baghdad Zoo. In the office, wires hung out from cavities in the bare wall and ceiling where a lightbulb and its companion, the switch, used to exist. In the corner stood a surgical table and autoclave donated days earlier by another animal welfare NGO. A representative had arrived, donated the table and left almost immediately. It seemed a bit implausible that those would be the two most desperately needed items in the circumstances, but I was new and bordering on idealistic. As exciting and appalling as Luna Park sounded to me I needed to see Baghdad Zoo so I could understand what I was getting myself into. As I left the room, Lawrence advised I stick to the paths. "They found some unexploded bombs of some sort lying around the zoo a few days ago. Cleared them, but there could be more in the debris and grass". Finally!

The cages were reminiscent of old Victorian menageries I had seen in books, except in this case most were empty of animals. Rows of bar-fronted structures stood among dusty, mature palm and eucalyptus trees. Dull, repetitive clattering sounded nearby as a small revitalised pump started to suck water from the murky, weedy Tigris-fed canals that weaved through the zoo grounds. The old, moustached (of course) trolley minder had carted the zoo's one car battery across to the next pump to get that cycle started. Water dribbled and spat out of the sprinklers onto the parched soil and a few clumps of sparse, dusty grass. This splutter alone was a sign of enormous progress given that many of the metal irrigation pipes had been crushed by armoured vehicles and that the original pumps and batteries had been stolen. Sporadically uprooted trees tilted over and shattered branches hung limply from mottled eucalyptus trunks or littered the paths and surroundings. Behind green bars a defeated-looking brown bear lay curled on a bare, stone-tile floor clawing gently at a seeping sore on her chest. Saeida was thirty-two, apparently blind, malnourished and frail. She had no access to an outside enclosure, and her tragic state represented all that was around her. She would not have been able to see the destruction but would have heard and felt the explosions, intimidating clanking of armoured vehicles, helicopters and overhead roars of jet aircraft. Parched and starving, she would have blindly padded around searching for the non-existent food and water once the facilities were abandoned. It was her fourth experience of war while locked behind bars at Baghdad Zoo.

A few cells on, past the empty cage with the "Beagle – Germany" sign hanging at a rakish angle, another self-interested bear loitered lethargically like a schoolboy bully outside a liquor store. It was, I assumed, the one rumoured to have killed a few looters a week or two earlier when they broke into the holding area. He still, at very least, had access to an outside exercise area. Quite honestly, and perhaps perversely, the small section I had seen appeared in an entirely better state than I had expected. Sure there was grime and filth engrained in the canary-yellow paint, and the animals looked restless or depressed, lethargic and a touch emaciated, but it was healthier than what I had been hearing about in previous weeks. Clearly, an enormous effort and much improvisation had already gone into halting the crisis and levering it from the brink of soiled despair. There was water in the drinking troughs, the faeces and piss that had accumulated over weeks had been scraped loose and washed away. There were remnants of food served the previous evening. They were mostly simple tasks, but the complex circumstances meant every basic step felt like a disproportionately immense achievement. The incarcerated animals were on a slow journey to physical recovery because of the unrelenting foreigners and returning Iraqis.

The aquarium building was uniformly segmented inside by columns covered with marble tiles. Every glass tank had been pulled off their respective platforms to the ground and smashed. The senseless destruction had quickly become depressing to see. Polystyrene tank bases lay among the glass shards, and tank remains, spread in a mess across the floor. The ceiling light fittings were stripped to bare wires.

Three dishevelled ostriches, formerly from the palace complex about a kilometre away, strutted aloofly around a paddock. The road alongside the paddock showed shrapnel scars and a shallow crater where a mortar round had killed the donkey. Lawrence had earlier described the transportation of the ostriches with great gusto. It was because there were insufficient vehicles available that the only option left had been to herd the running birds from the palace menagerie, through a checkpoint of startled troops and off to the zoo. The muddy, matted-hair camel across the road, rescued a few days earlier from the Luna Park zoo, gutturally gurgled as he ambled to meet us at the barrier fence. Photos of the rescue had shown him in a state of physical collapse, lying curled like a withered pretzel. Now with access to water, fairly regular food supply and memories of a ride across the city in the back of a Humvee, he was showing his sunny personality as he drooled liberally and mumbled appreciation for his lumpy head and neck being scratched.

    Over the bridge, a sizeable white-stone building housed a collection of lions. As we entered the building, Jaffer, allegedly a former Iraqi republican guard turned zookeeper, and a pint-sized spitting image of Sly Stallone, sat on the floor caressing the heads of two young lions. Pets of Saddam's depraved son, Uday, they had been rescued from the abandoned palace days earlier by Lawrence, Dr Hussam and some zoo staff. Jaffer had taken a shining to the lions. In compartments behind bars were more adult and sub-adult lions. They lounged in their washed cubicles next to chunks of donkey bone that heaved with the flies Lawrence had cursed so often. A cream crossbreed dog lay quietly on the cool tiles in the corner of the building's entrance. It was unexpected and as with so much else in this setting, absurd. War zones undoubtedly forge some odd alliances, and this case was no different as Lawrence later explained. When entering the lion enclosure at the palace, they had found that dog and a German Shepherd amongst the lions. It was assumed the dogs had been left in the pen as living larders when the palace was abandoned. Through some twist of nature's traditional role-playing, the felines had in fact bonded with their canine captives to the point of being inseparable. While the German Shepherd had been quickly adopted out, the woolly individual had refused to leave his feline companions and was now a fixture at the lion exhibit. Two cheetahs, also starving pets rescued from the derelict death trap the abandoned palace had become, lay restlessly in an adjacent cell. While the lions had access to a reasonably large paddock about four times the size of a basketball court, the cheetahs saw negligible natural light and had no outdoor space.

"Hello! I am Salman. Lion, Tigers, Beers. Thirrrty two yirrss. Good! Very good!" He seemed to materialise in a rush of surprising eccentric animation like a dysfunctional leprechaun caught on a day off. The bronzed 5-foot-tall figure with balding grey hair, a dirty beige t-shirt, even grimier trousers and sandals patted his chest as he beamed a grin. A cigarette drooped from the corner of his mouth. "I am Salman! Thirrrty two yirrss" he burst out again now waving his hands in circular cleaning motions like a disciple of Mr Miyagi from the Karate Kid. The cigarette wobbled up and down but never left his mouth. He stood staring at me. There was a disjointed pause as I registered Salman in my head. I shook his hands before he proceeded to walk down the row of the lion holding enclosures, playfully slapping the paws that lions rested out between the bars, exclaiming proudly "Good! Very good!"

Past the building a rhesus macaque that appeared to have aged rather poorly sat mournfully on the floor of her cage watching the world go by. Looking just shy of 109 years old (rumour was that she smoked about a pack of cigarettes a day which may have contributed to her haggard appearance) she stared blankly back. I stared. She stared. Suddenly she pursed her lips, pressed herself against the bars aggressively and her face transformed into a demented demonic expression as she held my gaze. I could see why she was the only monkey not stolen from the zoo. A few cages along another pair of macaques sat recuperating after their rescue from the conditions of Luna Park, hoping their placid looks would lure unsuspecting staff and visitors close enough that they could snatch dangling loot like digital cameras or food. On that account they had been highly skilled, swiping a soldier's camera before she could even get a fright.

Around the corner behind two sets of heavy bars was a stunning Bengal tiger. The vibrant colours of his auburn and black coat draped over a sleek, muscular frame showed a magnificent beast in his prime and entirely out of context given his surrounds. He lay in the shade on the bare soil of his hopelessly inadequate outdoor exercise area. A few cleaned donkey bones lay scattered around. The white-tiled plunge pool was empty. An oily, horizontal stripe plastered the walls and bars marking the territory definitively. His copper eyes stared with apparent indifference. Malooh was, without doubt, the most visually striking of the animals in the zoo. There was a palpable injustice that such a fierce creature, the physical and mythical embodiment of raw, wild power and wilderness was confined in that enclosure.

In a similar enclosure nearby, a healthy lioness named Suker lay asleep and unbothered by our proximity. Next door was an elderly, frail tiger; the father of Malooh. Apparently close to his final days, he had lost condition, was listless and could not generate the lean musculature to conceal his ribs and hips. By all the recollections he was an improved version compared to his pathetic, wasted state of a few weeks prior.

As obviously depressing as it was to see such conditions after recently having left an African game reserve, there was some fragile optimism that progress was being made. It was a miserable situation, but a collection of starkly different people and cultures were mobilising around what was needed to help those individual animals and their keepers. The zoo labour force had quickly grown into a motley blend, with remnants of the former zoo staff contingent, some of their relatives, and a few opportunistic individuals who had never been near a zoo animal but who knew the value of a U.S. dollar. Few knew anything about the biology or natural behaviours of animals. We would later discover some thought the rest of the world looked and was just like Iraq, which made them more confused about our motivations for arriving in their part of it.

Despite the veterinary backgrounds of Dr Abbas and Dr Hussam, their knowledge of zoological veterinary medicine was rudimentary. Any international exposure to knowledge of modern practices and protocols had stopped decades earlier. They had no diagnostic equipment and no experience with the few medical potions Lawrence had managed to source in Kuwait. Lawrence and Stephan had arrived in circumstances they needed to succeed in without having even the basic knowledge of what (or what quantity) some of the animals like badgers should eat in a captive situation. Whether anything appropriate was available at a market or store was another matter. The staff were feeding the bears morsels of bread and occasionally some meat. A wolf, a pelican and a camel would all need completely different diets.

Lawrence and Stephan had navigated those obstacles through cooperation with willing staff, Ali (whose title of *taxi driver* bore no resemblance to his relentless resourcefulness), military contractor contacts and the U.S. Army. Donkeys were $6 each, and the zoo needed three per day to feed the carnivores. Would it work to have a supply of donkeys at the zoo? Suddenly in an emergency zoo survival triage, donkeys were viewed by necessity or perceived priorities as commodities rather than a direct welfare target. That would require supplies to feed the donkeys. In one case U.S. soldiers trying to help the zoo had been conned into paying $100 to buy two goats to donate as food to the zoo. It all meant awful practical decisions and compromises to the somewhat comfortable and hypocritical suburban value systems we assign to animals we like. It was clearly a case of locking in emotions related to the conditions of animals and ensuring there was another forward step made towards a supposedly healthier, semi-functional zoo.

At the office, the logistical planning for the second Luna Park rescue, scheduled for the following day, continued between Lawrence, Stephan, William, Dr Abbas and Dr Hussam. Luna Park was a combination of a hellishly contained animal menagerie and small amusement park located on the edge of an artificial lake, adjacent to the Martyr's Monument in eastern Baghdad. With a rickety roller coaster and a colourful assortment of other rides, it was easy to understand its popularity for families in more peaceful times. The walls of the entrance were painted with deceptively exotic scenes of tigers prowling the forested edges of lakes. An enormous and cheery Mickey Mouse metal cutout welcomed visitors. Propped up by a rebar rod, Mickey appeared to float above the images of lions, peacocks, tigers, an elephant, a pig and a Dalmatian dog. The idyllic pictures were a curiously gross utopian illusion of animal camaraderie that attempted to complement the disgusting, abusive setting real animals barely survived.

Following the initial reports about the facility and its maltreated, starving animals, William had set about with colleagues to unravel the legitimacy of the U.S. Army getting involved in shutting down such a facility. A decision was taken that it was within the very vague framework of the Iraqi law that animals should preferably not be subjected to abuse. William had organised for a letter to be drafted in Arabic that explained the animals were being relocated to Baghdad Zoo on the grounds of animal welfare concerns. When the animals were sufficiently healthy, the owner could retrieve them. This laid the platform for the first operation aimed at moving the animals to the Baghdad Zoo. It fitted with the quickly conceived intention that care for the caged exotic creatures of the city would be consolidated at one facility for easier care management. As with all the previous days at the zoo, it was an operation that relied almost entirely on improvisation. The brown bear was considered the most dangerous captive to relocate. Without a dart gun (it was before I arrived from Kuwait) the plan agreed relied on luring the bear with bread and honey to hopefully stand against the cage bars. If that worked then, again hopefully, a volunteer would hand-inject the bear with immobilising drugs. Dr Hussam was adamant the gaggle of the press that had arrived to film the transfer were not to feed any of the animals even if the desire to help was overwhelming. Hungry animals could be lured by food into the assortment of transport cages cobbled together for the rescue. William's concern was for his unit to liaise with the 3rd ID soldiers to provide security and transport for the operation. Lawrence and Stephan would work with Dr Abbas and Dr Hussam and their staff to move animals into cages and onto Humvees. It was presumptuous to assume the team would have the necessary skills to shift those particular animals, but chance was a currency everyone was dealing with. Hilde was tasked to ensure the animals' welfare during the loading and drive.

On the 10th of May 2003, the descending swarm of military vehicles and personnel, media, foreigners and unfamiliar Iraqi's with cages had naturally come as an unhappy shock to the few lingering staff at the Luna Park. The intent of the convoy was unmistakable. It was not a welcome intervention. Dr Abbas and U.S. Army translators were quickly engaged in negotiating the fiery standoffs between Lawrence and a man who turned out to be Luna Park's owner, Karim Hameed. Hameed argued furiously that the facility was well managed and should not be any concern of the aggravated, irrational foreigners. The clash of perspectives was intractable. Reports surfaced that keepers had killed several animals for food to try to keep others alive. The already scant resources had dried up. This narrative contradicted Hameed's angry outbursts. It was a clash of personal values, and for Hameed, economics. He was overruled. The transfer was to go ahead. The military had every intention to ensure that. Birds flashed around their small, grimy, crap-spattered cages. At each turn was another pathetic sight. It was immediately decided the brown bear was too big to be transported, despite his dire living conditions. It was also quickly apparent there were too many animals for a single trip.

The luring, catching and loading began. Unwilling rhesus macaques, goats, vultures and a frail gazelle joined a filthy, wretched grey pelican that had been abandoned, tethered to a pole in the blazing Baghdad sun. More birds, porcupines, dehydrated Maltese, Pekingese and German Shepherd dogs, and a wolf and piglets were loaded. The stricken, emaciated camel refused to be lured by Hilde's fresh forage and anguished pleading. As Hilde was temporarily distracted, the camel only needed Dr Hussam's kick in its backside to activate its hitherto unknown desire to clamber along the path, down stairs and onto the Humvee's load bin. The transport cages were quickly filled. Bewildered piglets sat in the footwell.

With Noahs in Kevlar at the helms of their modern-day miniature arks, the menagerie-packed column of Humvees negotiated the heavy traffic back to Baghdad Zoo. In the minds of the soldiers, staff, Lawrence, Stephan and Hilde, they knew they were a slow-moving potential target for an opportunistic attack. There was always anxiety when traffic slowed. No attack materialised. The geographic and abstract sense of safety of the Green Zone finally enveloped them. They drove past the many palaces and former government ministry compounds that had either been bombed to crumpled, eviscerated shells or acquired as temporary Forward Operating Bases by the invading military, then under arches, past waiting tanks, through more checkpoints and finally into Al-Zawra Park. For all the personnel involved the relief of unloading the animals into the recently emptied Baghdad Zoo enclosures felt like an unmitigated success. That sense of joy was paired with the burden of knowing more food and supplies were required, and that it was only the start. They would have to return.

My arrival had coincided neatly with the plotting for the second rescue. As the planning progressed, they again tallied the available transport cages and guess-matched the sizes with what animals were believed to be still at Luna Park. William clarified which troops and transport the military could offer. He explained the route the convoy would take. Capture drugs and equipment were noted down. The final decisions made were where the different animals would be housed once they arrived at Baghdad Zoo. Ali, not one to be left out of the action, discarded his taxi driver identity and practised his darting skills with the zoo's newest weapon. There was no telling when in the dynamic state of Baghdad, he may need this unique skill. Air pressures were calibrated and tweaked, and packages of meat victimised as darting targets. Excessive grinning and back-slapping was evidence of how excited the staff and management were about their new technology. They had never seen one before and as far as we knew no one in the country had ever immobilised animals using a dart gun. It was viewed as a modern marvel – a quirky little moment serving to highlight how isolated the country had become under sanctions.

Lunch-time approached. The heat seared down on us. With the day's zoo food supply organised, the skeleton-crew of zoo staff resting and the following day's plans finalised, it was decided that a visit to the coalition headquarters palace for lunch with Lawrence and Stephan was in order. The tour also required a stop at some of the coalitions' administration offices to organise me the foreigner's hallowed lifeline, an identification card. Ali finished off another cigarette before settling in for a nap in his taxi. The three of us foreigners shuffled along with the pedestrian queues at the mandatory checkpoints to enter the palace grounds. Across an expanse of dirt, through the dishevelled eucalyptus trees, we could make out the partially collapsed layers of another enormous palace hit by cruise missiles. The barrage of noise from the pulsing, rapid *whupping* and whining of spinning rotor blades and turbines dominated our ears as Blackhawk helicopters hovered, landed and rose out from behind the trees across the road. The rotor wash forced out clouds of dust and leaves from their landing area adjacent to the parking area. It was exhilarating theatre. The former Republican Palace we were entering was an incredible spectacle. Bow shaped in the front, it extended nearly 250m from end-to-end. The dusty garden debris and a dry fountain remained from a once-manicured entrance feature, separated from the building by a road matching the building's curve, leading into and out of the grounds. A palace frontage of heavy-set, creamy-beige arches and pillars connected to massive square porticos, that extended over the road at either end and in the middle. At the central portico, the creamy stone arches flowed into eagle head facades pressed against a flat, blocky background of marine-blue stone. The palace, with its conspicuous aquamarine roof dome in the centre, dwarfed the few Humvees parked on the adjacent road. Most astonishing were the grand, imposing busts of Saddam Hussein. Each of the four 12m tall busts was cast with a military pith helmet, exuding egotism as they perched intimidatingly at points across the roof of the building. Even in the absence of the man himself, Saddam's threatening presence dominated here as it did almost every corner of the city.

The chunky wooden doors opened inwards to reveal a hive of foreigner activity, bustling to and fro across the grand marble corridors, staircases and rotundas. Chandeliers hung like inverted golden jellyfish in each foyer, reflecting flickers of light off the gilded doors and buffed marble. Military men and women, foreign civilians, even a few Iraqis (at the time we assumed it was to give the invasion some local cultural diversity - or at least an understanding of spoken Arabic), seemed to be heading somewhere with documents, weapons, water bottles and reconstructive zeal. With Lawrence and Stephan heading off to meet familiar contacts, I was free to explore the maze of spacious palace passages. The description of "palatial" was dictionary appropriate. The designers obviously had liberal encouragement to adorn ceilings and pillars with gaudy interpretations of Arabesque decorative facades and trims. Tall arches in the walls were filled with attractive symmetrical patterns of tiling while ceiling cornices decorated in pastel colours and gold paint clashed with cheap plastic decorative light fittings. Enormous pillars grew into elaborate coral-like whorls on the ceiling. The new authorities in town had deemed it appropriate to change a vast hall with its dramatically patriotic wall-mural of unleashed Iraqi

Scud missiles, into a makeshift chapel. The apparent ORHA impulse to create and display acronyms on closed doors seemed to reflect an almost gratuitous fetish for recycling the unused tiles on a Scrabble rack. Quasi-military abbreviations on door after door gave a brief insight into how many organisational cogs (and probably egos) were quickly manufactured and morphing to drive the complex bureaucracy of the regime-changing governance machinery. The snippets of jargon I was overhearing bordered on obscure alien dialect to my novice ear. It did not look or feel like an institution where concerns of a zoo or animal welfare would be viewed as anything but a fringe curiosity.

Lawrence, Stephan and I reconvened for a lunch that lacked the kind of dignity and ceremony that would have been fit for such an expansive dining hall. It was simply immense. It had been relegated to a chow hall crammed with tables covered in plastic sheets, commandeered red velvet-like chairs with kitsch gold paint trimming, and hordes of noisy infidels wolfing down soft drinks and sloppy joe hotdogs on disposable plastic plates. Stephan, severely unimpressed that his U.S. taxes were being used to produce such low quality, processed food, tried to vent his anger on a contracted KBR employee serving the meals. She was dismissive, adamant that cheap burgers, fried chicken, cola and lettuce could be combined into a nutritious, balanced diet. If nothing else, the futile, idealistic argument was entertaining as I watched from a distance with my nourishing, free Fanta soft drinks.

With the identification card organised, we walked down the marble stairwell into the belly of the palace. The corridors were laden with boxes of bottled water and MREs to which we generously helped ourselves. Shuffling along like pack mules with our new bounty we headed back up staircases and along more mazy corridors before Lawrence found his South African security contractor allies. They'd been tasked to protect Lieutenant General Garner, and at the same time had progressed to being valuable links for the zoo to the coalition hierarchy. Fortunately, the zoo had become their soft spot; it was where their compassion and empathy seemed most apparent. It had prompted their initiation of a visit to the premises by General Garner. That visit had concluded with a $20,000 donation to the cause, and with a few whiskies, it cemented the relationship between Lawrence and the most improbable of friends. With introductions completed, we lugged our boxes of water bottles along to *Space and Missile Defence Command's* office (SMDC – of course). Lieutenant Colonel Kuh, short and lively, greeted Lawrence warmly in the room swamped with maps and satellite imagery. The rebellious, tattooed "Harley chick" was well hidden and all that was projected was a motherly charm enhanced with an energetic glint in the eye. Socially connected to the South Africans back down the corridor, she had also become a staunch supporter of the zoo effort and as we would learn later, was only too willing to help us in almost any circumstances. Her friendship was invaluable to Lawrence. It was to become so for Farah, myself and William as the months rushed on.

Ali was still parked in the shade of eucalyptus trees, melting in a sweaty sleep at the wheel of his Caprice. We loaded in the boxes as a stream of beige Humvees with their staring cargo of troops and roof-mounted guns weaved between the nearby portable concrete traffic barriers that lay like discarded Jenga pieces in the road. Everywhere you looked there were men and women in uniform, stretched coils of concertina wire, Humvees or a Bradley grinding its way along the streets. Blackhawk, Apache and Kiowa helicopters seemed to take turns at whipping up the dust and drowning out conversations. The wafting smells of aviation fuel and diesel exhaust fumes embedded as the aromatic memory of the Green Zone. There was a palpable energy, perceived or imagined, that radiated from the circumstances. We drove along what would become a familiar daily route, under another large decorative archway over the road, past the 14th July circle with its dramatically heroic statue of soldiers representing the 1958 coup, past tall dusty walls and large houses and towards the parade grounds and conference centre. After delivering Lawrence and our supplies to the Al-Rasheed Hotel, Ali, Stephan and I made our way back to the zoo to collect buckets of meat for the lions at another nearby palace formerly occupied by Uday Hussein.

The skinned donkey head gawked out from between bloody ribs and legs as the checkpoint soldier at the palace inspected the vehicle trunk. A sight of a deconstructed donkey in buckets should have been disconcerting, but at a palace in Baghdad, it apparently wasn't. A soldier sat opposite us mounted in his APC. He lethargically aimed his machine gun in our direction at the entrance. "ID's please," another soldier asked. "I come here every day, same time, same reason and they still ask for fucking IDs. You'd think they would figure it out by now!" Stephan muttered at me. With a cursory, officious look at the tags, we were grumbled entry permission. Checkpoint duty looked like nothing other than prolonged, mind-numbing dreariness.

As the vehicle turned right, round the corner, past the high beige walls with carved Assyrian human-headed winged bulls and Arabic writing, a tall green-barred structure stood 40m in front of us. Three large lions loped out into their enclosure from the side of the small holding building of the right. It was a scrubby area of dried mud about the size of two tennis courts, partially shaded by three large palm trees planted in a row down the middle. Two bathing troughs inside the enclosure had apparently overflowed enough times that the minor floods and flow angles had generated a lush patch of grass outside the enclosure. It was into that small swampy drainage patch that Lawrence had accidentally dropped his camera. That moment and that patch erased all the celluloid memories of Lawrence's early weeks of emergency relief efforts. Inside the enclosure, powdery dust stirred into the air as the two lionesses and an auburn maned male bounded past the palm trees and paced excitedly along the fence line. Ali and Stephan meant meat in the belly. The lions knew it. Six animated, golden, furry bundles scuttled along behind. It was impossible not to be immediately captivated by the sight of the feisty cubs. We drove past the enormous hulls of parked M88 Armoured Recovery Vehicles and stopped outside the small building.

As with the other animals locked in menageries around the palace complexes that lined the Tigris River, those lions had been abandoned and left to starve. The savage "shock and awe" campaign had sent missiles slicing through key targets, pumping crushing concussion waves and thundering roars through the surrounds. As much as the civilians of Baghdad were dreading a missed target, animals would simply be terrorised by the ferocious assault on their overwhelmed, refined senses. The Baath party HQ, 300m across the road from the lion enclosure, was gutted by a Tomahawk missile directed through the roof from the Arabian Gulf hundreds of kilometres away. The lions would have undoubtedly been subjected to the expanding force of the shock wave.

U.S. Special Forces had made rapid incursions into Baghdad and were the first invading military units to enter the palace complexes. The abandoned lions, confined by the enclosure in the unkempt garden of that palace were discovered emaciated, dehydrated and pregnant. Adopting the lions as their mascots the men reportedly located and shot weakened sheep, gazelles, blackbuck and ostriches they found either among other palaces or on the lands surrounding the airport. They named the imposing male Brutus, the lionesses Xena (after the mythological warrior princess) and Heather (presumably a dedication to a less erotic and more contemporary princess back in the U.S.). Only a few days after their discovery, the cubs were born. Then seemingly miraculously Lawrence and Dr Hussam had arrived to assist. A decision was taken to leave the lions at the palace because the enclosure was bigger than the alternative, and had a water supply. It was better (emergency criteria were simple) than what was available at the zoo at the time. With the other lions already at the zoo, there wasn't anywhere else more suitable to put the feline refugees. Soon after the lions' discovery, the rumours surfaced of Uday having tortured prostitutes, abducted ladies, and other casualties of his twisted psyche before feeding them to the lions. Given his appalling reputation for torture, rape and irrational rage, it was entirely plausible to imagine his deranged merriment as human flesh was torn from limb. We later heard of accounts by individuals who claimed to have witnessed relatives mauled to death by packs of ravenous dogs in enclosures. Whatever the actual truth of the lions, it seemed it lay closer to sinister, monstrous and grotesque than Wordsworth-like romance. Investigative digs into the surrounding grounds were instigated by the Army to search for human remains. The findings of the excavations were inconclusive. The rumours persisted, but without evidence, we chose to take the line of neutral, feigned ignorance as the months progressed. There was no way for us to interpret if the lions were the man-eaters the rumour mill seemed to crave. We felt a simple approach was the best. Lions eat meat so logic suggested that if we went into the cage with them, we would get ripped apart, irrespective of the lions' history. Provided we stayed out of the cage when the lions were in it, we wouldn't get eaten. If there was an evil history, we could not rectify it. Beyond the simple facts of natural predation and survival, we did not believe the discussion had relevance to us or for the lions.

Stephan talked quietly and calmly to Brutus as he introduced me. I felt it was quite an unusual gesture, but then again, I had never really considered what was acceptable social etiquette when meeting a lion. Brutus's eyes suggested he was entirely unconcerned with our social modesty. They were firmly fixed on the bloody donkey leg Stephan held by the shin. Brutus wanted to rip the hell out of it. As Stephan lifted the meat through the bars, Brutus raised his immense frame onto his back legs and lunged with powerful forearms and sickle claws to snatch the morsel. The primal growl and slash as he wheeled away was a striking display of primitive, raw power. I was suitably impressed. Respect. Ancient fear. I was grateful for the bars between us. I had no intention of testing the man-eater rumour. Brutus lay on his broad belly, contently tearing away at the meat and sinew as Ali pushed in ribs and haunches for Xena and Heather to clasp with their declawed paws. The cubs hissed and snarled as they fought to protect their new caches from the domineering parents, before the entire mass of lions suddenly bolted outside, each with their quarry. After Stephan's arrival in Baghdad this had quickly become his and Ali's afternoon routine; one which they both prized. There, in that palace garden, it was impossible to escape the sense of having been suddenly transplanted into a world we could never have imagined and were never meant to see; a world of excess, brutal despots, world politics, opulence and cultural discovery.

Ali used his brute strength to crank the reluctant handle of the nearby diesel-powered water pump. As it chugged out black fumes and spluttered into life, cool, clear water gushed from the hose pipe. With the lions in their outside section and the sliding doors to the building closed, the inner cages were soaped and rinsed of hair, mud and the chewed food remains that the massing black flies enjoyed so much. Several soldiers had gathered as spectators to watch the lions. They immediately asked questions about the man-eating status. There seemed to be a primordial disposition towards violence that some of the visitors desperately needed satiated, either through the inferred slaughter of humans or witnessing some carnage. It would be a persistent theme. "C'mon throw in a live pig for us! If I buy a donkey, will you throw it in to be killed?" It wasn't the last time we would have to politely decline the suggestion with "yeah, there's not a fucking chance we will do that." Others stood quietly as they appreciated the uniqueness of having these magnificent beasts in their new Baghdad barracks.

As I entered the Al-Rasheed grounds, Ali wasted no

time whipping his "ZOO" Caprice into a U-turn, rounded the corner, slipped through the nearby checkpoint and headed out across the Jumariyah Bridge over the Tigris River. It was significantly safer to drop Stephan at his hotel and for Ali to make it home to his neighbourhood and his family before dusk enveloped the city. The dark was time for thugs and thieves and anti-American dissenters to stir into greater violent action than in daylight.

The stale, sweaty aroma of my one-day-old home was curiously comforting as I stopped for a coffee at Diehl's café. It already seemed routine. We debriefed the day's action like we actually knew each other and then it was the vertical slog up the dark stairwell to the 7th floor. The magnetic lure of the cold shower downstairs at the abandoned pool (and the need for a bucket of toilet-flushing water) meant an excursion back down the stairwell to sluice off the sweaty, muddy gunge from the day. It felt like a comical, surreal relief to stand naked with an awfully unfashionable farmer's suntan, bared to all and sundry at the Al-Rasheed, feeling the cold water and the memories embedding. It wasn't long after that, refreshed, excited by the days overwhelming sensations and starving, that the MREs were being wolfed down with a cold beer in the company of Lawrence and the entertaining 7th-floor mafia. The experience of factional exclusivity felt a bit like an adults' version of a high school playground. As would be the case each night, the palpable relief of solitude in the bedroom would give time to decompress and attempt to mentally process and file the day's overstimulation, culture and unfamiliar chaos. The sporadic, distant and then nearer clattering of machine-gun fire and interjecting snap of single shots started as dusk darkened. It was to become a familiar lullaby.

MRE's for breakfast, coffee stop at Diehl's, the thundering-whining of tanks waking up, Ali's "ZOO" taxi and a drive through the park to the Baghdad Zoo immediately became the standard morning routine. There was a tangible sense of anticipation as we arrived on the 14th of May 2003. Luna Park zoo was going to be closed once and for all. I hadn't seen the place, but the energy and ambition around clearing it of animals (and Lawrence's opinion it was the worst zoo in the world; ever!) projected a clear sense of how awful it was. The Humvee convoy from the 354th Civil Affairs filed under the gate arch and parked in the shade of the avenue of trees. Excited crews dismounted in their familiar chunky layers of body armour with long weapons clunking against the vehicle as they tried to manoeuvre in the tight spaces. William coordinated the loading of the myriad transport cages of different shapes, sizes and quality (basically anything the zoo staff thought could contain an animal) up onto and into the drab green and black camouflaged vehicles. With final preparations completed, weapons and ammunition were checked. Discussions on the safety and speed merits of different routes were agreed. We climbed into our assigned vehicles and the convoy snaked its way through and out of the Green Zone.

The second operation had been delayed by days as a result of the dart gun's unexpected vacation in Kuwaiti customs. With it in hand and the collection of cages being hauled into the Luna Park grounds, there was an urgency to snatch the remaining creatures and move them across town as efficiently and incident-free as possible. Immediately a posse of ragged looking Iraqis and one in smarter attire arrived to again protest the theft of their possessions. The gesticulations and irate remonstrations faded to barely disguisable seething as they realised they were obviously outnumbered and outgunned. In the commotion, William negotiated that there would be a token gesture of financial compensation for the loss of their animals. The concept of their return when the conditions improved had hit a reality check. Given the lack of cooperation and any desire to improve conditions at Luna Park, the option of Karim Hameed recovering his animals from Baghdad Zoo, once they were suitably healthy, was taken off the negotiation table. Any payment was also conditional; that the pitiful detention centre would not be restocked once our backs were turned. The soothing-by-dollars total was to be negotiated or assigned later once the animals had been removed.

It was decided to give the striped hyena the honour of being on the receiving end of the first dart of the day. The hyena began to look decidedly uncomfortable with the attention it was sensing from the paparazzi's knowing glances and hushed whispers. He began steady pacing in figure-of-eights across his concrete floor with erratic, seemingly mortified glances at the equipment being unveiled nearby. The few journalists who had joined the second mission primed their cameras as Dr Abbas and Ali, who was not shy of a word of advice, loaded the drug-filled dart into the chamber of the dart gun. Dr Abbas tweaked the air pressure and raised the weapon towards the chain link fence shielding the hyena. Not wanting to infringe on this splendid moment we decided against telling Dr Abbas he could remove the foot pump dangling like a tangled squid from the dart gun's end. We stepped back a pace as the rifle was being waved side to side as if it had an invisible string attached to the tail of the now frantically pacing hyena. After 30 more seconds of weapon waving, it was collectively decided to instead pick a target spot and hope the animal would be hit as it loped past. The tension mounted with the anticipation. The pressure was on Dr Abbas to deliver the textbook darting. His finger squeezed the trigger. Pfft! The dart reluctantly arced out the barrel and dropped onto the grass a metre away. After a few sheepish stares at the dart, it was retrieved and loaded again. The foot pump, singled out as the guilty party in the previous misfire was stomped vigorously to atone for the embarrassment it had rendered. The trigger was squeezed again. The dart propelled straight into the rump of the hyena that had become as frantic as a hyena in a dodgy Baghdad zoo with barbed darts being shot at it ought to be.

While the drugged hyena was being blindfolded and loaded into its transport cage by industrious Baghdad

Zoo staff and soldiers, attention shifted to the pigs. Dirty pink, irate after years of being pigs in a traditionally porcine unfriendly neighbourhood, and a little pissed off because of people trying to catch them, they stampeded around their tiny, rudimentary enclosure. It took some muscle to shove them through the opening in the fence and into the waiting transportation. Jaffer, dressed in his black sleeveless, muscle shirt and armed with rubber dishwashing gloves, looked more like a part-time wrestler gearing up for a marathon kitchen spring clean. He eyed the Eurasian badger cage, grinned, nodded at us knowingly (we didn't know what that meant) and climbed inside. My knowledge of badgers up to that point was primarily based on honey badgers which have a reputation of being obnoxiously hostile and belligerent despite their diminutive size. So as Jaffer climbed into the cage, I expected a whirlwind of pissed off badger reaping some revenge on the unsuspecting zookeeper. I watched, not wanting to interfere and with a hint of curiosity at how it would all turn out. As the two badgers scrambled and clawed their way up the chain-link fence, irritated, but weakened from lack of food and water, Jaffer snatched at their necks and in each hand held a writhing black and white bundle of muted anger. He stuffed them into the smaller cage, and the door was slammed shut. I was suitably impressed. A demented one-eyed fox, a hissing jungle cat and a variety of smaller birds were all collected from their uncompromisingly awful, filthy residences.

While the roundup had been taking place, Stephan had concentrated on feeding honey-laden bread to the previously abandoned Iraqi brown bear lounging in the squalid block close to the zoo's entrance. By all accounts, the bear had arrived as a cub eight years earlier and had grown up in the 15m x 4m cell with a concrete floor and grimy, once white, bathtub in the corner. The floor was littered with fetid faeces and torn up hose pipes the bear had pulled in as people teased it. The walls were smeared with 8 years of muddy filth. The top of the bear's head was worn to dark bald patches as it paced methodically against the blue rebar fencing. At each turn, it would run the top of its head against the bars. The only cleaning of the area since the bear's arrival had been hosing from outside the cage. A blue plastic tub was newly placed against the outside of the bars and filled with water so the bear could reach across with a furry paw, and slop water into its desiccated mouth. The blue tub was progress! It was pathetic. The reality hit us that there was yet again no space for the bear in the convoy. We were fully stocked, and there was no way we could squeeze him in even if he were drugged. We had completely underestimated the logistical considerations of moving a giant brown bear. The sole remaining animal in that menagerie would have to endure more suffering, and it seared our consciences with caustic frustration. We needed to leave. The sweat was dripping off us, and we anticipated traffic to be a severe test of our resolve.

The convoy of Humvees and a truck with its assortment of creatures weaved through chaotic midday traffic. Iraqi drivers, as jammed in the traffic as we were, craned their necks as they gawked in disbelief at the animals sprouting out the backs of the foreign army vehicles. We entered the underpass tunnel on Tayran Road heading towards Tahreer Square and were suddenly stuck behind a jam of buses, Volkswagen Passats and a battered green car being pushed up the slope. The heat radiated off the road and beat down from above. The hooting continued as usual, and pedestrians swarmed along the pavements as the convoy slowly exited the tunnel. "SNIPER!" was shouted above the clamouring chaos. The convoy slammed on brakes, soldiers dismounted, and weapons were pointed desperately in all directions in an attempt to find the danger. Taking William's barked advice, I made sure I was tucked well behind the driver's seat. A t-shirt didn't feel much like armour and being shot wasn't high on my to-do list. "Jesus! Day two only. Fuck!" I muttered sharply. Ali's taxi, with Lawrence, Stephan and Dr Abbas closed up to the convoy. The area had become well-known for sniping from surrounding buildings into that road. William's commanding officer Major Henry Norcom made the call. The "all clear" came through on the radios. False alarm. This time. From what we heard, on many occasions, it was not. The urgency to get the hell out of there was dramatically increased. With rifles pointed, wild gesticulations and swearing the convoy forced its way through the traffic, across the bridge and into the relief of the Green Zone, the Baghdad Zoo and a cold Pepsi. Dr Abbas issued orders and allocations, and caged animals were disappearing in different directions as the staff relocated the rescues into their slightly upgraded conditions.

Stephan swore under his breath as he again went through the routine of explaining what he was doing at the palace checkpoint in an Iraqi taxi laden with buckets of donkey and buffalo meat. The same soldiers from the previous day, and the day before that, grudgingly waved us through for the daily lion feed. The buffalo meat was packaged portions imported from India via Kuwait. Although expensive, it had been sourced by the assisting NGOs to reduce the reliance on the paltry daily slush fund for sourcing meat needed at the zoo. William's Civil Affairs unit had moved into a large villa commandeered in the lush, canal-laced *Little Venice* in the Green Zone. Crucially the unit had sourced two deep freezers (unofficial exchange rate: Deep Freezer x 2 = Thompson submachine gun and "a couple of Mauser rifles") and had a supply of electricity. It meant the meat could be stored there for a longer-term, rather than rot into stinky pulp at the zoo.

The lion feeding was for the first few days, our only zoo-day constant. Each new day brought new chaos, new problems to be solved and new novelties. The hyena needed to be darted and moved again after it was decided his new setup was inappropriate and the cells for the badgers, foxes and jungle cats were still horribly unsuitable even though they were several grades better than Luna Park. Baby steps.

CHAPTER 4

There was a constant need and drive to deliver a food supply for the animals. Vegetables were more easily sourced than meat because several open-air public markets were still open. Despite being a war zone, farmers still needed to sell their produce and residents still needed to eat to survive. Deeply wrinkled old ladies, hunched inside their black abayas, shuffled among the battered old cars and past the chunky wooden tables laden with greens, fruits and varieties of vegetables I had never seen in South Africa. The markets were an industrious mix of smell, noise and activity. The bespectacled Ahmed had been appointed as the zoo's greengrocer and took to the task diligently. He adored birds, and his compassion for the animals at the zoo was obvious. Plastic packets were filled with enough food to last for at least two days. Cucumbers, tomatoes, lettuce, carrots and freshly baked bread. He would also source pickup-loads of *jet* (alfalfa) from markets closer to the city fringes. Storage was still a significant problem. No refrigeration at the zoo meant the vegetables would spoil quickly in the heat. The only option was almost daily trips to markets. When possible, I would go with Ali and Ahmed to get a sense of the city and to try to understand the pricing of purchases. So much time was spent staring from inside the car, trying to mentally process what I had initially found was an utterly alien culture. It appeared as a city in chaos rather than a city at war. When Farah would join us, it immediately became easier to understand what was happening, because she could explain situations clearly to me in English, rather than me struggling through assumptions, mixed phrases of bastardised English-Arabic and hand gestures.

Ali was our best connection for meat, although it came at a premium price when cash was desperately depleted. The finances Lawrence and Stephan were juggling were already under pressure from paying staff and piecing together necessary infrastructure. Ali too commanded a high rate for his essential, reliable services. The heat was intense. It was always hot. Sweat continually seeped through the shirt. It wasn't even the peak of summer yet. As Stephan and I followed Ali and his plumes of cigarette smoke through the ramshackle corridor-like market, it was evident that without Ali's presence, we would definitely be unwelcome. Blank stares, curious stares and acidic stares all loomed out from smartly dressed, sweating men on stools waiting for business besides their stalls of clothing and vibrantly coloured material. Ambivalence did not seem to be an option. Some would continue to instinctively run prayer beads between their fingers. Tattered coloured cloth and corrugated iron sheeting provided dilapidated, improvised roofing above the passage to protect the wares and patrons from the sun. The stench of puddles of leaking effluent and fresh meat clung on the air in the oppressively humid, mazy, cave-like atmosphere. The first meat stall we arrived at erupted with greetings and hugs for Ali. Relatives. He waved his cigarette, his stout belly pressed against his sweat-drenched shirt, explaining all about us proudly in his comfortable, muddled setting. Nodding and pointing at us as a means of introduction, the butchers were inviting; despite the brutal surrounds of bloodied white tiles with innards and sheep carcasses in various stages of dismemberment hanging from rows of large steel hooks against the wall. The open-fronted stall filled with curious passers-by, all keen to have a stare at the unusual sight of westerners straining through the market with packets of meat and thigh bones. Stephan's adoption of U.S. Army camouflage trousers may also have raised eyebrows. It was clear that Ali had influence in the market as greetings and back-slapping lightened the tone. The crumbling concrete and mud paths which led between stalls continued to bubble in places with pools of sewage. River carp gasped for air as they lay horizontal, glinting golden in the water in a shallow wooden cart. Skinned sheep heads and varieties of white cheeses were for sale in another stall. A young fruit vendor sat under an umbrella, on a wooden box in a shallow, murky pool of stinking sludge with his cucumbers and tomatoes proudly displayed for customers. Life was going on despite the wretched circumstances and visible decay.

Driving through town, although initially unpleasant because of the heat and disastrously chaotic traffic, were experiences we came to perversely enjoy, only because they gave us a partial understanding of life in Baghdad. There was no discernible order, and with electricity more off than on, traffic lights were irrelevant and driving with civility was discretionary. Several of the larger connecting city roads had also been closed by U.S. Army checkpoints which created masses of deflected congestion elsewhere. Bombed or looted buildings (many with wide wisps of char on the brickwork from fires set during the looting), informal markets, hustling pedestrians, goldsmiths and fruit juice restaurants all added to the intense consciousness of the experience.

In Mansour neighbourhood, the Mamoun telecommunications exchange building stood next to Baghdad tower, a ruined shell of steel and concrete. Courtesy of two Tomahawk missiles, its metal innards and remaining exterior lay draped like contorted sheets of metallic toilet paper. Nearby the colossal, incomplete, bare concrete, multi-domed, Al Rahman Mosque stood surrounded by cranes like a futuristic disused set from a Star Wars movie. Across the Tigris River from the Green Zone, the iconic Firdos Square led to Kahramana Square in Karrada neighbourhood. The Palestine and Sheraton Hotels, popular with foreign journalists, looked onto the ornate turquoise dome of the 14th Ramadan Mosque and Firdos Square where the statue of Saddam Hussein was memorably toppled from its plinth by American forces in April 2003. Kahramana Square was recognised by its figure of a young girl pouring water (representing hot oil) onto forty pots of thieves referencing the folk tale of *Ali Baba and the Forty Thieves* in the collection of stories in *One Thousand and One Nights* (also known as *Arabian Nights*).

Young entrepreneurial boys sold freshly brewed tea at grubby stands on the pavement. A gas bottle connected to an old two-plate stove allowed them to simmer the leaves in the kettle to a rich, intense brew poured with flare and a smile into small, thin, shapely *istikan* (hourglass-shaped glasses) set on saucers. A liberal load of white sugar swirled with a spoon clinking on the glass held back the bitterness. The pavement was also where money exchangers would sit at tables in the shade of beach umbrellas with blocks of elastic-band wrapped Iraqi dinar currency. Their dexterity and counting speed was baffling as they instinctively thumb-whipped through the notes wedged between fingers. Farah repeated it faster to reinforce my distinct lack of coordination.

Ali seemed to have relatives on every corner and knew where to source a bargain deal. He also had the stamina needed for a bargain hunt. Even if it only meant a saving of a few dollars on a mop or broom, he would prefer to navigate across town through hours of traffic, melting slowly into his seat, rather than be conned into a higher price. Alleged crooks and thieves were chastised for ridiculous prices and u-turns against the coagulated traffic were common. Taking Stephan and Farah and me along did, on occasion, create difficulties for him. In search of bargain squeegee mops, he visited a back alley connection that refused to sell him anything because he had brought *Jews* into the shop. The mood soured rapidly as us westerners were repeatedly accused of being Jewish. Fuck facts. Fuck reality. Whatever the perceived characteristic features are, we apparently had them. As much as Ali refuted the charge – it made no difference. We purchased our goods in the next door shop and left briskly before the rumours of our presence, and alleged religious allegiances spread. Jews were notably unwelcome, a point made to us on several occasions. The Palestine-Israel geopolitical conflict was a volatile, sensitive topic of debate in Iraq. Fortunately for us, it was usually an easily avoidable discussion. Our focus was a zoo.

Beyond the excitement of the Luna Park rescue, each day distilled down to reactive problem-solving. The initial aims and tasks were quite simple despite the logistical hurdles – get food and water to the animals. Clean everything. We did not have the resources, the zoological knowledge or the stable circumstances to plan ahead. As we were out sourcing supplies and Lawrence was either assisting Dr Abbas and Dr Hussam or working a networking angle at the palace, the small crew of Iraqi staff toiled away sporadically at the zoo. It was a peculiar type of industriousness in that a genuine desire not to work, uncertainty about Iraq, Baghdad, fate, and who we were, meshed with opportunism, a willingness for dollars and in some cases a genuine love for animals. We would slowly learn to understand that their normal wasn't our normal. As outsiders, we certainly did not have the physical or logistical capabilities to cover all the tasks that needed to be completed to keep the animals alive and slowly improve the circumstances. Yet each day brought a step of progress (or so we wanted to believe), even if it only meant pilfering functional irrigation pipes, uncrushed by tanks, from another section of the park or scrubbing another layer of grime off a cage wall.

The facilities had been substandard, neglected and underfunded long before the war. The calamitous state forced onto the zoo in the previous weeks had served to exacerbate the situation. We had not understood what we had arrived in, and it would only be later in the zoo's progress that we would hear allegations from visitors of the permanent stench of animal crap which permeated the zoo in earlier years. Without that insight or information (not that it was entirely relevant to our increasing missionary zeal) we knew we needed to break down every challenge we perceived into manageable chunks. Without that approach, we knew the scale of the mess, and how we believed animals should be treated, would have overwhelmed us. Critically, we also knew that between us outsiders we needed to ensure that Dr Abbas was comfortable with any decision we wanted to make because, in the absence of a functional state, it was effectively his zoo. As foreigners, we knew we were only there temporarily. We understood making progress was about cooperation and the clichéd capacity building. We were guests and needed to behave like it.

With a reasonably steady supply of food being scrounged, the animals were recovering quicker than we had anticipated. There were still massive hurdles though. The sum of our shoe-box sized pile of veterinary supplies probably comprised fewer pharmaceuticals than an Ozzy Osbourne urine sample. Those supplies we did have were mostly symbolic anyway because realistically we had no idea what to administer since nobody there knew how to accurately diagnose the most basic ailments. There was no diagnostic equipment, no reference material, and nobody to ask for husbandry or veterinary advice. The Iraqi veterinarians at the zoo appeared willing to act but had been isolated from modern veterinary practices. They didn't recognise most of the meagre donated supplies and simply put, had no more knowledge of veterinary relief in such a disaster than we did. Sanctions and bureaucracy had combined to make it almost impossible for them to source appropriate veterinary supplies. They had no idea of the evolution in the accepted standards of progressive modern zoological facilities internationally. Sanctions and their government had cut them off from the rest of the world and fuelled an apathy or fear to challenge anyone for knowledge or curiosity's sake. Life was more about personal and family survival in the increasingly decaying and paranoid municipality. For us, there was no internet option, and Lawrence's satellite phone was the only contact we had with the world beyond Baghdad. Who did you phone for that information and who would pay the phone bill? We had to run on common sense and what we felt would be a reasonable adaptation from an animal's wild existence.

We knew we needed to put systems in place urgently to ensure basic daily routines became entrenched. That was simple and non-negotiable. That was what Lawrence and Stephan had focused on for weeks with Dr Abbas and Dr Hussam. Animals needed to be fed, watered and to have their living areas cleaned daily. The situation was still critical. That was done no matter what needed to be found to make it happen. Simultaneously zoo grounds were being cleared of debris to give a sense of improving order. As the water supply improved, efforts were made to resurrect lawns and gardens. There needed to be some noticeable visual improvements to rebuild the link between work and progress. The zoo could almost have been described as a proverbial hive of activity, even if only for a few hours in the morning. After that, workers would become disgruntled, feeling that they had earned a day's wage for their generous over-exertion. It was harder than they had ever worked before at the zoo. The new intensity had the potential to stir a mini-insurrection. Stephan actively toiled in the muck to set an example, although it was hard to notice evidence on him in the minutes beyond the labour, as his appearance would miraculously default to post-war reconstruction haute couture. Since it was money from Stephan and Lawrence that was paying staff wages, Stephan also tried to establish an incentivised work scheme where those who worked harder and completed more tasks would be paid more. This foreign strain of reward won a few immediately compliant hearts (those paid more), until a few minutes later those being paid less realised they were paid less. If only the spirited response could have been harnessed for more than disagreement. It unleashed accusations of favouritism and such heated arguments that to keep the peace, the idea was consigned to the "ok, ok, ok, no more" pile.

Small tasks or minor problems like a broken lock or punctured hose always seemed to take an astonishingly long time to repair or find a solution to. Although funding was a contributing cause, these challenges were also a manifestation of the setting. Tea breaks were significant. Even if taken in silence, except for the clinking of the stirring spoon, it seemed ritualistic enough to border on sacred. The numerous prayer times were obviously the most critical times of the day for the 99% Muslim staff. The language was a difficulty too. Between William and his colleagues (with very few exceptions), Lawrence, Stephan and I, none of us spoke Arabic. Farah was the only Iraqi we knew at the time who spoke fluent English. Dr Abbas and Dr Hussam and Ahmed initially spoke enough English that we could carry out an elementary conversation (their spoken English improved considerably, unlike our Arabic). So discussions around the zoo with working staff were often mostly in some sort of concocted sign language until we could find the doctors, Farah or Ahmed. Information was often mixed up between who was reporting and how many individuals it originally came from.

Frequently staff would not arrive at the zoo for work so there would be a reshuffling of those who did to cover the allotted tasks before we could hope to make any improvements. There was little sense of the conditions many of the staff lived in when they were not at the zoo. We did not know enough about them or the city. There would be genuine, compelling risks or problems they would be facing. What were the family pressures that may distract them from getting to work? The one certainty was most had little electricity supply and nights would mean a sweltering sleep generally without any means to cool down. At best some could hope to sleep outside on the house's flat roof, woken up by low-flying helicopters. Then there was the issue of roadblocks and sections of the city being locked down when the U.S. Army was trying to impose order. The number of animals had more than doubled at the zoo since Lawrence's arrival, which meant a growing set of tasks for us to help the few workers with. Moreover, of the workers available only specific staff were willing/allowed/able to carry out particular duties based on rank, skill-set or years of service.

There were shortages of supplies like cleaning equipment and repair tools which were often of cheap quality in the markets and would break after a few days or weeks. Finding replacements could take an entire morning's driving with Ali simply because of traffic jams. There was never one shop, like a Home Depot, where one could buy everything. A bag of screws, a squeegee mop and a car battery may well be located hours from each other in that traffic – and that assumed the shop was open. By the time we would return to the zoo, some staff would have left for home. At markets, the origin of the product often gave an indication of how soon you would return for another and how much you could afford to buy at once until there was more money. "China" often meant budget, poor quality. "German! Almania! Good. Very Good!" Back at the zoo, there were still the lengthy discussions and speculations about what dietary requirements we could source immediately for individual animals, and what improvements were critical versus nice-to-have. Every morning we would walk the zoo premises with Dr Abbas or Farah to check on each animal, discuss the keeper's observations and work out if a veterinary intervention was required and actually possible.

Farah would passionately explain to the occasionally exasperated staff why we were all doing this, why they needed to help the animals and us. Her life growing up with pets and a family with a veterinary history had engrained empathy for animals. It had been an immediate cultural overlap that, combined with her spoken English, sense of humour, biting determination and flirtatious personality, made us feel we had known her a lot longer than a week. Dr Hussam fought his daily battle to resurrect the zoo's water supply. A few of the nearly-pensionable workers, not quite so enamoured with the new intensity of working for their salary, showed impressively uninhibited nepotism and resourcefulness. One even brought his eldest teenage son to act as a proxy-labourer to complete the day's work. The father would briefly attend to water pump maintenance and then spend much of the day resting in the shade. His son would complete the shift. The father would invariably insist on collecting the day's wage, which would aggravate the son, who would complain vehemently to us. Since we had not employed him, we suggested he instead negotiate with his father; a suggestion which met with sour disapproval and days of overt sulking. We could only go on the guidance of our *hosts*. The father, apparently devoid of the capacity for awkwardness, wasn't bothered with any of the fuss. He had been employed at the zoo before the war, so could not be asked to leave. The cunning old fox was content to let the matter fester. Whatever the outcome, he would get paid for putting on his trousers in the morning and wandering to the zoo for a glass of tea and some conversation. Any extra payment for the son would be a bonus for the family.

With any physical labour, we felt we needed to participate for the sake of encouraging reciprocal effort among the staff. The heat was a challenge which left us sweaty messes before many minutes passed. We wanted the tasks finished. We wanted the zoo to improve. We wanted this to be visually obvious to military visitors, stray dignitaries or curious media. We hoped that would spark further interest and support. The trickiest factor was that the zoo staff were mostly a collection of individuals who knew how to guard against overworking or unnecessarily breaking a sweat. It was the most eclectic and peculiar aggregation of workers I had ever encountered; quite likely a reciprocated opinion when they considered us foreigners. In years before the 2003 invasion, most of them had been sent to work at the zoo as a punishment. Firing government staff wasn't an option but sending them to clean animal poo at the zoo was. Consequently, the zoo staff were mostly untrained and rarely well-educated. Any affinity for animals was welcome but incidental. Persistent infractions at another government department – to the zoo. Sheer incompetence – to the zoo. Incurably lazy – to the zoo. Possibly disabled or just odd – definitely to the zoo. Rejected – to the zoo. It was the classic not-in-my-backyard relocation of a problem. Dr Abbas would despair at the quality of individuals he was meant to manage to keep his zoo functional. The zoo was the bottom of the food chain.

A day's work schedule or progress was anything but consistent. Staff would generally arrive earlier than us foreigners, get their jobs partially done and then spend much of the rest of their shifts dodging work or supervision. They would get the same salary either way. That was the government way before the war, and we knew if any salary were held back, the staff member would either not return at all (and likely demand back pay once government systems were back and running) or cause significant problems. Still, Dr Abbas would sweat and swear and get angry to cajole the staff to get their jobs done correctly. He was not shy to deliver the occasional motivational head slap. In part though, we were just relieved staff made it to the zoo over consecutive days. We were never sure if they would make it home alive, or back to the zoo the following day. We knew little of the background of many of the staff. In Salman's case, he apparently had nowhere else to go and lived in the tiny storage room in the lion enclosure building.

From the periphery, it seemed a mostly dysfunctional crew, but there were terrific exceptions. Ayed, the diminutive 50 +/- year-old resident of Fallujah, was responsible for the gardens and grounds at the zoo. He barely talked but worked tirelessly. He was always working in his clean white collared shirt, dark office trousers and a cap. His productivity was clear to see, reflected in the grounds that improved weekly. When his staff refused to work, he would cover their jobs. He never showed malice or protested at their lack of support. When we made concerted efforts to thank him, he would merely smile without answering.

Jasem could easily have been any age between twenty and fifty. He had little education, was always dishevelled in his grubby clothes, and either dirty or wet from a task he would be assigned by Dr Abbas. He would shuffle with purpose, managing his awkward limp in a way it never impeded his work. He appeared to be perpetually smiling and toiling despite his lowly workhorse status. As with Salman, the eccentric lion keeper, when it was perceived that he had stepped out of line, he received a head-smack from his boss. As with Salman, he would grin, laugh and carry on as before.

Sa'ad was immediately noticeable as the cherubic young man growing into a sparse moustache. He was quick to laugh and beam a huge, uninhibited smile. He could never have been accused of being the hardest working soul or a stickler for repetitive duties, but his endeavour was usually cheerily focused on supporting whatever we were attempting. If any of us outsiders, or Farah, were working on a task Sa'ad would materialise like our overheating, sweaty genie, trying to take over the work without any intention other than to help. He preferred that to his routine work and would be insistent he help us. He appeared to genuinely enjoy our company and quickly became my personal teacher of the foulest Arabic words and phrases; enough to earn both of us rebuke from Farah who was herself rarely shy to unleash a torrent.

Akram was Sa'ad's emaciated, virtually blind (even through his staggeringly thick eyeglasses) companion with a tragic family background. That he was rumoured to be trying to marry a prostitute allegedly complicated matters further. It seemed his sinewy frame would never fill the clothes that hung on him and his casually gangly walking style gave him the air of a bipedal lemur. Much like his closest companion, he would readily beam an unmistakable smile, except in his case it would reveal an alarming array of irregular, coloured teeth seemingly in conflict with each other. He certainly showed no intent to overwork himself and noticeably viewed being exceptionally friendly as a means to avoid our scrutiny of his aversion to hard labour. He quickly understood our weakness and his disarming approach left us struggling to build up enough irritation to be openly annoyed, even though tasks were frequently left incomplete. Manipulative, yes. A suitably colourful character for the odd setting; absolutely. Our days were more entertaining and enjoyable because Akram was at the zoo.

Jaboory was another character defying the odds, and another of the staff crew we could not help but develop an affinity for. Aged somewhere "close to retirement" to quite possibly far older, he was a Yoda-esque figurine. He was short, hunched and bald with a waxy complexion and faintly opaque eyes. He struggled to hear and was virtually blind but would still break into a toothless grin in response to almost all Dr Abbas's comments irrespective of their venom or sweetness. That Jaboory consistently made it to work was admirable in its own right. It baffled us. Occasionally we would find him on a flat bench behind his wheel-barrow of alfalfa, sitting upright, but apparently asleep. We would leave him be, knowing the task would get done when he could. He never gave up. He clearly loved the ducks and pelicans he was assigned to care for, waiting patiently at each feeding time to ensure each bird had consumed enough. How he determined or saw that we didn't know. When the ducks were resting on the platform that arched out the middle of the pool, Jaboory laid a connecting wooden plank above the water and shuffled on his bum across to the ducks to hand-feed. When his bucket was empty, he would shuffle back to the outer pathway, set the plank aside, and with his singular focus, hobble onwards to his next task.

Among the other characters was Jaffer, the badger-catching, lion keeper formerly of the Republican Guard, who would sometimes be at work and then sometimes not. The frequent absences were never explained. He loved his sleeveless shirts, black rubber dishwashing gloves and to periodically squeeze my bicep to show me how strong he was. He would look into my eyes, press with his gloved hand and smile at me to let me know who was stronger. I never quite understood the peculiar ritual, but it seemed his perceived dominance cheered him to smug satisfaction. Majed was in his 30's but entirely hairless with a complexion like a waxed baby, allegedly because of living his childhood near to chemical weapons (which at the time seemed plausible and of little concern or surprise to his colleagues telling us). His red and white patterned *yashmagh* scarf was always wrapped around his head to protect him from the brash sun. Reliability was not his strongest point, but he was a solid performer who arrived more days than not and with some verbal motivation from Dr Abbas usually completed what was asked of him on the first or second invitation. Occasionally he would stand and glare at us foreigners with what was either a quizzical or bitter expression. As with many of the staff, it was difficult to clearly discern how we were genuinely viewed; as invaders or convenient, temporary help with money. Our lack of cultural understanding and language skills left us in a void of social interpretation we would often guess our way through, hoping we understood what we saw. Two months later two additional female vets arrived at the zoo, apparently under formal instruction by the coalition controlled municipality authorities. Always dressed immaculately in their lab coats and headscarves, faces layered with bold makeup, they were assigned to walk the zoo grounds in the morning with their supervisory clipboards to tick off the staff's completed duties. They were not the hands-on types of a vet, nor did they express any particular interest in the medicine, but it seemed lab coats and clipboards at least gave them a regular, measurable task with an element of authority. It encouragingly represented order, even if superficially.

A daily battle was to stop some of the staff from stealing food supplies, particularly packaged buffalo meat intended for the animals. Some of the theft was opportunism, or because the staff were short of cash. Some staff were desperate for meals. The problem was obvious and straightforward, but only once Lawrence and Stephan were made aware of it. Until then, they had not considered it. They needed to get daily staff lunches up and running as an urgent priority. Until then, the supply availability had fluctuated and made keeping everyone fed an impossibility. Little had been done to bring force down on the staff because of the need to find an amicable solution. We discussed the idea of hard discipline with Dr Abbas to stop the meat theft by workers. We also knew that would cause resentment among the staff we needed cooperation from. It was agreed with Ahmed, who was sourcing much of the food supply in his "new", old pickup (a battered relic that had only days earlier arrived courtesy of the U.S. Army), that chicken would be purchased daily for meals. It would provide an alternative food source and create a situation where Dr Abbas could be stricter on any theft. The tank crews at the Al-Rasheed once again came to the rescue on the food quest. It helped that they had access to the stockpiles of supplies below the hotel. It wasn't long before a request from Lawrence resulted in Humvees being loaded with bags of rice, tins of food and additional supplies to ensure the staff left their zoo work with full stomachs and perked up morale. For good measure, we took the loading trolley too, which became Ahmed's commissary truck for moving the animals' food around the zoo at feeding time.

Not to be outdone in supplying the zoo with necessities, William honed his scrounging skills and went to work sourcing furniture and desks for the zoo offices. Partially destroyed palaces were a treasure trove of tables and kitsch-painted chairs which we loaded into Humvees under the interpretation of "interdepartmental transfers". It gave the zoo offices a stylish new look, a combination of opulence and jumbled functionality. With new light switches, the offices were functional (when air conditioners arrived weeks later it felt like luxurious bonanza time). Simultaneously, the South African security contractors sourced two deep freezers for Lawrence. Through a generous stroke of timing, and we will never know how it was manipulated, a few anonymous soldiers arrived at the zoo in a truck with two generators to run the freezers.

Generators (and Ali's car) needed diesel. The nearest supply was the U.S. Army encampment at the crossed swords parade grounds adjacent to the park. Whether it was the audacity of the approach or some overall instruction, we never found out why those soldiers helped us. Nobody ever questioned our presence. Temporary residences were set up with camouflage nets and camp stretchers between the trees and parked Humvees. Soldiers would be wandering across the grounds with their M16s strapped over the shoulders or around the back. The smell of burning rubbish and diesel fumes lingered in the heat. We would trundle along the roads or dirt tracks in Ali's taxi, among the fuel and water bowser trucks until we would find a group of soldiers near enough to an appropriate truck. When we said we had come from the zoo, there was always a soldier willing to help. There was never questioning of us, never a doubt. The taxi, still with its ZOO tape stuck on the bonnet, and the extra jerry cans would be filled. We were grateful, and the soldiers content in their belief that they had helped the zoo. The support was invaluable, and word of the zoo efforts spread quickly amongst those troops stationed nearby. Every day that a group of curious and willing soldiers arrived at the zoo to offer assistance, we felt an extra surge of validation that the project was worthwhile. Soldiers, exhausted and annoyed from uneventful patrols, would arrive at the zoo to help with anything we could task them with. Squads of engineers would visit with jackhammers, welding equipment and muscle in return for some personal satisfaction and the occasional fresh steaks we could source from town. "Ya tell us, and we'll fix it" some would say with a wad of tobacco dip squashed in between their lower lip and gum. When cage doors needed welding or reworking to fit or be made sturdier, the engineers would jump at the opportunity, sweating away until they were happy with their product. At one point an idea to deepen and extend a reinforced-concrete bear pool in an empty, old enclosure had engineers arriving daily and hammering away; until we all agreed we could never make the enclosure even partially suitable for a captive bear. The engineers never complained about the extra effort. They volunteered eagerly. They had children back in the U.S. they knew enjoyed their local zoos. They had no control over the giant political beast they were entrenched in. They wanted the redeeming sensation they were making a positive community-level contribution. At that time, in combination with tireless efforts of those from the 354th Civil Affairs, it was those contributions which never made the international or local media, but which played a significant role in demonstrating to Iraqi staff at the zoo that there were some genuinely decent American troops on the ground. Those troops defied any negative perceptions that would spark up so quickly on the fuel of rumours.

The problem of looters raiding the park and zoo persisted, although not with the same intensity that William and other patrolling squads had previously encountered. At one point thieves were temporarily confined in zoo cages to restore some semblance of order. As we stepped out of the office, a young keeper ran across the paving to alert us to "Ali Babas" in the park. We stood under the arch at the zoo's entrance gate watching the thieves. If they were out in the park, then they were not in the zoo. It was a matter of outlook. I had always assumed that the lampposts with street lights had been knocked over by tanks or explosions. To see the small gang operate so slickly to only steal a light bulb put the scale of the epidemic into perspective. After unbolting the base of the lamppost with a spanner, the crew toppled and then gently guided the pole to the ground in a controlled manner. The light bulb was removed with the glee of fisherman finding a prized pearl in an oyster.

Iraqi night-watch guards were posted at the zoo to guard against the looting. They had no jurisdiction or power of arrest and so reported the problem of infiltrations to William. He convinced a few willing colleagues to join him setting up an observation post on the roof of a 6m tall pump station. Concealed from view, they waited patiently with rifles, grenades, night-vision goggles and a desire to scare the life out the parasites that roamed the night. The hours of darkness wore on tediously, and the occasional crickets and the distant stuttering and sharp popping of skirmishes of gunfire maintained the expected Baghdad evening chorus. Then they witnessed the moment they hadn't been waiting for. Through the green illuminated light of the night vision eyepiece, they watched as a badger dug his way out to freedom. Not quite the thrill they were anticipating, it was their last night-time foray to intercept Ali Babas.

A decision needed to be taken on the future of the petite gazelle that had been rescued from Luna Park. Initially found in a dusty hovel lying on a piece of corrugated iron next to a broken lawnmower (obviously an accessory every self-respecting gazelle should own), the gazelle had been moved to a spacious paddock. The improved variety of grass, vegetables and greens, ready access to clean water and space was not enough to stimulate a reversal in its health. Its condition deteriorated daily. There was a subtle swelling of the throat, but we didn't know if that was a natural characteristic (as with Goitered gazelles) or an indication of a health concern that was leading to the body condition worsening. There was no way for us to run blood tests, diagnose the actual problem or develop a course of medication. It was guesswork from the vets. The vitamin powder Dr Hussam keenly professed to be the universal answer to any illness definitely wasn't curing whatever ailment it was. With the gazelle declining to the point of emaciation and suffering from chronic diarrhoea, it was decided that it would be humane to euthanise it.

William had left a silenced Stirling sub-machine gun at the zoo, and I agreed that without the available drugs for chemical euthanasia, I would shoot the animal. It wasn't a pleasant task, and I hated killing animals, but I figured that it was what the situation demanded. I knew I could do it quickly, without any further suffering to the animal. There weren't any other volunteers. It was a quick lunge, grab and twist, and we had the gazelle lying on the ground. I squeezed the trigger gently but was a bit surprised when a few more than the one intended bullet burst out. The death was immediate. There we saw an opportunity.

Lawrence and I felt a necropsy might be worthwhile to allow the vets some hands-on work and to inspect the organs. "Not necessary," remarked Dr Abbas as he lifted the animal's head on the opposite side to where I had shot. "This cheek and side of the head are very badly damaged. Looks like cancer. Definitely cancer!" I looked at the barrel of the gun, looked at the head, looked at Lawrence, looked at Farah, looked at Dr Abbas. The matter was closed. I thought about mentioning that I had just shot it in the head. I held my tongue. I needed a cold Pepsi. In the new medical records, the gazelle was officially listed as suffering from thyroid cancer.

The days felt like they were passing so quickly we had lost all bearing on time. It was a case of everyone contributing in their own ways. Stephan, William, Farah and I would be at the zoo daily. It felt like an island of crude creativity compared to the city around us. We could pick our own priorities and then tailor them towards outcomes that aligned with Dr Abbas and Dr Hussam's ambitions. We were still trying to work out what were the best diets for the animals that we could muster with the money and market options available. Buying new taps or cable ties or trying to get broken tree branches cut or trying to make daily checklists always seemed to take all the hours of the morning when combined with roving inspections of all the animal enclosures, scheming zero-budget fixes and trying to track down errant staff.

Lunches would be spent at the ORHA palace and late afternoons feeding the lions with Ali. Farah started to engage more openly as her confidence and role in the manic hotchpotch situation became more apparent. She was a window into a side of Iraqi culture we had never known existed; young, feisty, motivated, intelligent, and ambitious to be productive. Farah seemed to live off cigarettes, Pepsi and chocolate. With her extroverted energy, rebellious streak, tight clothing, brightly dyed hair, quick temper, love of the dogs that arrived at the zoo and desire to help with any task, she stood out completely. She was the antithesis of what we ignorantly, culturally expected Iraqi women to be like; subservient. She was definitely unlike any other Iraqi woman we had met. Her friends and relatives sounded tech-savvy, musical, artistic and products of an active education system, which despite recent deterioration, had previously held a reputation for high quality. We had a lot to learn about the society we had arrived amongst. By her own admission, her veterinary skills were inadequate for the challenges, but her ability to speak Arabic and English became increasingly essential as more tasks were added to our collective to-do lists. She could organise, and she did not expect a salary. It was like a godsend at the zoo. Any foreigner, like ORHA officials or security contractors that were initially sceptical of the cute Iraqi girl from the zoo, were quickly charmed. Like us outsiders, she revelled in the opportunity and excitement of the greater project. She had the political and cultural understanding we lacked, which became crucial in us understanding the intricacies and context of why she thought specific individuals at the zoo appeared more obstructive than others. Iraq and Baghdad comprised exceedingly complex societies morphed through thousands of years of history, tribal affiliation, marriage, family pride, religion, landscape, location, ambition, war, brutality and resources and we finally had a tiny peephole of insight.

Although there was almost always overt charm and politeness from all the staff, there was still noticeable suspicion, apparent allegiances and social angling. It had a cultural context but was entrenched by the uncompromisingly ruthless reign of Saddam's regime. We had no idea of the genuine political or religious affiliations or ambitions of many of the staff. We had no idea who may have had former Baath Party links, who was bitter about the invasion or how they had been impacted during the recent battles. Who knew anything about family members detained before the war or more recently? Who had lost family members to abductions or conscription and war? Who thought we were Jewish spies? Who thought we were all American invaders? Who believed they would rather be oppressed by Saddam the Iraqi than Bush the American? Without that knowledge, we felt it was best to stay polite, patient, respectful, and observant. If we were fair and friendly with everyone, eventually the real social politicking at the zoo would reveal itself. In time the truth almost always squirms its way out. We had to be perceptive enough towards the subtle clues to astutely play the social game.

Lawrence was almost always scheming how to acquire more funding and supplies and working out how to facilitate additional international help. Securing resources was still priority number one. He was spending less time at the zoo and more time at the Al-Rasheed and the ORHA palace grooming potential connections. The immediate, inexperienced concept of only providing emergency relief to the zoo animals rapidly evolved to being about restoring staff functionality, enabling them to care for their families, and getting a city recreational area up and running. The context had become apparent and was crucial to understanding how to market the project. As a means to draw attention to the urgency of the zoo relief effort, Lawrence had been selling to the coalition authorities the broader concept of Al-Zawra Park being a "green lung" for Baghdad. Draped in that veil, we believed reinvigorating the zoo would be a significant step in offering some semblance of escapism for families of the city. Outsiders may have disagreed with the logic, but they were not there. Pragmatism trumped idealism. The idea gained traction. It had the *winning hearts and minds* flavour to it that the imposing power was keen to embrace. It was understood to be more than an animal welfare issue. This gave us substance in the inevitably obstructive and irritating debate of "why are animals' lives more important than human lives when there is so much suffering?" What we really wanted to say was "stop your whining, if you don't like what we're doing go find your own project to be pious about. This is where we have chosen to make a positive difference." The people who posed those questions tended to be sensitive, sanctimonious souls, so we had to explain ourselves with considerably more eloquence and tact. Animals are a far more significant component of the ecology of human society than many people care to acknowledge and, quite simply, we were not diverting funds from humanitarian initiatives. The binary *animals* versus *humans* debate administrators and reporters conceitedly and ignorantly engaged us with was as welcome as a recreational colonoscopy.

As well as employing Ali, Stephan had also made use of a translator, Haider, who offered to take us to Babylon. It was a city of ancient legend dating back to 2300 BC. Located on the plains between the Tigris and Euphrates rivers it was occupied by historical icons like Nimrod, Hammurabi, Nebuchadnezzar, and those two most modest rulers, Darius the Great and Alexander the Great. Under the Assyrians, it was reputedly home to one of the ancient world's great wonders, the hanging gardens of Babylon. Its fortunes and fate had risen and been savagely plundered by empires for thousands of years. It had long since decayed from neglect but remained an archaeological gem, despite further destruction by Saddam Hussein and the U.S. Military. We were told that in the 1980s Saddam had commissioned a reconstruction of Babylon, where many of the bricks were inscribed with his name to glorify his part in history. U.S. forces had subsequently occupied the position and levelled areas for helicopter landing sites and parking areas. Although it was perhaps an inappropriate time to go sightseeing given the zoo's needs and the war context, it was an opportunity we did not want to miss out on. If Haider was happy to take us, we were delighted to go. Ali was less enamoured with the idea and made it clear that any guiding should be his responsibility. Stephan placated the visibly disgruntled Ali by assuring him the zoo was undoubtedly in greater need of Ali's unique brand of resourcefulness and persistence than we would need for one errant day.

Haider's old car coughed its way south towards Hillah, passing sporadic defaced Saddam motifs at random junctions that appeared to be in the middle of nowhere. On tracks parallel to the highway a train lay burnt out next to an Iraqi tank. Upon arrival in the area Haider knew was close to Babylon, we struggled to find a route towards Babylon itself with the U.S. military blocking all roads and tracks heading to the site. We were told at a checkpoint that a helicopter had crashed earlier that morning and there was no chance we would be allowed in that day. Frustrated by the unfortunate timing, Haider suggested a visit to Hillah to make the trip worthwhile. From what we saw, it was a grimy clutter of decaying buildings with plentiful filth and refuse and no place for two pale foreign tourists to be strolling about. A quick tea stop and a few received stares later we were certain heading north back to Baghdad would make us feel more comfortable. The car that had been struggling throughout the journey finally spluttered to a halt. With much urging and manipulation, it bunny hopped to a conveniently placed roadside mechanic where it appeared to cough out its final breath. We were caught off-guard by how friendly and hospitable the grease and muck caked mechanics and children all were. Working amongst a scatter of clutches, brake pads and mechanical debris we were served the customary steaming hot, sugary tea as they took great interest in the car's death. Like every tricky challenge we had experienced so far in Iraq, there always seemed a person able to fashion a solution, however improvised. The resurrection defied expectations. What appeared a brisk two hours later, we were on the road northwards as the car wheezed back to Baghdad.

At the Al-Rasheed, Lawrence and I were still gathering with the tank crews after our afternoon returns to the hotel. Their days had become more mundane as active fighting had evolved into routine patrols and checkpoint duty. The rumours about deployment back home to the U.S. were discussed with a mixture of relief by those wanting to see their families and eat alternatives to MREs and others fearing going back to comparatively dull, routine barracks life.

The cultural eye-opener of being in Iraq was not only limited to working with Iraqis. As white, suburban South Africans during apartheid, we had grown up watching American culture through television shows and Hollywood films. It was not a refined intellectual understanding. Guns, ammo, MacGyver, Corvettes and bikinis. We perceived *'Merica* promoting its exceptionalism with unapologetic pride, in love with its identity and cultural bubble, while simultaneously trying to dominate the world. Not many other countries would call its annual domestic championship the World Series as Major League Baseball does. Lawrence had spent considerable time in the U.S. while I had never been there. He assured me I was in for a cultural education.

The most jarring social difference from where I had grown up and travelled was in the general American sense of humour. Apparently, the easily digested comic lines of

Friends and Seinfeld were not the norms. The timing, intent and literal bluntness of comments in Baghdad left little room for self-deprecation, sarcasm, general ridicule and irony of the British-style humour we grew up with. That reality was made abundantly clear to me at a checkpoint as I responded to a query with a joking observation about a brand of knife, as I was being patted down for weapons. The soldier's immediate response was to stare at me as if ziptying and detention were inevitable. I kept quiet. It seemed explaining the wisecrack would only dig a deeper hole. He carried on the search. It was a social quirk I hadn't adapted too in the first few weeks. Fortunately, when a U.S. soldier asked us what state of the U.S. South Africa was in, his colleagues saw the opening to mercilessly mock him. That cultural difference was only reinforced by a brief stop at the old British Embassy in the Al-Shawaka neighbourhood. As Ali and Farah delivered an impromptu tour of parts of Baghdad, they wanted to show me the formerly prosperous area with its carved wooden window frames and latticed shutters. It had miserably decayed when its residents were both squeezed and neglected for holding anti-Saddam tendencies. The British Embassy was a landmark. The joking banter with maroon-bereted British Paratroopers behind the gate was immediate. The relief at not having to explain a sarcastic comment was oddly so comforting that I remember pointing out the difference to Farah. Even the cocky street children that energetically clustered and jostled at the gate seemed to have done so purely because they could engage in back and forth playful mocking and smiling verbal abuse. "Hey meester, what your name? Hey meester gimmee dollar. Hey fuck you meester."

Like many of the foreigners in Baghdad, we spent time absorbing the notable surrounds of the parade ground with the crossed sword arches at either end. Being an iconic Baghdad landmark, the officially named Swords of Qadissiya monument became a familiar *I was in Baghdad* photo opportunity. It was constructed to celebrate a supposed victory over Iran during the eight-year Iraq-Iran war which ended in 1988. Although the swords were modelled on that of the victorious Arab general from the 7th century Battle of Al Qadissiya (fought against the Persians), the hands holding the swords were designed as enormous replicas of Saddam Hussein's hands. Helmets of approximately 2,500 Iranian soldiers were kept in nets at the bases of the hands and were also embedded into the parade ground road as speed humps to be driven and walked over. Many of the helmets had visible bullet piercings in them.

By early May the ORHA had been replaced by a new entity, the Coalition Provisional Authority (CPA). It was led by L. Paul Bremer who was appointed the U.S. Presidential Envoy and Administrator in Iraq. Despite being an experienced diplomat, Bremer had never been to Iraq, never served in the Middle East and did not speak Arabic. Bremer was in. Garner was out. Through Tim Carney, a senior administration staff member whom Lawrence had been liaising with during his time in Kuwait and Baghdad, Lawrence was introduced to Pat Kennedy, the Chief of Staff for Paul Bremer. Lawrence explained the zoo efforts, progress and challenges and over days, approached Kennedy with updates and a request for the CPA to provide vehicles for the zoo. It was crucial for the logistical demands and despite Kennedy's empathy with the zoo task; he politely declined the requests, clarifying that all vehicles were already in use in the city's reconstruction effort. When Lawrence pushed the point further and let him know the zoo would be grateful for any of the abandoned vehicles the U.S. Army cleared from Baghdad roads daily, he hit the jackpot. The following day two worn-out pickup trucks arrived at the zoo. The excitement was palpable. The consideration of the zoo as a reconstruction product to be delivered had been recognised. It was a crucial development.

Lawrence was introduced to The Mayor, the CPA coordinator for Baghdad. He was in effect the caretaker mayor of Baghdad through his office Baghdad Central. The Mayor was reportedly an old-hand at the diplomatic game, with a distinguished career in parts of the world where people tended to emigrate from rather than immigrate too. Lawrence quickly recognised The Mayor's broad sphere of responsibility. In the palace corridors, where influence and persuasion were currency, Lawrence engaged his narrative skills for the zoo cause. The angles were initially the potential public relations hype for the American administration and the social benefits of restoring a reinvigorated Al-Zawra Park and its zoo to the Iraqi people – and all they at Baghdad Central had to do was enable us to do the dirty work. The Mayor obviously had more pressing priorities to keep his bosses' ambitions fulfilled; like overseeing his departments' restoration of all Baghdad's municipal systems including electricity and water supplies, but he was open to Lawrence's propositions. They quickly established a professional rapport. The Mayor hardly radiated enthusiasm when Lawrence later introduced me, the minion. At best The Mayor's painfully unnatural smile was reluctant and hardly worthwhile under a veneer of tolerance; the "Thanks, but no thanks" look reserved for Hare Krishna pamphlet wavers. I rarely made good first appearances. My entrance as a dishevelled youngster in a sweaty T-shirt and Zululand-distressed Chinos and boots was apparently not the office-chic that drew approval as representing earnest endeavour. I clearly did not master the illusion of projecting myself as a professional zoo trouble-shooter.

  I was courteous but impatient. I didn't enjoy the token fluffy talk, tactical bullshitting and preamble to build a rapport (I would later regret that). Where Lawrence was a deft persuader, I was more introverted and did not understand or care for the nuances. I had a job to do and viewed success in simple terms; either we were succeeding, or we were failing. It was how I had worked for Lawrence at Thula Thula. As a grand, cultural hodgepodge collective at the zoo, we were making noticeable progress despite the tensions, ambitions and political differences we were engaging with. The Mayor's seemingly disingenuous, condescending approach immediately riled me. Perhaps I misinterpreted his manner, or he thought I'd stood on his family hamster, but my immediate sense was that the fragile relationship would likely be hard work. To be fair, I had little understanding of the intense pressure he was under to birth Baghdad into the new world. But I was conscious of how his personality compared with that of Pat Kennedy, who was higher up the pecking order and appeared to project calm and genuine, unruffled courteousness even in brevity. Kennedy never failed to act graciously or interested in us, which encouraged straight, quick answers to get to a potential solution. With The Mayor, it usually felt like an honest answer rather than an insipid diplomatic one was more likely viewed as provocative or at best, ignorant. Back at the zoo, William took great delight in laughing at my post-meeting mutterings, suggesting on more than one occasion that I needed to work on my diplomacy skills.

The news that both Lawrence and Stephan were to leave Baghdad caught William, Farah and me by surprise. Three days later, at the end of May, they departed. Stephan needed to resume his WildAid responsibilities in Cambodia and Lawrence left to London and the United States to rally international support for Baghdad Zoo. Suddenly the dynamics changed. While Farah, William and I had quickly bonded through shared values and humour, we could not make that same assumption about anybody around us. The reality of the scale of the task at hand hit home, and from only contributing, we felt directly responsible for the change. Farah, William and I would have to work closely with Dr Abbas to ensure the zoo staff continued to improve on their productivity. Realistically, Dr Abbas, despite his years at the zoo was short of ideas and appeared to still be adapting to an overturned life at the newish Baghdad Zoo. His working world had been dramatically changed through no fault of his own. Following years of stagnation, every day was lively, charged, and perceptions of power shifted like a tidal wash in a city facing colossal uncertainty.

Improvements were critically needed, but most importantly, they were possible. It was a genuine opportunity to capitalise on, not just empty words. We had all arrived to alleviate an emergency. Once there, we saw exaggerated opportunity to improve the lives of animals, the staff and their management. We wanted the poor zoo to mature into a better zoo (entirely subjective - I understand), but we needed Dr Abbas's approval, cooperation and participation. It quickly seemed clear he wanted it too – he wanted to see what we would deliver. We wanted him to enjoy the chance to invest in improvements. We tried to persuade and assure him where he had doubts. We believed it would be the only way changes would persist beyond our departure. We knew we needed to project humility. We could not be perceived to be arrogant foreigners (or a young Iraqi woman) imposing change by telling the director of twelve years what to do. It was vital Dr Abbas had the final say on all matters and ideas we concocted. It was clear that he appreciated all the attention on his zoo, but it was also clear that with years of a resilient, ingrained survival instinct under the Baathist system, gaining a personal advantage in the fluid situation was also on his mind. That was natural and understandable. We all saw opportunities. None of us was there altruistically. For us, it was partly about a hint of self-gratification if we could engineer a favourable situation compared with the zoo's state of early 2003. We needed to be shrewd to ensure a satisfied director and progressive, lasting change. Through our tea time discussions with Dr Abbas and Dr Hussam, we agreed we could develop a zoo with a significant recreational, educational and conservation purpose. We saw the potential but knew that was a long-term concept. Perhaps it was a little over-ambitious. There were undoubtedly moments of laughably blind optimism. First, we had to try to get the staff paid, the animals fed, the poo-shovelling and cleaning routines embedded and the team willing to arrive each day. "Step-by-Step" and "We'll make a plan" became entrenched in the vocabulary.

I had a small bundle of U.S. dollars from Stephan and Lawrence stored at the hotel for daily zoo supplies and emergencies. That gave us some operational relief. Meanwhile, William was our official link to the U.S. Army and was returning to the zoo daily to help us plan improvements and rescue projects and to liaise with other useful units for logistics. He and colleagues in his 354th Civil Affairs unit like Captain Mark St Laurent, Lieutenant Heather Coyne and "Lynge – the medic" had quickly become valuable additions in the zoo restoration efforts. Significantly, they had personal and professional links into the CPA. A bonus was they were a regular source of social relief when the intimidating reality struck me that I was the only foreigner then permanently based at the zoo. There was still no operational phone network so Farah and I would have to rely on William's arrival at the zoo or find him at his unit's house if we wanted to make contact. That I was getting to navigate that experience with an energetic, quick-witted and savvy young Iraqi lady, heightened the insight, intensity and enjoyment of each day. It was impossible not to sit in a quiet moment and think how oddly I had strayed from trying to emulate David Attenborough.

With Stephan gone, Ali appointed himself as my official transport and unofficial protection. When Farah and I needed supplies from around the city, we would only go with Ali. We had complete confidence (or more likely blind faith) in his inspired, domineering driving skills and ability to assess where was safe to drive with a conspicuous ginger in his taxi. Despite speaking almost no English, he would always have an unrestrained opinion on the quality of equipment or the price paid if another zoo staff member provided us with a quote or item. It became a source of reliable entertainment that predictably the quote was always too expensive, the item of inferior quality and the supplier untrustworthy. Credit given where it was due, Ali was usually correct.

After weeks of Stephan's muttering, the checkpoint soldiers at Uday's Palace had finally begun to recognise Ali's white and orange taxi, *sans* Stephan, and relented on their overly officious approach to us. A cursory glance at the ID cards and the buckets of meat would invite the boom to open and prompt a wave from the soldiers in the APC or Bradley Fighting Vehicle providing the checkpoint's backup firepower. Farah would follow us in her Passat so she could also enjoy the excitement of meat-tossing to lions. Soldiers quickly congregated to enjoy their daily flirt with "the lion lady". It also helped to have willing extra hands to swab the floor and stoke the little waste bonfire.

Farah, Ali and I had quickly assumed an acute sense of responsibility towards the palace lions, but more than that we developed an almost possessive air around our recent acquisitions. We felt that if we didn't keep these lions healthy, nobody else would. First Special Forces, then Lawrence, then Stephan and Ali had kept these animals alive after the Hussein's had fled. It was our turn.

Brutus's approach to donkey heads and thighs was absolutely brutal. When Ali passed donkey thighs between the bars, Brutus would raise his powerful body up onto his hind legs, claw the meat with ten opaque hooks, and rip the limb from Ali's grasp. There was no subtlety. Donkey heads were too large to pass between the bars. Climbing onto the car roof, and then onto the holding building to drop in the bigger bits wasn't always appealing. In a macabre game of Highland Welly Throwing, we would attempt to launch the heavy head over the 8m high enclosure fence patrolled by the pacing lions. A firm grip under the moist jaw bone helped prevent the head slipping away, and a big arm swing usually did the trick. Ali was my tutor. When it didn't arc over, the head would bounce off the upper bars and clatter back on the ground near us. It became a matter of refined hurling technique; a bit gruesome but a practical solution. On occasions when soldiers would watch and get particularly cocky with their comments about how strong they were, or implore us to throw a live animal into the enclosure, we would offer them the head-tossing option to divert attention onto them. It was undoubtedly grisly, but their egos wouldn't allow them to back down with their friends watching. After all, if an Iraqi or a South African could do it, surely they as Americans could. Most attempts ended in repeated failure, their companions would mock them, and we could carry on with our tasks undistracted. We would often have to fling the head in to rub in the soldier's humiliation. Brutus would pounce on the bouncing head and then slowly lick his fresh possession before beginning the potent crushing, tearing and chewing. If the adult females or cubs walked near to Brutus and his quarry, a deep, penetrating growl and a bearing of teeth stopped the interference. If he lost interest with feeding, he would rub against the bars and chain-link fence, expecting a scratch of his neck and mane; which Ali always obliged. Ali, despite his staunch bravado and macho approach to most situations, could not hide his soft spot; his affection for the lions in a palace compound that months earlier he would never have conceived he would be allowed near.

The six cubs, as cute as they appeared with their golden fur, chubby spotted bellies and bluish eyes were hostile little wildlings. They would hiss and swat at any attempt by us to contain them while herding them back into the inside cages in the holding building. Being small enough to slip between the bars at a point where the barriers were more widely spaced to allow the operation of the sliding-gate handles, they made a habit of trying to escape. They could only realistically then play in the viewing area within the locked holding building, so we were not too concerned that this happened when we were not at the enclosure. With persuasion, they would eventually scramble and dive back through the gap as a cluster of cubs, over our temporary collapsed barrier of stone water troughs that they had pulled apart to escape. They would then solicit a dose of playful grooming from their mother(s) in the most innocent of manners. It was impossible not to feel affection for them, even if we were reciprocally viewed purely as a source of food.

As Ali would crank the water pump into life to wash the floors, I would stoke the fire of burning palm fronds, meat packaging, donkey bones and skulls, and lion poo in the pit next to the building. The pile would flare and smoke and flare again until smouldering as collapsing grey ash. It was the only way we could maintain any semblance of hygiene. There was nowhere else to remove the waste to. The stench locked into my olfactory memory, but rather than wretch, I quite curiously began to enjoy making the daily bonfire. Today the smell of burning rubbish takes me instantly back to that surreal and rather happy fire-stoker role in the palace grounds.

CHAPTER 5

The gossip filtering among military circles in the CPA dining hall was that there was a bear at "the far end of town" in a ghastly zoo. Nobody was doing anything about it! Surely it was our responsibility to find the bear and save it! How could we not have known about it? We did know about it. We wanted that bear out of Luna Park for its own sake, and we wanted the rumours of its neglect and our apparent lack of conviction or action to finally cease. Our biggest problem was that the bear was too big to load in a Humvee. That was all we had access too, until William once again delivered the goods. By our estimation, his scrounging had reached tremendous new heights. Having befriended an Army engineering unit with a HEMMT (Heavy Expanded Mobility Tactical Truck) with a hydraulic arm, William knew we had a potential solution.

The idea simmered. We discussed it at length but the reality was we were still short of equipment and had no experience of moving bears. We improvised a plan. Once again, the idea was that we would initially dart the bear with immobilising drugs. Assuming the drugs worked, we would load the bear into a cargo net, wrap and tie the net closed like a string bag around a boneless ham. That would be hoisted onto the back of the truck, and we would hope like hell that the bear slept the entire journey back to the Baghdad Zoo. If it did not, it would probably be the most significant talking point of several soldiers' tour of duty. We recognised that to say it was a refined and safe plan would have been an exaggeration. We knew there was a severe probability for it to go completely, chaotically wrong. The idea of a rogue, stoned bear rampaging through the streets of Baghdad after having climbed or fallen off the back of a U.S. Army truck would not have played well as a narrative on Al Jazeera news. We preferred to be cautious but unrealistically optimistic about the litany of potential risks because if they dominated our thoughts, we would never give it a try. There were so many unknowns. What was the strength of a brown bear? Could it tear through an army cargo net? How much of the drug should one use at the suggested concentration? How would that impact the bear's breathing? The package insert page gave some information on dosage, but it relied on us knowing how much the bear weighed? None of us had any idea how much that bear weighed. We didn't have access to a reference that would tell us even a rough estimate. What was likely too much of the drug? Was it feasible to imagine a bear could sleep safely immobilised for a potentially hour-long trip through Baghdad traffic jams? Would the bear overheat? What does an overheating bear do, shit itself or die? Could we ethically or physically kill the bear if it broke loose? What would the implications be for soldiers joining this rescue if any of the above scenarios happened? That we were in that situation likely meant we had converged at a time in our lives where an appetite for the daft and overly-ambitious generally took precedence over sound reasoning.

  Our convoy of three Humvees and Ali's taxi pulled into the grounds of one of the many palaces in the Green Zone. Humvees and the prized HEMMT truck baked in the parking lot. After some gentle persuasion by William, with the conversation progressing along the lines of "do you still want to rescue that bear from across town?" the commanding officer agreed. The opportunity for a great adventure and a positive outcome was too good to miss. The convoy, with a HEMMT following, ground its slow way out the Green Zone checkpoint at Assassins Gate over the bridge crossing the Tigris River, towards Tahreer Square, and off to whisk away the suffering beast. Despite being early morning, the traffic was already thickening like it was moving through corn-starch and it was a chief concern that we would get stuck in a gridlock on the return ride from Luna Park. A convoy of conspicuous U.S. military vehicles is difficult to miss in the chaotic civilian traffic of Baghdad. The opportunity to let off a rifle shot, or better, fire an explosive munition in the direction of such a convoy was a treat for people hating the foreigners now occupying their country. We stuttered on. Anonymous dull, blocky brown buildings lined either side. Some stood with sooty licks on the walls, gutted by fires blamed on the rampaging looters. We passed the gutted Ministry of Oil building. Beyond the surrounding parched land and dirty waters of a small artificial lake in the distance stood the two colossal turquoise sections of the split dome of the Martyrs (*Al-Shaheed*) Monument. At 40m tall, they dominated the beige, flat landscape. The surrounding circular platform from which they rose up was ironically a provisional parking bay for a mix of U.S. military vehicles.

There was the anticipated delay as staff at Luna Park objected to the attempted removal of the bear. As he did previously, Dr Abbas played peacemaker and explained the bear would be well cared for at Baghdad Zoo. To those at Luna Park, the bear's health was not even close to the issue of contention. It was difficult to avoid a curious crowd of spectators (Luna Park staff, assisting soldiers and randomly arriving members of the public) gathering to watch the events unfold. The bear saw more people, more animation, more tension. It spiked the bear's stress levels, translating into its stereotypical pacing against the metal bars, turning and repeating, again and again. Farah mixed the drugs with Dr Abbas. The final agreed dosage was calculated through speculation and cordial, uninformed consensus. The only certainty was that the drugs had recently passed the expiration date. They had unquestionably been exposed to heat which we understood would likely compromise potency and effectiveness. It was all we had, and we needed to get that bear out of there ASAP. The move quickly started to feel more attritional than swift and effective. Thankfully, Dr Abbas was on his A-game. The first dart pegged into the bear's backside. The animated ursid continued to harass the chewed hosepipe in his cage, oblivious to the dart. We waited. In intense anticipation, we all observed quietly hoping like hell that the bear would fall over, asleep, and ready for loading. Darting bears was new to all of us. It felt like it. Speculative theories and options were raised. The heat made the sweat dribble down our faces. We knew we could not wait much longer before personal safety concerns dictated we would need to leave. We didn't know what direct risk we were at being where we were, particularly given that we had irritated the Luna Park staff. Too long in one area as an obvious target was not a smart practice. We were already testing a few boundaries. The bear sat down, head upright and watched us. We observed the bear for twenty minutes. Stalemate.

The second dart whipped into the rump. The bear spun round to find the offending sting. The dart with its fluffy orange rear bobbed up and down as the bear made a lazy attempt to swat it off. It was clear Dr Abbas now understood his weapon. He was chuffed, but we could see the plunger had only pushed half the new drug cocktail into the bear's butt muscle. The bear sat and watched us. We waited anxiously, trying to keep the spectators quiet. Ten minutes passed. Another ten minutes passed, and the bear was once again pacing confidently in his cubicle. "Shit!" We needed a better plan. We were increasingly concerned about the time we had spent at Luna Park. Ali and Dr Abbas agreed that Iraqi brown bears were deceptively tough, in fact much tougher than American bears and that none of these western drugs would be able to knock it down. Farah and William and I suggested what we thought was a logical argument about the concerns of dosage and expiry dates. We were wrong - "Iraqi bears very tough. Strong!" Despite the frustrations, Ali and Dr Abbas appeared slightly conflicted by the pride they felt that the bear was resisting. The few Luna Park staff nodded in agreement.

As the third dart was being prepared, Specialist Mitchell and I found the nearby decrepit cable car rides. We felt that if we could disconnect one of the small funfair cable cars, it could be used as a cage to house the bear, even a semi-drugged bear. It was undoubtedly optimistic and fanciful, but the bear wasn't cooperating. We thought it would be a potential improvised alternative to what was looking like an increasingly doubtful cargo net-wrapping plan. Our biggest initial concern was we suspected that in the interests of public safety, the bolts would be too tight for us to disconnect the vehicle from its overhead tracks. How foolish we were. As we unscrewed the bolts with our fingers, we considered ourselves lucky we had not come for a day at the funfair. A small delegation of fuming, sweaty Iraqis stormed across and yelled venomous abuse at us in Arabic, apparently under the impression we were stealing the valuable item. Our attempts to explain we might use it to capture the bear were unlikely to have gained traction even if they could have understood us. William, distracted by the uproar, arrived to display authority and quell the tension. We agreed in the interests of community relations to cease the theft of the impromptu bear sedan and focus instead on the theft of the bear as the seething delegation made sure to call it. I couldn't fault their interpretation.

The third dart caused the bear's pacing to slow noticeably. He stumbled, likely for the first time ever in his instinctive, repetitive rut. We grinned, satisfied that the drug was finally, definitely taking effect. He lay down gingerly as if unsure where the floor was. He lurched forward slightly and vomited a little splash of goo, another sign that the drugs were working through his system. Fighting the demons, he rose drunk and defiantly to his feet before once again resuming the monotonous, stereotypical pacing. We were stumped. "Iraqi bears very strong", Dr Abbas reminded us. The heat was scorching, straining our concentration as we were running out of patience, time and ideas. An unkempt, dusty teenager who had been watching the events play out, chirped out unexpectedly that he and his friends had often spent time drinking alcohol with the bear, plying the willing hairy companion with vodka in the evenings when they were all bored. He was adamant the bear's preference for cheap liquor was the reason for its resistance to these weak western drugs. Collectively, our Baghdad Zoo team decided a fourth dart was the last resort for the dazed, alcoholic, very tough Iraqi brown bear. Our reasoning at the time was callous but tainted with empathy and ignorance. We agreed the fourth dart would either knock the bear out or kill it. The situation felt that grave, that tense, that those appeared like the only alternatives. We backed our collective judgement. Dr Abbas agreed. Either way, the bear would be out of its miserable circumstances. We felt that familiar strained, soupy tension inside our guts. We did not want the bear to die.

The fourth dart did neither. The bear stumbled, slumped onto its chest and lay down. His lips twitched with the makings of a contented snore. He was on the verge of sleeping. We stared, willing him to sleep. He lifted his groggy head and stared towards us with glazed eyes. Fifteen minutes crept along mercilessly on the watch. We needed him to bloody-well sleep! He dragged his limp front paws forward, lethargically staggered to a wobbly stand, fighting the sensation of the drugs and resumed the pacing game like an unrelenting boxer recovering from a powerful but inconclusive uppercut. Defeated, intensely frustrated and severely deflated, we decided there was no alternative option. We would have to leave the bear behind. Again! As this battle of wills and physiology ensued, William was once more attempting to negotiate a final financial settlement for the removed collection. It was made clear to the makeshift mob of the Luna Park owner Karim Hameed that unless the bear was fed and watered until we could return, there would be no deal. We needed a proper transport cage, urgently. We needed a cage big enough and strong enough to hold a bear. Ali, resourceful as ever, made it his personal project.

A message reached the zoo through Dr Abu Bakr, a tall, portly veterinarian. His oversized office attire, and stubbly moustache, combined with his affable character concealed the calculating insight previously responsible for the care of Saddam's private collection of Arabian thoroughbreds. Looters had raided the stables and stolen almost everything that could be taken, all animals included. The whereabouts of the horses were apparently unknown, but he had been approached about another curiosity. A stray pony had recently been adopted at a luxurious house in the neighbourhood of Karrada. The pony had wandered from those same nearby stables, and when the owners of the house saw the pathetic state of the animal, they felt compelled to try to care for it. They quickly realised that frail ponies and war zone suburbia were not an ideal mix. Despite the dangers of slowly-fermenting Baghdad, Dr Abbas and I sat with Abu Bakr on the open back of a Humvee, with Farah and William's Civil Affairs crew on the other as we drove off to find another casualty. There was no sound logic to taking the risk to save the pony, mainly since we would later that day be feeding slaughtered donkey to the carnivores, but it seemed like a good, almost sensible, idea at the time. Those targeted moments of seemingly inexplicable empathy and compassion felt like they made immediate, obvious sense, even if they didn't when we attempted to rationalise our priorities and decision-making in the bigger context.

The diminutive blue-grey pony's attempt to stand on the marble path was earnest but pathetic. As it wobbled and resisted assistance, it finally stood upright, not much more than a metre tall at the shoulder. Its hooves had been neglected for many months (which had us questioning the quality of pre-war care) and had grown curled forward like mutated Dutch clogs. It was malnourished, elderly, and had slick sores on one hip from lying prostrate for such a long time. The owners of the house had tried to feed it bread and fruit but were at a loss with how to help the animal. We shunted, pulled, dragged then carried the pony across the manicured lawns. Inelegant lifting and shoving finally sprawled it on its back in the Humvee load bin. We got it to stand up, tethered it to the railings and were zoo bound with our quarry as we held it upright.

Kadhim, the zoo's butcher, grinned through his twisted, drunken face as we offloaded the pony at its new enclosure, but was deeply disappointed when Dr Abbas told him it was out of bounds of the axe. We couldn't explain the logic, and it wasn't the last time he would have to be advised to consider alternatives to the pony. The illogical decision had a magnetism for him, and he would, again and again, offer to kill the pony. With the hooves trimmed and a steady supply of grazing, the pony survived another four months before its age, and presumably, undiagnosed ill-health, caught up, and it died. Kadhim remained mystified by the mercy shown.

It seemed that the more problems we solved, or the more questions we asked, the more work needed to be done. Each day was chaotic but adventurous and it felt like we were holding the entire project together with a frayed reign of thin thread. Our attempts at creating order were fighting the natural direction of events. If the thread snapped, any cohesive plan would spiral out in unravelling directions. It was a curiously liberating experience to be working without any direct guidance, no salary and no rules. We made it up as we went along using what we believed was a logical approach. We convinced ourselves that if we isolated and addressed small problems rapidly, the bigger picture will improve. Nobody told us we were wrong – it is an exhilarating experience to try out potential solutions without fear of failure or being reprimanded. We knew we functioned with high expectations of ourselves, and failure was only what we perceived it to be. That was the joy of being an island in a dysfunctional sea. Nobody there knew any more about how to fix the situation than we did. We could say what we wanted to the media because our agenda was only to be as honest and practical as reasonably possible. There was no risk of offending donors or breaching some protocol. We didn't have either. Crucially, there was no oppressive bureaucracy reigning us in at that point. Our most significant limitations were skill, knowledge and money. We considered risk and consequences, made a plan and acted on it.

Lawrence, with his inimitable enthusiasm, had been explaining the plight of the zoo to newspapers, radio stations and all who would listen. He had made contact with Dr David Jones at North Carolina Zoo about funding options and liaised with Sarah Scarth at the South African branch of the International Fund for Animal Welfare (IFAW) regarding logistical support. Jones, through the North Carolina Zoological Society (NCZS), had been the coordination point for an international fundraising appeal to assist the devastated Kabul Zoo two years earlier. Jones's practical experience and calm demeanour would prove a heartening sounding board, and he appeared to have little hesitation with assisting in whatever way Lawrence thought he could. IFAW was organisationally and fundamentally opposed to zoos. Yet they knew that they could also generate some funds, the publicity and a relief team to assist with this high profile animal welfare disaster. As we understood it in Baghdad, a plan was taking shape with the intention being that IFAW would field a relief team to work with us until such time the zoo was stable enough for re-development to be overseen by a zoo management expert funded by the NCZS.

It was early June. Ali was sluicing away the last water, hair and blood from Uday's lions' freshly cleaned holding building. I answered a call from Mariette Hopley of IFAW on the satellite phone. We had been running short on meat left from Stephan's visit, our money for vegetables was running low, and the ability to purchase the desperately needed supplies to repair and maintain the zoo was almost at an end. The staff required money. Ali needed money. We were still reliant on any goodwill we could generate among CPA and military personnel. We were begging, borrowing and scrounging almost all our supplies. It was abundantly clear through that phone call that Mariette was an imposing, no-bullshit, ex-South African Air Force Major, with a raucous laugh and an incredible ability to work logistics. She asked appropriate, direct questions and seemed to understand what would really be required to get supplies to Baghdad. They wanted our wish list. It was an immediate, seductive feeling of relief that the cavalry was on its way to help. Lawrence had played to his strengths and made the connections work for the zoo.

Meanwhile, the CPA administration was quickly gathering bureaucratic momentum. Logistical systems were evolving rapidly, and we marvelled at the Al-Rasheed's resurrected water supply in the bathrooms. It meant no more open-air showers next to the empty swimming pool. A KBR-run dining facility, mirroring the one at the CPA palace, was set up as an alternative food source to MREs. It quickly transformed from a makeshift barracks into a hotel of occupation and reconstruction. With those changes, we lost the freedom of social manipulation and unconstrained choice - rooms were registered to individuals. Use it or lose it. The need for official CPA or U.S. government contractors to get rooms was becoming increasingly pressing. Lawrence and I did not fit that description. Fortunately, individuals in the system were sympathetic to the zoo and by association us. With our identification cards, we maintained an illusion of legitimacy despite having no other paperwork to say why we were there or who we were responsible too. Between the D.O.D. filming crew who had dominated Floor 7, they would ensure several extra rooms were maintained in a *used* state to meet their operational requirements beyond what the planners would allocate. We did not want the newly contracted housekeepers to report an unoccupied room. My standard morning routine included going into Lawrence's room, making a mess of his bed linen and splashing some water on the basin. I would leave a few discarded MRE items on the countertops for an added hint of occupational authenticity.

The greatest excitement was reserved for the rumour of the CPA contracting a company to provide CPA contractors and military personnel with communications. The anticipation infiltrated mealtime conversations. It was the most significant upgrade in the logistical evolution we were witnessing, a cellular phone network. We would be able to make plans without having to physically find each relevant individual somewhere in or near the Green Zone. Simultaneously a project was initiated to build a civilian cell phone network across Baghdad, the first in Iraq. That all-powerful identification card meant I was eligible for a free cell phone with international calling credit. The rumour was that the calls were monitored through a computer network with sets of security-related algorithms. That seemed a bargain price to pay. I had nothing to hide. Apart from being able to contact my family, which was prohibitively expensive on a satellite phone, it would mean we had access to outside information when we finally knew who to contact. Through contacts in the CPA, we also managed to arrange for Farah to register for a cell phone, which would give us more planning flexibility when the network started to be built around Baghdad. It also gave the illusion of greater safety, in that in the case of life-threatening emergencies, we could phone William or security contractor friends, hoping they could rescue us. That illusion was an upgrade on the "I hope Ali can fix this" or the "yup, Ali can't fix this, we're fucked" defaults we had assumed until then.

Farah's statement "I've heard there is a bear at a nursery in Al-Adhamiya, we should probably go check it out" started a rollercoaster chain of events that would last for the year and give us insight into the unregulated and depressingly cruel trade in exotic pets in Baghdad. The nursery, nestled amongst a grove of mature date palms, was combined with a veterinary clinic and a collection of assorted dogs in cages or tethered to trees waiting for new owners. Farah steered her white Passat up the driveway, weaving past the animated chickens and ducks. A pelican ambled towards us and then in a panicked moment of clarity flapped past us nervously. Our intention was only to see the bear and offer assistance. With it being a veterinary clinic, and given the lush surrounds, we trustingly expected the bear to be a well-cared-for pet.

It was an appalling sight. A rebar cage stood on bricks. It looked similar to the disgusting images circulated by international welfare agencies of bears being drained of bile in torturous Chinese facilities. The young bear was almost too big to turn around inside the cage. Blood mixed with faeces as diarrhoea trickled through from somewhere in the plate-sized wound of a festering, suppurating anal area. Its paw pads had been rubbed to weeping raw flesh as it paced weakly backwards and forwards on the metal barring; spaced apart for the faeces and piss to run between onto the concrete below. It was staggering that an animal could be so badly treated. Dr Nameer greeted us warmly, if somewhat suspiciously. Farah and I knew the only way to get the bear out of there was to play the game, suppress our disgust, act sympathetic to the vet's problems and fluff his ego. A grimy, overweight assistant walked over. Smiling widely, he pointed to his prize specimen; the pathetic bear. He mock-charged the bear to get it to react and animatedly slapped me on the back as if I was a long-lost companion.

The vet introduced us to his animal-trader friend, a tall, glowering, stubbly man with imposing, dark eyes and a scruffy black moustache. It seemed more a snarl than a reluctant smile as he watched us like a clichéd spaghetti Western movie bandit with the refinement of an Iraqi black market operator. With Farah translating, we talked about the clinic, the bear and life before the war. Dr Nameer said he had occasionally helped with pets at the Hussein's palaces and had then been ordered to take over management and welfare of the police dog unit. Although he claimed he had not been keen on the idea, he had no choice, since denying Saddam anything was the incorrect option. He had grown to enjoy being the master of the dog unit. It was financially rewarding for him; until the war put an end to all of that. We declared sympathy for his dilemma. We discussed exotic pets in Baghdad with the trader and were offered any animals we wanted, like tigers or bears which could allegedly be sourced through Iran. Naturally, revelling in our proximity to the predator pimp, we feigned gratitude at this prospect. He invited us to come to the animal market held on Fridays where he sold flamingos and other exotic animals. We debated the bear again and the need to transfer it to the zoo, even if temporarily (although we knew that once we had it at the zoo, there was no chance we would let it return to such an appalling and incompetent set up). Dr Nameer clearly wanted his job with the dog unit back again, and when we mentioned we might have U.S. Army contacts who could put in an influential word for him if he cooperated with us, he took the bait and offered his help. We had leverage. He asked for a meeting with our "contact". He wanted to ingratiate himself with the U.S. Army by showing them around areas of the palaces he had become especially familiar with as Saddam Hussein's vet. He was as subtle as a thrown brick. As a token of his goodwill in the matter, he walked across and tried to spray purple, antiseptic wound spray on the bear, admonishing the bear for not standing still. The dribbling faecal-bloody mess was impervious to such limp efforts. "Wounded–Ass bear" as she affectionately became known to us, had to be moved!

A day later, Dr Nameer arrived at the zoo to flatter William, offering up any help he thought the Army could use in exchange for a new opportunity at the police dog unit. He was the personification of cooperative and believed he knew of secret areas in palaces which would be of great interest to the "Amrikan Army". William contrived boundless personal curiosity, and as a demonstration of goodwill, Dr Nameer agreed to bring the bear the following day. Dr Abbas, shrewd as ever, warned us in a hushed tone not to trust Dr Nameer. By then, we had already learnt (with some helpful cultural tutoring) that almost every Iraqi we had met was working angles with us apparently naive foreigners, to their own benefit. It was the system. William departed the zoo to work on his unit's growing list of other responsibilities.

Farah handed Dr Nameer the drugs to immobilise the bear. He gave them back. We could fetch the bear ourselves he muttered. He evidently believed that he held enough exploitable information to be of great use to the Army, and reasoned he did not need to waste his time and take the risk of trying to move the bear. The following day Dr Abbas, Farah and I navigated the chaos to Dr Nameer's clinic in the zoo pickup. We had the drugs and dart gun ready to immobilise the bear. Having driven with Ali and Farah, and adapted to the white-knuckle, cursing-fuelled, stock-car-racing approach required to survive Baghdad streets, Dr Abbas's cautious driving scared me more. It felt like we were drifting along in a fragile origami chariot. Those roads were no place for the timorous or oblivious. Other drivers, hell-bent on fulfilling their perpetual obsession with being in front of the driver in front of them, responded to our approach with the obligatory contempt. A car bumped into the back of us in a jam of traffic. I immediately looked across to Farah thinking the incident would mean unwillingly spectating a slanging match while standing among irate drivers. Without even a cursory blink at the jolt, Dr Abbas carried on serenely until we reached the nursery. His enigmatic personality across differing scenarios continued to puzzle me until the day I left Iraq.

Dr Nameer wasn't at the clinic, but we decided to carry on without him. The confined bear, wise to all the sudden attention, spun around aggressively in her stressed, wounded state. The Neanderthal-like assistant from the previous visit tried inexplicably to jam the bear into a corner with a piece of rebar which the bear swatted at high speed and mangled with ease. Its adrenalin was pumping. The deceptively weak, frail bear plainly still contained massive fight despite the chronic, festering wounds. Dr Abbas had a quiet instructive word with the assistant. With the assistant relegated to the bench inside the clinic, Dr Abbas mixed the drugs and fired in the first dart. No effect. "Oh hell, here we go again," we thought. The second dart embedded in the shoulder, but the plunger failed to press in the drug. After a third dart, the bear started to slow, the effects of the drugs eased her into a light slumber which she fought by trying to lift her head. We sat patiently on the nearby plastic chairs and waited, hoping that it would be the break we needed. A visitor to the nursery walked up the path as we sat there staring at the bear. We ushered him to move on. He stopped, looked at the bear, looked at us looking at the bear and launched a kick, strong enough to clatter the cage and jolt the bear awake. "What the fuck are you doing?! You..." Farah interrupted me with a deluge of foul Arabic. Dr Abbas hurled further abuse at the visitor. Disgusted and fuming, and knowing that we had now run out of immobilising drugs, we decided to leave until we could get a new supply of non-expired drugs. As we distracted it, Dr Abbas jabbed a syringe of long-acting antibiotics into the fired-up bear's rump before we headed back to the zoo. As with Luna Park, another bear would be left behind to test our conscience.

Over beers and MREs, Lawrence and I speculated with others about the disappearance of Saddam's famed Arabian horse collection. We would raise the topic again with Farah and Dr Abbas the following days. Saddam's collection was rumoured to be of high quality and significant financial value. Saddam had allegedly authorised his staff to be prepared to pay generously from state coffers for suitable horses. It was apparently a self-aggrandising source of personal and national pride for the Arab nationalist president. It super-charged the iconic Pan-Arab warrior image he craved. Patriotic paintings had been commissioned of Saddam in military fatigues on Arab thoroughbred stallions. Video footage showed imposing Saddam riding an elaborately decorated white stallion across the parade ground below the crossed swords. Statues across Baghdad represented the national hero, Saddam Hussein, on horseback in various majestic, combative poses.

Rumours were whispered that the horse collection had been stolen during the looting phase. There were always rumours. Stories that subsequently emerged claiming we actively sought information on the horse collection at that time are untrue. A story about a horse that had run into a checkpoint and was killed in a tangle of razor wire, which then somehow was evidence of Saddam's horse collection being in the vicinity, was only partly true. The incident of a horse being killed at a checkpoint occurred, but at a different time and it was unrelated to us. It was a breakaway cart horse that became violently entangled in razor wire. Soldiers shot the frantic, flailing horse to end its suffering. In a nod towards pragmatism, the meat of the horse was delivered to the zoo to feed lions. Additional stories asserting that the bloodlines of Saddam Hussein's Arabian horses could be definitively traced back to Salah Al Dein's horses used to fight the Crusaders are unsubstantiated.

In late May 2003, Abu Bakr, the former veterinarian for Saddam's Arabian horse collection, who had days earlier led us to the pony in Al Karrada, had arrived at the zoo again. In a curiously surreptitious visit, and therefore suspicious to us, he took Farah aside to a quiet area beside the zoo office. She suspected she had been approached, rather than Dr Abbas, since there was a perception that she was linked to "the Amrikis" (Americans) and Abu Bakr might be rewarded for his information. He claimed to know the location of many of the stolen horses. He left as anonymously as he had arrived, which was particularly strange since by then we knew who he was. Back in the office, Farah told William and me. We knew we would have to discuss it with Dr Abbas. Abu Bakr had claimed to be able to source the studbook records for all the horses from the former Director of Saddam's collection, Abu Marwan, but the offer was conditional. He and Abu Marwan wanted a guarantee of them being reinstated as horse collection managers and financially rewarded if we recovered the horses. We agreed, without having any authority to do so or any idea how we would engineer such an outcome. Lawrence had taught us well. We would have to find a way. It felt like it was likely to be the most absurd venture of our brief collective time at the zoo. Us, an odd little crew at the zoo - recover Saddam Hussein's stolen horses!

Among all the other operations that were brewing, and the daily battle for supplies, trying to put together a mission to rescue the horses became an essential task for us. We needed more evidence. We needed to separate what was fact from what was a rumour. Dr Abbas began to make enquiries among sources as to where Abu Bakr lived. We had no phone contact options. We were also never sure who to trust, or if the information was genuine or a trap. Would it be a scheme to snatch someone associated with the Americans? Based on that information, Farah volunteered to take the risk and make a reconnaissance drive early one evening to validate the house location and other information about the neighbourhood. All seemed sound. The following afternoon Farah spoke with Abu Bakr with the intention of sourcing more tangible evidence of his claims. Although it may have been more sensible from a security point of view to get Ali to drive us, we wanted as few people as possible to know about the initiative. We anticipated that the fewer people who knew about the evolving plans, the less likely we were to encounter risk. The downside was that it meant no security backup option beyond William knowing where we were going. Late the following afternoon, Farah and I drove out to Abu Bakr's house. In the dusk it was less likely I would stand out as a foreigner, but it wasn't too late for the night threats to be out in full force. We hoped the timing would enable Farah to be able to drop me back at the Al-Rasheed and still get back home to Mansour safely. I waited in the car while Farah knocked on the front door. Once Abu Bakr opened up, we both moved quickly into the house and lounge. There, on the table, were piles of registration records from the World Arabian Horse Organisation. We paged through the assortment of folders. They looked legitimate to us; not that we had any other reference. Between Abu Bakr and Abu Marwan, they had taken the records home for safekeeping when it became apparent war was imminent. When it seemed the Baghdad experience could not get more surreal, there we were in a stranger's house looking at the records of Saddam Hussein's stolen horse collection. The rumour was of 41 horses being stored at the Abu Ghraib racetrack stables. I finally felt like I had a gem of information I could casually slip out in beer-time conversation with the D.O.D. contractors that evening.

Back at the zoo the next day, with William and Dr Abbas and Farah, we debated what to do with the new information. How would we carry out a rescue? Where would we put any horses we may find? Forty-one was a lot of horses to suddenly be responsible for. How would we source food for them? The most likely facility to stable the horses was the Cheval Equestrian Club at the extensive Baghdad University campus in the Jadiriya neighbourhood. Situated on the eastern side of the Tigris River, it was the equestrian complex where many of the horses were stabled before the war. It was where they were mostly stolen from. As with parts of the university, the stables had been ransacked. We didn't know to what extent the complex was damaged, and we didn't know whether we could arrange permission to use the stables. It was an advantage that Farah at least knew the campus well. Her family had socialised at the University Club during her childhood since her uncle was a veterinary professor. Later during her years at the College of Veterinary

Medicine at the Abu Ghraib campus, she had visited many of her friends who studied at the Jadiriya campus.

William immediately initiated contact with the commanding officer of the U.S. Army unit tasked to restore and maintain security at the university. He facilitated a meeting for Farah and me to assess the plan's feasibility, and a day later, we were walking through the powder-like sand into the makeshift, tented command camp at the university campus. The whole unlikely idea gathered some traction with the military unit because of its novelty. Because of the confused state of the university administration post-invasion, the commanding officer had the authority to allow us to use the stables. Beyond that, they would not be able to help us with anything other than security and perhaps to facilitate meetings with university management. That was enough for us.

The stable structures were standing mostly intact. A neat series of permanent stalls faced onto a central concrete courtyard. Stall doors were stolen, and several of the windows of the stables had been broken. All the cleaning and maintenance equipment and horse tack had been taken. With a quick walk around the outside facilities and exercise areas shaded by palm and eucalyptus trees, we found all the heavy, stolen stable doors that had been hastily discarded. It was all looking promising, and we left buoyed and eager to see William and Dr Abbas back at the zoo. This rescue could be done! We could reallocate some of the zoo funds for a hasty stable restoration. It would severely curtail the remaining funds for the zoo, but we agreed the opportunity was too compelling to miss. We idealistically dreamt of a legacy project. An equestrian centre could be built where the Baghdad public could learn to ride and be educated on their cultural links to the breed. This could happen in the context of some of the most beautiful Arab horses in their country, assuming the rumours of quality and lineage were true. It could be our chance for a little cultural revolution, taking a dictator's private collection and starting a positive public initiative. Over the following week, we returned to the stables with Abu Bakr, the recently resurfaced director Abu Marwan, Dr Abbas and William and colleagues of his Civil Affairs unit. The plan was to resurrect the facilities first, ensure their continued protection and then work on the logistics of securing the horses. We did not want to fix it all and fill it with horses, only to have the trophies stolen again. Crucially, Abu Bakr was able to reconnect with former stable hands and jockeys who had abandoned the facilities as the ground war neared Baghdad. They were excited to be returning to work and quickly set about repairing and cleaning the complex with the supplies that we had arranged. It felt industrious, and each day we returned the progress was obvious and proudly presented.

William had been promoting the grander idea among his unit, and fortune smiled. U.S. Army veterinarians from 414th Civil Affairs Battalion had found a stockpile of twenty tons of rye grain in an abandoned warehouse complex. The commanding officer, Colonel John Huntley, needed to get rid of it and apparently could not directly distribute to local residents since this conflicted with other food aid programs. They needed an outlet. William ensured we were it. Abu Bakr, of course, was confident he could sell most of the stockpile, the funds of which would then be used to source more appropriate horse feed. Unsold rye would be used to supplement the horse feed. The quantity of rye sold meant they would be in a position to feed the recovered horses for several months. With Civil Affairs logistics mobilised, a staggering volume of bags of rye began to arrive at the stable complex.

Lawrence fleetingly returned to Baghdad. He had made critical contacts with IFAW and North Carolina Zoo and had wanted to check on progress at the zoo. He also just enjoyed the addictive energy of being an outsider in Baghdad at that time. With his gift for spinning stories, it was that much more entertaining in the evenings when he was around. In the brief period he had been away a startling amount had happened. He could even shower in his own en-suite bathroom instead of at the communal pool shower. But it was with greater excitement that we could discuss the rapidly evolving horse plan. It was real. After all those evenings of lively speculation, he was thrilled. His timing of return worked well with our logistical requirements and bigger ambitions, and he immediately set to work on Pat Kennedy at the CPA. Together with Farah, he explained the enormous cultural significance of the horses for the city, and how it could be a delivery win for the coalition administration. To reinforce the importance of the opportunity at hand, Lawrence made comparisons to the rescue by the U.S. Army of German Wehrmacht-managed Lipizzaner horses from Czechoslovakia before the Soviet Red Army occupation. That rescue was forever associated with instructions by General George Patton. Persuaded, Kennedy promised Lawrence and Farah the full U.S. military support he could arrange for any rescue attempt. Beyond promises, there were no details finalised. We needed more detailed information to plan the logistics.

It was a quiet Friday morning when Ali, Farah, Lawrence and I drove to a portion of the Abu Ghraib stables. Friday is the weekend in Iraq and the most important day of prayer in the Islamic week. The large, usually chaotic nearby race track was closed that particular day, and it meant we were less likely to be noticed as we scouted for information. Farah and Ali initiated a conversation with a stranger at the stables and convinced him we knew about stolen horses being held illegally at the complex. Farah's reciting of names of specific horses, information that Abu Bakr had supplied, was enough to alarm the stranger into ushering the four of us into his isolated cordon of grubby white, brick stalls. Disinterested horses heads in halters, poked out from the stalls like mounted hunting trophies. It was a quick meeting, rattled along in Arabic, to confirm that stolen horses were indeed being held by several of the different owners throughout the area. The stranger proclaimed innocence, obviously; and pleaded ignorance when asked where particular horses were kept. If he did know he wasn't forthcoming with the information to us unfamiliar, suspicious humans. As quickly as the meeting was initiated, we were back in the taxi. Lawrence and I were conspicuous. We knew we would be noticeably unwelcome if anybody malicious saw us and that the risk was unacceptably high for the four of us. Lawrence and I had joined Ali and Farah to contribute to the investigation. It was likely we only compromised it. Still, we could not help feeling protective of Farah despite our evident scarcity of Iraqi street smarts. Suspicious activity seldom went entirely unnoticed. To be seen to be collaborating with western foreigners could lead to kidnapping and/or summary execution. Ali decided when it was time to leave. We feared that the stranger would likely report the encounter to others at the stables, but there was little we could do about that other than hope horses would not be moved out. With no covert support, we had to play our hand to confirm the potential for a raid.

A few days later, Lawrence was scheduled to fly out of Baghdad again. The timing of his visit coincided with the closure of a significant chapter of the experience. The troops of the 3rd ID at the Al-Rasheed, who had become close companions and the conduits to an entirely different perspective of daily events, were redeploying to Fallujah. Discussions of them returning home to the U.S. were soured. Fallujah, set on the Euphrates River 70km west of Baghdad, had become a scene of obstinate resistance and public unrest. The battle-tested division was being sent to restore order. There was a tinge of sadness at the end of what had been a brief, original and familiar core component of our Baghdad experience. Suddenly it felt like we had a small emotional investment in familiar faces going to war, even if only by short-lived association. It was a curious sensation to feel a hint of inexplicable assimilated pride and concern. We had no particular allegiance other than through passing camaraderie of shared space, a broken zoo, intersecting values and banter at Diels café. We would never know if everyone survived. We watched from a distance as the convoy of striking firepower gutturally roared, ground and clanked itself away from the rendezvous area at the Tomb of the Unknown Soldier. It was an insight into the transitory nature of where we were and who we had begun to know. The 1st Armoured Division would replace the 3rd ID.

A week later, in early June, Farah and I joined William's unit to head back to the Abu Ghraib race track. It was partly to see the scale of the race day spectacle, but also for William to liaise with the Army unit based nearby. The discussions were to inform the group of the intended plans for a raid on the horses of the Abu Ghraib stables and to request security backup. The armoured unit at the stables had both troops and imposing, heavily armed Bradley Fighting Vehicles. The more security that could be arranged, we presumed the more likely it would be that we could retrieve horses without us being shot or captured. We would still need to arrange a security escort for the 40km journey from Abu Ghraib back to Jadiriya.

The Abu Ghraib racing area covered a vast expanse, mostly bordered by a sandy-coloured wall with horse head motifs imprinted into the concrete slabs. This enabled the locally based unit to establish a security checkpoint, at least for race days. The column of old cars and beaten trucks extended far from the cluster of soldiers and razor wire. As each car systematically became the front vehicle, all the doors would be opened, and it would be subjected to a cursory glance for weapons or bombs. Each driver was physically pat-searched while standing to one side and then allowed to drive the vehicle through. It was laborious work in the extreme heat and more frustrating for all those in the choked queue. They wanted to get to the races. Their perception was that the Americans were unnecessarily complicating matters. In our convoy of Humvees, we were able to skirt around the queue, flash identification and bypass the search. Four massive, flat-topped, cylindrical towers stood evenly spaced apart in a line in the front of the enormous beige buildings and track viewing stands. The parking area behind the buildings was a hive of activity. Men in dishdashas, sporting clothes or dishevelled office attire gathered against the white railings and partitioning coils of razor wire to watch and animatedly comment on the race-ready horses being paraded past. It was a spectacle of social escape and passion in the intense heat. The racing track was one of the first recreational enterprises to be resumed in postinvasion Baghdad. The zonation of the larger area between Iraqis and U.S. troops was definitive, neither engaging with the other. As we surveyed, enjoyed and photographed the scene, William confirmed consent from the local unit to assist with whatever security backup they could spare on raid day. There was no guarantee of a full force, but they were excited by the prospect of being able to contribute. Our quick drive on the crumbling perimeter roads and tracks showed the rear walls of several stables partly obscured by patches of scrubby bush, grasses and tall reeds. We began to sense an emotional weight in the scale of importance of the horse-retrieval but the CPA was silent about authorised assistance. We believed we could not delay any longer. The longer we waited, the more likely word would spread of our speculative visits, and the more likely target horses would be moved out from the area. The prospect of us being ambushed nagged in a suppressed corner of doubt.

William engaged with the engineering unit based in Al-Zawra Park about any additional convoy security that they could provide. The troops on the ground were immediately energised by the prospect of the mission and agreed without hesitation. They would have to feed the request up their chain of command for permission, but were confident there would be no resistance to the idea. It was a mission to help, and one that could be viewed as constructive and positive. Through Abu Bakr, Farah had arranged a collection of medium-sized, open-back delivery trucks to load horses onto. Those of us organising the logistics of the raid had almost no practical experience with handling horses and certainly knew little about Arab horses, other than that they were allegedly temperamental. The returned stable hands and jockeys from the Cheval Equestrian Club would be vital to the safe handling of the horses. William made contact with the international World Arabian Horse Organisation (WAHO) to explain the rapidly evolving situation. He also wanted to verify WAHO had been the providers of Abu Bakr's registration documentation, to validate the purity of the bloodlines and ask for advice on such a move. They responded with polite confirmations and a hefty digital manual extensively detailing the behavioural traits and qualities of the breed. It included the best-practice protocols for loading and transportation of the potentially volatile animals in appropriately designed horseboxes. Charming. This was Baghdad, June 2003 with no Pimms in sight. Shabby medium-sized, open-back delivery trucks and some sketchy rope would have to suffice.

The afternoon before the raid was scheduled, the last details of the preparations were being finalised. Logistics had shaped up as intended. Under the circumstances, we had what we felt we needed. We recognised the flaws. There was no standard protocol to adhere to in the event plans hit drama. We would need to improvise, rely on our ability to adapt and move forward. William's unit was confirmed ready-to-roll. As Farah and I were exiting the zoo with Ali and our meat-laden buckets to feed the palace lions, William arrived in his Humvee. The engineering unit was out! Authorisation to provide additional security detail had been denied by their commanding officer. We knew we would not be able to transport the horses out of Abu Ghraib without convoy security. Intense, petulant frustration welled up immediately. "Fuck"s were released. Suddenly it felt like none of the new administration understood the significance of our ambitions. We knew how rare and fleeting it was for opportunities to execute such a plan. It was abruptly scuppered. An agitated Farah immediately changed course, the Passat speeding into the suburbs to find Abu Bakr and cancel the trucks. Without security detail to support us, we knew the risk outweighed any possible reward. Sporadic small arms attacks, indiscriminate mortar fire, and detonating roadside bombs were increasing in frequency. Suicide bombers had shifted in the daily consciousness from opportunistic fringe maniacs, or enslaved gofers, into determined killers with targets. The reality of risk was changing rapidly. We needed a new security option.

CHAPTER 6

Mariette Hopley arrived as the spearhead of the International Fund for Animal Welfare's (IFAW) Emergency Relief Team. There was no mistaking her intentions. She was a booming personality, with a raucous ever-ready laugh, generous attitude and a commitment to make a change. She was the team's logistics coordinator, and from the first minute of her arrival, it was evident that she had no time to waste. She had been planning the supply chain through Kuwait since we had spoken weeks earlier. There were no flies on her. She had been a senior officer in the South African Air Force and arrived in Baghdad ready to operate. Her efforts to engage the zoo staff were immediately welcomed by Dr Abbas and his team who loved her energy, and the supplies she arrived with. Almost as importantly, she had also appeared with Johnny Walker whisky, U.S. dollars and fresh socks for me!

Her baptism into the ever-morphing daily schedule was to join Ali and me on a scouting visit to Luna Park. It was in preparation for the fourth attempt to rescue Samir, the stranded Luna Park bear Lawrence had nicknamed "Last Man Standing" in recognition of our previously thwarted attempts.

The previous day Ali and I were standing on a busy pavement, shuffling through boxes of trolley wheels at a grubby side-road hardware shop that looked more like the final destination for all those *just in case* jars hiding on shelves in suburban garages. Ali's bear cage was almost complete. On the pavement, we argued about the merits of different wheel sizes. He was angling for the sleeker, smaller, cheaper option. I was adamant we needed to upgrade, considering the weight of the bear. We could afford the extra few dinars they would cost. I can only imagine how the conversation would have looked to the wheel proprietor given that Ali spoke almost no English, and I spoke no Arabic. It was in a bastardised mixture of language combined with overly animated, bear-describing gestures which became more so as it became increasingly likely Ali would not concede. We paid for the small wheels.

The cage was more medievally brutally functional than aesthetically pretty, and Ali was putting on his final strokes of welding before the three of us left Baghdad Zoo in his taxi. Was the bear still alive? Could conditions have deteriorated? I feared we might arrive at a zoo beginning to restock its depleted animal collection.

At this time William was trying to organise another Army HEMTT truck with the hydraulic lifting arm and a suitably armed convoy to cover security. The route to Luna Park had become increasingly restless, and the relatively long journey was difficult for units to secure permission to drive, especially for a bear rescue. We assumed, perhaps incorrectly, that the recently acquired zoo pickups would not be able to handle the combined weight of the cage and a large brown bear, even if we could hand-lift that somewhat risky package.

It was one of our initial encounters with the "Old Ironsides", the 1st Armoured Division (AD) which had taken over Baghdad security responsibility from the 3rd ID. We arrived on the fringes of the Luna Park to a protective perimeter of sandbags and coils of razor wire. The scepticism of the troops at our arrival was evident, but before long, we hit on a common concern; the bear. The unit was garrisoned around Luna Park and at the nearby Martyr's Monument and had been taking MRE food rations to the bear to supplement whatever meagre provisions it had been receiving from the menagerie staff. The 1st AD platoon had also been considering moving the bear but was not sure where the people who took the last lot of animals to Baghdad Zoo were, or how to make contact. Whatever we needed, they would help. After a quick check on Samir's conditions (fortunately, only as disgusting as before) we headed back across town to finalise retrieval plans with William, Dr Abbas and Farah.

Lunchtime the following day arrived, and we had still not been able to make contact with William. He had not come to the zoo, so we assumed he was unable to source the HEMTT we urgently required to transport the cage. Being naturally impatient, Farah and I drove with Ali back to Luna Park. We had no other way to contact the unit stationed there and needed to let them know of the postponed plan given the cage transport problem.

We arrived at Luna Park to an unexpectedly rousing sight of a convoy of Humvees and a HEMMT truck. Their green and black European woodland vehicle camouflage was a little incongruous, but the Old Ironsides were waiting for us and chomping at the bit to move a brown bear across the city. Body armour was Velcroed on, weapons were ready, and the heavily armed convoy had been cleared to roll out. We felt a surge of camaraderie. Our new logistical glitch was no issue. Captain Little, the commanding officer, knew he had a limited window of opportunity to assist. The equation was simple. His squad were mission-ready. They wanted to make a contribution. They wanted to be the ones to move the bear. They were motivated. If the only stumbling block was getting the cage to the bear, they would drive the 10km, hour-long trip through congested traffic to fetch the cage. No problem. Every day's patrols were tainted with risk. At least retrieving a cage and rescuing a bear seemed novel and like it had a positive point. Fortune smiled again. It was another incident-free journey. With Ali's taxi at the head of the convoy, we arrived to find William at the Baghdad Zoo office. It was a stroke of unplanned but excellent timing. He and his team steered their Humvee into position in the convoy. Dr Abbas joined Ali's taxi. The pit stop was quick. Hydraulic arm extended. Bear cage loaded. The convoy headed back out the Green Zone, across the river and into the familiar disarray. Luna Park. Finally.

The HEMMT arm protruded over the Luna Park perimeter wall. It was a relief to watch the bolt cutter-armed soldier break the padlock off Samir's door. The transport cage, dangling from a hook-ended cable was lowered down. Guidance from soldiers and Luna Park staff directed the cage against Samir's cell door. Despite the prospect of their bear being taken away, the few Luna Park staff were surprisingly cheery and keen to help out the soldiers with their bear catching ambitions. While Samir was pacing and glaring at the activity from the opposite end of the squalid cell, we tied the cage to the enclosure with nylon rope with the blind faith the bear wouldn't push them apart and escape. The holding cell door was slid out sideways, and the transport cage door slid upwards by two of the Luna Park staff standing on the low enclosure roof and tugging on fastened ropes. All we needed was for a sober Samir to walk through the gap from his home of eight years into the unappealing, smaller, iron transport cage. The raised door was ready to drop down when the bear entered the cage. Naturally, since nothing else had gone to plan on either of the trips, this was no different. The bear showed little intent on moving and in fact, for the first time, seemed quite comfortable in his familiar cesspit. He rubbed up against his worn load-bearing stripper pole. He was lured slightly with fresh vegetables and bread, sprayed with water, poked with iron rods and shouted at; as we had witnessed, all were excellent Iraqi techniques for moving a bear. Samir stayed put. He was wet and stubborn. A small crowd gathered to watch. We dispersed them in the hope Samir would settle, but it was a routine to be repeated. The game carried on for nearly an hour.

Eventually, he cracked. He was finally tempted by some food. Our optimism spiked. He moved through the doorway and into the cage. We gesticulated to the keeper operating the door ropes to release his grip. He did. The door jammed in its sliding groove. We watched in despair as Samir calmly turned around and walked back into his home. We could not tolerate the thought of another defeat. The frustration levels were rising. Patience was being usurped by volatility in the incredible heat. Dr Abbas discussed options with the keepers who passed another half an hour of alternating between spraying the bear with a hose and plaintively luring it with food.

A Luna Park keeper staff walked across with a gnarled old cooking pot and handled fistfuls of burnt rice through the bars onto the plywood floor of the transport cage. Samir perked up immediately, sauntered over to the doorway and unhesitatingly into the cage. The soldier, who had taken over door duty, slid the door down and Samir was trapped. Not that he cared. He had burnt rice. It was so simple. Dr Abbas hand injected the distracted bear with a mild sedative, while we cable-tied the door fast. The bear-filled cage was winched into the sky above the perimeter wall with its perversely idyllic paintings of flowing rivers and a tiger in a forest. After being lowered onto the back of the truck, it was strapped down tightly to avoid any potential escape.

We repeated the journey. Along the highway, through traffic, over the bridge, through the checkpoint of gawking soldiers and queuing civilians, into the Green Zone, past the CPA palace, past the crossed swords and into the zoo. The mildly stoned bear on the back of a U.S. Army truck watched the world go by as his temporary orange tarpaulin sun protection flapped in the breeze on top of the cage. It was quite a sight for us, and likely for the bear too. We would later be entertained with stories from soldiers at dining halls about the day they saw a bear being driven past the CPA palace.

A small cluster of zoo staff, random visitors and media who had spent the day with Mariette gathered to watch the spectacle of the bear being winched into the sky again. We bathed in the intoxicating, collective satisfaction of seeing Samir finally relocated into his new enclosure. Ali smugly enjoyed another cigarette, appreciating his role as chief advisor in another odd task well done.

Samir was lowered back to the ground without incident. As we pushed the heavy, reluctant cage over the brick paving to the new enclosure, the four wheels collapsed. I couldn't help chuckling with childish satisfaction as Ali cursed his capitulated wheel selection. He still stubbornly refused to concede it was the actual wheel quality and size, despite us needing to lean our shoulders into pushing the paving-grating cage on the bricks to the enclosure. The new enclosure was far from ideal, but it was cleaner and marginally bigger than the Luna Park cell, had a resting portion out of public view and a small outside exercise run. The IFAW-led modifications would later turn that into a frequently assaulted plunge pool. Samir was also guaranteed a daily diet of fresh vegetables and meat and primary veterinary care. It was a start. Our ambition was that in the coming month or two, we could develop a plan for a large, wooded, outdoor enclosure.

William finally negotiated a deal to shut down the Luna Park Zoo for a $10 000 compensation payment (although we can't recall if it ever reached a point of handing over cash). The commitment from the owner was not to restock his menagerie. We assured him that if he did try, and we suspected he would, we would relocate the collection again and he would have wasted his money. We couldn't be sure he would not screw us over. We had to bluff as best we could. Months later, when a U.S. Army General visited Baghdad Zoo and asked how he could help, I asked if he could roll a tank through the remnants of Luna Park. He said he would. It never happened.

There was seemingly endless speculation as to what happened to the hundreds of animals stolen from the zoo when the sweaty hordes of looters pillaged parts of the city.

Pets, plucked for the pot or being sold at the black market were the most popular theories. So with Ali at the helm as our brawny navigator, negotiator and self-imposed bodyguard, Farah, Mariette and I went to the swarming Al-Ghazi pet market in the city centre. The market, restricted to Fridays, was utter mayhem. A myriad of sellers crowed out to potential buyers; virtually anybody in the seething crowds of gawking, squawking onlookers including us two pale foreigners. The pungent stench of litter and general filth was enhanced as the crowd squeezed us past rope-tethered guard dogs and desperately dejected-looking ducks contorted and bound into positions yoga gurus would avoid. Chickens lay sprawled out with their feet fastened together by plastic grocery packets. Metre-long aviaries stood stuffed to bursting with blue, yellow, white and green budgies, and doves. A jovial man in his promotional "Visit Hungary" T-shirt held out a partially throttled monitor lizard as his colleague subdued scorpions between his fingers. Downy yellow and black ducklings awaited their fate in grass-filled cloth shopping bags. More novelty animals were squashed into awful cages in the litter-strewn, overheating public square between worn-out city buildings.

The expressions of the masses of faces were curious, hostile, frustrated or at times welcoming until it was all a confusing blur. Ali's hairy fist reached through, grabbed me by the shirt and yanked me through a bottleneck of noisy, sweaty shoppers. Ever the protector he turned and pushed open gaps in the crowd, dragging me to Farah and Mariette. An ibex, with its chunky curved horns arching towards its back, stood tethered in a pile of cardboard and plastic litter. We knew several ibexes had been stolen from the zoo, but it was no situation to start causing a row about tenuous ownership rights. We walked around a corner of wooden huts and were immediately recognised by the brute of a man who had offered to source us tigers at Dr Nameer's veterinary practice where the Wounded-Ass bear was. He appeared genuinely excited to see us, although it seemed he was also courting our business.

We accepted his vociferous invitation and stepped into a small room with aviaries of pigeons lining the walls. In the middle of the room behind the office chair were two grimy, traumatised pelicans fending off two panicked, filthy grey flamingos (usually filter feeders of algae and invertebrates) that were vomiting up forearm-sized fish. The response of the other man in the office was to wave and shout. Helpful. It was depressing and pathetic and the foul stink of partially digested, regurgitated fish rushed around in the heat of the room. The trader beamed in delight at his stock and was disappointed at our declining his offer of tea. In hindsight, even though we had refused respectfully, it was rude of us not to accept the gesture. We needed better control of our emotions. At that time, he had known we wanted his bear from Dr Nameer, so we politely made our apologies and left the depressing hovel with forced, cheerful smiles. Seeing the squalor of the market amplified our desire to improve Baghdad Zoo's conditions far beyond what the average citizen could conceive as possible. The reference to how animals were treated needed to change. We had seen enough and found sanctuary in Ali's Caprice with closed windows and air-conditioning to temporarily turn us into spectators in a bubble.

As so often when ploughing through the city in the heat of the day we stopped at Mishmisha juices, the small patch of psychedelic heaven with rows of blenders pulping piles of melons, apples, pineapples and other extravagant fruits into fresh, cold juice. Among the muck, grinding heat and lurking threats of the streets it was a sensory mind warp with its cleanliness, exotic tastes and welcoming staff. We thanked the heavens it had not yet been discovered by the flurries of westerners who complained daily about the bland KBR fare coughed up in the Green Zone.

Mariette was mobilising in preparation for members of her emergency relief team to arrive. They would consolidate the situation over several months until long-term international support was prepared to take over. At that point, Lawrence and I would exit, unlikely to return. That was the plan or at least our understanding of it. Transport was her first target. Where we had been content to utilise Ali's taxi and the two pickups donated to the zoo and had focused on the rescue plans of the bears and horses with Army logistics, she wanted more independence to operate in the Green Zone. Within days of arrival, she had organised a new GMC Suburban SUV through Pat Kennedy at the CPA and had Ali searching through the searing 40+ °C Baghdad heat for vital equipment in addition to what she was jostling buyers to source in Kuwait. Since the 3rd ID had closed camp and rolled out of Baghdad to Fallujah, our access to diesel had become restricted to black-market purchases through Ali. Pre-invasion the stories were of petrol and diesel being cheaper in Iraq than water. Post-invasion Iraq's oil production and fuel supply had collapsed, and functional commercial fuel stations were scarce. Fuel prices naturally skyrocketed as the grimy opportunists, and intense demand dictated the cost of fuel syphoned from plastic 20l containers with pieces of hose pipes. With her new GMC Mariette now had access to the CPA fuel depot behind the palace compound. We would fill up extra Jerry cans; until a CPA contractor doing that accidentally set his car ablaze. Policy changed.

Her team arrived over several days. Amir was listed as a U.S. based logistical expert with previous UN disaster relief experience. Jason was a veterinarian from New Zealand, Jackson was a zoo management expert who managed IFAW's Moon Bear Sanctuary near Hong Kong, and Dr Ashraf was a wildlife veterinarian from India with extensive interest and experience in zoological park management. It was immediately apparent the team was an eclectic mix of cultures, skills, ideologies and attitudes. Although I had dealt with Mariette over the telephone, and she was the one who had sourced the extensive supply of equipment in Kuwait, it was Amir who confidently projected himself as the senior member of the team. Personal swagger was in abundant supply as he regaled us with anecdotes of his time allegedly working for President Clinton's administration and in African refugee camps. We had no legitimate reason to doubt his experience, but what was becoming evident was his sureness that his résumé would impress us and that he would have the zoo relief situation quickly resolved. He positioned himself as the IFAW team's media liaison officer, general negotiator and link into the CPA. Beyond the initial few days, we saw little of him, he was seldom at the zoo, and for all the charming talk he delivered little noticeable product. Through his commentary in the evenings, it was apparent from the outset he believed the zoo effort was a waste of his time. It irritated me immensely because I knew Amir would be paid a small fortune for agreeing to participate, while Lawrence, Farah and I were volunteering.

Jason did not agree with the principle of zoos. He made it clear from the outset. His blunt proposition that the animals be euthanised humanely and the facility be shut caught us by surprise. We were baffled and then pissed off. It seemed a dubious attitude to send along with a representative veterinarian for an emergency response to a war zone zoo. It was coldly pragmatic. Sure. Yet while it was clear the Baghdad Zoo situation was still bordering on awful, it had improved radically through ballsy decisions and sweaty cooperation. We empathised fully with that idealistic sentiment of free-ranging animals, but Baghdad Zoo at that time wasn't the place for that debate. Despite his reluctance at apparently being shoehorned into the overall Baghdad Zoo situation, his professionalism towards animal welfare was indisputable. Unfortunately, idealism and pragmatism rarely seem to be the same outcome. He immediately became the point of veterinary expertise we could rely on in the zoo. We finally had somebody at the zoo who could educate us on modern immobilisation drugs and dosages. He brought skills we desperately needed and promptly set about compiling a health and condition registry of all the animals in the zoo. It would provide the starting point from which all veterinary care and routine assessments could be tailored for each animal.

Jackson proved immediately to be sensitive and affable, characteristics seemingly entirely out of place in a war zone. Yet, his intellect, extensive animal husbandry knowledge and resolute commitment to the cause of caring for the zoo's animals had him immediately working solutions to improve conditions. His patience and dedication never faltered despite the heat and constant frustrations which would upset him. He quickly set about with Jason, assisting with health assessments and working with Ahmed (the zoo's daily buyer of food supplies), Dr Abbas and Dr Hussam to develop more relevant feeding programs for each animal based on requirements and what supplies were available. It was a more structured result than what we had produced up to that point.

Ashraf appeared to live in an emotional realm quite unique from the rest of us. He exuded the calm detachment of the clichéd, brilliant yet absent-minded professor. He was going to use his extensive zoo experience in India and abroad to develop a strategic plan for the zoo. The ad hoc recreational menagerie approach at Baghdad Zoo was to be replaced. Enclosure designs, thematic zoo layout, a horticultural plan and educational delivery would be the future. Priority 1; improve the living conditions of the animals. He was also tasked with using the available biological information to develop more appropriate and informative educational signage than the existing "Beagle – Germany" and "Carnivora – Felidae – Tiger - India". In his guise as an introverted zoo philosopher he created options quietly, deep into the evenings, designing workable modifications of the many enclosures.

Ashraf brought a new dimension to the zoo perspective. He started to discuss the merits of indigenous animals versus exotic animals for display. We were thinking pool = good, and food in + firm poo out = good. He was debating about collections created on zoogeographical concepts and about the educational and conservation qualities of the facility in the context of modern zoos. He wanted his first stop in discovering Iraqi wildlife to be the Natural History Museum of Baghdad. With Ali sourcing materials for Mariette to build temporary recovery pools for the pelicans (another withered pelican had been delivered to the zoo by the U.S. Army), Farah agreed to drive Ashraf and me to the museum.

Piles of rocks on either side of the entrance provided mounting points for a metal-cast lion on one side and a gazelle on the other. They stood in front of a broad, high, stone-tile covered wall, bare except for a sign saying "Natural History Museum" in English. As we walked into the reception area, a lady in a black abaya and headscarf shuffled quickly past the bare mounting plinth that stood amongst broken tables, boxes and papers. The reception and opening hall of the museum had small clusters of staff sitting around on chairs amid some damaged and other intact display cabinets. Farah and Ashraf managed to explain our intentions for a walkthrough as I stared at glass cabinets housing ghoulish-looking foxes and wild cats in various mummified stages of anguished dementia. Startled fake eyes gawked out from behind the gnarled noses and dental nightmares. The rudimentary taxidermy of what appeared to be the few remaining specimens was still curiously compelling in much the same way vintage freak shows attracted an indelicate audience. Yet it seemed to be in keeping with the character of the battered, old-fashioned surrounds. The specimens were held together with stitching that gave the impression of dried, contorted parasitic worms at rest, inadvertently lending the collection a more Frankenstein-like quality than was perhaps intended. While I had admittedly been naive in my expectations of elegant specimen mounting, I was still excited to see what samples of Iraqi wildlife from past decades or even centuries had been saved.

Farah and Ashraf had attracted a small crowd that quickly begun to lament the destruction the invasion had unleashed on the museum. They were frustrated, animated, demoralised and angry. They didn't care about the politics they said, but the looting had torn the collections and equipment apart. Hordes had descended on the museum. The staff were powerless to stop the destruction. There was no help from the U.S. Army. The museum was plundered. It mirrored the story of the National Museum of Iraq that William had been tasked to archive the antiquities of in his early weeks in Baghdad. "Why America does not stop this!?" they vented. Farah explained in detail what was happening at the zoo, the efforts to resurrect it and to care for the animals. She explained what information Ashraf was looking for. Slowly the anger dissipated and a small entourage of men and women gathered to tour the museum. It was led by the museum's director, a short, passionate man, with a fuzz of balding grey hair, in a shiny, blue, short-sleeved suit.

His interest in our interest fed a growing smile with each article or exhibit we showed curiosity about. The majority of public display specimens had been stolen or broken. The sample storage rooms were a depressing yet fascinatingly diverse collection of smashed specimen jars, ransacked cupboards, ripped-apart filing cabinets and hurled documents. Attempts were being made to shuffle the debris into some order. Symmetrical piles of remains somehow seemed to return the finest of slivers of dignity to the mess. A human hurricane had battered the rooms. Some of the preserved vultures lay dishevelled on their racks, while others had been tossed across the room in a peculiar response to a dictator's downfall. Each new room would bring increasingly contorted facial expressions of grief from the entourage of staff. It was impossible to not feel utter hopelessness with them. They were so clearly passionate about their collections, whatever the quality and condition. The ignorant or uncouth masses had treated their carefully catalogued treasures with contempt. Ashraf photographed the destruction and curiosities with a forensic fascination as each new find caught his attention. The director was keen to tell us about his experiences training at the Natural History Museum in London. He spoke with reverence as he reminisced about another era, another time in his life when the world was open to him. His staff had spent many decades collecting and classifying specimens, but the museum had deteriorated under Saddam's regime as competing priorities drew funding elsewhere. International sanctions meant additional isolation from world exposure and evolving standards of curatorship.

My increasing cynicism wondered if all the travel opportunities in the world would have changed anything. The system appeared so deeply decayed. When I recognised some of the director's common insect specimens, he was surprised and asked about my qualifications. At my explanation of having studied entomology at Rhodes University in South Africa, he erupted into the sort of nerd-like frenzy unique to biologists who eagerly want another biologist to gush over a discovery. He hurriedly ushered us into the next room to show us his most prized specimen. He radiated relief at the ignorance of the looters as to its significance. They had only discarded it onto the floor and left. Another old fish!

It was immediately recognisable. It lay dehydrated amongst the scattering of papers and smashed glass on the table. A Coelacanth! A fish talked about as a living dinosaur. It was a stout deep-sea fish, nearly two meters in length, but had been so elusive that fossil records had led scientists to believe it had gone extinct about 66 million years ago. A chance discovery in 1938 changed all that speculation. A specimen was caught by an angler off the East coast of South Africa and taken to the East London museum. It was identified by the Rhodes University ichthyologist J.L.B. Smith as a Coelacanth. Few intact specimens existed in museums around the world. There was one in the debris of a ransacked room in Baghdad. It was a legitimate moment for some unbridled geeking-out at the privilege to see one. The animated director fussed over his star specimen like a proud parent. The context seemed to once again reflect the scale of the havoc that had taken the city from mildly worn out, to completely humiliated. As the morning passed, Ashraf trawled through files of journals and research papers for information he deemed useful to his grand zoo redesign. We finally extracted ourselves from the mauled museum with the director apparently at least mildly cheered that someone had listened to and shown empathy for their despair. The dejected, demoralised staff stared at us impassively.

The following day was a return to the Baghdad University Jadiriya campus. Not only would it allow Farah and me an opportunity to check on the maintenance work at the stables, but it meant Ashraf could meet zoology staff at the College of Science. After a month of being in Baghdad, and Farah being the only young Iraqi woman I had seen, I had begun to wonder if young Iraqi women existed or whether Farah was a complete anomaly. The other women we encountered, admittedly usually in markets, were middle-aged to old, and predominantly in black abayas and headscarves. The university campus was a revelation. There at the College of Science were dozens of beautiful young women, some conservatively dressed in headscarves but others were in tight denim jeans and collared shirts with flowing hair. The makeup was painted on in theatrical layers, but suddenly what Farah had explained about her university years had context and made sense. And they were studying zoology! Irrespective of the limited information Ashraf was to find at the university, I was cheered by the demographic discovery. The one useful piece of information offered to Ashraf was of the existence of a "The Mammals of Iraq" field guide developed decades earlier. The Jadiriya campus did not have a copy, but the zoology professor suggested we approach the Mustansiriya University College of Science further to the north of Baghdad.

Later in the week, with Ashraf occupied with his designs and cataloguing of the information he had already gathered, Farah and I headed north to the recommended college. Given our experiences until then with Farah, it had not entered my thoughts at all that she may be harassed for walking through an academic institution with a foreigner. That changed. As we walked along a corridor the sight of the petite, tight-denim wearing, dyed-hair Farah with a conspicuously pale and ginger alien, the chirping comments from a small group of male students began. I began to feel self-conscious since the cocky jibes were undoubtedly targeted at us. They were in Arabic, so I didn't understand, but the intent and pouting noises seemed quite clear. Since Farah carried on walking seemingly unperturbed, I assumed that was the best approach. Once we were past the students, she turned and unleashed a verbal tirade which stunned them into silence except for a few muted whistles. Their response and what I recognised as insults related to donkeys and dogs seemed to set the record straight. She was on fire. The meeting with the professor was a far more cordial affair and although he knew he had a copy of the book we were looking for; we would have to return once he had a chance to find it.

The return visit to the college gave some indication of Farah's feisty, provocative temperament. I cringed, thinking selfishly of my own safety given what was becoming all too frequent lessons in the mostly indistinguishable, seemingly shifting parameters of a new quasi-liberal, quasi-conservative culture I was trying to understand. While my personal approach would have favoured subtlety to avoid attention, Farah arrived in tight short pants, with her sleek legs exposed for male students to gawk at. It elicited the expected response of chirping. Farah's verbal barrage was less tactful and again invoked the apparently offensive qualities of the much-maligned dogs and donkeys. Fortunately, the still amiable professor was able to provide us with a copy of The Mammals of Iraq, and we could head back to the relatively sedate setting of the zoo.

To expedite reconstruction progress at Al-Zawra Park, and within the Baghdad Zoo, the U.S. Army deployed more engineer troops to the area. As part of the initiative there was a permanent battalion representative, most frequently Lieutenants Dietz and Wise, stationed at the zoo to ensure coordination between what the zoo required and what the engineers could offer. Much of the initial effort still focused on removing collapsed tree debris, organising paving contractors and fixing the water supply system which Dr Hussam had so dutifully nursed to life. The subduing of looting by coalition forces in the broader city was reflected in the park and zoo, and armed U.S. Army patrols frequently visited the areas as a show of force; and because it was more fun to patrol the zoo than most other places nearby. Armoured Personnel Carrier and Humvee visits to the zoo were regular, with commanding officers stopping in to check on progress and consult with Dr Abbas and the rest of us. The two main rooms in the office building contrasted starkly with each other. Dr Abbas's office of smart furniture (leftovers acquired from a ransacked palace), new light fittings and guest seating was always the lure for those seeking the executive experience. The other room had been turned into a clutter of an operations room the rest of us would all share; for those seeking no-bullshit answers. Boxes of equipment were stacked up against boxes of MRE's. A whiteboard had the ever-growing list of tasks. William had printed out a satellite image of the park (there was no Google Earth accessible to us then) for structured planning. When there was visiting military, the floors would be the place for piled-up sweaty body armour and helmets, while weapons would be stacked against the walls.

Encouraged by the rapid health improvements of Samir following the Luna Park move, and the availability of a squad of willing U.S. Army engineers, we decided Wounded-Ass bear was the next target (again). They had a HEMMT, and we had the cage. William had quickly coordinated the logistics with Lt Dietz, and in a small convoy with Farah, Mariette, Jason, Me and Kay Chapman (who was organising the CPA room designations at the Al-Rasheed Hotel) we were driven to the nursery in Al-Adhamiya. The location within a cool grove of palm trees seemed a pleasantly serene setting in contrast to the jumbled background of enclosures with numerous dogs, pelicans, hustling ducks and the tragic bear scene. Dr Nameer was not there, but as we had come to expect, his portly roguish assistant was. The sudden arrival of a U.S. Army convoy at the nursery seemed to induce cooperation, and the engineers were quick to attach and offload the transport cage. The bear paced rapidly in its tiny holding cage. Its ass wound still leaked blood, pus and diarrhoea and the disc-shaped injuries where its footpads had worn through into gaping sores were still infected and weeping discharge.

The transport cage was rested on cinder blocks to position it at the same level as the bear's cage. The sliding doors were opened, and with some unsubtle encouragement from the excited assistant, the bear leapt into the transport cage. Door shut. Cable ties zipped. Hydraulic arm and chains clanking. Cage in the sky. Cage strapped down. Convoy safely to the zoo. Bear seamlessly offloaded to the enclosure adjacent to Samir. After a period of rest days, fresh foods and meat sprinkled with the vitamin powder Dr Hussam had become so fond of distributing, she was finally anaesthetised by Jason for a comprehensive medical. The wounds were deep, scarred, infected and heart-breaking to see. The awful reality was that she would still need to walk on those severely wounded footpads every day. Bears are not fond of extended bed rest in hot climates. Despite the improved conditions, her wounds would require treatment into the following year. While William, Farah and I always referred to her affectionately as Wounded-Ass bear, the zoo staff named her Warda; meaning Flower in Arabic. Within a few days, we had managed to relocate both of the bears to Baghdad Zoo after enduring weeks of frustration and failure. We started to brim with confidence that we may actually be learning something AND making progress.

The evenings at the Al-Rasheed had become a changed affair of social dynamics since the D.O.D film crew contractors were mostly absent, Lawrence had left, the dining hall was fully functional, and the 3rd Infantry Division soldiers had moved out. It meant fewer evenings of utterly bizarre anecdotes and MREs. Although there was still a robust U.S. Army presence, the Al-Rasheed was undoubtedly becoming increasingly like a post-conflict aid agency establishment than when we arrived. The IFAW team all had rooms on the 7th floor, and while I had grown irritated by Amir and Jason's constant negativity about the zoo mission, socially they could be hilarious company to drink a beer with. On one evening, and against my better judgement, Amir had been agitating to leave the Green Zone and head across the Tigris River to the Al-Hamra Hotel. On the surface of it, the idea seemed harmless; nightlife in Baghdad was on the upturn and despite the risks of attack, night markets and a semblance of normal life had been returning to some neighbourhoods. The instinctive caution that helped us avoid any trouble or high risk since we had arrived suggested it was poor judgement to leave. With Jason, we walked out of Assassin's Gate and caught an old taxi across to the Al-Hamra.

The streets were busy as we lurched through the crowds and past the vibrant, neon-light decorated shops. Throngs of lively, animated pedestrians swept past the ice cream shops and the piles of boxes of fans or bargained for televisions, satellite dishes or suitcases. As lucid moments of rational sense hit me, I texted Farah on our CPA phones to let her know the plan, in case something went wrong. She replied with fury what a stupid idea it was. Noted. I felt considerably better once we were at the Al-Hamra swimming pool on that warm evening and the first beer had gone down like Ronaldo feathered near the penalty area. There were many beers emptied before we woke up on the floor of a journalist's spare room. The next morning under Farah's instructions, Ali fetched us to guide us from our strayed ways.

At the zoo, the initial inundation of equipment that IFAW had delivered was being put to use. There was tangible progress, and importantly, the keepers who cared to notice started to observe how animals responded. The temporary pelican pools that Mariette had fashioned with help from keeper staff gave an indication of how a simple, cheap solution could achieve a remarkable change in behaviour. When Mariette first attempted to spray the pelicans with water from a hosepipe, Dr Hussam responded aghast as if the mad woman was going to kill the prize birds. Until then, the two pelicans had been in a large shaded aviary with a small container of drinking water. We did not have an enclosed pool for them to use, and quite simply, we had focused on ensuring they were receiving daily feeding more than anything else. We had no experience with pelicans, and it had not crossed our minds to hose down the birds. Mariette confidently reassured Dr Hussam the experiment had merit. She had brought so much equipment to the zoo and had won the confidence of Dr Abbas, so Dr Hussam somewhat placated, watched sceptically, confident he would be proven correct. The birds immediately started to preen; flicking their bill tips against the oil gland at the base of their tails, and over and under their wings. Dr Hussam was horrified. It was apparent to him that the birds were going into a sort of shock and with contorted twists, were desperately trying to get the water off their bodies. Mariette kept spraying. Dr Hussam pleaded with her to stop while trying desperately not to offend her. He had never seen a bird preening. He had no concept of preening as a natural mechanism to waterproof birds' feathers Mariette, in her inimitably pleasant manner, explained the process and took the show a step further by hustling the two clumsily stepping birds into the pools in the adjacent aviary compartment. The pool was simply a bright orange, rubberised tarpaulin with a fringe of supporting sandbags and rocks. The pelicans, unleashed to awkwardly hop and splash into the pool, begun to preen themselves further. They dropped onto their bellies, splashed with their wings and stood up to preen further. Muscovy ducks that the zoo had acquired also took the opportunity to join the pool party. Still slightly unsure, Dr Hussam smiled at what may have been progressive. Keepers like Sa'ad and Akram were delighted at the new discovery.

I had requested large ropes and shade cloth for the austere and sun-baked outside recreational areas of several enclosures. IFAW delivered. With Mariette, Jackson, and Jason we profusely sweated as we climbed up and cable-tied shade netting over the lattice of rooftop bars of smaller enclosures for the collection of rhesus macaques, the hyena and the large cats. At times the exposed rebar stung our skin with its absorbed heat. Several of the areas, like where the wolf and the bears were housed was mostly shaded by large trees. Initially, we created a series of knotted climbing ropes interspersed with orange traffic cones (it was what was available) to give the monkeys a few alternative options to clinging depressingly to cage bars hoping to steal digital cameras and cigarettes. Where logs could be sourced from cut down trees, they were added to the large cat areas as scratching posts. Ashraf had worked with local craftsmen to build a series of log pole and palm frond shaded areas in the main, huge but bare and exposed lion enclosure. Under the shading were raised tables for the lions to lie on. Irrigation piping had also been laid in the outer area to start the watering of sparse scatterings of recently planted grass sods. Seeing us admiring the progress from beyond the extensive boundary wall, Salman would walk among his lions with his supposedly protective stick, waving to us joyfully proclaiming stridently "Lion, Tigers, Beers. Thirrrty two yirrss. Good! Very good!"

Despite this progress, we heard rumours via the CPA that Amir had been working to have the CPA shut the zoo. From general daily conversations, we knew Jason fully endorsed the opinion of closing the zoo, but he at least had the professional courtesy of continuing to carry out his veterinary assessments, minor surgeries and working to improve the veterinary protocols.

All of us foreigners engaged in the relief effort viewed the zoo's conditions as unacceptable. We definitely differed in opinion on what to do about it. It was the national zoo. It would be refilled when us foreigners left, irrespective of whatever excitable short-term animal welfare public relations such a shutdown would generate. As outsiders, we were only as effective as the cooperation we could create. We had already experienced the stubborn, resilient Iraqi mentality and resistance to overbearing foreign influence, and we knew Dr Abbas would never sanction the zoo's closure. It wasn't our place to impose that decision on the country's only government zoo. Openness to change was the exception, not the rule. Our (William, Farah, me, Mariette, Jackson and Ashraf) logic was that if this zoo was shut, the main facility in the city, the demand to see animals would still dictate that zoos of any foul sort would continue to exist or be created in the Baghdad. It was naive to believe that shutting this zoo would have any positive long-term spin-offs. It was a misplaced, transient first-world ideal entirely out of place in the harsh durability of a third world setting. We strongly felt that the best chance of educating people against awful facilities was to take the only one with any potential and make a positive example of it. The pragmatic approach was to try shift opinions towards the animals, teach willing staff better husbandry practices, implement easy-to-replicate routines and develop an ethic of acting responsibly towards animals in captivity. We knew it would be a hard slog, but then perhaps we also knew we were not going to leave a month later as had been intended.

The undermining of the efforts to rehabilitate the

zoo, by individuals who had spent so little time and energy at the facility, risked so little, and were being adequately paid was fuelling a simmering frustration within Farah, William and me. It demonstrated a lack of cultural sensitivity and sporting team play. However, we knew that in Mariette, we had an outspoken mediator on our side and had full confidence she would be able to relay the positive progress to any potential detractors. Between power outages, she would spend hours each night documenting progress and filing the combined daily team reports over the slow, patchy internet signal that had recently graced the hotel surrounds. But we knew it wasn't IFAW's mandate to rebuild zoos, and the worry lingered that their support could turn on public opinion and their support base. Until that point, those of us at the zoo without an NGO association had focused little on public opinion. We really were not too bothered about it because we were mostly disconnected from it - and didn't try to engage it. We focused on getting the task in front of us completed. That was innocently optimistic and may have been why we were at best sporadically scraping together dollars. Lawrence was our link to potential funding sources, and we knew he was skilled at winning support. We had made it that far. Just.

The ensuing weeks were to be a pile driving, frustrating introduction into how fundraising in the real world worked. It was also a humbling lesson in how easy it was to feel territorial over something which didn't belong to us anyway. At first the deluge of boldly branded containers, clothing and stories seemed reasonable for a relief effort. As the news stories filtered back to us at the zoo it seemed like all the efforts we had sweated through with the U.S. Army, Stephan and the Iraqi staff had been consigned to bit parts. The marketers far from the battle and politics were getting creative. In media outputs generated far from Baghdad, truths were massaged, animals were given western names and weaved into false but alluring stories. Lady and the Tramp were two of the lions which were suddenly part of a contrived Disneyesque romance. In my quite literal, blunt approach to events and understanding, I could not reconcile why reality was manipulated to generate support. Was the true story of despair and cooperation and progress so unpalatable to the donating public that it needed softening or culturally consumable emotional triggers? I was ignorant and again apparently wrong about the psychology of persuasion because the approach generated substantial interest.

It didn't sit well that in that chaos, there were also still fly-by-night opportunists, organisations that appeared sporadically with banners and barely a box of medicine, to promote their support. We would accept the gifts (beggars can't be choosers) but were left cynically wondering whether support for the zoo was being given as a means to generate funds for an organisation, rather than funds being generated to provide the zoo with support.

When working with Mariette and Jackson, it was clear to see their passion was solely on delivering a facility better off for their immense efforts. Mariette was continuing to facilitate the procurement of an extraordinary shipment of supplies for the zoo from Kuwait. However, the obligatory visual NGO-washing of the mission in the wake of Amir's simultaneously cynical efforts at trying to cut the task at the ankles by engineering a shutdown felt viscerally irritating. Regarding what seemed like an increasingly impending closure, it was not only the animals that were at stake; it was the livelihoods of all the staff and their families, the recreational opportunities for ordinary Baghdadis and a story of international cooperation that was being risked by misrepresentation. There was also a clear risk that had Dr Abbas or other zoo management staff heard of foreign meddling to shut down the Iraqi zoo that we, the outsiders, would all be considered complicit in the guilt despite our conflicting views. I wasn't particularly subtle about airing my frustrations to Mariette who provided the mature, logical sounding board. She knew the risks to the bigger picture. As with all the tasks she set herself in Baghdad, she somehow enabled a way forward to a point where the likelihood of Amir's vision coming to fruition was dampened. His influence faded until he exited the stage almost as quickly as he had entered the fray.

The CPA decided to implement a comprehensive policy intended to dismantle any remnants of the Baath Party still operational or influential within the Iraqi government. Employment by the state traditionally required Baath Party membership and without such association, mobility up the government hierarchy was almost impossible. Along with the dismemberment of the military and police forces, the consequences of de-Baathing was to collapse Iraqi government structures and fuel the acute grievances of dismissed employees and their dependents. Families went from earning an income to unemployed panic at the sweep of an ill-conceived, vindictive foreigner's order. The CPA appeared to be entirely blind to the social upheaval the initiative could cause.

At the Baghdad Zoo, Dr Abbas and Dr Hussam fell under the accusatory spotlight. As both were led away by the U.S. Army for meetings at the CPA, we were left wondering how it was all going to play out both for them as people we had come to enjoy the company of, and as leading allies in the zoo cause. Although they later returned, none the wiser of their impending fate, the fear and concern of the almost arbitrary process became immediately tangible to us. They had families that relied on their income. Selfishly we worried that if they were dismissed, it would likely be another disastrous blow to the zoo. Both men had been at the zoo for many years and appeared well versed with the city's corners of middle-management bureaucracy. Dr Abbas appeared outwardly less concerned about the impending questioning than Dr Hussam about whom rumours began to circulate at the zoo. From our outside perspective, it seemed Iraqi culture was dominated by rumours and insinuations. As foreigners, we seldom knew what to believe entirely, what was deceptive, sinister or intended to manipulate us.

We did not have a clear understanding of who was allied to whom and what the association would be. There often seemed to be a performance in motion, and we had to learn the hustle without having a relevant cultural reference or speaking Arabic.

What seemed apparent was that despite their respective positions within the zoo, Dr Hussam was a higher ranking Baath cadre than Dr Abbas. It was allegedly his responsibility to feed information back to the regime about the staff; yet whether that resulted in any direct, malicious targeting or knowledge of insidious actions, nobody was prepared to openly discuss with us. We knew little about Dr Hussam's background, but we unilaterally concluded that since he only worked at the zoo, and was not the director, that inevitably meant he was not a vital cog in the greater Baath machinery. If he had somehow been responsible for menacing acts then, of course, we might concede his removal would make sense, but in reality, nobody would let us in on redeeming nor damning evidence. That was not even considering how odd and archaic it was for a foreign power to invade and then implement such sweeping rules. It was a situation better suited to being resolved by a judicial system. From our comparatively recent perspectives, Dr Hussam worked hard and showed ingenuity. In Lawrence's eyes Dr Hussam had been the first Iraqi back at the zoo after the invasion, he had slogged away tirelessly in the heat, resurrected the water pumps, encouraged the return of staff, and always arrived neatly dressed in the same ironed trousers and shirt. He impressed Lawrence without reservation. Dr Abbas, despite being the senior zoo official, only came later and preferred to be administrative and advisory than get his hands dirty. He was openly charming and hospitable, but it was also clear he knew his rank and understood how to survive within the doggedly hierarchical system.

When the rumours of the impending process and its targets initially became apparent, Lawrence immediately engaged with the diplomat Tim Carney at the CPA.

Lawrence hoped that his highlighting of Dr Hussam's significance to the restoration of the zoo would offset any potential *justice* the CPA intended to deliver. Unfortunately, Carney made it clear that the U.S. administrations pervasive, partisan bureaucracy hamstrung any opportunity he may have to influence the authority of such final decisions. That responsibility fell to The Mayor of Baghdad Central. Lawrence engaged his highest gear of suave, sugary diplomacy. In a conceited tone, The Mayor consummately deflected the queries, quite determined not to be swayed nor to issue any clear insight into his stance. He certainly did not owe us an explanation, but we hoped he would at least show enough empathy to explain to us the reasoning behind any decision relevant to the zoo management. When Lawrence left Iraq, I made an ambitious attempt at diplomacy. I wore a clean shirt and was as polite and subservient as dignity would allow and attempted to engage The Mayor on the importance of Dr Hussam to the zoo. To The Mayor's credit, he at least let me in the office. Yet his dismissive demeanour quickly made it quite clear that his morning decision to choose a tie that looked as garish as an exploded trifle, was likely a more significant five minutes than my visit. I was obviously attempting to punch above my weight. I needed to learn my place. I thought his initial mention of planning a visit to South Africa was encouraging. As I moved closer, and in case I had mistaken that as an opportunity for a friendly chat, he let me know that following his internet searching, he believed the accommodation prices at Thula Thula, the establishment I represented, to be far too high for the product on offer. "Awkward moment," I thought. I didn't have the subtle skills to navigate that salvo. I couldn't decide whether he was trying to goad a petulant response out of me or if it was another opportunity for him to reinforce that my presence displeased his lordship. He followed up that revelation by curtly making it clear de-Baathification was none of my business. I needn't have wasted my clean shirt. I earned another "F" grade for diplomacy and left the headmaster's office subdued and irritated.

On a scorching, sweaty morning in early June, Dr Hussam, Dr Abbas, Ali and I sat waiting for The Mayor at the Baghdad Municipality headquarters. Instruction had been relayed to us to meet regarding the de-Baathification. We waited expectantly. We sweated. There was no electricity, so no fans turned. The air felt stuck to our skin. The Mayor and his entourage filed along the passage towards us, then passed us briskly as he strained a greeting and indicated the room into which Dr Hussam and Dr Abbas should enter. We hopefully thought that the gathering would resolve the concerns, evaporate the dark cloud, and we could focus on the zoo's recovery. I tried to enter the room as an act of solidarity with the two men. That intent was stopped with a *speak to the hand* gesture as Ali, and I were tersely ordered to wait outside the office.

There was obviously no weighty deliberation. The verdict had been predetermined. The Mayor and his makeshift jury asked both men for brief, irrelevant clarifications of their former responsibilities. It played to the cursory façade of impartiality. The outcome was brutally swift. Minutes later the entourage swept out the room with a decisive air. The Mayor turned his head and brusquely uttered, "Abbas's still in, Hussam's out." My attempts to request clarity were sharply deflected by the protective capsule of arrogance and crisp marching shirts. "None of your business". The Mayor strode away down the passage, ready for his next task. He left the confused Iraqis in his wake. Dr Hussam and Dr Abbas, clearly baffled by the swiftness, language and authority of the unofficial trial and decision asked me what had happened. They assumed that perhaps as a foreigner, I would have insight. I was embarrassed and seething. Two adult male Iraqis, in their own independent country, were asking a 26-year-old westerner about their fate, fates that directly impacted them and their families and that were imposed on them by a smug, dismissive outsider. I had no information to work with and no right to assume I had any authority over them. What could I possibly say to the anxious-looking men nearly twice my age that would soothe termination of employment? I called "bullshit", repeated what The Mayor had said to them and then flailed mentally as I tried to conjure up meaningless words of consolation. All I could really think was "What assholes. How do they think they are going to win over Iraqis like that?". Dr Hussam was dismissed. We brooded in a bitter, deflated, stunned silence as Ali drove us back to the zoo.

Captain Hoybach was a U.S. Air Force finance officer on a visit to the zoo after some gentle persuasion by Captain St Laurent, a 354th Civil Affairs colleague of William's. We were desperate for funds to keep purchasing supplies for the animals. Mariette assured us there was a consignment of meat that was due to arrive from Kuwait within weeks, but we did not have time to wait. The animals needed to be fed daily and not all the animals ate meat. We were cautiously self-satisfied about the progress the zoo was making, but Hoybach didn't appear impressed. He held the purse strings for an enormous amount of U.S.-controlled cash. As we walked past Suker's (an adult lioness that was older than the other lions but for reasons unknown to us at the time had been separated before the war) cage, I was taken aback when Hoybach stared at me and challengingly asked if I was happy with the state of the zoo. The tone of question felt for a moment like I would have to defend our progress.
"Of course not, but it's a damned sight better than it was a few weeks ago" I replied.
"How much do you think you'd need to fix it up properly?" he probed.
"Honestly I haven't a clue. We really haven't thought about it like that. It's been a case of scraping together what we can to patch up the disaster on an hourly basis" was all I could say.
"Well, it looks pretty awful! Come see me tomorrow, and we'll make a plan".
I was taken aback. This was the kind of blunt approach I had

been waiting for from someone with funds. When it arrived, I was caught off guard. It was another lesson. I had been in Baghdad less than a month – I was struggling to keep up with the lesson-learning!

The following day I entered Captain Hoybach's office, still sheepish at not knowing how to handle a man clearly holding the keys to the future of our cause on a personal whim. I had no experience with fundraising, especially not of this impromptu kind. We could use hundreds of thousands, but I feared asking for too much would frighten him off giving us any. My concept of what funding could do was entirely skewed by the shoestring budget we had made a plan with every month in the start-up years at Thula Thula. Even $5 000 seemed like an extraordinary amount of money to be given.

"Hi, so have you got a figure for me? How much do you need?"

I was hopeless. "We need a lot, probably as much as $20 000". That was what Lawrence had initially received from Lieutenant-General Garner. I thought that was a sound benchmark figure that may get a bite.

"Do you honestly think you're going to fix that place with $20 000?" he retorted.

"Well, how much can I get? We need vehicles, pumps, food, irrigation, equipment etc." It seemed the easiest way to avoid the verbal dance.

"What about $50 000? $10 000 goes to the Department of Irrigation to get the water in the park and zoo up and running, and the rest is used to fix the zoo."

"Sounds good to me," I responded. It actually sounded miraculous.

"Right, go get the request signed off by Baghdad Central," he instructed bluntly.

I cringed at the thought of having to take the document to The Mayor, but grabbed it and headed down the marble corridors. For $50 000 I'd rub his back! The Baghdad Central offices were all devoid of staff except for an American interpreter. I asked her to sign the document which I told her was of no significance, found an official-looking stamp on a random desk and zapped the front page. I rushed back to Hoybach before anyone could change the decision.

"Ok. Come with Dr Abbas tomorrow because the money has to be signed out by an Iraqi manager since this is Iraqi money".

I was surprised at how easy it was. In my thoughts THAT was how fundraising should be. Back at the zoo, I quietly told William, Farah and Dr Abbas of what had transpired. I was feeling quite chuffed with that result, although I was frustrated that I was such a hopelessly unpersuasive novice in the game of convincing people to part with their money. Over the past few weeks, I had seen how quickly money could be spent so played down the excitement and emphasised to Dr Abbas how the funds would potentially need to stretch out until the following year. There was no need to raise expectations beyond making steady progress and Dr Abbas also confided it was best that the fewer people who knew of the transaction, the less the risk of future exploitation or theft there would be.

The following day Dr Abbas and I stood with Captain Hoybach at the entrance to the staggeringly enormous vault. It was 20m wide, 10m deep and about 5m high. I had brought a small backpack in the expectation of the volume of bills that would constitute $50 000. The vault was stacked with cash a few meters deep, from the left wall to the right wall. Columns of bills almost reached to the ceiling. I suspected I had underestimated the size of the backpack I would require. Dr Abbas was quietly staring at the volume of money and partly mentally processing that he was in Saddam Hussein's former palace which was now a coalition nerve centre.

The bookkeeper handed Dr Abbas the $50 000. It was an elfin sized pile of crisp, sequenced, $100 bills. Each centimetre-tall block was $10 000. That was it! It could fit in my trouser pockets. I woke up. Properly! That vault was likely holding billions of U.S. dollars. I realised the scale of what we were in the middle of, and again felt the realisation of having been frustratingly naive. I could have asked for extra but thought it was too late to return to Hoybach with my begging bowl. The money was signed out. There were no expectations of accounting or follow up receipt submissions required. $10 000 was allocated for the Ministry of Irrigation. I explained to Dr Abbas that I would keep the remaining $40 000 secure at the Al-Rasheed since it had safety deposit boxes. I also quietly suspected that if the money were to be held at the zoo under management responsibility, it would be infinitely harder to make it last for the months I intended it too. Under Ali's tutelage, I had come to see how quotes for goods were almost always inflated to allow anyone in a procurement chain to include their personal fee. I immediately ensured a ledger was kept of every dollar, feeling that apart from it being sensible bookkeeping, if there was any chance of securing additional funds we could show where and how the money had been spent. The cold beer that night was delicious.

CHAPTER 7

The plan to retrieve Saddam's stolen Arabian horses had stalled because we could not find security backup for the raid and route back to the stables. We were short of ideas and influence to unlock progress. Mariette and I met Pat Kennedy at the CPA palace in an attempt to revive the promise made to Lawrence of officially sanctioned security clout. Kennedy presumed the raid had taken place and immediately apologised for the delayed support. He assured us he would flag the matter again for attention. Within a few days, a squad of imposingly large, square-jawed Texan soldiers arrived at the zoo. They epitomized the clichéd Texan of Hollywood folklore. Their side of the office looked much more like a Men's Health photoshoot than our side of the desk as William and I sat with Farah to discuss the raid. Farah noticed that quite quickly.

The soldiers weren't shy to let us know how they would be running the raid and how they all had considerable experience with Arabian horses at their respective ranches. Their confidence bordered on unnecessary arrogance, but we attributed that to being Texans. If they were going to help us execute our goal, we were happy to defer to them. They candidly professed to have the horse wrangling credentials we did not and reconfirmed that on numerous occasions in case we hadn't heard their initial declarations. William outlined the background to the initiative, how much planning and information gathering had been carried out, where the horses would need to be retrieved from and relocated to, and what route would be taken. The plan and date were agreed. As with the previous attempt, Farah and Abu Bakr ensured truck transport was available.

Late in the afternoon before the raid, William made contact with the squad to confirm final timings. They were out! They felt it was unsafe and security arrangements inadequate. "Fucking chickens!" was all I could think of saying. The hulking martial warriors had flaked out. Of course it was unsafe. That was why we wanted security. After all the confident bluster we had seen in the meeting we couldn't believe that they had pulled out the afternoon before the scheduled mission. We fumed in the office. It was getting dark and was too late to cancel the trucks. Farah had no other way of making contact with the drivers since there was still no functional city-wide phone network. At 6 a.m. the following morning, William and I met Farah and Ali at the zoo to confirm there was no alternative but to cancel the mission again. Farah and I drove to the rendezvous location with Ali to pay the truck drivers for their scheduled work. Abu Bakr would have to let the jockeys know to wait until another day.

William found a way. A squad of U.S. Marines, technically operating as a Civil Affairs team allocated to archaeological artefact recovery duty in the Babylon area, was staying briefly with William's unit in Baghdad. "Do you want to go save some horses?" was all it took. Captain Gavino Rivas leading the squad had no doubts. The Marines were in. It was likely against direct orders. The mission was a go. The final touches for the plan were cleared. Farah and Abu Bakr made arrangements for the trucks again. We went to check on the restored stables and to reconfirm the willingness of the jockeys to participate voluntarily. They had been keenly involved since their return to the stables, partly because they missed working with their horses and partly because it was money in the pocket. But this step was the riskiest, and they would be integral. We did not have time or experience to laboriously try to match up horses at Abu Ghraib with the available records. We needed the jockeys to hopefully recognise and then identify the horses for us. It was one of several frailties in the plan, but it was also the only option we had to work with. The inherent risk was to the jockey's safety. Some people working at Abu Ghraib stables would undoubtedly recognise some of the staff now collaborating with "the Americans". It needed to look like the three helping us were being forced to cooperate. They guessed it might give them some plausible deniability when confronted and accused. The plan was that each of the jockeys would have their wrists cabled-tied together, as if under the custody of the soldiers. Abu Bakr would not be with us. He was big, bald, widely known and conspicuously recognisable. It was too much personal risk if word spread he was behind the horse recovery. It had to look all American driven. He had given us a small hand-drawn map of where he understood particular horses were held. That would theoretically help us target specific stables directly. They appeared to be near to each other, so despite having limited security cover, we could hopefully move in quickly, extract the horses, load up and exit. If there were more horses than we could fit on the trucks, we would consider the risks and practicalities of returning for a follow-up raid the same day. The availability of only six cattle trucks for 41 horses and the brevity of the Marines stay, made that option potentially overambitious but very likely.

Raid morning finally arrived. There was no cancellation! The assembly point was the fuel station about 500m from the stables. 6.30 a.m. The temperature was already intensifying quickly towards the scorching forties. Six cattle trucks and four Humvees made up the convoy. Abu Bakr was still there to check on the willingness of the three jockeys he had transported to meet us. In addition to the eight Marines with their shotguns and M16s, William had soldiers to drive the Humvees and brought three cameramen from the 372nd Military Public Affairs Detachment to provide backup. Cameras may have been their tool of choice, but at very least from a security point, they held weapons. Although Mariette had been keen to join us, the IFAW team was reportedly under instruction from their base in South Africa not to be involved. We never talked openly about being shot at during the raid or what a contingency plan would be in the face of a reactionary assault. Perhaps because of that, we did not anticipate we would be casualties that morning. Blind faith in our determination and the outcome excluded any genuine consideration of fear.

We headed towards the U.S. Army 2/6 Infantry – 1st Infantry Division's temporary compound at the race track, anticipating the additional backup of a squad of infantry and a platoon of Bradley Fighting Vehicles they had initially committed weeks earlier. On that day, it was not the case. Naturally! Only one Bradley could be spared. There was no accompanying infantry. "Sorry." A Bradley with its crew would have to suffice. Bugger. The search was rolling. Our small eclectic convoy arrived at what looked like a main entrance into the stable complex. From Abu Bakr's map and our previously brief recce with Ali to another separate section, we anticipated the gates to lead directly to a small complex of stable stalls we needed to target. Objective: retrieve 41 horses. Our convoy and foot traffic ground through the opened entrance.

"Oh Fuck!"

More than one of us said that. It was like a citadel gate opening into a suburb. We looked around us at a network of roads, houses, joined stable complexes, scrubby fields with patches of burnt rubbish and manure, and sink areas growing full of tall reeds. The small page with a map scrawled on it was useless. Intense frustration welled in me. We had questioned Abu Bakr at length about what to expect, distances and precisely which stables we needed to concentrate on. What he relayed to us was nothing like what we anticipated (*A quick look on Google Earth a few years later showed the total area covered roughly 800m x 400m. That space was comprised of three enormous fields, bisected by a central road – all of which was flanked by nearly 150 stable buildings that were each further divided into dozens of horse stalls and many courtyards. The network of dirt tracks gives an impression of a dusty circuit board).*

In the flurry to rapidly re-plan the heist according to the distinctly underwhelming security support and intimidating new target scale, we forgot to cable-tie the hands of the jockeys. The illusion of their coercion never even started. Our small gathering of vehicles and volunteers clustered. During our previous fact-finding recce, we had obviously entered a single stable building from a side entrance – in the interests of being discreet we had missed out on seeing the complex. The only comfort was the brutish Bradley rumbling next to us for firepower. William and Rivas consulted. About a hundred meters to our right two elderly men moved their table aside, picked up their white plastic chairs and habitual glass teacups and slipped back into an adjacent stable. The doors closed after them. It felt uncannily like the calm before the storm in a western movie.

We needed an area to consolidate. Quickly. We had immediately lost the initiative and any momentum and needed it back. In the distance, a sizeable centralised dust and gravel plot was the obvious location. It was where several roads intersected and was closer to the majority of what we presumed were all stables. It had a clear view of the area around it, making us an easier target but also allowing us time to see what was happening nearby. The Bradley would be tasked to ensure that the area remained secure for us. A cluster of soldiers would move with each of the jockeys to a stable building to start identifying horses. The available sand pile from nearby bulldozed patches would be used as a convenient makeshift ramp to walk the horses onto a truck's load bed. A truck would be reversed against a pile and the tailgate lowered. Once we had as many horses as we could load, the next vehicle would replace the loaded truck.

A small swarm of about twenty people quickly converged on our cluster of vehicles to unleash a torrent of questions and accusations or just to stare. Other onlookers stared from a distance. Some panicked children ran away as fast as they could. Several young men ran down the road shouting in Arabic "they're here! The Americans are here!" The one thing we were sure of was that could not be good for us. The volume spiked. Why were we there? Others knew exactly why. As they shouted accusingly among each other, Farah relayed to us what was being said - it wasn't about their enthusiastic willingness to cooperate. Farah took charge quickly, dominating the space. With characteristic Iraqi subtlety, the hand gesticulations amplified the verbal flogging. She made it uncompromisingly clear to all those surrounding us that the military knew there were horses there and that the shouts to disperse them were only further confirmation. Despite her slim frame, blue mirror sunglasses and turned-around baseball cap she projected an intensity we had become accustomed to and were almost embarrassed by. Cute, cheerful Farah was gone. Her biting intent was unmistakable. In a bluff, she waved the useless map threateningly as an indication of our documented information. Cooperate or be arrested was the ultimatum. The jockeys quick-wittedly confessed to horse owners they had been jailed for a month and interrogated by the military about the horses.

With the Bradley parked as a central point of protection and intimidation near the trucks, we set off in a posse of marines, jockeys, cameramen and with embedded freelance journalist Micah Garen. Staying together seemed the safer, sensible alternative to splitting up. It wasn't hard to spot those of us in civilian clothing, and we needed to ensure we didn't stray from possible military protection in the melee of moving from yard to yard. The doors of the first stable were already open. Worn brick stalls surrounded the courtyard, the decor we had seen during our previous visit. There was an immediate lucky strike. The jockeys recognised a dusky-grey mare. There was no argument from the passive, staring stable manager as the jockey led the horse out by its halter. A scuffle broke out outside the stables. A young ratty-faced man yelling abuse at the Marines and shouting for people to hide their horses was being hoisted, hands cable-tied, into the back of a camouflage-netting shaded Humvee. The message projected was clear. The quicker we recovered the stolen horses, with or without cooperation, the faster we would leave. I am not sure we entirely believed we could pull off the bluff, even briefly. We didn't know if or at what point we would be attacked. We had no desire for the situation to turn violent or spark a gun battle. Any extraction plan to the armoured protection of the Bradley would be improvised and chaotic, at best.

The mare was led up the earth ramp onto the truck-load bin. The WAHO documentation had advised against regular tethering of horses to the transport vehicle because of the temperamental nature of the animals. It could cause further stress and possible injury. This was not the place to test the best protocol. The horse was tied by the halter to the crossbar above the truck cab. As it stamped a back leg, the hoof broke through a rusted patch of the load bin. The horse collapsed with its leg piercing through the hole of torn metal. Its eyes bulged as it panicked when the tether rope on its halter jerked tight. Blood gushed down the shivering, jerking leg from where the rusted shard sliced and embedded into the mare's inner thigh. Fuck! This was NOT the plan! A mass of observers instinctively clambered onto the truck to try to collectively wrench the horse up to gain slack on the tether rope. As the horse attempted wildly to break free, additional men tried to pull the horse's leg back through the blood-spattered hole. The twisted shard gouged horizontally, deeper into the flesh and stopped any movement of the limb. The blood flowed out the wound. More men crawled in the dust under the truck to push the leg up by the dripping hoof. The fucking metal shard! The frantic horse struggled furiously against being constrained by men and rope and truck. A man forcefully manipulated the leg off the metal spike as another shoved the leg up by the slick, red hoof. The leg was free. The tension of the choking neckrope was eased as we immediately compressed the wound with dirty clothes to staunch the bleeding. The shock of the incident galvanised neutral support to help the horse. In an instant, it was the focus of all our energy. Remarkably the accumulated men and jockeys standing on the truck settled the mare. The flow of blood stopped, coagulating sticky on hands and cloth. With a makeshift bandage torn from fabric, the leg was strapped. We all sweated uncontrollably as the sun scorched us. Untether. Reverse horse. New truck. Horse reloaded.

Farah and the remainder of the search groups were still working their way from stable to stable. The jockeys were making slow progress gleaning actionable information. We glanced at our watches. Too much time had already passed beyond what we initially hoped and anticipated. The realisation set in that there was no option to maintain a straight sequence of searches because doors were locked or tip-off information led us to stables in unexpected areas. We struggled to be sure whether new information was deflecting us from other potential targets. Somehow there was a slow, if irregular, accumulation of horses. One horse in that stable. Another sour, resentful owner. A passive owner in a dishdasha stroking his prayer beads recognised it was better to consent to a stable search than be detained. None of Saddam's horses in that one. Two there. Some horses were looking gaunt, some had small, wet or scabbing wounds and most had been shoed for racing; despite them only having led a ceremonial life until that point. The father of the detained man complained furiously and begged for his son's release. The Marine's message was clear. His son would remain confined in the Humvee until the mission was over. The father pointed out another stable where he knew stolen horses were held. He pleaded to keep helping. His son was released. An argument erupted between Farah and a jockey, and two track-suited men who refused to cooperate at another stable. The Marines brusquely instructed cooperation and detained one of the protagonists, hands cable-tied behind his back.

A smaller group of us split off to try speed up the search. We were all feeling a growing urgency to get the horses and leave. Locks dislocated under the force of the wrenched crowbar. "That one" the jockey would gesture. Another stable hand was instructed under a guarding overwatch to walk it down to the trucks for loading. Search momentum increased. We lost overall cohesion but became increasingly productive. Humvees were driven between stables and search parties to enforce the illusion of a dominating presence. The vehicles were a potential emergency extraction option for us. They also acted as roving tether points to tie horses as more were gathered before all being walked down the road to be loaded. More than once, frayed tethers broke, and the horses bolted down a track with a jockey in pursuit. The horse would slow, be caught, and returned to a tying point. We kept moving. One hour passed, then another. It felt like twenty minutes had passed. The stables to be searched were increasingly further from the load trucks. The operation spread thinner over a larger area. It was far from ideal. The more ambitious we got, the more risks we knew we were taking. We reasoned, correctly or not, that if we were going to be attacked by the rumoured armed thieves in the complex, it would have happened in the first hour of our retrieval.

Athool, a robust mottled grey stallion was reputed to be one of Saddam's favourites. The jockeys were thrilled to find him. As one led Athool out to the road, another jockey continued to search stall to stall with the military standing guard and Farah clarifying details of what was stolen and what was legitimately owned. Athool cooperated at first, walking with some arrogance and resistance; but still walking. Within a few hundred meters of the truck collection point, he began to trot and fight the halter rope. As he launched forward, the jockey's arm was twisted. He stumbled and tried to run to keep up with the equine force he was battling to control. He had no chance. Athool had smelt mare and with the strength of a rutting male, fueled by pent-up lust, broke free. He galloped down the road, hooves clattering on the asphalt before he swung off onto the dirt loading area. Shouts erupted from the gathered crowd as he arced round to his target, a nearby filly. She was about to be loaded onto a truck and kicked violently backwards at Athool who changed direction. It was too late for a chestnut-coloured horse that burst free of her handler and tried to gallop out of Athool's sex-crazed beam. He reared up onto her as she fired a double-hoof kick into his chest with her back legs. It stopped him briefly in mid-mount. One man lurched behind a protective lamp post to avoid being swept up in the chaos. Other men waved their arms in fury while yelling in a futile effort to chase the butt-thrusting Athool off the fighting mare. A man in a dishdasha bravely lunged and grabbed her halter rope to attempt to control her. She fought the tether. Her wild eyes and flinging mane left no doubt about her objections. She bucked and repeatedly kicked at the obsessed stallion. Athool tried mounting her from any possible angle and reared again onto his back legs. The man holding the female's tether waved a threatening but inconsequential stick at Athool. She broke free again, and in the shadow of the Bradley fighting vehicle and its chuckling crew, Athool mounted her with his unleashed rig reaching animatedly like a gibbon's arm for its target. Comically, another dishdasha'd man wielding a log pole rushed forward like a zealous vice officer to try to knock the horse's massive searching penis off target. The fantastically implausible setting against the outline of the Bradley was one for the memory bank. The ambitious attempt to joust away the enthusiastic violation was futile. Athool was working out his surging desire. With Athool distracted in his leggy Jiu-Jitsu clasp of his victim and partly fulfilled, men were able to grab hold of the mare's and Athool's halters and drag the horses apart. Athool, the sexual assaulter, would get his own truck.

Progress slowed. In the mounting frustration, dust and heat we had only found 16 horses, one of which the jockeys knew was not from Saddam's collection. They believed it belonged to Uday Hussein. It was loaded. We did not have the anticipated 41 horses. Rumours were circulating that other target horses had been relocated following our reconnaissance visit. Others had been moved even before that visit. Rumours started that two of our target horses had been moved slyly beyond our view while we were raiding. They were allegedly on a truck at the fuel station we had gathered at earlier in the morning. We were not going to risk going after those. In the commotion, our anticipated two hours had turned into nearly three of replanning, searching, lock breaking and loading. William made the decision. We needed to leave. Nobody had attacked us until that point. We had extended any possible cooperation far beyond sensible time, and the horses needed water and shelter. The wounded horse needed a veterinary examination. It had been hours since its leg had smashed through the truck and the wound was unclean. William and Farah ensured the trucks were lined up and ready to move, while the rest of us headed towards whichever Humvee was nearest. For shade, I climbed into the back of a Humvee with a canvass cover. It felt like an age before the vehicle jolted. It was at least five minutes since I had climbed in, yet we were meant to leave immediately. The Humvee jerked forward again, then again before it started to move slowly. I was thinking "surely after all that I could have climbed into a Humvee with a proper fucking driver!"

When it next stopped outside the perimeter of the stable complex I climbed out, relieved we were all out and alive, but baking hot and irritated enough to find another vehicle with a driver who could actually drive. There weren't any other vehicles nearby except the Humvee up ahead, to which the one I had been in was hitched. One Humvee was towing the other. I had inadvertently climbed into a Humvee which had broken down during the raid. Fuck! To make it worse, the two vehicles in the towing process had become separated from the convoy. We loaded up again, and they drove as fast as they could muster. Minutes later they stopped again against a curbside.

We were lost. The feeling of fear began to seed in my belly. We were stranded, lost, with troops I didn't know, with one broken-down Humvee and none of us spoke Arabic beyond about ten words. We couldn't see any landmarks and the traffic was in the usual messy state. Red double-decker passenger buses, as if from the streets of London, added a perversely comical texture to the situation when they passed. The soldiers consulted their map and grid references. Agitation grew as it became increasingly clear that none of them knew where we were. I was game to abandon the defunct Humvee and have the four of us move out in one. Just keep moving. They did not agree with the civilian assessment! The asset would not be abandoned. With the help of a pedestrian who knew where *Hadyqa Al Hiwan* (the zoo) was, a travel direction was decided. That would only mean the stopping of traffic, a U-turn with one Humvee towing another, mounting the middle barrier pavement into the dense traffic, all the while hoping nobody would attack us as easy targets. When we finally arrived at the zoo, Ali gave us the raised eyebrow and a little lecture. Our absence had sparked a hint of concern. Some of the IFAW staff had already seen the horses offloaded at the university and returned to the zoo. It had taken us that long.

Arriving at the stables, the sensation of concentration waning and emotional release of surviving, and securing horses, was immense. William, Farah, Rivas, the Marines, Abu Bakr and the jockeys were all there. The jockeys had efficiently and systematically started to feed, water and groom the recovered horses. Sixteen. Given the prolonged planning and logistical confusions it had taken, the frustrations and that every person involved was safe, we settled on that as a success. Members of the IFAW team returned to view the haul. To our relief, Jason had the experience to assess and treat the leg wound of the injured horse. It was clear that despite the depth of the flesh wound, major veins, arteries and tendons had been missed by the rusty shard. In the following months, it would only be the narrow, hairless scar tissue that would physically hint at the drama of those few minutes. As we recalled all the stories of the day William recounted "The thing I remember most is running across our video cameraman with his camera under his arm watching us clear a stable. I asked him why he wasn't filming any of this. His response was, 'I'm trying not to film anything that would make the Army look bad.' I stared at him for a minute, laughed, and said 'Then you better put down the camera and help us out.'"

As weeks passed, we continued a routine of checking on the horses, jockeys and supplies each day. There was a seed of media interest growing, and at times William would be able to get permission and a small convoy to join the daily inspections. Even that did not always go to plan. Within the university grounds, a Baghdadi pickup driver ignored a stop sign and entered an intersection at speed from the right as we entered the same intersection to turn left. Thinking it would plough into us, and feeling exposed without a door or any other illusion of protection, I lifted my knees up to my chest as William reactively steered us right into the pickup. The front of our Humvee punched the vehicle to the side of the road. Its windows burst out with the impact. Despite failing to stop at the intersection, a furious driver and passenger climbed out to accost William before interpreters and Abu Bakr agreed on a symbolic fee to settle the matter. Just another day.

At the stables the short, plump Abu Marwan, surfaced. Abu Bakr's former boss sported a robust, greying moustache. He appeared, at least superficially, to be grateful for our efforts to retrieve the horses. We were slightly taken aback by his casual, affable personality given that he was supposedly the director formerly responsible for Saddam Hussein's horses. Nobody refuted his claim. He did not overtly project any air of seniority or authority as we would have expected. We had no idea whether that meant he was in an elevated Baath Party position before the war or not. Was he imitating a subservient waiting game with us to see how it would play out financially for him? How did one acquire such a position? We had no idea what his ambitions for the horses were, whether it was a personal gain or a love of the herd. As was almost always the case when we met new people who claimed to be in previously high-ranking positions, we chose to be cautiously polite but suspicious in his presence. We knew opportunism and graft had become entrenched in the social fabric as a survival mechanism. What did he want and how could we use that ambition to benefit the horses?

With the horses settled, the university management (that had by then started to exert some basic governance) had become increasingly excitable about their desire for us to pay stable rental fees. Surprise! They wanted to extract $2 500 per month. The threat to us was pay-up, or the university took ownership of the horses. It was a ludicrous but accepted power play. The military unit we had previously liaised with regarding university security was no longer operational at a management level, and it was left to Farah, Abu Bakr and me to negotiate through the impasse. Meeting times would be set by a departmental secretary and Farah, Abu Bakr and I would wait seemingly endlessly for an administrator to arrive. We would remain in former lecture rooms or offices, with cracked windows held together by brown box tape. The views from the elevated floors were unexpectedly outstanding. Beyond the campus, stretches of the Tigris River were flanked by palm plantations on the floodplains. Houses clustered tightly on the plains, dwarfed by a small number of grand palaces, and towards the zoo, in the distance, the swords arched out above the tree line.

When an administrator or two arrived at the office, the warm tones and façade of politeness seemingly took an age to meander towards actual demands and potential resolutions. There would be much smiling and reminiscing of days gone by when Baghdad University was an internationally renowned educational institution. We would nod sympathetically. There would be the talk of how much funding the university needed to be restored to former glories. It was always about money, less so about quality, planning and accountability. The administrators were adamant stable rent would have to be paid. That we had repaired and were then maintaining the stables daily, was of no interest to them. Our flawed thinking that the case would be discussed on merits was immediately apparent. That wasn't the game at play. They looked at us and saw the obvious U.S. link. They could barely disguise their belief it would be an opportunity for them to enrich themselves through the guise of the university. The administrators' attempts to manipulate us were initially irritating until we considered the reality of the situation. There was no protocol they were claiming to adhere to and requests diversified from cash payments to televisions and satellite dishes (for the lecture theatres of course) to office air conditioning. The game was on.

We agreed to take such demands to our superiors and would return in two weeks with an answer. We offered that, of course, we were not in a position to make such decisions given the coalition bureaucracy. Yet we knew we had no superiors. Two rent-free weeks later, we returned with a revised deal that would be subject to negotiation. We would make up outlandish tales of a bureaucratic grind and infighting, and yet demonstrate a sympathetic desire to accept the administrator's obviously reasonable requests. Nothing was ever written down, and the administrators would forget their initial demands. This allowed us the opportunity to exaggeratedly drag out meetings, reminding them of each item while also acknowledging the obvious merits of such requests. Of course, we would need another week or two to consult, or set meetings on days we knew the university would likely be closed. We would leave a message with a secretary on possible meeting days that our movement was restricted by security threats. At times it was the truth. We knew it was unscrupulous but felt little remorse given a clear intention to fleece us. Our "superiors" would want to come to such meetings, but their schedules would be full. We would miss meetings (which inherently bugged me because I had been raised to be reliable) and return incredibly apologetic and subservient. The administrators felt they had manipulated us enough that the university (rather, *they*) would, in time, be generously rewarded. When needed, with William's guidance, we would source coalition-written letters that would buy us additional time. All this time, the care at the stables continued. Later, when we had run out of distractions and plausible delays, Dr Abbas became involved in the negotiations on behalf of the horses and the zoo. His authority and skill in the territory was an education in itself. It would be another eight months of that game before we would arrive without warning, without having paid a bogus rent, and relocate the horses to facilities at the Baghdad Zoo.

We stressed about how we could continue to pay the jockeys after weeks paying them from zoo funds. They had mostly been reliable and dedicated to the horses despite the limited riding equipment and supervision we could offer. IFAW had supplied additional cleaning supplies which meant that the feeding, watering, grooming of the horses and hygiene of the facilities were of a good standard. Anticipating projected zoo costs and the reality of the meagre funds still available, we knew our payments to the staff was only a short-term option. There was progress within the coalition authority to restore municipality staff from the previous administration back to their posts, usually at pay rates far higher than what the Baath regime had paid. For the period before inflation and cost of living spiked to catch up, there was genuine excitement among staff at the financial windfall. If the horse-related team could be reconnected to the government payroll based on their pre-war positions, we would all be smiling. The dread I felt was that I would need to approach The Mayor at the CPA with this request.

I went with Mariette who I had seen was a persuasive negotiator. I wore what was as close to a cleaned, ironed shirt as I could muster. I felt confident with Mariette we would get the desired result. From the weak, familiarly condescending smile it appeared The Mayor was more pleased to see Mariette than me. She launched into a clear explanation about how we had investigated, retrieved and secured the horses and how the zoo was funding the daily maintenance costs of the horse collection. The Mayor listened intently. He immediately responded by suggesting that the director in charge of the horses sell several of the horses to fund their care. His mind was made up. It was the only obvious solution. We had already considered that option, and it was only an assumption we could raise a fortune selling horses. We didn't want to deplete the herd so soon after the retrieval and without precisely understanding how the game worked. I explained that given our lack of background information on the director, and the risks taken in securing a small portion of the culturally significant collection of horses, that it would be of great help to have the staff returned to the reconfigured government payroll. They had formerly been government-paid staff so it would be a small extension of the process already activated. The rest of the husbandry we could fund through the zoo. There were only 16 horses. Once the situation stabilised and matured, and the breeding records and value of each horse was confirmed, we could find money for a formal equestrian and cultural establishment that we believed should be run commercially. This suggestion appeared to displease The Mayor. He didn't look to grasp any of the cultural significance of the rescue operation. Horses should be urgently sold to fund the jockeys! I suggested it was premature to adopt that knee-jerk approach given we were already managing, just, to support all daily requirements. What we needed was less than ten former government staff to be re-registered as was already happening under his jurisdiction throughout the city. Obviously, I was no entrepreneurial badass. The Mayor's response was a blunt, patronising pontification on the countless virtues of commodity capitalism. A recently renovated cement factory had just turned a profit! The verbal lactation of economics advice-for-dummies frustrated me. I argued that some government systems shouldn't merely be immediately dismantled because they could make quick money by selling off assets. We didn't need an economics lecture. It distracted from the straightforward purpose for which we had requested the meeting. I could feel myself getting warmer as my frustration simmered. For a third time, after soothingly confirming that I understood the principles of capitalism, I broached the idea of returning the jockeys to the government payroll. I thought I was rather tactful and subservient. I only wanted the pragmatic, simple, "yes". The Mayor's tone curdled. He stood up, visibly irritated and glared at me. "If you're not prepared to listen, this meeting is over! I've told you my answer!" But he hadn't. We had received a lecture on free enterprise. Mariette and I were escorted out of the office by The Mayor and his assistant. I was seething internally. There was no logical reason for him to be so obstinate other than his belief that I was an acute irritant. Could he not see the significance of what we had all achieved until that point? Could he not see the opportunity for a positive outcome? Was it just because I was an annoying prick? Several weeks later it emerged that the jockeys, Abu Bakr and Abu Marwan were reinstated on the government payroll. We never heard how that came to be the case, whether it was the turning cogs of the powerful bureaucracy or a word from The Mayor.

CHAPTER 8

Through Lawrence's persistent liaison with the coalition authorities, politicians recognised the opportunity of using the zoo and Al-Zawra Park in the escalating campaign targeting *winning hearts and minds* of Iraqis. William had achieved similar recognition in military circles. The US-led administration needed to promote reconstruction efforts as a positive legacy of their occupation, however temporary or long-term their stay would be. It was not only to offset destruction in some sort of engineering and cultural algebraic equation but rather to demonstrate a campaign of liberation underpinned by humane and civil values (slightly different to the initially rousing ambition of finding weapons of mass destruction and avenging 9/11 or securing oil and logistics tenders, depending on who was talking). That elevation of priority status translated into an increased commitment by engineering units to deliver daily progress under the calm direction of the ever-obliging and seemingly all-knowing Lieutenant Colonel Porter. He was, for the brief period he was in that role, Mariette's guaranteed go-to for any zoo related infrastructure assistance. In a move that would inspire us all to persist, the CPA later authorised an additional $250 000 through Baghdad Central to ensure delivery of the reconstruction and refurbishment of the extensively battered water supply infrastructure, restaurants, roads, gardens, public pool, train network, boundary walls, and entrances of Al-Zawra Park. Security consolidation and the restoration of a park administration were to become a priority. Later.

Mariette left Baghdad on a military C-130 to Kuwait. She needed to finalise logistical arrangements for the supply trucks delivering urgently-needed supplies to the zoo. Confident her plans were on schedule, Mariette returned to Baghdad on the 26th June on the same flight as Lawrence. Farah, William and I drove Lawrence to the horses, smugly satisfied as we recounted the unravelling plan of the unconventional heist. We reflected how far the zoo had progressed since he had last seen it. Lawrence was noticeably upset and angered at the course of events which had led to Dr Hussam's dismissal. To Lawrence, it seemed to reflect an incomprehensible injustice given their initial bond forged in the zoo's darkest days. It was a *status quo* he felt compelled to address irrespective of the CPAs presumed righteousness of their punitive actions.

Much as I had delighted in the novelty of arriving to see Lawrence's Baghdad world in May, he seemed energised by the changes in his absence. There had been the adjustment in the Green Zone to the pseudo-colonial post-2003 invasion phase. He was particularly delighted that we could buy a cold beer in a makeshift nightclub in the basement of the Al-Rasheed. It was noticeable that the tempo of each day was faster and more cluttered. More people than ever before seemed to be committed to transforming post-invasion Iraq into a model world of reassembled justice and wealth. Within the manic surrounds, we received an invitation to watch the inaugural concert of the Iraqi National Symphony Orchestra post-invasion. Their former headquarters had been ransacked by looters, and as a result, they were to perform at the Conference Centre across the road from the Al-Rasheed. As evening set in, Farah was delivered to the Green Zone by her father. Lawrence and I mustered the smartest combination of khaki and green clothing we could. With Farah, we enjoyed the brief taste of sophistication, serenity and culture. The following day Dr Abbas was openly laughing as he recounted to all who would listen that he saw me on television, fast asleep. My disagreements were futile.

Lawrence's return was unfortunately not only borne of a desire to re-immerse himself into overstimulation through proximity to tanks, lions and sweltering heat. An incendiary munition of emotion arced into Kuwait with animal transport crates. It was heading to Baghdad, unwittingly threatening to scorch a wake of political wreckage. Before Lawrence's arrival, I had received phone calls from international journalists asking for comment on our imminent plans to move Uday's lions to South Africa. On each occasion I answered honestly; I didn't have any opinion on a matter that I knew nothing about. I was assured by journalists that had never been to Baghdad that the lions were suffering and were being evacuated to South Africa. Similarly, Dr Abbas was asked by a local journalist about the impending move. Dr Abbas also quashed the rumour; no lions were moving. Naturally, he approached me given the alleged destination was South Africa. Despite my assurances of ignorance on the details, but admission that I had also been contacted for comment, it was clear he was guarded about accepting my version. Understandably. It wasn't like he'd encountered many South Africans at his zoo. South Africans at the zoo were taking the lions to South Africa; the journalist had unwittingly planted the root of suspicion in fertile ground.

I had urgently phoned Lawrence thinking he may have engineered a plan without informing us. It was unlikely, but contact between us had been irregular. He was none the wiser about the lions. His search for answers revealed alarming headlines. The content international news agencies had been fed was provocative and infuriating.

"Uday Hussein's Lions Find Home in Africa"; "Saddam lions head for Africa"; "Baghdad's lions making a comeback in Africa"; "Baghdad lions to be relocated to South Africa" were all headlines.

"Refugee lions on their way 'home'" reported *'South African conservationists are rescuing nine lions in war-rav-*

aged Baghdad from certain death by giving them the chance to spend the rest of their lives in the African bush...Now abandoned, they are starving, shell-shocked and have no future in Baghdad....One of the objectives behind the move is to use the predators as "ambassadors" to help raise money for the Baghdad municipal zoo.'

And then there was the added confirmation that the blind brown bear, Saeida, would be moving to a sanctuary in Greece!

We were still invigorated by the rapid progress being made at the zoo, excited by the horse rescue a few days earlier, and had bypassed the hurdle of IFAW's Amir trying to shut the zoo. In a matter of days, Hilde, without arriving in Iraq, had swept in a pall of suspicion, anger and belligerence. Dr Abbas was understandably unamused. The question of the palace lions moving to a foreign sanctuary had been raised with Dr Abbas when Lawrence, Stephan and Hilde were in Baghdad a month and a half earlier. At the time, Dr Abbas considered it might be an option, but there was never a formal agreement. Realistically it wasn't Dr Abbas's decision given that they were not zoo assets. With the Hussein's fleeing, the lions were likely state property, and a choice would need to be made by an interim Iraqi authority. The tipping point for Dr Abbas was Hilde's assumption she could not only take the lions but the zoo's longest-serving resident (after Salman, the lion keeper), Saeida, the bear. Dr Abbas would not sanction that, ever.

With this unexpected escalation of tension, the trust we had been deliberately building between Dr Abbas and us foreigners was suddenly in serious jeopardy. In a land of rumour and obvious risk, it was embarrassing and galling to suddenly be viewed as a potentially deceptive foreigner conspiring with western arrogance against the Iraqis. We relied on trust and relationships to make progress and survive. There had been an invasion and Iraqis were watching to see what the foreign intervention really meant. The little zoo debacle spotlighted the problem at a local level. It was a situation entirely insensitive to the politics and ignorant of the culture on the ground. Genuine collaborative cooperation was the only way we could all relieve the zoo's critical state. It was how Lawrence had engaged from his first day in Baghdad. I feared it would unravel rapidly the more momentum Hurricane Hilde gained. Bluntly, I was thinking "who the fuck is this lady who thinks she can come and take the zoo's animals and wreck any progress we've all slogged away for?"

To aggravate matters further, Hilde's passionate declarations of her intentions to military personnel in Kuwait was making its way along the ethereal grapevine to the communal dining halls in the Al-Rasheed. I lost count of the occasions that soldiers would discuss the delightfully unappetizing news of a lady in Kuwait "who is coming to take the animals from the zoo. They're going back to Africa. She's gonna move lions, bears and a wolf!" Without knowing the context, the soldiers relaying the news were animated by the prospect of that noble outcome.

IFAW feared the potentially damaging political and public relations repercussions of the impending debacle. Their emergency relief involvement in the zoo had been an extraordinary measure given the organisational stance on captive animals. They would distance themselves from the debate, although in principle supported the animals' relocation from a welfare perspective. Sarah Scarth, Mariette's senior manager, made contact with Lawrence requesting he urgently fly to Baghdad to mediate a constructive end to the situation.

Lawrence and I disagreed on how to manage the situation. While I felt Hilde's efforts should be shut down while she was still in Kuwait, Lawrence had coincidentally met her in Kuwait while he was en route to Baghdad. He was adamant that she was so enthusiastic about having finalised the move she would arrive in Baghdad anyway. He arranged for her to stay at the Al-Rasheed. His logic was it would be easier to mitigate her impact, and less likely she would spread inflammatory rumours if she was close to us. He also harboured the optimism that the most amicable solution would be for Uday's palace lions to be relocated to a South African sanctuary and for animals in the zoo to remain in the zoo. In principle, I agreed with that idea, and I believe we were all (even Dr Abbas) slightly seduced by the romantic story of Uday's lions free in an African savannah. Lawrence was deeply concerned though that while he was still in South Africa, his attempts to contact the South African sanctuary to explain how political sensitivities in Iraq may delay or prevent the move, had immediately resulted in a need for defensive legal counsel. It didn't seem a pragmatic approach to a complicated situation to aid war zone lions.

Dr Abbas, William, Farah, Mariette, Jason and I had discussed this at length when we first heard the rumours. In South Africa, the scandal of captive-reared lions being shot in *canned hunts* was prominent in the news. As a result, there were estimated to be thousands of lions in oppressively inhumane captive conditions in South Africa. Did they not deserve priority of *freedom* over potentially inbred lions of questionable origin living in Iraq - Brutus was allegedly bought from a Russian circus, and the females were rumoured to be from Sudan. The palace lions were not suffering, as reported, and were well cared for despite the need for a larger enclosure. Were the palace lions definitely genetically African lions? What if the rumours of them being man-eaters were actually true; how would that impact a release location? How would the females hunt, given that they were declawed? Was anybody going to perform disease screening on the lions before they were imported into South Africa? How was it possible that the lions would generate enough money, as a news article suggested, to return funds to the Baghdad Zoo? Would that be ethical given the concerns related to captive lions in South Africa? Was this not rather about a public relations coup by animal welfare organisations to generate publicity and funds rather than considering the welfare of the lions? But the most complex of all was, who had the authority in Iraq to decide whether or not the lions or zoo animals could leave the country?

As a means to help navigate the state of affairs, Lawrence had also made contact with Stephan Bognar from WildAid to see if he would return to Baghdad. He believed Stephan's insight and diplomacy, combined with the good working relationship he had previously had with Hilde in their earlier days in Baghdad, could help defuse tensions. Stephan had planned to return to the zoo, just not that soon. He departed for the Middle East without hesitation. Although I was happy Lawrence had returned and was eager for Stephan's return, I found the sudden change of dynamic at the zoo personally aggravating. Between William, Farah and I, we had achieved an enormous amount with the zoo staff in the previous month and felt we understood the evolving political nuances at the zoo better than anyone. We worked with the team daily. We had initiated a comprehensive rescue initiative and retrieved some of Saddam's horses. We had recovered two bears. With Ali, we were the ones caring daily for the lions in question. Additionally, Mariette had proven herself a force of logistics and negotiation. Surely we could deal with Hilde. Within less than a week we were relegated to the side-lines to advise rather than provoke.

Before Hilde's arrival, Lawrence made sure to get the counsel of Dr Abbas on the quickly escalating concern. It was clear, Dr Abbas would prefer the lions not to go, but he didn't believe he had the authority to decide their fate. No animals would leave the zoo. Jason, the IFAW vet, had reinforced our concerns that even though the relocation of the bear may have been planned with the best welfare intentions, the likelihood of it surviving sedation and transport to Greece was slim. And if she were blind, would it not be cruel to remove her from a location she had known almost all her life to an entirely alien landscape? She was old, frail and not likely to survive another five years; if there were a bear that would really benefit would it not be the young Wounded-Ass? Strictly speaking though, she wasn't a Baghdad Zoo possession. At the very least the expenses incurred in relocating a bear to Greece could be used to improve the lives of all four bears at the zoo. Either way, Dr Abbas's assertion was no animal would leave the zoo.

Dr Abbas took Lawrence aside to quietly explain a sinister reason for his views; the threats to his life in this situation were a reality. It was Iraq. If animals left the zoo, it would be perceived to be only with his consent. Giving his permission to foreigners to take animals out of the zoo would mean personal collusion, and an assumed financial kickback. Foreigners working at the zoo could be construed as imposed from beyond his control; removing animals invited an amplified perception of complicity. There were South Africans at the zoo, and the animals were moving to South Africa. The local media would definitely pick up the story. There were already stories surfacing of Iraqis that worked with foreigners, being shot dead. Whatever our perception and involvement, the Iraqis would believe Lawrence and I were behind the move. That meant risk to Dr Abbas and to us. The zoo project would likely implode. At best, Dr Abbas could distance himself from the palace lions' debate given that it would probably be a decision for a government entity if one existed.

Hilde's arrival at the zoo was as we had anticipated. Lawrence had tried to warn her the night before. I avoided her. Her overtly sweet and animated demeanour rapidly soured as Dr Abbas made it clear her plans were sunk.

Lawrence called a meeting with Dr Abbas, Farah, William, Jason, Hilde and me to discuss the matter in depth. Farah was to translate the details to ensure Dr Abbas understood the discussion entirely, and that we understood his considered replies. Except for Dr Abbas, we all agreed an idyllic sanctuary living with the pride kept together would be ideal for the lions. Dr Abbas sat quietly, obviously aggravated. Hilde launched into her explanation of how the relocation would work. The crates were in Kuwait, a vet was waiting to assist, and all that she was waiting for was military approval to fly the containers to Baghdad. The rest was settled. The sanctuary was waiting for the lions. Media coverage and South African permission had been finalised. The bear would be heading to Greece. The wolf would also be sent to an international sanctuary. I had to hand credit to her, her apparent inability to read a political minefield enabled her to thunder forward fuelled by an unrivalled determination. The meeting degenerated quickly into accusations and counter punches. All our concerns were spurned by Hilde as irrelevant. In response to my concerns that the adult females were declawed, and wouldn't be able to hunt, she lashed out in her clipped German accent that "This is no concern. The cubs will hunt for them". Maneaters? "This is no concern. They will not encounter humans". Disease screening? "This will be done once they are in South Africa!" It was clearly single-track, irrational logic and pointless to argue the matter. I couldn't believe they were still debating the topic and felt the next step would be to contact the CPA and get the issue shut down for good. We needed to guard against forgetting we were uninvited guests in Iraq. Adopting condescending, preaching attitudes was disrespectful and unnecessary and would never end cordially or in improvements. She was trying to slash open the door with a shrieking, smoking chainsaw when it required the tenant to quietly unlock it from the inside. Unfortunately, it appeared that Hilde was so immensely consumed by fanatical righteousness she had one strategy – full throttle.

Lawrence attempted to play peacemaker. Hilde was incensed to the point of exasperation. Her contention was it had been agreed she could take the lions when she was last in Baghdad. She had interpreted the concession to consider the idea as final approval. The matter of inflammatory, ill-considered, pre-emptive global press releases, she blamed on the sanctuary. The reality was it didn't matter who had drafted out the press release; the concern was that it alerted the Iraqi public to a situation which could endanger Dr Abbas. Zoo staff had begun to question us about why we were taking the lions. It was bad enough that looters stole most of the zoo's animals, now us foreigners, who pretended to help, were stealing the remainder. That afternoon, around the buckets of buffalo meat at the palace lion's enclosure, Farah and I took considerable effort to explain to Jaffer and Ali that despite Lawrence and I being South African, we hadn't engineered the lions move, and we agreed that Iraqis had to make the final decision. Maybe they believed us. Maybe they didn't.

Back at the Al-Rasheed, we were acting like childish high school teenagers in our attempts to avoid contact and discussions with Hilde. At the communal dinner tables in the KBR dining hall, our efforts were futile, and she would attempt to engage in conversation to which Lawrence would oblige. My muted, simmering contempt for her at that time resulted in a flash of fictional tension release. A brief vision of thwacking a plastic fork in her cranium passed. I recognised the potential diplomacy flaw in that approach, but it was the only moment of pleasure I experienced in her company. I left Lawrence to try and explain the subtleties of avoiding Iraqi death threats to Hilde. That night, over cold beers, Lawrence, William, Mariette, and I ran through all the potential scenarios. Each conclusion was the same. Without Iraqi permission from an authority higher than Dr Abbas, the zoo director would be at genuine risk. If animals were moved out of the country, we would be considered complicit, and the staff would likely ensure cooperation at the zoo was untenable. Any trust would be dismantled. Lawrence and William drafted a press release addressing the issue of authority. The makeshift zoo committee would not support any move unless it was sanctioned by an appropriate Iraqi authority.

More pointless days of stalemate followed. More circular arguments, caustic politeness and wasted breath. We should have just told her "Thank you, now jog on!" Instead it irritated me intensely that despite Hilde claiming to have the welfare of the lions at heart, after nearly a week in Baghdad she hadn't enquired once about their condition nor been with us to feed them. "I have nine crates for nine lions. I don't care which lions I am taking but I am taking nine! The bear and wolf are going too!" A Lebanese television crew arrived at the zoo and began to interview staff about the imminent relocations of the lions, bear and wolf. Dr Abbas intervened to defuse the growing cluster of irate staff. Media, craving new sensational stories, sniffed the whiff of controversy. The situation was spiralling out of control.

William suggested that since the zoo was soon to come under the direct control of the new Iraqi-controlled *Amanat Baghdad* (Baghdad Municipality) that any decisions be postponed until they could be engaged. This was a delay Hilde could not tolerate. Lawrence decided it was appropriate to contact The Mayor at Baghdad Central, who would in time transfer his department's authority to the Baghdad Municipality. It was likely that if a decision to approve the lions' export from Baghdad needed to be made, at that time, The Mayor would be the approving authority. "I thought the animals were already gone," he said, "what's the delay?" We were stunned. Hilde had already been in contact with him, and with her infectious enthusiasm and manipulative cunning had sold the move. Dr Abbas's increasingly surly disposition was inflamed with contempt. "This is not an American decision!"

Lawrence, recognising a new angle of approach, went with Dr Abbas to meet with Dr Faris Al-Assam, the soon-to-be authorised deputy-mayor of Baghdad. For Dr Faris, the decision was simple. Lions had been historically native in Iraq and are intrinsically linked to an expression of national pride. The few remaining lions observed along the Tigris and Euphrates River systems were documented to have been killed at about the time of World War One. He recognised nineteen lions were too many for the zoo to sustain, but there were intentions to develop a drive-through safari park once Baghdad settled. The lions at Uday's palace would not be exported.

Stephan's arrival buoyed our mood. Once again he arrived in a bustle of charisma and energy. Once again, he was confident and determined that he would make the difference that was needed. Believing he could encourage Dr Faris to reconsider his stance on the lions while conceding that the zoo animals remain zoo animals, Stephan donned a suit and headed with Ali into central Baghdad. Lawrence and I agreed that if Dr Faris changed his mind willingly and consented that the palace lions would be taken to South Africa, then that was the final decision. Likewise, if he did not concede, we would respect it as the Iraqi decision. I returned to the Al-Rasheed with Dr Abbas as Lawrence had requested a private meeting to navigate a pragmatic way forward. As the three of us sat in the lobby discussing the options to avoid the vitriol of the zoo staff spilling over into something increasingly dramatic, Hilde walked past, glared at us and requested a ride to the zoo. I grudgingly obliged at Lawrence's insistence. As we entered the vehicle, Hilde facetiously asked if we had enjoyed our "threesome". "Very much so" I replied. We sat in brooding silence for the rest of the short journey.

Stephan had returned with Ali from his meeting with an unmoved Dr Faris and offered Hilde and me a lift back to the Al-Rasheed. Jaffer, as had become a new routine when we went to feed the lions with Ali, decided it was an opportunity to join us. The moody awkwardness of being jammed as a buffer between Hilde and Jaffer on the back seat of Ali's taxi was tangible. Jaffer, in his crisp white branded T-shirt Hilde had given him, leant forward, grinned, looked past me at Hilde and ran his finger across his throat.

"Oh, jeezzzus," I thought. "Here we go."

Hilde's initially startled expression turned to a tirade of gesticulations, and the pitch of her voice grew progressively higher.

"Did you see that?! Did you see that?! He threatened to kill me?! I'll show you. He threatened to kill me."

Although I was quietly amused at how quickly she rose to the blatant provocation it made for a backseat ride reminiscent of childhood family road trips. I half expected Ali to threaten to stop the car and make us walk. I claimed to have seen nothing. Jaffer smiled and waved as he and Ali drove away from the Al-Rasheed. Hilde was apoplectic. I chuckled, reassured her whatever she saw was likely merely provocation and headed to the serenity of my bedroom.

In the middle of this row, journalist Graham Spence had arrived in Baghdad from leafy English suburbia. Graham was Lawrence's congenial and curious brother-in-law who would later write "Babylon's Ark" about Lawrence's experiences in Iraq. Loosened by cold Bavaria beers at the Al-Rasheed's downstairs nightclub, Lawrence and I recounted recent events to him in the comforting surrounds of pink velvet décor. Cocooned by the unglamorous synthesiser tones of 80's disco music, we were able to reflect how our benchmark of a typical day had evolved rather radically in two months.

William phoned us the next morning. The zoo staff were demonstrating with placards. They had gathered at the zoo entrance to protest. It was remarkable in that under Saddam's reign of fear the mere discussions of such a plan would likely have incurred violent retribution, yet now they were emboldened by a common cause. Incredibly, the reason was that they wanted their animals to stay in Iraq. They genuinely cared. They also disliked being dispossessed of anything. The day's work at the zoo stuttered with more small gatherings of agitated staff at Dr Abbas's office. The IFAW team resolutely avoided intervention, continuing to instead focus on the reason they were there, to improve the facilities and animals' conditions.

The scene in the Al-Rasheed lobby was as bizarre as it was unexpected. I had returned with Lawrence to the hotel by mid-afternoon, and there was lively Hilde in a camouflaged flak vest, in animated conversation with a clearly captivated cluster of brawny soldiers we didn't recognise.

"Don't you know? The zoo staff have threatened to kill her. Fuckin' hadji motherfuckers. She's trying to save the animals." They had handed her a 9mm pistol. Farah was there too. Earlier in the day, Hilde had insisted Farah join her at the Al-Rasheed. Unknown to Lawrence and I, Hilde had set up a get-together for the officer of the group to meet Farah. The reason; to turn Farah on her Iraqi zoo colleagues. He used his charm to offer Farah the American dream, full protection and immediate evacuation to the United States in return for her cooperation. Farah's response - "Go fuck yourselves, both of you, I'm going back to work".

The *status quo* had rapidly escalated to madness. Three months earlier we had not even heard of Baghdad Zoo. Lawrence tried urgently to intervene. I phoned William at the zoo to warn him of the impending posse that was determined to deliver some justice to protect the innocent lady saving the animals. As William was working with Dr Abbas to settle the volatility at the zoo, Lawrence continued anxiously to calm the spiralling rhetoric, urging logic, dreading how the sudden turn could lead to bloodshed. He insisted the officer of the unit speak to "Captain William Sumner of the 354th Civil Affairs" who was at the zoo. We were nobodies. What we said held no sway. The unit had been spun into the web. As the military group mobilised behind Hilde, Lawrence and I rushed to the GMC and raced through the narrow lanes of Al-Zawra Park to the zoo. At the entrance, the staff were still gathered, some with placards. William and Dr Abbas were making progress in urging them to disperse. Lawrence implored them to go back to their workstations.

Two hurtling black SUV's turned sharply off the road into the paved area in front of the zoo entrance arch. The doors swung open in unison and armed, helmeted soldiers and Hilde exited to confront the alleged massed hordes. William rushed forward towards the posse urging restraint, explaining who he was. Dr Abbas rushed forward, arms out demanding to know why they had come to kill his staff.

Farah arrived in her white Passat. If the unravelling performance hadn't been so unpredictable and explosive, it would have been farcical. This was only a zoo in Baghdad. This is what Hilde had generated in a week. William wasn't the ranking officer (there were Majors involved too) but acted like he was in charge and immediately defused the aggravated bravado. "It seems to work a lot in those kinds of situations where nobody is supposed to be doing what they are trying to do," he said. It was pragmatic wisdom beyond the power of his authoritative moustache. He urged restraint and tried to explain the complexity of the situation. A riled-up Hilde was still seething, urging that at least Jaffer be detained. She was encouraged to return to the vehicles. As quickly as they had arrived the troops left with Hilde and the evaporating fumes of any potential cooperation from the Iraqis.

The following day The Mayor arrived at the zoo. The decision was clear. No animals would move without Iraqi municipal government consent. With The Mayor onsite Lawrence saw it as an appropriate time to also try to negotiate a return to the zoo for Dr Hussam. The Mayor's first response was that Lawrence needed to reign in his aggravating sidekick (me). Lawrence laughed. The Mayor's second response was that Dr Hussam was old news; collateral damage in the Baath Party ruins. That case was closed. Later that day a brown-enveloped letter generated by Dr Faris at the Baghdad municipality arrived at Dr Abbas's office for Hilde. She was banned from the zoo. Lawrence fed the envelope under her hotel door. The matter was closed. In her wake, we would need to carefully restore the frayed trust of our Iraqi colleagues.

The release of tension amongst us at the zoo following Hilde's departure was immediate. Quite perversely, given her intention to relocate animals had at least partly been about securing better living conditions, we could immediately re-focus on improving living conditions at the zoo. The storm had passed. The furnace-like heat, the occasional rattle of gunfire during the day, the high pitched whizzing sound of cicadas, and overhead patrols by Apache helicopters once again felt normal and irrationally serene. Where irrigation once again encouraged lawns to grow, Faaiz was reluctantly pushing the IFAW-bought mower in the morning sun. An astonishingly nimble, diminutive old man in a white dishdasha shuffled up the palm tree trunks like a seasoned man-squirrel, to deftly slice off dead fronds with his sickle. Staff still sloshed the soapy water across the enclosures tiles in the morning, squeegeeing the collected hair, poo and food remains into the gutter. Work gangs in Al-Zawra Park still lethargically toiled and tilled the hard, chunky soil in the soon-to-be beds of roses and petunias. Farah and I would go back to our familiar checkpoints with bottles of frozen water to help the soldiers through punishingly hot days of standing alert and sweating profusely under the weight of energy-sapping body armour. Soldiers would, in turn, discuss their curiosity about the zoo or their growing attachments to stray dogs that were adopting soldiers and their food. When any of us needed to wait for Ali's taxi outside the Al-Rasheed, the corpse residue that had leached into the paving still remained an oily stain. By then it was an unremarkable memory of war dead from three months earlier. I would find myself not reflecting on the sacrifice, but with macabre curiosity on how the anatomical outline morphed into an increasingly abstract shape with time. Our version of the Baghdad experience was like a perpetual highlights reel and life continued to be a barrage of change.

Less than a week after Hilde left, Jason left too; partly to fulfil personal commitments but partly because he had wanted to go since his arrival in Baghdad. To his credit, he had conducted necessary health checks on all the animals and provided valuable assessments on the severe cases like with Wounded-Ass bear and the Arabian horse that had gashed its leg on the truck. His professional contribution at the time had filled a desperate need for veterinary advice. It had been reassuring to us, and with Jackson's expertise, brought clarity to welfare protocols we had little experience in compiling. Beyond the disagreements though, Jason's piercing comic relief had added a comedian's edge to daily reflections over a cold beer. Amir had apparently also left. We hadn't noticed.

The following day all the talk was about the 4th of July. It was a visible indication of our new cultural immersion into little America. It wasn't a date that had any meaning to me, but the Independence Day of the United States was cause for celebration and caution to those around us. We, as with all foreigners within the Green Zone, were advised against all but essential travel beyond the Green Zone boundaries for an apparently heightened risk of a retaliatory attack against coalition personnel and their associates. There seemed to be intense concern an attack was increasingly likely and would be more significant if it struck American targets on a day the U.S. held as hallowed. Although we adhered to the travel recommendations, any discussion on the potential escalation in violence seemed a slightly nebulous sensation to us given Baghdad was about as calm at that period as we would normally experience under the guidance of Ali and Farah. The incongruity of the political and clashing cultural identities playing out against each other was rarely more evident than at the CPA's adopted palace. Outside the coalition-controlled zone was the real Baghdad. Inside, as nightfall gained traction the unlimited beer and buffets of burgers and hotdogs were patriotically guzzled by hordes of contractors, foreign civilians, me, CPA officials and military personnel clutching soda cans. They delighted in the chance to party in and around Saddam's enormous, gorgeously inviting palace pool and palm tree dominated gardens. It was a spectacle. The diving boards were opportunities for bomb drops, classy dives and beer-fuelled belly flops.

"You must come. Old weapons. Maybe mortar" the work squad supervisor beckoned to William. Throughout Al-Zawra Park, small municipality-funded teams had been digging, raking and restoring basic geometric order to the extensive grounds. We didn't know what they had found but, not for the first time, William was called to take a look at possible unexploded ordnance. He was the familiar, approachable face wearing a military uniform and so was usually the first call for any ordnance finds near the zoo. Depending on what he saw he would decide whether to call the Army's Explosive Ordnance Disposal technicians. It was a short drive in the Humvee to the location between restored irrigation piping and a children's climbing frame in the shade of tall Eucalyptus trees. In the churned-up clumps of dry clay soil were a few spent bullet shell casings. Rather disconcertingly for us, the worker was slamming his shovel into the soil in exaggerated digging motions so we could all hear the "klak, klak, klak" sound as his shovel tip slammed into whatever was solid and metallic below the surface. I never claimed to be an ordnance disposal expert, but that seemed to me to be a slightly careless approach to mysterious, potentially explosive remnants. William tried to quickly explain that caution may be the better option. "Klak, klak, klak!". "Look more Mister William" the supervisor indicated excitedly as the spade wielder continued his particularly unsubtle approach a few paces further on. "Mortar for sure," they said to William. In a moment of self-preserving clarity, or perhaps unwarranted cowardice, I decided to casually stand a little further away, with a solid tree between the investigation and me. It may not have helped survival chances if something exploded, but it still seemed a prudent vantage point as the "klakking" evolved into shovel thrusting and levering of the mysterious items. The grunting and sweaty efforts of the two shovellers suggested a large find as they levered out a 1.5m long, solid, heavy, pipe and then another. They grinned in satisfaction at the validation of their assumption. With no more metallic sounds hiding in the ground, it seemed a good time for William to photograph the discovery and record the grid location and GPS coordinate before relaying the information to his colleagues. We then loaded them into the back of the Humvee until he had the time to find a suitable disposal spot days later.

It would not be the last ordnance related request. A gardening squad later found a small cluster of artillery shell fuses under a bush, and a few artillery shells had been lined up for William to inspect. Again we were somewhat concerned with the cavalier approach, but since I had no reference to what pieces did what when they were separated, I took photos while William penned the relevant details into his notebook. From the side of where a small crowd of workers had accumulated around us, came another worker walking towards us carrying what seemed a weighty artillery shell given his apparent straining. Ignoring the suggestions of caution, he promptly dropped it at our feet and stared at us, smiling at his find. "What the fuck?" were the first words that instinctively burst out my mouth. It had become increasingly apparent that my comparatively sedate middle-class upbringing in suburban Cape Town had made me more inherently cautious around unexploded ordnance than the workers in Al-Zawra Park. It was to be the last time I went out to see what the treasure hunting had unearthed.

Ashraf had been working industriously with the construction contractor to ensure modifications to the badger, bear, porcupine and pelican enclosures would be finished by early July. Given the expense of importing materials, the quality of locally available goods and our budget, the designs Ashraf had conceived and initiated were more about immediate relief to the animals than being ideal in the long term. We had to concede that many of the zoo's animals would remain in enclosures or cages which we were either simply appalled by, or we knew would preclude almost any natural behaviour. Even in cases where dimensions may have conformed to an arbitrarily designated international standard, we knew changes to enclosure size, design, husbandry and enrichment were imperative. Ensuring a proper diet and clean water was one thing, but our ambitions had progressed significantly beyond only keeping the animals alive. We intended to improve facilities and societal expectations of what was, unfortunately, the frequently dreadful benchmark for captive animals. How to make that a reality and not sound like self-important foreign emissaries was another problematic and possibly over-optimistic task. Still, we were adamant there was merit in persisting, showing some fortitude and cheerfulness.

Samir, the brown bear evacuee from Luna Park, was showing physical improvement. He had enough hair slowly advancing into his bald spots to be the envy of Wayne Rooney. The diverse mix of fruits, vegetables, bread and occasionally meat he was eating thanks to Jackson's work with Ahmed, Sa'ad and Akram was encouraging given the comparatively bleak menu at his former cell in Luna Park. Ahmed's pride in feeding *his* animals reflected a commitment beyond standard diligence (fortunately he took the same approach to plying me with highlights of Iraqi cooking). Although the outdoor recreation area of Samir's enclosure was undoubtedly oppressively small, and behind thick iron bars, he would later get an outdoor plunge pool and wooden footballs to entertain himself with as he leapt and dived to submerge.

The pelican pool enclosure best represented the eclectic mix of adaptations needed to creatively retrofit an enclosure. Ashraf's concept was simple. Clean water. Shade. Netting to stop the birds flying away. The pool already existed and was surrounded by a set of low, flimsy bars better designed to stop obese geese waddling out rather than children climbing inside. The pool's pumps and drainage system were restored to working order with small fountains bubbling out water. The central platform for pelicans, ducks and geese to sunbathe on stood behind a set of two concrete blocks which were each the foundation for 10m tall, green painted metal masts. The masts provided the centre point over which tent-shaped netting would drape, tethered to the freshly reinforced fencing and guy ropes around the sort of circular exhibit. Ashraf's big initial headache was the shading assembly which was anticipated to be a simple affair. Beneath the netting would be a welded frame of metal lattice, mounted from the back wall to be braced against the mast poles and then covered with a canvas. Structural rigidity seemed to be an optional clause for the workmen and the first time of mounting the assembly wasn't the last. Nor was the second. But with some encouragement, solemn consultation and extra welding, the endeavour was finally finished; four months later. Completion was much to the delight of the birds (transferred from the smaller enclosed aviaries) that were able to holler squarks and quark-quarks as they cavorted, swam and flapped around each other on their way to the abundance of alfalfa, bread and fish that Jaboory diligently rained down. It was refreshing and uplifting progress given the initial state rescuers had found the pelican in at Luna Park.

Over the following months, the contractors would knock holes in walls to slightly improve the space available to the badgers, foxes and jungle cat but until a new area could be constructed the chamber would be undeniably poor. Areas of solid flooring were replaced with sand, gravel and piles of palm frond husks to allow digging, and sleeping boxes were included to allow some escape from public view. For the porcupines, Ashraf had used the footprint of a previous small enclosure to develop an exhibit, raised off the ground and shaded by woven palm fronds. The central core of the display was a space packed with sand and stones for the porcupines to tunnel into. As can be imagined, the concepts took several rounds of explanations for the initially mystified contractor to understand. The difficulty was also in allocating space to animals of the same species that were definitely not socially compatible. I had never realised the vitriol that could be stirred up between spiteful porcupines until we saw the wounds of a male attacked by another. The entire rear half of one's back had been de-gloved in an overnight feud, leaving what looked like a raw, bloodied rugby ball under an arc of black and white patchy quills.

Suddenly it was time for Ashraf to leave Baghdad and return to previous commitments. Before going, he had suggested the zoo develop a clear animal collection strategy, clarity in its reason for existence and an enclosure organisational concept. Those would likely remain unfulfilled long-term aims, but the suggestion of a collaborative technical board with representatives from universities, botanical gardens, animal welfare NGOs and regional zoo bodies had merit and could be targeted. The difficulty was that few such representatives existed in Iraq, and even if they did were likely not in a position to offer any useful technical expertise for modern, progressive zoo management.

Coincidentally, Lawrence and Graham also left Baghdad the same day. It was becoming increasingly evident the intended plan, at least as it had been explained to me, for IFAW to transition the Baghdad Zoo to a state where an international team of zoo experts from the American Zoo Association would build upon progress, was unlikely. Despite planned changes being initiated, and facilitating the delivery of critical supplies, in little over one month since arrival only Mariette and Jackson were left from the IFAW team.

The number of stray dogs adopted by soldiers was increasingly influencing our zoo days. U.S. military General Order 1A was issued to maintain good order and conduct among U.S. troops in war zones. Watching pornography, drinking alcohol, having sex with a foreign national, and adopting local dogs and cats were all considered nefarious deeds. One could argue that all of those itemised acts improved morale but our exposure to U.S. troops engaging in those obviously despicable evils was limited. Except for dog adoptions. That particular horror, doting soldiers showing compassion, was front and centre in our lives. Soldiers who arrived at the zoo with their newly adopted pets readily confessed the animals were enormous boosts to personal or even squad morale. Judging by the whippy tail-wagging responses of the dogs, the feeling seemed mutual. Frequently though, units were being relocated or redeployed back home, and they feared their adoptee would suffer neglect or death by being abandoned. Soldiers confided that their bonds with their new pets had lifted the drudgery or fear of many dull days in-country and the thought of leaving the unquestionably loyal mascots in Iraq would be heart-breaking, and bordering on immoral. Farah alone, under Lawrence's initial urging, had become Iraq's first, though informal, animal welfare charity. Any soldiers arriving at the zoo with a stray dog were directed to Farah. We had no initial concerns beyond how we would feed the regular arrivals; until puppies were born into the equation. The majority of the dogs enjoying a Humvee ride to the zoo were pregnant. That meant the dog population at the zoo swelled rapidly, to the consternation of Dr Abbas and some of the zoo staff who believed dogs to be unclean, fearsome or taking up cage space that could exhibit wild, exotic creatures. The real problem was that despite two vets working at the zoo (excluding Dr Hussam who was no longer there) neither of them had hands-on experience of surgically sterilising animals. In the case of Dr Abbas, it had been many years since he had qualified. For Farah, her university exposure had been limited to theory and watching a lecturer perform the surgery; once. Lieutenant Colonel José Lozada, a veterinarian and reservist from the 490th Civil Affairs Battalion, had been liaising with William to help the zoo and agreed to demonstrate the surgery to Farah and Dr Abbas. So as the sweat poured off Lozada, Farah, Dr Abbas, Jackson, Stephan and I, we watched as our office turned into a makeshift educational operating room. The dog lay splayed out on the donated surgical table as Dr Abbas shone the tiny torch onto the bloodied opening among the drapes and Lozada demonstrated the snips, twists and sutures of a spay.

There had been a simmering sense that IFAW was unlikely to spend many more weeks in Baghdad. Only Mariette and Jackson remained from their original emergency response team, and it was increasingly clear that the generation of a final report was about a handover of recommendations, not long-term implementation by IFAW. The consolation was that the zoo was visibly better for IFAW's intervention and the contributions of Mariette and Jackson in particular. They had been a consistently energised, transparent and constructive force. The common purpose we felt with them, particularly Mariette's pragmatic approach, was invaluable in growing our confidence.

A trip to the vegetable market expedited IFAWs intended leaving date. Mariette, Jackson and Ali arrived to source goods for the zoo, an activity which wasn't particularly risky most days. Volleys of bullets were unleashed as a chaotic gunfight erupted at the market. The firing forced Mariette, Jackson and Ali to lunge for cover to avoid being struck. When it subsided, they hustled a quick exit and returned to the zoo, somewhat shaken by the events. Once settled, Mariette could joke with Ali about his facial expressions as they hid, and in the comfort of the zoo grounds again, life and work carried on. It was Baghdad. Unfortunately reporting the incident back to their South African headquarters morphed into a decision that the team would have to leave Baghdad earlier for safety concerns. Mariette, frustrated by the choice, knew the decision-makers in South Africa were not prepared to risk the lives of their emergency response crew. Certainly, the perception of risk between those of us inside Baghdad and those outside seemed to differ, despite our attempted reassurances about threats being sporadic, incidental and unpredictable. On reflection when compared to potential all-out carnage, that seemed a comforting and reasonable scenario to rationalise when inside Baghdad, rather than from afar. The ensuing days passed quickly in a flurry of activity. Mariette worked to hand over the equipment and remaining finances to Farah and regular email contact would remain the umbilical cord from South Africa.

As Farah, Ali and I stood with Mariette and Jackson in the searing heat on the edge of the runway, Blackhawk helicopters skimmed over the surface beyond the masses of storage boxes, C-130 aircraft and hustling vehicles of the temporary U.S. Air Force base. There was that sensation again that our support network was leaving. There had been frustrations, but the reality was that the IFAW intervention had given an enormous impetus to some of the work at the zoo. We had been educated. Through watching Mariette, we had better understood how to manage the details of logistics and prominent personalities. The expertise of some of the team had been invaluable, and the equipment was a blessing. In Mariette and Jackson, friends were leaving. It felt like it. Yet we were also excited – we were still there. They headed off towards the lingering soldiers at the enormous, tan-coloured departure area tents as we exited the departures parking lot, through the checkpoints, and took our new acquisition, the GMC SUV back to the zoo.

Lawrence returned, a visit that coincided with two significant changes. The first, and more meaningful, was that Dr Hussam returned to the zoo. We weren't sure if this had anything to do with Lawrence's persistent agitating for it with The Mayor or Tim Carney, or whether it was a bureaucratic bungle. Either way, he was back as a veterinarian, demoted from his previous position of Deputy Director. We were delighted to have him back in the fray, but it was harder to tell which of the Iraqi staff were happy and which were concerned to see his return.

The other oddity was the restoration of a television

video service at the Al-Rasheed Hotel. We felt it was a strange priority given the general circumstances but quickly capitalised on it. One afternoon as Lawrence and I were savouring the treats of an MRE ration pack, we turned on the television to see what this new rumour of entertainment was about. There it was. Fierce Creatures. A farcical zoo-based comedy with former Monty Python icons. Given our zoo context and the hilarity of the film, we found enormous entertainment in every viewing. Lawrence and I quickly found the small cave-like media room in the hotel basement where an Iraqi contractor randomly selected pirated DVDs to screen. Randomly that was, until we paid him a steady small bribe to ensure the entire hotel was regularly subjected to our cinematic habit.

On the 19th of July, approximately three months after Lawrence had initially arrived at a bleak and assaulted Baghdad Zoo, the refurbished facility was reopened to the public. A smattering of Baghdadis mingled with the crowd of U.S. soldiers, Al-Zawra Park staff, journalists and delighted politicians. The Green Zone perimeter had been re-demarcated, contracted to exclude Al-Zawra Park, to again enable public pedestrian access. The zoo was now in the "Red Zone", although politicians wouldn't express it like that. More of Baghdad for the Baghdadis! We're handing it back, we promise. It was media gold for the CPA. Politicians, including The Mayor, wasted no time in promoting the grand occasion and their apparently considerable input into the restoration. In noble gestures, they would claim to be champions and custodians of the zoo's vision. Appropriately, The Mayor did accurately gauge the sense of occasion with "This park is for families, this park is for friends, and it is especially for children." Iraqi officials, a blend of anonymous faces to us at the zoo, took to the podium to brazenly promote their contributions. It was terrific public relations fodder, and the small crowd cheered appropriately to herald the new beginning. It was a distraction from the chaotic electricity and fuel supplies in the chaotic city. Colourful party balloons and tables laden with treats greeted the first official post-invasion visitors. Journalists lapped it up, scribbling print-worthy quotes in notebooks as photographs were snapped of enchanted children seeing lions, tigers, bears and wild boars for their first time. Farah, William, I and later Lawrence stood back at a distance, watching the crowd below the entrance arch, and reflected briefly and contentedly on the horde that had gathered to inaugurate the improved conditions. Yet there was still so much work to be done. Badgers don't care about political dances. Stuffed with enough pastries, the bureaucrats and media swept out again; job done.

We knew the opening of the zoo was a landmark, but the celebration was a tick-box exercise in a long process of necessary restoration and rehabilitation. We were thrilled the milestone was receiving the attention, but hoped beyond that, that it wouldn't lead the global public to assume the zoo was fixed. We needed international support to continue and wanted the opening to merely be a spectacle to reflect what had been, and what could be achieved with steady development.

Lawrence, Farah and I also had a little pang of urgency for the whole occasion to be wrapped up so we could feed the palace lions earlier than usual and then head out of the Green Zone to find a television showing the Tri-Nations rugby match between South Africa and New Zealand. These were the small, but significant luxuries we relished in the extreme environment. Farah had never seen a rugby match before. Explaining the sport (adult men throw a ball backwards while running forward as other men try to snap them in half) gave us a sound idea of how alien it was in Iraq. Yet, she had spent so much time with Lawrence and me, and she knew how much being able to view the game meant for us. She went well beyond sensible friendship, contacted hotels, and visited others in an attempt to find someone screening the match via satellite television; a recent development in Iraq. Through a series of social networks, we eventually heard of a hotel in central Baghdad where a small international group of United Nations staff had rigged up a satellite dish which would feed us the South African sports channel *SuperSport*. Farah rushed Lawrence and me through the uncooperative Baghdad traffic in her Passat, in a bold and successful attempt to arrive in time for the national anthems and kick-off. We squashed into the small room filled with strangers. The crushing defeat by New Zealand somewhat took the gloss off the novelty of the occasion.

Two weeks later the South African security contractors Lawrence met in his first week, and who had subsequently become our neighbours on the Al-Rasheed's 7th floor, were also particularly keen to watch the rugby. This time our convoy of SUVs was more official and ruthless in the traffic. Assault rifles were positioned for ease of access. Standard protocol. SUVs with foreign occupants were recognised targets to be attacked by Fedayeen, urban militias, insurgents, Saddam sympathisers, disgruntled de-Baathed citizens, criminals, opportunists, nationalists or dismissed former military or police. The contractors had lived through multiple wars, considerably worse conditions, and were recognised as among the elite of ex-special operations, close protection staff on the industrial war circuit. We needed to make kick-off time in a hurry, again. Again we witnessed the South African team take a beating. At least the charitable conciliatory beverage on offer was cold.

The return back was as rapid as our journey to the match viewing, but as usual required passing through one of the Green Zone access control checkpoints where identification badges were verified, weapons were declared, and the safety status confirmed. Lawrence and I had both been supplied 9mm Beretta short pistols and ammunition by a military friend early in our Baghdad stay. We seldom carried them with us unless we were sure we would leave the Green Zone. It was not a particularly gutsy, intimidating weapon but we felt it was better than nothing and if we had needed to use it, it might buy us precious time until a better plan was an option. At the checkpoint, the security contractors were not always required to clear their weapons, but as civilians, it was a protocol that we showed the soldier that our guns were clear. The soldier on the 14th of July Bridge tried to insist that the security contractors leave the vehicle and demonstrate all their weapons were cleared. They argued it wasn't required protocol which left the sweating soldier slightly irritated and flustered. Lawrence and I passed the soldier our guns through the open window. I had removed the magazine of rounds from my gun and had checked the chamber was empty, before demonstrating this to the soldier. Lawrence was in the seat in front of me and handed his gun to the soldier who, unfamiliar with the Beretta's weapon anatomy, and still slightly irritated at the contractors, slipped off the safety catch and pulled back the slide aggressively as some sort of masculine display that he was checking a weapon. I could have sworn I saw him load a round into the empty chamber before he worked out the safety and re-clipped it. I second-guessed myself, thinking I may have been mistaken. He handed the gun back to Lawrence. The vehicle weaved in the Green Zone at high speed between the concrete barriers. I mentioned to Lawrence what I suspected had happened, but in the raucous conversations with the contractors, my statement was lost. I left it. We turned into the grounds of the Al-Rasheed. At the entrance gate of the Al-Rasheed, all military personnel were required to check the safety status of their weapons while they pointed the weapon barrel into a barrel of sand in case a round was accidentally discharged. We had driven through the hotel entrance checkpoint without going through the routine. Instead, as Lawrence exited the vehicle, he flicked off the safety of his weapon, and immediately pulled the trigger with the barrel pointed at the ground. BAH!! We leapt as the unexpected sound jolted us in the confined space of cars and paving. The bullet ricocheted off the brick into the parked car next to us.

"Fuck! I thought so," I said. Soldiers came running from the nearby checkpoint. As Lawrence tried to desperately apologise the soldiers glared and swore at the fucking civilian before confiscating the weapon. The contractors laughed at Lawrence. "You're fucked boet (brother). But don't stress." They tried to make light of the situation as we walked away grinning, leaving Lawrence explaining himself out the hole. He was sheepish as they led him into the hotel for questioning. Any accidental discharge was a severe offence. We'd heard the serious, but in hindsight undeniably comical, story of a soldier in the early days at the parking lot of the CPA Palace not clearing his MK 19 Grenade launcher correctly, and firing a round into a senior official's parked vehicle, blowing it up. Many apologies later, some intervention by Lieutenant Colonel Liz Kuh and assurances to be more careful in future, Lawrence was reissued his weapon by the officious hotel security coordinator later in the week.

As we later laughed about Lawrence's predicament and plotted the ongoing series of changes at the zoo with the management, Stephan's time in Baghdad sadly drew to a close. He was taking his functional-meets-elegance style and field organisational skills back to Cambodia. For a few days, the chaos seemed a little less colourful, a little less organised, and a little short of outrageously smutty innuendos that always guaranteed a laugh.

PART 2: TEA AND DEATH IN MARGARITAVILLE

CHAPTER 9

Lawrence was talented at projecting confidence. He had a presence, fortified by wickedly sharp wit and intellect, and persuasive charm unlike anybody I had encountered. He was masterful at articulating what he believed was needed or wanted to advance progress. Facts were, at times, malleable. Laughter was frequent. His gregarious personality made him equally at home in a boardroom, designated smoking area or a bar if people were listening. He hated being alone. "C'mon boy, just one smoke, and then we head upstairs for a beer." We would stand in the hotel parking lot, roasting to bright pink, waiting for him to enjoy his nicotine-infused reflection of a complicated day in a complex Iraq.

Lawrence valued loyalty, friendship, work ethic, marshmallow animals and the guitar riffs of Deep Purple. Everyone it seemed knew him, yet he treasured only a few, unwavering friends. He could be as inspirational and breezy as cutting, obstinate, relentless and demanding. Effectiveness was his priority. Yet it also seemed that his life and character needed to be fuelled by apparent paradoxes, where flaws and occasionally exasperating turns of temperament accentuated charms, sentiment and aptitudes. He made quick, stubbornly unwavering judgements; so rapid, self-contradictory changes of a detailed plan or sentiment on a whim were occasionally infuriating. Sometimes they were just brutally hilarious. After enduring countless sermons about owning responsibility for vehicle maintenance (I had no such skills), it was hard not to laugh when (before we went to Baghdad) we found him unhurt, partly wet with petrol, attempting to light a cigarette, under an overturned quad-bike. They lay stacked in a deep, wide erosion gulley that Lawrence momentarily thought he could ramp over. The short relapses to teenage bravado masked an usually deep analytical intensity as he reflected on situations and people while sitting tall and dishevelled in his dissipating trails of comforting cigarette smoke, surrounded by incongruously elegant handwritten notes. He appeared oblivious to criticism, threat or the social protocols arbitrarily associated with hierarchy. Chain of command was only an indicator of who generally wielded the most beneficial influence. To him, it did not represent a list of bureaucrats to be sycophantically pleased before making another step upwards. A setting like the Baghdad Green Zone was a fertile habitat for Lawrence.

He could also be a pedantic perfectionist, and it was impossible to suppress my upwelling laughter as he earnestly explained spelling mistakes on the menu in a new Al-Rasheed Hotel restaurant to the bemused Pakistani waiter. The waiter, with little understanding of English, stared and asked again if we wanted a kebab. Lawrence animatedly took out his pen, crossed out the incorrectly spelt words and re-wrote the menu items with correct spellings. The waiter, confused, left the menu behind as he went to place an order for the westerner expat usual, kebabs, hummus and Pepsi.

After the re-opening of the Baghdad Zoo, Lawrence spent little time there. His focus shifted to another of his passions. He had championed the exposure of psychiatric human rights violations under the political system of Apartheid South Africa. In his capacity as a commissioner with the Citizens Commission on Human Rights he made a submission to the South African Truth and Reconciliation Committee on the links between psychology, psychiatry, state abuses and political repression in South Africa. At the CPA he advised Tim Carney, and then Pat Kennedy on the toll that psychological abuses and associated social manipulation had exacted in South Africa. It wasn't difficult to see that Iraq was a brutalised state and beyond traditional hospitality and resilience, the national psychology was heavily impacted by intimidation, perpetuated violence and frequent retribution.

Posting cloth banners in prominent parts of the city had become common. Banners posted under the regime were usually death notices on black cloth or advertisements. As the hint of freedom of speech grew in the absence of the dictatorship, so the opinions became increasingly politicised, some memorialising victims of abductions or government executions. Lawrence saw it as an opportunity to promote human rights values. Banners would not change anything but maybe stimulate a little dialogue. Logically, Ali the taxi-driving, meat-sourcing, lion-feeding, cage-welding, Johnny Walker-providing fixer was the go-to for banner production. "Human rights must be a reality and not just an ideal dream – L. Ron Hubbard" the 5m-wide white banners declared in red Arabic script.

In the sweltering heat, the banner day became a guided cultural tour of Baghdad's highlights and infamous institutions. Farah had been persuaded by Lawrence to join us despite her feeling nauseated. It was more enjoyable when she was around, and her translation skills trumped ours. I think Lawrence also trusted her aptitude over mine for using the modern technology of a digital camera. So with Ali waiting at the steering wheel of his car in case there were objections to our actions, we initially posted a banner at the symbolic Firdos Square where the statue of Saddam Hussein had been toppled in front of international media. At Tahrir (*liberation*) Square another banner was fastened below the dramatically incongruous frieze of *liberated* figures. Traffic swirled around the traffic circle as the remaining manicured hair, and a shoulder of a vandalised Saddam Hussein portrait glared at us from across the road. The banner drew the brief attention of a local news crew. It was an opportunity for Lawrence to gain approval. Thumbs up. "Good! Virry good!" With Farah, they navigated their way through a brief interview.

The next destination was the Al Rashad Psychiatric Hospital of Baghdad located in Thawra (*revolution*) neighbourhood (also known as Saddam City). The area was later renamed Sadr City after the Grand Ayatollah Mohammad Mohammad Sadeq Al-Sadr, father of the firebrand, vehemently anti-Sunni, anti-American, Shiite Cleric Muqtada Al-Sadr. Along the highway burnt-out buildings stood beyond wreckage after wreckage of blown-up or burnt cars and trucks scattered over the litter-strewn, desiccated mudscape. Shredded plastic bags clung to patchy grass among piles of fetid or burning rubbish and murky pools enveloped broken water pipes. It was visceral decay. Horses pulled carts along the side of the road as old *Folgas-vagen barazillis* (old Volkswagen Passats from a batch originating in Brazil) whipped past. Lawrence had visited the hospital during his initial weeks in the Al-Rasheed Hotel as he accompanied the Department of Defence contracted journalists Peter Jouvenal, Alastair McLarty and their interpreter, Qais. Over evening beers and MRE's they had discussed the tactics of suppressive regimes at length, and the hospital was an obvious target for their investigative recordings. In the chaos of "post-liberation" the information on incarceration of sane political prisoners among insane people, the liberal use of psychiatric drugs, surgical lobotomies and the indiscriminate use of shock treatment was openly discussed by some remaining staff. The institution stood cheerlessly like a mud-coloured prison in the bleak, dusty fields among sporadic palm trees. On video recorded by the contractors, zombie-like patients had drifted past, while others rocked maniacally on filthy soiled beds. Fortunately for us, our visit was merely a blip in time to post a banner at the location and document it photographically for the records or later media exposure. It gave a context for some of the tormented spirits in the country and perhaps, by creative assumption, some revealing insight into national values associated with caged animals.

The next stop was the notorious Abu Ghraib (*Father of Raven; Place of Ravens*) prison complex, 30km away, to the west of Baghdad. It had been the fortress setting for extensive sadistic torture, mass cruelty, amputations and death under the Baath regime. Towards the end of 2002, with war almost certain, the prison was emptied of its nearly 10 000 inmates. They were free to go home or cause mayhem. After a brief redecoration in 2003, the U.S. military began to repopulate the prison. Building a modern facility would take too long. It would be in 2004 that evidence of beatings, sexual humiliation and severe psychological abuses perpetrated by members of the U.S. Army's 372nd Military Police Company would be released to the world. It was a hell between walls. The drive out to the prison was more of the same setting from earlier; life carrying on among war detritus. Old trucks, pickups and cars sped on the highways past dismembered, burnt-out armoured personnel carriers and random tank turrets which looked like they had been swept into the palm trees and dust by a petulant giant baby. T-72 tanks still hid behind palm trees, except by then the trees were scorched and a flaccid turret barrel drooped from the charred metal remains. Abu Ghraib to us was, fortunately, only another generic, big brown perimeter wall with concrete watchtowers. Once again a prowling local film crew saw an opportunity for an interview with the conspicuously tall, ginger, bannerman.

Then it was back into the city to Baghdad Gate, on Mosul Road heading out the city towards the north. The "gate" was an imposing 30m tall battle-damaged wall with massive pointed Islamic arches curving over each of the two directions of highway traffic. At either end of the wall stood taller rectangular towers. The wall stood isolated in a bleakly flat landscape. The most common theory encountered was that it was an arbitrary Baath Party construction rather than an iconic historical site from the city founded in the

8th century. Unsurprisingly the intricate beige tiled façade of the wall had been partly chiselled off by explosions, like Pacman had eaten his way across a Tetris wall. One tower base showed the deep blast scar of a rubble-surrounded hole with rebar reinforcement thrust out like metallic anemone tentacles. The skeleton of a small contorted Ferris wheel stood nearby. Perhaps it was only my cultural ignorance that it seemed an odd location for a playground. It was hard to imagine a child boasting about how cool their father was because of a weekend visit to the most despondent Ferris wheel in the region. The white banner was hooked up amongst already-mounted black banners on the central wall between the two arches.

The final stop was the concrete stage on the corner of Mansour and 14th Ramadan Streets in Mansour neighbourhood close to the zoo. As a child, Farah and hundreds of children from other nearby schools would be transported by bus to the area to welcome, wave and chant for cavalcades of foreign dignitaries in black, open-topped cars. A reluctant, adoring rent-a-crowd. Suited presidents and Kings would stand in the vehicles waving to their devotees. Ali Abdullah Saleh of Yemen. Hosni Mubarak of Egypt. King Hussein of Jordan. King Fahd of Saudi Arabia. Yasser Arafat of the Palestine Liberation Organisation. Omar Ahmed Al-Bashir of Sudan. Countless security officials. Berets. Multitudes of black sunglasses and thick moustaches accessorised the glossy suits. "Bil ruuh, bil dem, nafdeek ya Saddam!" (*With life, with blood, we sacrifice for you Saddam*) the children would all repetitively chant as instructed. It was less than a hundred metres from the popular Al Sa'ah restaurant near to where the private house had been pulverised by the U.S. missile Farah and her father had seen whip past their home four months earlier. Across lanes of the intersection opposite the stage stood two large, slim, powder blue art deco arches with earring-like discs of the Iraqi flag dangling from each bow. Below a tangle of electrical cables and heart-shaped street light decorations, the wall behind the stage was a mix of amateurish Saddam-era patriotic art and rebellious graffiti partly covered by banners. Stern soldiers were painted next to the image of the iconic crossed swords. A warrior rode an Arab stallion. Flowers. Flags. Arches. A white-suited portrait of Saddam wore a new, fresh, yellow smiley face with an edging of squiggly black spray-paint hair. An educational poster pasted on an adjacent electricity box highlighted to children the dangers of playing with explosives. Ali and a newly acquired accomplice posted the banner as Farah took the necessary photographic evidence. Ali returned Lawrence to the hotel and "zoo girl" and I went to engage checkpoint soldiers over the usual buckets of flesh and bottles of cold water on the way to another palace lion feeding.

As I finished reading for the evening and was readying to sleep there seemed to be an unusual amount of gunfire noise outside. With the extravagance of functional electricity, it meant the rooms were luxuriously cooled by air-conditioning, and we kept the windows closed. Our setting was undeniably very comfortable, while much of Baghdad endured the dark, baking hot nights without electricity. The heavy glazing on our room windows muffled the noise slightly. *Duk duk cak cak duk duk*. Every night there was still habitually little bursts of gunfire nearby. The stop-start exchanges usually finished after growing into what sounded like a customary rapid, intense finale. It wasn't even a talking point anymore except when the security contractors would grumble that the U.S. soldiers patrolling at night were "just fucking scared children who fired wildly at anything in the dark that they assumed may be a threat". The genuine fear was that there was a greater likelihood of being shot by a squad of freaked-out U.S. soldiers than by the supposed Iraqi enemy.

I opened the curtains to a scene of coloured tracer fire arcing into the blackness above building silhouettes. Flares of different colours shot up until their momentum slowed and they would drift back down like a bright, pulsing ember. I opened a window. The gunfire clatter was intense and sounded like it was echoing down alleys, above buildings, around nearby corners and far in the distance. Assault rifles on semi-automatic. Single shots. .50 Calibres responding. It wasn't localised. It felt like a war had erupted through the city around us. "Shit," I thought "it seems like a proper bloody attack". I closed the window and went across the hallway to find Lawrence at another bedroom's window. It was the same scene westwards out over the park towards Mansour and Kindi neighbourhoods. Flares. Tracer. Bursts of disconnected gunfire. We wondered if we were genuinely at risk and why there would be such a concerted, coordinated attack after so many weeks of relative calm. What was unique about 22 July? I tried to phone Farah to see if she and her family were OK and to let them know what we thought was happening. Did she know what was going on? Was this only in our portion of the city? It seemed to extend far into the distance. The phone rang. No answer. Lawrence and I stared out at the scenes reminiscent of the night vision television footage of anti-aircraft fire shown across the world during the 1st Gulf War. The phone beeped with a text message from Farah. "Uday and Qusay are dead." Saddam's sons. The rumours were circulating rapidly and excitedly that Saddam's sadistic sons, frequently linked to acts of arbitrary savagery and cruelty, torture, rape, opulence and vile excess had been slaughtered in a gun battle against raiding U.S. forces in Mosul. The gunfire around us was celebratory! The scale of the spontaneous celebratory eruption gave some indication of the hatred towards the tyrannical overlords. While there were also rumours that the media would be shown evidence of their deaths the next day, some weren't waiting for confirmation. The parties in the suburbs carried on late into the night. Two days later, head photos of Uday and Qusay's mangled corpses made sweeping international headlines as U.S. authorities attempted to convince sceptical Iraqis the deaths were genuine.

In our intensely parochial world of the Al-Rasheed, the momentous news circulating was the completion of renovations to the hotel swimming pool! The hotel was quickly turning into a quasi-expat resort with its series of restaurants, bars, a nightclub and shops selling standard local trinkets like paintings, carpets, kitsch Call to Prayer alarm clocks and quirky Saddam Hussein watches. There is nothing like a few months of slaughter to turn sycophantic, dictator-chic collectables into desirable novelty memorabilia. The hotel was unashamedly in U.S.-dominated post-war reconstruction mode. Rotations of soldiers and bureaucrats and diplomats let off steam among the swathes of support staff. There was open optimism and secretive pessimism and scepticism in bundles. The array of accents meant walking into the hotel was an immersion into a disconnected parallel universe to what was beyond the fortified Green Zone boundaries. It felt disarming, guilty, luxurious, compelling, comforting, historical and undeniably exotic. It was home. For Lawrence and me, our link to the zoo was still as novel to many people as we had encountered in the very first days or our respective arrivals.

Apparently throwing a Jimmy Buffet party was the best way to initiate the pool's grand revival. Americans we encountered talked excitedly about the opportunity to guzzle cheeseburgers and Margaritas. They would check if we were going to bust out our finest tropical attire as if that was an item in everyone's luggage in a visit to a desert war zone? I didn't know what they were talking about and didn't know what type of food Jimmy was. Every day at the KBR canteen was buffet time, so I didn't see the grand appeal of that unless a Jimmy buffet was unique. There was apparently a cultural "Lost in Translation" divide at play. It seemed we had insulted an American icon with our ignorance.

Over beer and cocktail-fuelled hours, we achieved enlightenment. As soldiers outcompeted each other from the diving board, a sound system boomed out an endless set of musician-songwriter Jimmy Buffet's tropical hits. *Marga-*

ritaville captivated the clearly unquenchable karaoke spirit of Americans pining for a mythical paradise. The grandmaster of island escapism music was worshipped as an idol at the quite decadent temple of the hotel pool and bar. Through the inky blackness of the sky above our bubble, blacked-out military helicopters would periodically, suddenly roar and clatter past at treetop heights, reminding us of Orwell's alleged sentiment that "people sleep peacefully in their beds at night only because rough men stand ready to do violence on their behalf."

The social construct within the hotel was an intoxicating mix of mind-bending novelty. Having emerged from comfortable South African suburbia and life at a Zululand game reserve, the Al-Rasheed felt like a newly constructed planet. Exposure to the characters and contrasting personalities was constant. It ranged from people genuinely intellectually committed to trying to improve Iraq through improvised governance, logistical projects or human rights interventions, to those blustering and posing to satisfy egotistical cravings. There were others for whom the circumstances were an opportunity for reigniting camaraderie from other shared war zones, enduring risk, enormous financial reward and validation of being incredibly efficient and skilled operators. Paying off the mortgage and children's school fees was a lot quicker process at those daily rates than working at home. The security contractors, in particular, appeared to fall loosely into the latter grouping. They were a mix of respected and/or feared elite military or police personnel from around the globe. Americans, British, South Africans, Australians, Zimbabweans (they preferred to be called Rhodesians) and Fijians had experience in the British, Rhodesian, Australian or New Zealand SAS, the British Parachute Regiment, the Royal Marines, the French Foreign Legion, Delta Force, the South African Police Special Task Force and military reconnaissance units. Business appeared a foggy mix of police and military training, protection of high-value clients and occasionally supporting sanctioned military operations under the U.S. Department of Defence. We were unlikely to ever encounter or engage with such people in our *normal* world.

As an outsider, it seemed prudent not to ask details, instead to listen to extraordinary insider anecdotes of past battles, to watch the emotion around memories of lost comrades and near-death experiences. Anything I could add would have likely seemed "civilian". And it was easier and more entertaining to listen to the banter and absorb the history. With beers, Jack Daniels and Johnny Walker, the reminiscing was seemingly endless and *almost* always captivating - I'm still not going buy a subscription to Scootering magazine no matter how big and hairy its number one fan is. It was standard banter with a twist. Women met, relationships lost, regrets, loves, the best night vision goggles (In 2003, Russian 3rd generation!), whores, adrenaline-pumping tales of testing night time HALO jumps, or songs which drew out silent reflection or raucous memories. It was a testosterone-driven scenario, but there was still room for a hint of chivalry. A female military contractor insulted at a barbeque by an intoxicated male colleague about "bleeding every month", smashed him squarely in the centre of his face and retorted about him "bleeding tonight". The rest of the men at the barbeque drank to her recalibration of the respect scale.

In the case of the South Africans, our political views would probably be unlikely to reach consensus, but it was compelling to hear another raw side to our country's cultural mix and its history. Among all that conversation I would never have thought Roger Whittaker singing "Streets of London" or U.S. country singer Jim Reeve's Afrikaans renditions would be a security contractor's music of choice. In many cases, it was the humility that was most striking, most contrasting from the Hollywood portrayal of modern warriors. They had nothing to prove in stories. They were the real deal. Their good mates knew it, and they knew it. Facts were facts. They spoke plainly. They had seen and done so much they didn't need to bullshit to inflate their egos. They certainly didn't need or seek any validation from us civilians. It was refreshing. The situation was almost equally captivating for them too. Many returned after the familiar "...this is my final tour. I'm going back to be with my wife and children" discussion. Some ended up in a Zimbabwean jail convicted as mercenaries while "on leave". We didn't need to have an opinion on their backgrounds. It felt best not to think about it too much, to find disagreement - even if we did, the outcome was likely to be irrelevant or academic at best. It satisfied a curiosity to be around them, and in that particular setting, they were especially likeable and welcoming. It was comforting to have their phone numbers and assurances that if we were in trouble, they had offered their assistance without reservation. After initial scepticism about the "Iraqi girl", they extended that same offer of protection to Farah whom they had warmed to because of her zoo commitment, cute looks and hustling, charming, cheeky approach.

Evening beers in their rooms were never dull. One discussion led to a disagreement again on the merits of trophy hunting. One man couldn't understand the point or the thrill of slaughtering animals for a set of horns or a specimen mount. "Nothing compares to the thrill of hunting humans. Once you've done that, trophy hunting animals seems fucking pointless." It wasn't unlikely for a discussion to be interrupted by a mission. "Don't worry guys. There is cold beer in the fridge. Make yourselves at home. We won't be long. My brother from another mother" Leon would laugh as he assured Lawrence about the beer fridge. AK-47s would be lined up on the bed as ammunition was counted. Pistols were holstered. Magazines would be taped to each other inverted for easier changing during a battle. "Where the fuck is the knock-knock?" (The shotgun used for shooting out door locks in a house raid. Of course!). A shotgun would be pulled from under the bed. Skateboarding knee pads were pulled up over old tracksuit pants. There was no fancy attempt to look fashionable. Why would you? They wholeheartedly believed they were warriors clearing the city of evil arseholes one raid after another. It was exclusively about being functional. Camouflage or black tactical chest webbing was fitted over the head, Velcro-sealed, loaded with extra magazines of ammunition, a torch and maybe an additional knife. They would leave and Lawrence and I would stay sitting, enjoying a relaxing beer, in an abnormal setting.

They would return, recounting the blow-by-blow events of the previous hour. The composed thrill of delivering another professional, merciless result was evident as they cracked a beer, unpacked and stored their kit. They thrived on their relationship with units like the U.S.'s Delta Force. They thrived on being respected for being efficient and exceptional. They thrived on beating their previous record time to clear a house and reach the roof. It sounded impossibly ruthless given the friendly chatter over beers the same evening, yet statements like "I shot him through the fridge" or "he used her like a fucking shield" or "these are evil men" left us in no doubt that they were delighted at having eliminated *scum* from the Gotham-like city. Since it appeared the coalition hadn't found the *smoking gun* of Weapons of Mass Destruction the focus was emphasising the kill or capture of people delivering ruthless armed resistance, kidnapping and bombings. It was a job and a delivery of justice. It was what it was.

Brent and Douw's primary responsibility was training the new Iraqi police force. Given their highly skilled technical abilities from their respective military and police force backgrounds, they were often infuriated by the slack approach of many of the local police recruits. On a lucky day, Lawrence and I were finally exposed to what they considered *acceptable* levels of weapons proficiency and marksmanship. They offered us a chance to join them at the shooting range of the police barracks, where they conducted daily training. A standard morning of aggressive tactical driving, including a few high-speed pavement hops to bypass choked traffic, got us to the barracks without incident. On that day it was only the four of us, a small range of weapons and plenty of ammunition. The range itself was slightly disconcerting. Its perimeter was large sand berms. At three intervals set back about 40m and beyond from the targets were a series of beige walls stretching the width of the range, raised on 3m tall brick columns. Each raised wall was severely pockmarked from years of poorly aimed bullets striking the brickwork. The supporting columns were protected by stacked sandbags. One column was barely the remains of chewed up concrete and a few rusty reinforcement wires. Recruits under Saddam's government were allegedly tied to it and executed. Range day allowed us to experience the joys of being on the right end of an Mp5 submachine gun, AK-47 assault rifle, FN Fal rifle and Glock pistol. To watch the precision handiwork of skilled professionals was undeniably impressive. Watching a single hole being incrementally opened up to the size of a coin by firing a full Glock magazine from 5m let us know how far off the benchmark we were. We could recognise why the recruits would take so long to reach *acceptable.*

   To enjoy the opportunity of a social setting beyond the Al-Rasheed, and to thank them for their hospitality, Lawrence invited the South African security contractors to the zoo for an evening barbeque. In his inimitable style, he made the announcement late in the afternoon as he headed off for a meeting. We had no meat, no grill and no alcohol. Farah and I suggested perhaps another day would be a better option, but he insisted he felt that evening would make for a lovely setting once we had arranged the logistics. Farah was heading home but fortunately was still able to make quick plans with the security guards and the concession restaurant managers at the zoo. They would arrange meat. Ali, as so often, came to the rescue on our liquor front. He knew a guy. Of course he did. Off we went across the Tigris to Karrada. I had not seen a liquor store anywhere in the city before so was curious as to how the plan would play out. The street bustle was building up as the stores reopened after the afternoon siesta. As we entered the blandly anonymous shop, I started to doubt Ali. Regretfully I should have shown faith. We stood at the counter as Ali discussed the business with his friend behind the counter. The shelves behind him were sparse, almost to the point of the tins of food being token items. But we weren't in the market for beans or tomato sauce. He opened the false wall by pulling the shelf forward, revealing his illegal business, a stockpile of liquor to excite a university fraternity. Cases of beer stacked high and boxes of vodka and whisky lay waiting for an emergency. We quickly loaded the taxi's trunk and headed back to the impromptu barbeque. Lawrence had not left for his meeting, nor had he arranged a cooking area. The gardener's wheelbarrow had to suffice as the fire pit, the spade as a makeshift barbeque grill.

It felt particularly unusual to be at the zoo in the evening. It was sedate, unlike during the day when it was all about feeding, cleaning and improving. By the evening, the animals were mostly resting. They had eaten their afternoon feed. Brent, the security contractor, sat quietly and watched Malooh, the tiger, as it flicked up its tail and sprayed the oily territorial marking on the brick wall and metal bars. A lion pushed out a deep, rasping moan which seemed amplified in the still, quiet, stifling air and could be heard well beyond the zoo boundary. Wandering the zoo at that time provided a moment to reflect on the changes in the past three months. A mongoose scurried past. Mongooses had always just been there. Or so the staff had told me. It was likely an escapee, but who was I to argue? In the shadows, a few stray dogs that roamed the park and zoo stirred while others dug deeper sleeping scrapes to reach the cooler soil. They would partly feed off the scraps of bone and flesh discarded after the keepers cleaned out the lion areas. In some cases, where the keepers had buried remains in the zoo grounds, the dogs would dig up the morsels. It wasn't entirely abnormal to find a furry donkey leg in the grass in a remote corner of the zoo. Back at the barbeque, Jaffer had joined us along with the restaurant staff and the security manager. Beyond being a little arbitrary social gathering, it was good for both the Iraqis and us to see each other in a relaxed, sociable setting; no work, no agendas, just camaraderie. So it appeared to us.

CHAPTER 10

Dr Mohammed Ihsan was the Minister for Human Rights for the semi-autonomous Kurdish regional government in northern Iraq. His imposing, thickset frame and thinning hair appeared to be secondary features to the intensity of his eyes. As a human rights advocate in an ethnic community subjected to extreme regional geopolitical struggles (Kurds occupy a contiguous, frequently contested region spanning parts of northern Iraq, northern Syria, southern Turkey and western Iran) and violent persecution by the Baathist regime, there appeared little room in his day for light-hearted banter. He was accompanied by an entourage of uncompromising security guards led by his less erudite younger brother, Azad. Azad was unreserved, loved a smoke, enjoyed the brash nature of his status as a protector, wasn't shy to test the capabilities of his SUV and relished starting any conversation which may lead to a discussion about Farah.

Kurdistan was a region of Iraq which had generally sided with Iran during the Iraq-Iran war of the 1980s. In response to Iranian forces, supported by Kurdish guerrillas, taking control of the northern Iraqi town of Halabja (241km northeast of Baghdad) in 1988, the Iraqi government unleashed extensive gassing of the town. Iraqi Migs and Mirage jets let loose bombs of Mustard Gas and nerve agents including Sarin on the residential area. It resulted in the mass slaughter of up to 5 000 people in the immediate poison gas attack, and thousands died later or reported subsequent debilitating injuries and birth defects of babies. A massive genocidal campaign to terrorise and systematically destroy the Kurds (and other ethnic minorities) in northern Iraq from 1986 to 1989 was known as *Al Anfal*. A combination of scorched earth policies including bombardments of lethal gas, ground assaults, mass deportations, executions and abductions was led by Saddam Hussein's cousin Ali Hassan Al Majed – who would consequently become known as *Chemical Ali*. Part of Dr Ihsan's responsibility was to unravel the paper trails of documented brutality and disappearances of ethnic Kurds at the hands of Saddam Hussein's government. Through deliberations in the CPA, he had heard of Lawrence's involvement in South Africa's Truth and Reconciliation Committee (TRC). Discussions on the topic led him to invite us to Kurdistan, partly to get a sense of the potential for Lawrence to aid with the formation of an adapted TRC. Because of our game reserve backgrounds, he also wondered about the possibility of developing such an industry, or formal conservation of wild areas, in Kurdistan.

Ali was the clear choice of driver for the 370km journey from Baghdad to Erbil (the capital of Iraqi Kurdistan). He had the requisite skills on the roads, and importantly, we believed we could trust him. It was known to be a road journey which could be anything from uneventful to terrifying. That excluded the unnecessarily insane driving. We had heard of occasions when impromptu checkpoints had been set up by militias (at times dressed like newly uniformed Iraqi police) to extort money, kidnap foreigners or execute rivals. Erbil though was regarded as considerably safer than Baghdad and walking around in the city in the evenings appeared to carry far less risk for foreigners. The most startling revelation of the journey north was that beyond the faded ends of the parched plains, we saw mountains. It seemed peculiarly exciting to have an actual structure beyond seemingly endless horizontal uniformity. We immediately realised we had only lived on or seen flat terrain for nearly three months in Baghdad.

Erbil was historically remarkable in that reports suggested the area had been continuously inhabited since 5000 BC. At the centre of the city was the thick-walled Citadel of Erbil, standing on a 30m tall mound. It was a dilapidated landmark that had been occupied by impoverished families. Erbil 2003 had become the City of Hooting. It was incessant, and one could easily believe the vehicle hooter was connected to the accelerator, the brake pedal and the cigarette lighter. It seemed the hooter was an essential tool of urban navigation, a modified vehicular version of bat echolocation. Ali adapted quickly, pushing through the seething traffic, his cigarette-stained hand pulsing on the hooter.

With the thick windows closed, the inside of the hotel brought initial respite from the cacophony. Since there had only been two rooms booked, Lawrence quickly decided I would share with Ali. The relief of bedtime finally arrived. As the lingering inner-ear ringing from the persistent hooting eventually faded, the rasping hacksaw of Ali's alarmingly unhealthy snoring ensured silence would only be found in luxuriously peaceful toilet breaks.

The meeting with Dr Ihsan was scheduled for late in the morning, and we took the opportunity to visit the highly recommended zoo. We were curious to see the apparently entertaining facilities next to the luxurious Sheraton Hotel being built to cater for the influx of wealthy foreigners. We entered a graphic disgrace. A small maze of whitewashed low walls, dried fountains, stairs, blocky pens and miserable cages held an array of suffering inmates. The sun and about 40 °C heat reflected violently from every surface. The highlight for the keeper who was delighted by our arrival, was the centrepiece, a rhesus macaque chained to an ugly concrete log-jar-pedestal artwork in a waterless fountain. A chain around the macaque's waist ensured that when it wasn't trying to hide in the tiny central spot of shade and protection, it could barely reach to the foot-high perimeter wall. For our viewing pleasure, another keeper attempted to force a second chained macaque in the adjacent pond section, which did have water, to drink. It looked like a confession-inducing drowning attempt as the monkey resisted having its head dunked. The language barrier was a problem too. We implored the jackasses to stop the harassment. Our efforts at explaining how fucking awful we thought the facilities and his behaviour was, led the staff member to start spraying hose water at two sets of macaques locked into stand-alone cages baking in the sun. One of the oppressively small cages looked like it had been improvised from the remains of a scrap metal recycling project by a demonic magnet. It seemed to all be held together with a big brick resting on the corrugated iron roof. A chained camel lay listlessly on the concrete floor of its pen, below another row of uniform small concrete pens. Patchwork scrap fencing enclosed the front of the bare concrete cells. Neither of the hawks appreciated their token log. Feather piles and desiccated flesh debris suggested they had eaten several of their cellmates. A vulture was housed next to a cell of dogs and what were possibly hybrid wolves. Porcupines. Owls. A sleeping bear. We walked and gazed in disbelief. It was worse than Luna Park in Baghdad. More birds in cages. A tiny cage with a plank on its roof for shade held a wildcat. Next to it, a smaller cage the size of a hand luggage suitcase confined two badgers and an empty water bowl. Only the shallow breathing of the badgers gave any indication they were still alive as they lay dehydrated and contorted. The keeper smiled and pointed to the badgers. We coerced him into filling the water bowls when what we instead wanted to do was club him with a spade. Behind him, the windows of the Sheraton Hotel glistened with modern chic. It was unbearable. Lawrence came over to say he had negotiated to shut the facility down for $10 000. It seemed a strangely trivial amount considering the Luna Park bear had cost that much in compensation. We would try to work out the logistics when we returned to Baghdad.

We turned our backs on the hellish facility and headed off to Dr Ihsan for Lawrence to discuss human rights and social justice amid the stories of gassing, sadism and abductions. On the walls hung paintings of columns of refugees desperately making their way to Turkish safety. The frustration and depression were compartmentalised. It had to be. And although Dr Ihsan was genuinely curious about the prospect of a Truth and Reconciliation type process in Iraq, he feared the sectarian divides, the slaughter and the regional temperament would never result in forgiveness. The blood of revenge would likely be preferable to the majority.

Dr Ihsan insisted we enjoy his hospitality and instructed that his brother Azad whom we had met in Baghdad, take us on a tour through Kurdistan to spend a night in Dohuk. Ali joined us as Lawrence and I, being driven by Azad, learnt a new level of fear as passengers. It seemed ironic that an armed, bulletproof vest-wearing security guard was appointed to us to ensure our safety against potential threats. Hurtling up mountain passes on the wrong side of the road around blind corners, or overtaking other SUVs driving down mountains at 140km/h seemed the odds-on bet to snuff us out long before we came under armed attack. But what did we know? Azad was raucous and loving the opportunity to show off his country. The scenery was spectacular. We quickly ran out of superlatives. Seemingly impossibly rugged mountain passes fell away to reveal dramatic brown valleys cut by swollen, winding rivers of gushing, turquoise snowmelt waters. Olive trees dotted the rolling hills, and scattered farms speckled the tanned plains with vibrant greens. It was a relief to the senses after the time in Baghdad and Erbil. There was wild open space. The clean air smelt and tasted delicious. Not even the abundant gardens of roadside litter could steal away the relief we took from looking out into the distance. Through Shaqlawa and onto the heaving tourist magnet of the Bekhal waterfall. It poured and spilt out into streams tumbling down the mountainside into cold pools surrounded by tarpaulin-shaded restaurants. As we lunched at an isolated restaurant beside an idyllic tree-lined river, a man in traditional Kurdish dress of baggy pants and a large waist sash tied the ends of his pants tight against his legs to form an improvised flotation device. He lay back and bobbed on his air-filled pants. We presumed his female companion would wait until he had finished swimming. Nope. She walked into the river in her tight jeans. With her delicate abaya floating out around her, it looked like she was suspended in a black hole.

The night in Dohuk was like a world apart from our earlier months. We were able to sit outside in the cool air, enjoying the freedom of a city at a restaurant overlooking city lights. It felt improbably safe. The following morning was an appropriately suicidal drive back to Erbil via more gorgeously rugged backdrops as Azad tried to discuss the compelling virtues of Farah. A rushed meeting with Dr Ihsan about the prospects of setting up a national park was ticked off (with no budget or mandate or support that idea would eventually be shelved), we took a final hit of the hooting mania and stared and processed the barren landscape of central Iraq as Ali raced us back to Baghdad. It had been less than a week away and I realised I had bizarre anxiety, and an unexpected problem; a Baghdad Zoo craving.

With a week living outside the daily zoo entanglement, thinking about what needed to be done, I could see a new reality; the calculation had changed. The initial one-month assessment and patch-up was a woeful underestimation. Nobody else was coming. We were on our own on the ground, and there were serious decisions to be considered and made. Leaving wasn't an enticing option. For Lawrence, he had persistent commitments back in South Africa. He needed to head back, but his focus had also shifted. He had opened the door. Before his departure, he engaged Pat Kennedy persistently until he managed to negotiate that both he, and I would receive a token payment for time spent at the zoo. It was a great relief to at least know I would be able to afford an air ticket or taxi fare out of Iraq.

At the zoo, it was once again Farah, myself and William who were coordinating the recovery with Dr Abbas's consent. The much-heralded outside support had come and gone.

CHAPTER 11

Pairs of black helicopters would hang high overhead, search and drift off like giant spider-hunting wasps. Processions of Humvees were increasingly juiced up by units who welded on metal slabs for added protection against incoming fire and shrapnel. Processions of black, tinted-window SUVs raced along the roads, weaving rapidly between barriers and into palace complexes. Their arrays of roof decorations were rumoured to have barrages of capabilities from simple communications to signal-jamming pulses to stop the detonation of cell phone-controlled roadside bombs. The speculation was whether the occupants were Bush's diplomats, CIA spooks, Special Forces or young political minions playing emissary. It was difficult not to stop and gaze at the massive logistical, money-spending machine attempting to entrench a debatably welcome empire. By loose association, an energised daily dynamic had become our new normal. The citywide mood was unquestionably changing. It was perceptible. Among CPA staff, between the usually bland policy fluff and office gossip, there was revealing chatter in the dining halls, or over beers. A sniping incident. Grenades being dropped from bridges into Humvees passing below. Another detonation. Another U.S. soldier in torn pieces in a Humvee. Iraqis being shot for collaborating with U.S. forces. Iraqi interpreters risking their lives for dollars or to help repair the city. Sporadically, explosions would rumble, boom or thud in the distance. Perhaps it was the military destroying ordnance. Maybe it was an attack of sorts. Farah had told us of a report of a suicide bomber whose hands were found cable-tied to the steering wheel in the remains of the detonated, charred vehicle. The apparent fermenting discontent in the city seemed to amplify any little progress we perceived we were making at the zoo.

Feeling we were competing against the odds made us fight harder. 50 °C day. Fuck it. Your skin feels like it is cling-wrapped in simmering sweat. "We'll set an example of how to work in the heat". Given how horrifically wet and pink I ended up, like a boiled Vienna sausage, I'm not sure it made the prospect of such work enticing to those Iraqis hiding in the shadows who probably noted the efforts as those of foreign, ignorant lunatics. For them, the personal benefit was unclear and thus the effort best avoided. Yet we were still growing in confidence in our progress at the zoo, and generally in our engagement with some of the staff. Some just listened and settled back down to drinking tea. Some would carry out any task Farah requested. Dr Abbas ordered around his few *reliables*. I found working seven days a week felt like a hobby rather than a chore. It had a compelling, challenging, fun, attraction to it. I felt I was chained to the wrong grand adventure each day that dehydration and diarrhoea knocked me out from work.

Ashraf's drawn plans were being worked to fruition by staff and contractors and over time each animal enclosure was modified with added items of creative entertainment. We always knew conditions could be better, and we felt guilty for shouting at Samir (the Luna Park bear) as he broke open the overhead bars above his outside pool and had almost leveraged his hairy bum out to freedom when we saw him. We shouted, he dropped back between the twisted bars and shuffled inside.

Water pumping was still a daily concern. The taps flowed enticingly after so many dry months, but as the engineers around the city tried to repair and regulate the larger canal water supplies, we would find parts of the zoo flooding if the pump cut-off timings failed, or the relevant engineer didn't arrive for work. Or so we would hear. The canal walls were a layer of permeable concrete and stone, so the level of water in the canals reflected the temporary, localised water table. The lions' moat would fill or drain as the water table fluctuated. The wild boar enclosure quickly turned from a small grassy paddock into a small wetland of reeds and mud. It gave an indication though of the complexity of trying to resolve problems. With Dr Abbas at the helm, we would have to understand the city's canal pumping network, navigate through layers of bureaucracy and denial of responsibility until we could track down the responsible engineers in the exact office in the right building in the correct department. Invariably the murkiness of the responsibility swamp would test sanity and patience to a point where we decided boars preferred an unpredictable marshland. It was easier to believe that than resolve each problem. It was a coincidence that in Iraq's southern marshes the boars actively thrive in that habitat.

Each day we encountered setbacks. They would diverge sporadically from a bit baffling to totally bloody infuriating as if at the whims of some drunken celestial nut. Broken equipment, fuel shortages, dirty black market fuel, politics and food logistics, but we knew that by approaching each task systematically (in theory) we could make any situation work. The challenge level was often beyond our knowledge and skills, but to counter the unpredictability, we set simple goals to at least make progress while we tried to sweat the details of solutions to the complications.

The daily Iraqi cultural immersion contrasted with the life of living at a makeshift U.S. Army base with soldiers, chow halls and Stars & Stripes newspapers. For Farah and me, it was like a cultural porthole into a new world. PX shops were small shops set up at U.S. Army bases to sell essential goods to soldiers. Torches, knives, sweets, crisps, toiletries, Gatorade, unlubricated condoms (war zone lubricant was obviously only for weapons, not deviant genitals). The store that had been established at Camp Victory, a huge but expanding base complex near the Al-Faw Palace 5km beyond Baghdad's international airport, was a giant warehouse of military kit, camouflage anything, souvenirs and home comforts. It sold an array of patriotic t-shirts with bold slogans. *Operation Iraqi Freedom. Sandstorm Survivor. Humvee. Who's your Baghdaddy? Got Sand – Sand provides 100% of your MDR of silicon and is 100% fat-free.* It was the most unusual supermarket queue we had ever stood in; soldiers with M16s, military contractors and bruisers with the shaved head meets ample beard combo, and a shopping basket. The holy grail for me in the enormous PX was a Time magazine. It felt like the antidote to vitriolic Fox news or the glitz of CNN. We could potentially see what the outside world had to say about where we were living the story. It still had a media angle, but it seemed reasonably reliable text. Propaganda-lite.

The deliciously soothing taste of a water bottle filled with a cold beer shandy helped defuse and catalogue the memories of each day into some semblance of objective reality. It became an afternoon ritual. I sunk into a quiet, reflective moment of normality staring out the bedroom window at the brown, blocky, hazy city. Sometimes such earnest reflection was confined to the traditionally male thinking-cocoon, the bathroom, as my colon would revolt against some newly acquired pathogen.

Zoo days were usually peppered with reminders of the cultural cocktail we were living through. That was expected. Several times a week Farah and I would journey across the Tigris to inspect the horses and stables, and occasionally engage in the psychological dodgeball of rental payment negotiations with the university administrators. That was routine, as was feeding the palace lions. It almost seemed like what should have been surprising was no longer surprising. To prove me wrong, there always still seemed leeway for the new-normal to be punctuated by another grinning cretin pretending to be rational.

"Why would you want to do that?" I rolled my eyes at her driver who appeared to be a young, rational human. "I just want to see what the lions will do to them. It would be quite fun to see them play with them and then tear the kittens apart" she replied sincerely but almost with the innocence of a curious grandmother. "Ja, we won't be doing that. Thanks for the offer but that seems pretty strangely cruel and unnecessary don't you think? A little fucked up?" The attractive Marine had been quite disarming with her first smile and questions when she was watching the lions being fed. And then the crazy crept out. A cat at her accommodation had birthed a litter of kittens. Someone apparently didn't grow up with a kitty to cuddle, and it seemed reasonable to assume that may have impacted her empathy development. She appeared genuinely disappointed that she would have to find another way to kill the kittens - for fun. Her driver sensibly took a step back so he could hide his grin from her as I attempted a rational discussion on perhaps not killing kittens.

At a period when there was a shortage of bed space in the Al-Rasheed a pleasantly polite but reserved, young British government official was allocated to share my room before he left on his mission; to provide direction and governance for a large slice of the southern portion of Iraq which included the city of Basra. I suspect having to share a room with a slovenly zookeeper probably felt like a letdown in the world of high diplomacy. He didn't have much experience, and wasn't much older than I was, but seemed apprehensive about trying to over-tax my brain with intellectual discussion. I naively presumed at the time such an elevated position of imposed governor would naturally be the domain of an experienced career diplomat and Arabist. It was a revelation to me that he wasn't. What could one say to that at the bedroom door as he left, other than "good luck"? It seemed better than "mate, don't get your head split open." In a world when policies seemed to be made on the fly, it was a little disconcerting to think the country may be being run even slightly like we were improvising at the zoo.

One of the occasional evenings in the Al-Rasheed bar resulted in a slightly inebriated effort to reach the hotel roof with a lively young lady contracted by the British government. In the circumstances, it seemed a suitably novel jaunt, and an opportunity to view Baghdad at night. So I thought. Curiosity had captivated me. That I was in the company of a sensationally pretty, apparently equally eager woman added to the sense of adventure. I had the seduction skills of a brick, and Lawrence had previously described my radar for flirtatious behaviour to be somewhere in the range of catastrophically hopeless. He may have had a point, yet the elevator's ascent seemed to match our excitement levels. I fleetingly considered if Farah were there instead, the anticipation of both the view and the potential exploration would be heightened. Where the elevator reached its end, a set of stairs among a lattice of air ducting presumably led to the roof. As we clambered up into the darkness "Hey whaddya doing here?" blurted out from somewhere nearby. Any lust-tinged thoughts were quickly quelled. Stone-cold sober that unexpected challenge would have likely been an alarming test of our mettle. Not that night. "Just coming to see the view," I said as our eyes quickly adjusted to the dark and the two armed young soldiers at their observation post. "No problem at all. Join us" he replied without the slightest hesitation or scepticism. Since I believed our reasoning for being up there, and my excitement at reaching the roof had temporarily distracted me from any considerations of opportunistic recreational novelties, my explanation must have appeared entirely plausible. The soldier immediately reached across to us with a pair of night-vision goggles he and his colleague were surveying the surrounds with. They seemed genuinely pleased with the extra attention and company as we all sat against the perimeter wall, taking turns at watching clear, magnified greenish imagery of trees and stray dogs across the road down on the edge of Al-Zawra

Park. It felt so utterly surreal that I worked beyond those trees. By the time we were finished, it seemed a great night to lay back on the bed alone, hang on and seal the chaotic novelty with a room-spinning nap.

It was 9 a.m. on the 7th of August when the short, deep bass, rumbling of an explosion sounded a notable distance from the zoo. It was like a condensed soundbite of a passenger jet lifting off from a runway with the characteristic loud peak and then fade of sound tailing off. There was no doubt. The slightly muted but dragging growl gave the impression it was a massive but faraway blast. The volume was compelling enough for us to momentarily stop, involuntarily cock our heads slightly, as if almost trying to judge the threat with our inner ear and muscle memory. Then we carried on as usual. News filtered through in patchy reports. The Jordanian Embassy had been bombed. It was a little further than four kilometres north-west of the zoo. The windows of Farah's family's house had been blown out; again. Their home was only a few neighbourhood blocks from the embassy. A mini-bus filled with explosives had been remotely detonated. Eleven Iraqis were killed, 57 were injured. The blast ferocity whipped, crumpled and tumbled a car from the road onto the roof of a nearby house. Body parts were reportedly strewn across the scenes of carnage. A mob of Iraqis stormed the building shortly after the blast had breached the perimeter walls and gate. Images of King Hussein and King Abdullah were smashed, allegedly in retaliation for the Jordanian ruler's decision to grant asylum to Saddam's daughters Raghad and Rana.

Days earlier Farah had driven to the zoo, and en route (about 2km from the zoo) noticed a white SUV parked in a location which to her seemed odd; on the side of the busy road where there was no shoulder for parking. It was adjacent to a fence outside the Baghdad International Fair and across the street from an International Red Crescent Hospital and a primary school. Before she had reached the zoo, the SUV had detonated.

The middle of summer, when temperatures were reaching an obscenely hot 50°C (122°F), was also a turning point. The lull in violent, explosive resistance to U.S. occupation we had experienced in the previous months seemed to slowly thaw and ferment. Aggravation had many guises. The service delivery of utilities in the city had partially collapsed when compared to the pre-invasion memories. With government department staff contingents gutted by de-Baathification, looting of buildings, theft of equipment and U.S. advisors trying to reconstruct an administration in a foreign land, the results were scrambled. Curiously, private enterprise in the city seemed to flourish while the governing authorities floundered. The electricity was often at best available for 12 hours a day, in bursts of three or four hours. It was enough to restart the fridge to save the groceries or to perhaps get the fan or air conditioner running to enable a less fitful night's sleep. The heat never relented, even in the middle of the night temperatures stayed near 40°C. The water supply was erratic. Fuel shortages dominated logistics for families with cars or generators, with the black market supplies drawing in queues of frustrated citizens. Hospitals strained in conditions worse than when they had battled under oppressive and manipulated sanctions. The apparent target of blame was the occupying American military force and its administrators. The perception of being occupied for a lifestyle worse than under Saddam stoked resentment. Society seemed to fragment increasingly into loyalists and militias of different factions, some driven by religious ideology, others by social dogma. It would lead to pro-Saddam, anti-American protests and anti-Saddam, pro-American protests. It was an opportunity for conservative clerics to gain increasing traction among receptive audiences. Explosive attacks fed a growing sense of dread. Scores could be settled against enemies real or imagined with impunity. Justice only seemed to be delivered through revenge. There were no clear enemies nor allies. Iraqi politicians like

Ahmad Chalabi, previously sentenced for banking fraud in Jordan, but a darling of the Bush administration and strong advocate of the invasion, agitated for power within the interim Iraqi Governing Council. Politicians (particularly those wealthy ones returning from decades of exile) were viewed as opportunistic, powerless American puppets by many Iraqis, and seemed to create more confusion with their rhetoric than define a clear path to stability. Quickly, the risk intensity in Baghdad felt increasingly real.

The animals had made remarkable physical recoveries over the four months through improved nutrition and necessary prophylactic measures against parasites. The gardens were developing quickly. Ayed, the gardener, was sweating away with his quiet, earnest approach. Hosepipes sprayed out fine mists of water where the creases and bends had resulted in small holes. It was a world apart from the parched facilities of April and May. Some staff began to show more aptitude for their jobs than their colleagues, and with squads allocated for morning and afternoon shifts, the cleaning of animal enclosures became increasingly effective. This though was relative to expectation given that the officially designated job titles on the newly printed municipality identity cards included observer, agricultural guide, breeding, worker, watcher, and work watcher. There was also a growing understanding by security guards about their responsibilities. Detentions of unmarried couples for holding hands in a public area suggested a need to progress to public and animal safety rather than nosy social vice monitoring. The challenge remained convincing some guards that handholding did not equate to instant sexual deviancy.

We were never quite sure who supported us and who perceived William, me or any other assisting troops as overlord occupiers or an opportunity for positive change. By association, Farah could very quickly have been judged a traitorous collaborator given the ease with which she had integrated into our approach. She had become an active, integral link between the Iraqis and us foreigners. The suspicion by some Iraqi staff and Dr Abbas of her potentially dishonest influence through a non-Iraqi network remained, given that she had initially arrived at the zoo with U.S. Special Forces. The most straightforward approach from our perspective was to engage everyone in a friendly, patient, validating, respectful way; and try to keenly observe every behavioural subtlety and group association. How did they respond to our requests? Who would regularly ask us for favours? Who worked without engagement? With Sa'ad I knew we could happily jokingly swear at each other in the Arabic filthy enough to irritate Farah, but for everyone else, nothing but polite would suffice. Observation and awareness were crucial to work out an understanding of those we could rely on, and those we needed to remain cautious around. One of the inherent cultural difficulties in this approach to interpreting Iraqi interaction was how rapidly seemingly friendly Arabic conversations erupted. There would be furious gesticulation, the rapid increase in the cycling of prayer beads between the fingers and what I would easily interpret as being pissed off. It was like watching water suddenly reach a boil in an electric kettle. When I questioned Farah about the abrupt arguments, the answer was always the same, "No, no it's all fine. They agree with each other."

Sa'ad became a particularly thought-provoking person to observe. Besides being young and friendly, we had learnt of his troubled family background and health issues, and that he responded well to being validated for his efforts. He never had formal zoo training, nor was he the hardest working individual we encountered, but he showed terrific, essential traits; keenness, a willingness to learn and an undeniable affinity for the animals. The general perception we had of the local culture was that dogs were perceived as unclean and usually only useful as guard dogs. Some people had dogs as companion animals, but it wasn't especially common. At zoos, dogs were displayed as novelty items. The arrival at Baghdad Zoo of so many dogs had been met with widespread scepticism and substantial concern by some staff and management, particularly Dr Abbas. It was a zoo mostly for exotic animals, not a stray dog shelter. The reality was that circumstances were unique, and there was a broader plan developing to deal with the pet situation. Sa'ad, Ahmed and Akram took on the responsibility for feeding the dogs, and Sa'ad, in particular, was delighted at the response from the dogs. The dogs, as expected, were excited to be fed, and once the mutual suspicion faded, they showed enormous affection towards the keepers. Sa'ad relished it. He would ask Farah if he could exercise the dogs by taking them on a leash for walks around the zoo. She encouraged it. The relationship grew. As the bond with the dogs strengthened, so did his (and several other keepers) affinity for other animals at the zoo. It was a completely unexpected evolution and the direct consequence of the temporary holding of dogs. Ali had already adopted one dog from the zoo (a German Shepherd puppy previously held with the young lions at the first palace of Uday's that Lawrence had encountered) although we had to suggest to him that locking it in the boot of his taxi for the ride home was not the ideal approach. Sa'ad was the second person at the zoo to adopt a dog, and beamed with excitement as he led it to the car for the ride home.

It was with Sa'ad and Akram that I had also decided on a little behavioural experiment with the Egyptian vultures. We didn't know the origin of the Egyptian vultures (wild or captive-reared), but either way, I was curious about instinctive behaviour. We were always on the lookout for opportunities we hoped would boost the perception that we outsiders knew what we were doing. It was partly to convince ourselves of our credibility, but we trusted that if small suggestions went to plan, it could help us influence more-significant future decisions. I had never seen Egyptian vultures before arriving in Baghdad but had seen television footage of them using their beak to break eggs against rocks. They would then gobble up the goo that ran out from the broken shell. Until then the vultures had only been fed slabs of muscle meat and some donkey organs. Sa'ad thought it was ludicrous to feed birds eggs. Birds *laid* eggs! They didn't eat them. Bears ate boiled eggs! Naturally. I arranged two fresh eggs on the gravel substrate in the large aviary and Sa'ad, Akram and I hid behind a tree to watch. Less than thirty seconds passed when the two vultures hopped and skipped across the stones to the eggs. They tilted their yellow-skin covered faces to observe the eggs before each picked up an egg in their beak and hit the objects against the stones. They immediately snapped away at the yolky slick spilling from the cracked eggs. Sa'ad swore in surprise. Akram beamed his wildly toothy grin.

I also thought it would be an excellent opportunity to try to implement some increasingly humane practices in the carnivore feeding system. Hawks and an eagle had been delivered to the zoo as rescues or gifts. There was also the resident owl. These birds were fed young chicken chicks, batches of which Ahmed purchased several times a week from the market. A strange quirk of the region seemed to be to dye the chicks a multitude of different colours. There would be a box in the office of pink chicks, yellow chicks, green chicks and blue chicks. We were quite certain any dying was probably an unpleasant process and asked Ahmed if he could rather source uncoloured chicks. "Noh noh Brandee this is the way. There are many colours. All baby chickens are coloured."

I felt I was on a losing path. The next task was to convince Ahmed to kill the chicks before they fed them to the birds. I hated to see animals suffer or die. I freely admit it was soft – in every respect, it was me trying to convince Ahmed my beliefs had merit. In some tiny, arbitrary way, I believed it was more compassionate to give the chicks a quick end. Ahmed genuinely loved birds. He did not want to kill any. "The eagle killing is the nature way" he explained. It was clear I was again heading into strange foreigner territory, but after several minutes discussion on the merits of humanely snuffing a chick and still feeding it fresh to the birds of prey, Ahmed conceded to humour me and let me try show him. I hated the idea but slipped my fingers around the chick's neck. A quick pull and twist to break the neck. The head came off in my fingers with a little squirt of blood. "Fuck" I muttered quietly. Fail. Ahmed stared at me with a touch of horror. I tried to explain a bit gentler would be better. He would "give it a try" as he left with his box of chicks. I couldn't help but feel it would be better to let the hawks and owl do the job.

Iraqi hospitality seduces one easily given how dominantly food-oriented it is. I am a sucker for that approach. It elevated camaraderie through stuffed bellies. With Ahmed, Dr Abbas, his assistant Fatima and Farah, there was regularly a chance to indulge. The style is simple and unremarkable, yet the new, striking, exotic smells and tastes of spices were intoxicating. For William and I, and the engineering soldiers temporarily based at the zoo, it was an immersion which undoubtedly enriched the memories locking into place daily. Piping hot shots of bitter tea transformed with industrial quantities of sugar fortified us in the mornings. Coffee and ground cardamom was brought to a rapid, brief simmer in a small long-handled *dallah* for mid-morning injection of thick *Gahwa*. On ordinary "special days", Farah would fetch plate-sized Tea Time burgers bloated with thick meat patties, mayonnaise, ketchup and a generous stuffing of potato chips. On special, "special days" Dr Abbas would organise with Ahmed for *Khouzi*, an impossibly tender and oily lamb shank embedded in a mountain of rice with almonds, raisins, cardamom, pine nuts, cloves and spices. At least five to ten fistfuls of glorious, flavour-soaked rice and meat would be added to William's, Deetz's or my plates during a meal until we could hardly move for fear of incurring a further top-up. Other days it would be meaty *kubba hamudh* dumplings in a tomato broth. The ultimate treat from Ahmed was the rare morning where he would arrive with thin, delicate layers of *kahi*, breakfast filo-pastry layers drenched in a sugary syrup and topped with cool, refreshing, clotted *gaymer*, buffalo cream. Most days even the staple bread, *samoon*, was a delicious doughy, pita-like rhomboid with enough attraction to keep us from opening up a nostalgic U.S. Army MRE or heading back to the CPA palace or Al-Rasheed for lunch (realistically the only KBR culinary competition was the over-sized serving of chicken Kiev the Pakistani waiters would hold for Farah and me in exchange for updated international cricket scores).

Masgouf was another Iraqi signature dish. River carp was split at the belly and butterflied into a flat disc shape before being pegged vertically with small wooden stakes around the edge of fiery coals. The meaty inner section is regularly basted as the fish grills to perfection. Farah had organised a *masgouf* lunch with Ali, the concession restaurant manager on an island within the zoo. It was an occasion when Dr Abbas could invite the recently appointed (by the now semi-autonomous Baghdad Municipality) Al-Zawra Park director whom we'd quickly nicknamed Mister *Bachir* (Tomorrow). He was an exceptionally agreeable man, and Dr Abbas appeared to promptly strike a healthy working relationship with him. Mr Bachir's inherent difficulty was ensuring delivery of any request to any sort of timeline. The answer to any probing on the start of a task, delivery of building supplies, arrival of flowers or even a meeting was always "*Bachir inshallah*" (Tomorrow, God willing). At first, it was quirky but frustrating, then infuriating, and then we conceded it was comical. A *masgouf* lunch was a way to build the relationship, and with William, we devoured three meaty fishes with the usual accompaniment of onions, radish, salads and a dessert of juicy peaches. It was times like that, in the shade of lush trees and a newly renovated restaurant, the complex of war and carnage meeting residential life and resilient culture seemed incomprehensible, surreal to the point of being entirely alien. "How on earth did we end up here?" would flick into the thoughts.

War was unfortunately always either a subtle but present shadow or a brash reminder of what was fuelling the adventure. The 19th of August was yet another day I was knocked out with dehydration and stomach troubles, and was recovering in the hotel room. The day before there had been reports of improvised explosive devices (IEDs) going off on the airport road, and across the Tigris River in the Karrada neighbourhood; both killed U.S. soldiers. Late in the afternoon, the recognisable deep rumble of a distant explosion was unmistakable. From my hotel room window, the view beyond kilometres of flat, dusty city was of a peaceful white column of smoke being gently drawn up by the lazy, rolling vortex of a horizontal ring of smoke. Reports of the carnage at the scene were quickly reported on news channels we could get headlines on through the sketchy internet link. An estimated 600kg of mixed munitions and explosives had been packed into a cement mixing truck and parked beneath the office of the United Nation's chief envoy to Iraq, Sergio Vieira de Mello. The savagely powerful detonation had wrecked the concrete compound, collapsing three floors of the building, killing 24 people and injuring at least 107. The blast tore a 3m deep and 5m wide crater in the solid ground. The roar and rumble of explosions were to become familiar punctuation of sound as the weeks wore on. The difference for us foreigners compared to Iraqi citizens was that irrespective of the targets of the bombs, it was almost always Iraqis who suffered the brunt of the vicious maimings or deaths.

The social and political context within which the zoo stabilisation was taking place seemed to mean that surreal, strange, previously inconceivable situations materialised. Perhaps it was the influence of the psychedelic painting of bricks on the perimeter walls of some of the enclosures a park contractor graced us with. Or the bizarrely enormous Mickey Mouse in a wizard outfit painted on the side of another enclosure wall. On one afternoon we got a call from Sa'ad saying that two young men had been taking drugs under one of the bridges near the lion enclosure, ended up in the water and drowned. The police arrived to remove their bodies to the morgue. That in itself was an unusually low-key affair and once the bodies were removed, the afternoon schedule carried on as per usual. On another occasion, a military unit asked us if we would like an assortment of iconic weapons and alcohol they had acquired from a palace on their arrival in Baghdad. They were concerned an internal Army inspection of their quarters would cause them undue bureaucratic nightmares, irate finger-wagging or worse if the contraband was discovered. We obliged, although we realistically had no use for Lee Enfield Rifles, a Martini-Henry from the 1800s, Sterling submachine guns, Beretta submachine guns, a Tommy Gun, ammunition, smoke grenades and a Czechoslovakian sword. There were some undeniably finely crafted specimens among the cache, but we didn't want the responsibility of being the caretakers or have formal accusations levelled at us. We swiftly passed those on to security contractors we understood could relocate or dispose of them; after we tested out the Sterling on some unsuspecting soft drink cans. I finally had favour-requesting leverage in the Green Zone with a supply of whisky and cases of beers.

At a similar time, rumours began to surface of an underground prison within the Al-Zawra Park complex. Unsurprisingly there were always rumours and conspiracy theories that made it to us. Some Iraqis mistakenly thought we were influential in the CPA. Some outsiders saw us as a useful link to Iraqis. The stories were almost all absurd yet almost all plausible in the kingdom of strange. We were regularly told how enormous caches of weapons had been disposed of in the canals by Fedayeen militia or the U.S. Army. We had heard of mass graves in the park and that Saddam was hiding in a bunker under the zoo. The underground prison rumour was taken seriously, and we were requested to assist a military unit search several of the unusual displays and recreational monuments in parts of the park for any signs of access. We never found anything despite the group assuring us the information was allegedly from a dependable source.

On one occasion a chaplain requested Farah's assistance with translation when a squad from his 40th Engineering Battalion was going on a boat patrol of the Tigris River. She had already been temporarily registered as a translator through the KBR network and had security clearance into the Green Zone. The opportunity seemed exciting, and so she agreed. It was there she met Captain Kevin Brown, an engaging and charmingly polite engineer seemingly direct from a Men's Health catalogue. Any hesitation by her to help out evaporated. He thanked her for risking her life to help. She hadn't thought of it that way! She thought she was going on a boat ride with some soldiers who may need some interpretation help. What life risk!? They handed her a bulletproof vest and helped her onto the boat. To reassure a slightly exhilarated but by then anxious Farah, he showed her the place in the boat she could duck into if things got a "little rough". He would let her know when it was safe to emerge. A simple plan. They were hardly into the patrol when they encountered a small boat on the river with two teenage boys and an older man. She called across to ask them if they had any weapons, specifically AK-47s on board. She automatically chose to ask them in accented Jordanian Arabic to mask that she was Iraqi. Whatever their load was, they claimed they were only carrying fish. That was good enough, and the patrol continued. Suddenly sounds of gunfire broke out from the river banks. The concern on the soldiers' faces was immediate, and Farah was directed to twist herself into her hiding corner. After five minutes, the flying bullets stopped as suddenly as they had started. Farah was given the all-clear to stretch out her contorted body and stiff neck. The patrol briefly continued before they headed back to shore, to the Humvees and returned Farah to the zoo for another ordinary afternoon.

It would only be a few weeks later that Farah arrived at the zoo sobbing, having received the news that a close friend of hers, acting as interpreter for an NGO group, had been shot dead by a sniper. Another energetic, educated individual cut down callously in the circumstances they had no ideological vested interest in; friends and family left behind as a statistic to mourn the heartbreaking loss. What could one possibly say to comfort a friend in such a situation? I didn't know.

The defrosted blood oozed out the flesh as the young lion sniffed lethargically at the pile of meat. His pride siblings sliced, graunched and chewed on the sinews of their deliveries of buffalo. Jaffer spent considerable time feeding, playing with and talking to his lions. Salman frequently revved up the lions with a playful paw slap as they lazily rested their agile, claw-filled mittens through the bars of the cool inner holding enclosures. The keepers developed a sense of their lions' moods. Outside was too hot to be an appealing lounging area for the animals, however, despite the expected sluggishness of the lions under normal conditions, it appeared several of the lions were eating less than usual. It began to reflect in their physical condition, enough that Jaffer had called Farah and me aside to express his concern. He didn't feel Dr Abbas was as actively concerned as he was. In Dr Hussam's absence, Farah had been temporarily appointed as the assistant director of the zoo and remained so after his unexpected return. She was energetic, direct and compassionate. We were increasingly finding sanity in each other's method of organising to deal with challenges. The keepers who cared respected her and believed she could assist and influence Dr Abbas positively. Initially, the only apparent signs in the lions were simply those that ate less were contracting slightly to a bonier physique. Dr Abbas and Dr Hussam were aware of the gradual decline but perceived the weakening state to be an exclusively nutritional concern. It was said to be the fault of those cursed packages of donated foreign buffalo muscle meat. They were adamant.

Dr Hussam increased his already liberal dustings of vitamin powder onto the meat, and Dr Abbas ordered additional supplements of donkey meat and organs. The apparently healthier lions continued to eat whatever meat was provided. Those that had alerted Jaffer and Salman's concerns continued to appear fatigued, and the skin started to wrinkle like the covering of a new-born puppy on a dwindling frame. Days passed. As constipation set in, the forced abdominal contractions to squeeze out anything increased. Loss of neuromuscular coordination followed. The sixteen-month-old lion walked like it was stoned and unable to work its bubble-gum feet. Over days we were watching a distinct, disturbing decline for which we had no answer. It seemed the vitamin powder was as likely to reverse the symptoms as hitting a nail in the head to release an evil spirit. As a speculative concession to our clear concerns, a cortisone injection was administered along with an oral antibiotic. We had no means of diagnosis beyond the visual and no veterinary laboratory in the city, even if we could extract a blood sample. Even if the lion could survive an anaesthetic for a detailed examination, we still didn't have anybody with us that would know what to look for. More vitamin powder!

William and Lieutenant Colonel Lozada had raised the veterinary profile of the zoo among the U.S. Army and in weeks before the lions' decline there had been growing interest from several veterinarians from the Coalition Joint Task Force 7. Beyond initial visits from veterinarians Colonel Mark Gants and Lieutenant Colonel Frank Miskena, they had introduced the eager young veterinary technician, Specialist Erin McLoughlin to the Baghdad Zoo. The higher-ranking officers were shouldering multiple responsibilities in the city, particularly in the public health sector, and Erin was tasked to assist the zoo and provide a conduit should additional assistance be required. William, Farah, Erin and I had been attempting to engage Dr Abbas and Dr Hussam in facilitating a broader discussion on our lion concerns with the U.S. Army veterinarians, but it appeared the severity of the case was touching on nerve endings. The more emphasis we attempted to place on trying to create a collaborative investigative process into the lion health, the more obstinate the resistance was. We didn't understand why that was the case. Perhaps it was pride, perhaps our doggedness, but we relented to keep the semblance of peaceful cooperation.

Jaffer stared with simmering rage. Nobody had helped his lion. It lay dead and stiff on the floor. Bloody discharge from its nose smudged on the concrete. Black, sludgy diarrhoea had pooled around the base of the lion's tail. It was the first opportunity we had to cut open a lion to try to understand what had transpired inside the animal. Dr Abbas reluctantly agreed, and hours later the Army veterinarians Lozada and Miskena arrived to perform and demonstrate a necropsy. Coagulating haemorrhage pooled among the viscera, and slim worms twisted in the intestines. Fluid accumulated in the air spaces of the lungs. None of these observations indicated a definite cause of death.

There were still lions showing symptoms to concern us and it seemed plausible to Farah, William, Erin and me that there was a viral outbreak. I suggested securing the lion building as a quarantined area with rigorous disinfection of walls, floors, equipment, clothes and shoes. It was a token gesture, but it seemed logical that if there was a mysterious illness in the zoo, it would be best confined until we could identify and eliminate it. Dr Abbas and Dr Hussam ignored the suggestion. Lions had never been ill at the zoo before the foreigner invasion, and the precise cause of the lion's death was a nutritional deficiency! The accusation wasn't subtle. We had stopped the donkeys being killed and forced in a supply of packaged meat because that was donated. Of course, there was merit in the nutrition accusation, but it didn't explain the deaths. More vitamin powder!

It became increasingly apparent that the battle to remedy the lion dilemma had distilled down to a stubborn force of vastly different realities and the toxic ingredient of wounded pride. Dr Abbas and Dr Hussam had been isolated from modern veterinary practices for more than a decade, and entirely disconnected from international zoological medicine. A suggestion or emergency which only served to highlight and reinforce that reality was dismissed with disdain. There would be no concession. More vitamin powder! My frustration smouldered at the infuriatingly illogical approach by the zoo director. Farah tried to maintain thoughtful discussions with Dr Abbas, but in the circumstances, she was a woman and young and aligned with the Americans. Suddenly the emotional reaction to the emergency was for all of us to retreat to underlying suspicions and prejudices. The lions continued to display the by-now-familiar symptoms. While Jaffer and Salman walked through the bath of disinfectant at the lion building entrance, Dr Hussam refused.

Between William, Farah and I, we had discussed the potential viruses we thought may be responsible for the lions' condition. Canine Distemper. Rabies. It was a quick discussion. That was all we could think of. Erin's online research had resulted in her finding research literature documenting the deaths of lions during Canine Distemper outbreaks in the Serengeti National Park in Tanzania. Descriptions of many of the symptoms resonated with what we had seen in the zoo. It was worth considering. The zoo was resident to known potential carriers of the virus, stray domestic dogs and roaming mongooses. Erin printed out copies for the veterinarians. The response from Dr Abbas stumped us.

"Impossible. Canine means this is a disease of the dogs!"

Erin and Colonel Gants had facilitated contact with both Cornell University in New York and the Smithsonian's National Zoo in Washington D.C. to seek advice and blood sample processing. Both establishments were keen to assist, and again discussions distilled down to the likelihood of Canine Distemper as the problem at hand. Gants navigated the wounded pride, and Dr Abbas conceded to allow blood samples to be taken. Later in the afternoon, assisted by Jaffer and Majed, he set about the grim task of bleeding the ill lions. Jaffer grabbed the young lion's tail through the bars and dragged the unwilling, enraged, but weakened animal to the edge of the cage. Its ears creased flat as it hissed and snarled with defiance. As Jaffer and Majed gripped tightly onto the tail, Dr Abbas attempted to draw blood from a reluctant vein. The stressed lion squirted and dribbled tar-like diarrhoea as the blood drained through the needle into the test tube.

A week passed. More vitamin powder, donkey meat and "we treating for parasite!" I had no additional possible answers. It seemed inevitable more lions would die. Dr Hussam, still smartly dressed and a busy presence around the zoo, viewed our irrational foreign interference with increasing belligerence. It appeared to reflect a growing discontent with attempted foreigner domination around the city.

Dr Abbas introduced us to the stocky, moustache-free, quietly spoken Dr Waseem, a young vet appointed to the Baghdad Zoo by the municipality. Only a few years older than Farah and I, he was a cultural mix of mostly Kurdish and Arab background and had studied his degree partly in the northern Iraqi city, Mosul. He was reserved by nature, and we heard his mother was working at the mayor's office. We had become so frustrated at the "jobs for mates" approach, which seemed to usually involve arbitrary appointments of incompetent people to jobs they were unsuited for. There were already enough inexperienced veterinary staff at the zoo, and Waseem spoke little English and had limited veterinary experience. We had almost no zoological veterinary skills to teach him and felt given the lion concerns, the municipality could have at least appointed an experienced vet. Yet Waseem was polite, friendly and we reckoned that if he showed interest, the U.S. Army veterinarians would be willing to train him as they had been doing with Farah.

In our jaded state, we had misjudged Waseem's

work ethic and capacity to contribute. We could not have been more wrong! He was never demonstrative, and worked quietly and tirelessly, avoiding any of the political baggage which simmered in the wake of the first lion death. He immediately recognised our concerns at the haphazard approach to donkey slaughtering. He set about ensuring it was carried out as humanely as possible and that the area remained suitably clean of blood and excrement. He had noticed our frustration with Dr Hussam and Dr Abbas on the nutritional discussions. He was a new neutral party and immediately requested to take responsibility for the lions' feeding. He would ensure they received extra bone and mineral-rich organ meat in addition to buffalo meat. "Brendan, don't worry" he would say in his heavily accented English every time I voiced concern. "Leave it to me."

19th September. The phone ringing woke me up. It was William. "The tiger's dead. Shot. And another lion is dead!"

"Fuckin' hell," I muttered. My trip to Babylon, scheduled with the South African security contractors, was off. I ran to the lift, through the lobby, to the car and drove to the zoo as fast as I could.

"Why did you do this?" was the outburst to William from the Iraqi Facility Protection Service (FPS) guard at the zoo's front gate. William was confused by the greeting. Early mornings at the zoo, before staff arrived, almost always felt tranquil and soothing. The trees, canals and birds seemed to temporarily hold back the inevitable crescendo of Baghdad energy, noise, politics, traffic, threats, progress and thrill. It was not one of those mornings. "Why did you do this? Why kill the animal?"

William, still bemused, persuaded the guard to lead him to the dead animal. As they approached the tiger cage, William felt a creeping dread. A trail of dried blood drips led to a smear on a nearby concrete bench. Malooh lay motionless on his side, stiff and dead on his caged lawn. Glazed eyes stared, devoid of menace. The imposing, captivating star of the zoo was dead meat in a richly coloured cloak. Dead like one of Kadhim's donkeys. Malooh embodied the galvanising fight, strength, and a reason to keep improving the zoo. It had always been disheartening to see such a vivid animal in such an inappropriately bleak, Victorian, barred enclosure. His sheer presence had made it impossible to ever pass him without stopping to acknowledge him. It always felt like a guilty apology was the only consolation to offer until his situation could be improved. Too late.

Members of the 422nd Civil Affairs battalion had been hosting a morale-boosting birthday party at the central island café area the previous evening. Something had spun desperately out of control. It wasn't the first time groups had held similar events in the evening, and in all cases, they had been approved by the zoo administration. The guards at the zoo maintained a presence throughout the evening, as usual. That soldiers had been drunk was open to speculation and, of course, allegations.

The trail of blood led from the bench to an open maintenance gate at the side of the enclosure adjacent to the holding building. Drips of blood led along the channel between the outer perimeter of bars and the draconian inner layer of barring built to ensure it was impossible to reach the tiger from the public viewing area. From the dust, patterns wiped off the bars, and the blood remains it was easy to see where the culprits had pushed along the shrubbery between the sets of bars to a point where all that remained was blood smeared bars, a patch of dry blood and a bullet casing. Even then, the outcome seemed so implausible. The gap between the inner barring was so narrow, the only way to reach the tiger was to turn the hand vertically and slide the fingers between the rebar. There was no physical way the tiger could extend any of its limbs between the bars. The reports from security guards suggested up to four soldiers had left the island and walked towards the tiger area. Two shots were heard fired. A second blood smear at chest height suggested more than one person had been in the channel. There was another bullet casing. The first was from a standard-issue 9mm weapon. The second casing was from a .32 Smith & Wesson revolver. The angles suggested the revolver shot was the fatal blow. After phoning Dr Abbas, Farah and me, William quickly made enquiries through his network. A soldier was in the Combat Support Hospital near the CPA palace, admitted the previous evening after being mauled by a tiger. There couldn't have been many of those.

We arrived to a state of anger and disbelief. The toxic talk about the U.S. Army flowed. First, the lions were dying, and now the tiger had been shot. William was firmly wedged between being a man in U.S. Army uniform and a man devoted to helping the zoo. The fragile trust we had repaired after the "Hilde lion-relocation saga" was creaking. We stared at the tiger corpse in the centre of the cage as William filled us in on what he knew. Dr Abbas and Farah questioned the guards and zoo staff in Arabic to try piece together a coherent story. After the two shots were heard fired the visitors immediately started leaving.

We needed that bullet to confirm which weapon killed the tiger. It was a curiously uncomfortable sensation to run our hands over the tiger's smooth fur searching for a bullet hole. It felt privileged and dismal. William, Farah and I rolled the animal over. A small bullet entry point had split a black stripe on the right side of the chest near the shoulder. There was no exit wound. The Leatherman sliced through the fur and flesh as flies immediately swept in to taste the bloody moisture. More cutting. Farah peeled back a portion of the chest, and the sloppy, gelatinous coagulating blood wobbled and poured out of the cavity. We fingered the bullet hole and traced the path to find the shiny, coppery slug in the meaty, bloody soup. Malooh had bled to death internally. We muttered and swore at the indignity of it. Our collective rage was impossible to contain as we stood there with bloodied hands staring at the split open tiger. William had spoken to Erin on the phone. She was on the warpath to find the responsible Sergeant Mitchell at the hospital. Dr

Abbas seethed as he ordered his staff to bury the tiger under the lawns adjacent to the enclosure. More outraged workers arrived. "Why? Why? Why Amricans do this? Why Amrica killing the zoo?"

We entered the lion enclosure. Another young lion lay dead on the floor as bloody discharge oozed from its nose onto the tiles. It wasn't one that had appeared outwardly unhealthy. It had choked while eating its donkey meat, struggled to dislodge the stuck meat, started turning and stumbling, and dribbled tarry diarrhoea before collapsing and dying. We made the call to the Army veterinarians requesting necropsy assistance.

William and I sat on the chest freezer in the office contemplatively sipping our Pepsis. Farah fidgeted at the desk. We were pissed off and simmering. The emotional jolt of the incident, the injustice for the tiger and our attempts to understand what responsibility we bore for the episode and in trying to mediate the fallout, had us stewing in our anger. There was a pulsing heat radiating from us after our exertion in the high temperatures. We stared blankly for a moment. The sensation of the cold liquid and fizzing bubbles down the throat was briefly, compellingly distracting and soothing. Briefly. I was seething. William's phone rang. Did we "inspect the tiger's digestive tract for barbequed food or human remains"? Of course not. Information emerging was that soldiers had attempted to feed the tiger a kebab, at which point the tiger bit the fingers and with dramatic force wrenched the soldier's arm through the narrow gap between the bars, de-gloving and shredding a part of his broken arm. Someone, perhaps Mitchell, had fired a weapon in panicked response as his colleague fired another round into the body of the tiger. We needed to search deeper into the tiger.

It hadn't been ten minutes since we had left the tiger enclosure and I was digging with a staff member to exhume it. A few tossed shovel loads revealed the pink, glossy side of the partly skinned tiger. "What the fuck?"

"Kadhim!" blurted out the labourer to deflect any guilt when he saw my brooding expression. Farah unleashed a livid torrent of questions. When we left to inspect the lions, Kadhim had tried to skin the tiger, and halfway through either feared the wrath of Dr Abbas or grew tired, but either way, he had mumbled to the staff to keep burying the animal. We cut deeper into the body and digestive tract. No kebabs. No human fingers. Whatever had transpired to leave a dead tiger and a mauled soldier it was simple, the only way for the tiger to have made contact with a human hand was if the hand was slipped between the bars. Revised recollections of the incident later emerged that suggested the tiger had reached out from its enclosure and with a swiping of a claw-fringed paw, grasped the unwitting soldier's arm and wrenched it between the bars. The configuration of the protective bars meant this version of events was physically impossible.

To our minds, there was only one way the matter could be resolved for the Iraqi staff and Dr Abbas since it seemed unfeasible that the tiger could be replaced. We believed the U.S. Army commander responsible for the soldiers involved needed to defuse the immediate hostility and tension by offering a formal, publicised apology. To soothe the political fallout around the perception of American impunity and malicious intent, there needed to be a conciliatory offer to assist in some tangible way with the construction of newly planned zoo facilities. There was a need for a new lion enclosure for the nine palace lions, discussions in play regarding a new bear enclosure, and intentions to develop an educational facility. Although all the Army officers associated directly with the zoo, but not the tiger killing incident, expressed their sympathies to Dr Abbas, the 422nd Civil Affairs refused to engage us. That decision to deliberately refuse us access to a ranking officer so we could mediate a solution for the pissed-off zoo staff infuriated Farah and me. In the context of "winning hearts and minds," it seemed a foolish approach by the hierarchy. William attempted to use his military influence to facilitate discussion between the appropriate officials. There was no concession by the 422nd Civil Affairs to consider the circumstances from the perspective of the zoo's Iraqi management. The closing of ranks around the event reinforced the simmering rumours that killing the tiger was intentional malice. It would take many months before a formal U.S. Army apology was issued; by a General who recognised the value of such a simple gesture but whose only link to the evening incident was that he also served in the U.S. Army.

By the following day, the international media headlines were carrying the emotive story of the drunk U.S. soldier shooting the rare tiger. Subsequent investigations concluded that soldiers had consumed beer, a violation of General Order No.1, for which Mitchell was temporarily demoted. The limited evidence did not suggest enough alcohol was consumed to consider any of the soldiers' situational awareness to be impaired. They weren't drunk. They couldn't use that excuse. It was most likely a momentary surge of bravado, naivety, or stupidity that unleashed bitter consequences. Sergeant Mitchell and his colleague were briefly, unintentionally, infamous as poster boys for U.S. Army abuses towards Iraqis and their assets. For Mitchell, he would carry with him the visible scars of those unfortunately reckless, terrifying few seconds in the form of a mangled, unusable arm. In subsequent years he reportedly endured 24 reconstructive surgeries in attempts to restore the functionality of the mauled limb. Deterioration in his health led to his death in 2007.

Lieutenant Colonel Miskena arrived with another veterinary colleague to conduct the lion necropsy. The animal had considerably better body condition than the previous lion that died. The vets speculated that it was possibly unrelated to the first death. Perhaps it was a bacterial infection. What fun. A potentially new confounding variable. We needed blood sample results to return from Cornell. We needed to get clarity beyond the speculation. As a precaution, it was recommended the lions be separated from one another and antibiotics administered to all the lions in case of bacterial infection.

Days later as Farah and I conducted the routine morning rounds of the zoo, we noticed two lions lying in Malooh's former enclosure. We were baffled. There had been no talk of bringing new lions to the zoo, and they definitely weren't lions from the palace. Given the outbreak concerns at the zoo and the two deaths, it seemed the worst possible time to be adding lions. The last outcome we wanted was more infected animals or spreading whatever was causing the deaths. We found Dr Hussam to ask if he knew the circumstances or background to the lions. Of course he did. He, with keepers and a transport cage, had moved them the previous afternoon from the lion area we had been trying to isolate and quarantine. "They are healthy" he proclaimed.

It seemed a typical morning at the zoo. I'd arrived early, boiled up tea on the gas stove and settled down to the laptop to plan out required logistics. It was unusual for Farah to arrive later than about 9 a.m., but when she occasionally did, we had always assumed there was no cause for alarm. Likely a hairdressing appointment. On this occasion, 10 a.m. had passed before she phoned. She had bought her standard breakfast en route to work, a Pepsi, a Crunch chocolate and cigarettes. As she neared a congested intersection close to the park entrance, she realised traffic access was being blocked and diverted by police. She had already passed a white SUV with police cars parked around it, but with no obvious explanation to indicate otherwise, had carried on as usual. The diversion was frustrating, but it was Baghdad, and there were frequently ad hoc diversions. She knew if she continued along her new route on Damascus Street the road would feed towards another Green Zone checkpoint. The distance wasn't particularly far, and although traffic was jammed, we knew to expect her shortly. We waited. She did not arrive. The phone rang again. The traffic was grindingly slow. Her concern was spiking. Closer proximity to the Green Zone quickly felt like it was carrying a higher risk of a random attack. The anticipation of the unexpected needed to be blocked out. Over an hour had passed, and I had become progressively concerned as she sounded increasingly stressed out. It was easy to anticipate gut-gnawing consequences; a random abduction, or charred and bloody smears of remains from a blast. We had seen images and heard stories that fuelled the imagination, but we had also made a habit of talking ourselves through such thoughts. I had phoned William, and we discussed potential options for finding Farah and extracting her if we felt it was desperately required. He didn't waste time and arrived quickly at the zoo through back routes and military access gates of the Green Zone. Our options to navigate our way to Farah were restricted because William would need to justify to his commanders the need for such a potentially risky response for a zoo staff member. Justifications would have to consider the liability and consequences, including the threat to life. Could we call on a private security option we had phone numbers for? How would we navigate through the stuck traffic to her? He was trying to find out through the Army network what was actually happening, and which checkpoints were still open. We decided to wait. We had little option but to blindly trust circumstance, and that Farah's savvy would guide her to a more secure, reachable position. As she neared her intended checkpoint, U.S. soldiers had blocked the road ahead where a suicide bomber had detonated himself at a pension pay point outside an Iraqi military facility. The location was later reported as a site of the fleshy, mangled slaughter. Panicked people had been running along the pavement past the traffic to get out of the danger area. Some drivers, not knowing what was happening, had abandoned their vehicles in fear. Farah phoned again, crying, panicked. The traffic had been diverted again. Would another attack hit? It was a case of blindly believing it would or wouldn't. You have no data to know one way or the other. I tried to calm Farah down, knowing that sitting in the zoo office there was almost nothing William or I could realistically do given the gridlocked traffic. Her fear and helplessness overshadowed any hollow words we could try to convince her with. We paced the office. Sat down. Stood up. Made phone calls. Paced. Waited. Hours had passed since her first call of the morning.

We tried to phone her back. No answer. That wasn't a good sign in the circumstances. We tried again. She had stopped crying, but the fear in her strained voice was unmistakable. "I'm driving right next to an American tank towards Assassins Gate." Two brothers in a car next to her saw the state she was in and had wound down their window to ask if she was OK. Clearly she wasn't, but she was hesitant to tell them she was heading to the Green Zone with a valid identification card to enter. She feared who they may be. She was frightened enough though that she took the risk and told them anyway. By a stroke of good fortune, they were heading to the same checkpoint. One of the brothers climbed out of their car and sat in the passenger seat of Farah's to talk and calm her down. They had seen a tank ahead grinding along in the direction of the checkpoint and quickly worked their cars up to it. Usually a dangerous-to-fatal move on open roads, in the traffic jam they judged it was the one way for protection. We stayed on the phone line. It was finally at that point we assumed she would be safe and we could settle. Assassins Gate was an especially choked checkpoint at the best of times, but Farah and her chaperone vehicle navigated into the official, express queue. Two Iraqi cars in that queue usually channelling CPA or military vehicles could arouse suspicion, but it was a chance to show identification and explain the panicked scenes and chivalry of the two brothers. She calmed her nerves as she sped through the Green Zone streets to the zoo.

The randomness with which one encountered risk was highlighted again by Farah on a quick car ride into Karrada, the busy neighbourhood across the Tigris River from the Green Zone. We drove through it regularly in her car or with Ali, without incident. Traffic there was always busy, and frustrating gridlocks developed quickly. Pedestrians would be sweating profusely in the heat as they shuffled quickly between the cars to cross the road. Sitting stationary in traffic was a period that sent the nerves into a jitter, particularly in light of the recent bombings. Adding a convoy of Humvees or Armoured Personnel Carriers (easy targets for attacks by militias) to the traffic jam only served to increase the anal sphincter pucker factor. On this occasion, Farah found herself in stuck traffic, between the pavement and a Humvee. Every driver seemed to be looking around, waiting for something to go wrong. A policeman casually walked along the pavement to chat with a group of gathered civilians and policemen who gesticulated and argued about the danger-merits of a cardboard box near the gutter. They were close enough for Farah to understand the habitually vigorous discussion. Some said it would be best to leave the suspiciously placed box alone. Others argued there was no way it could be a bomb at that time of day, a seemingly arbitrary piece of evidence given the potential risk. Not satisfied with the progress of the discussion the policeman that had walked over with certainty, stated it wasn't a bomb and kicked the box into the air. As he launched it, the box erupted with an explosive bang loud enough to shock Farah with fright, but fortunately only with enough force that the stunned policeman stood amongst the drifting leftovers of box pieces. It was the incentive needed to create enough panic to dislodge the traffic jam and have cars, Farah's included, jousting and wheeling away at high speed.

The evolving security situation in the city heightened the emphasis on securing the Green Zone against potential attack. When Al-Zawra Park had initially been excised from the Green Zone to allow public access, William and I had been provided with a key by army engineers which allowed us to enter a locked rear gate in the perimeter fence between the park and the crossed swords parade ground.

Tightening security measures meant it was becoming increasingly logistically complicated for William to gain permission to visit the zoo since he was leaving the Green Zone each time he crossed that boundary and entered the park. In another new development, a series of enormous, interlocking concrete blast walls were laid overnight along the centre of the 14th July Street between the Al-Rasheed Hotel and Al-Zawra Park. It cut off my access route and required exiting at a newly established checkpoint near the crossed swords. At the entrance checkpoints, it had become standard practice for vehicles with the appropriate accreditation and vetted personnel with identification to be allowed through a fast transit lane. Depending on familiarity with soldiers, or their temperament during what was a hot, onerous, tedious and potentially risky job, one's access could be smooth or exasperating. Shortly after the establishment of the checkpoint the usually cordial troops, always excited to see the meat cargo of "lion guy" or "zoo girl" were changed. One rotation of African American soldiers had been hilarious to talk too, especially after they found out I was South African. The cultural novelty was clearly mutual. "No shit! A white guy. South African. No dawg! Hey y'all check it out, the lion guy is fuckin' South African and white! That's crazy shit. Where's that smokin' zoo girl at? Donkey heads! No shit man!"

    A new rotation of soldiers changed that game in an afternoon as I returned to feed the palace lions. No quicker transit lane for the big black SUV with the KBR accreditation. "But I feed the lions, you know the ones. I'm from the zoo. I come through here every day. I've done it for months."

"I don't give a shit who the fuck you are. Back of the queue. One queue. Go!" the sour soldier barked. The queue was at least 30 old Iraqi vehicles long, each vehicle waiting to be subjected to a thorough inspection for weapons and explosives. A black SUV couldn't have been more conspicuous, and my one guilty luxury was another representation of foreign occupation; especially after it could have easily been perceived I was arrogantly trying to cut to the front of the queue. That is exactly what I was doing. It was one of the few times I genuinely regretted driving that beautifully air-conditioned meat wagon as I grumpily drove to my naughty corner.

As I sat in the queue with my gun on my lap in case anyone decided to exit their vehicle and opportunistically vent "Bush donkey, Saddam good!" retribution on me, I had time to think about the absurdity of the situation. I hoped that if any sociopathic driver with munitions decided to detonate their car, it would either be far away enough to not maim me or that it took me out instantly. To exit the queue and navigate through suburbs and traffic to another checkpoint would also mean encountering potential threats. So it was a case of sitting and waiting, rolling forward, waiting, rolling forward. I wondered what local drivers thought while they waited to be subjected to the suspicion, inconvenience and risk by grumpy young invaders. Was there festering contempt (the constant electricity blackouts, water shortages, heat, fuel queues and obscene traffic were enough to enrage most people) or were they still delighted that Saddam's reign was being dismembered? Many of those entering the checkpoint would be doing so either to work or to meet a family member living in the excluded area. I stewed in the thought that despite being so generally risk-averse and trying to help, I was sitting in a situation enforced by bloody-minded, officious troops. After finally making it between the barriers for a thorough examination of my dismembered donkey bits, I thanked the soldiers for my period of meditative contemplation.

Shortly afterwards that checkpoint option was taken out my hands anyway. A Major in the 1st AD responsible for overseeing Al-Zawra Park security heard about my and William's park back gate keys. They were confiscated. It was a risk to the Green Zone perimeter for which he did not want the liability. We must use access routes and checkpoints like everybody else! "Actually while we are talking about it, what are the lions still doing at the palace? They need to be moved to the zoo!" he commanded as the sweat seeped alarmingly from his forehead and cheeks, dripping to his body armour. Attempts at a renegotiation on the keys were ignored. Our explanations responding to the ratcheting up of pressure to move the lions also fell on deaf ears despite the evident lack of suitable enclosures for them at the zoo. The new directive would mean exiting the Green Zone at a checkpoint on the same road as the palace lions and then driving briefly along suburb roads to the zoo. Although it frustratingly increased my daily travel risk as a single, unguarded SUV driving near the Green Zone perimeter, for William, it became a significant logistical headache. His back gate park access had also been revoked. It meant he would require a formal convoy escort to travel the suburban route and visit the zoo. He could no longer visit the zoo on a whim. It would require the availability of additional vehicles and armed soldiers for support.

It was early morning, almost time to get out of bed. Duf! Pause. Duf! It sounded like the short, dull thud of a sledgehammer on a concrete wall. Duf! It was an odd sound for the usually quiet early morning. I left the bed and looked out the window from behind the potential protection of the bedroom wall. It seemed a strange time for maintenance. "Is that what an attack sounds like?" I thought. I opened the bedroom door slightly ajar and peered into the hallway. A few other people were doing the same down the length of the corridor. It all appeared still. Nepalese former British Army Ghurkhas had been contracted as private security by the coalition authorities and assigned as protection to each hotel floor. On the 7th floor, the Ghurkha shrugged his shoulders. There was no report of a threat. He calmly suggested those of us enquiring should go back into our rooms and remain there until there was a situation report. "Fair enough." Minutes later, the rushed knocking on the doors started. "Evacuate! Immediately!" Backpack. Laptop. Passport. Gun.

Ammunition. Keys. For an inexplicable reason, I put shoes on without socks, thinking it was a waste of time. Down the seven floors of the stairwell and into the increasingly crowded hotel lobby. I removed the envelope of remaining zoo money from the safety deposit box into the laptop bag. Nobody seemed to have a clear idea of what had happened nor seemed to be overly concerned. Rumours were there had been a rocket attack. We were evacuated across the road to the convention centre until a makeshift risk assessment could be conducted. I had what I needed for the day and headed to the park for an early morning start. We were still in the middle of the possible viral outbreak at the zoo and tensions remained high. We needed to find a way through and were hoping for fewer distractions than the situation kept firing at us.

Later in the day, William showed me photographs of the located launcher, still pointing at the Al-Rasheed from a neighbourhood street below. A crudely improvised welded frame held eight pipes, four still holding small 85mm rockets. A series of wires linked the launcher to motorcycle batteries and a box with firing switches. With minimal damage and no casualties resulting from the attack, the hotel was reopened to carry on as before. It was a period of sharp increase in violence in the city. In a matter of weeks, car bombs were detonated at the UN headquarters (again), in Rasafa neighbourhood, at the Baghdad Hotel and the Turkish Embassy. A Spanish intelligence officer was killed. A bomb detonated at the Al-Aike Hotel killing a hotel clerk and mortars were fired into the Green Zone. Smaller, notable incidences became commonplace. A protest. A small riot. A shooting. There was increasing talk of violence possibly spiralling into insurrection in the southern towns of Karbala and Najaf, and northern towns like Tikrit or Mosul.

The morning following the Al-Rasheed attack, keepers on the first cleaning shift reported urgently to Dr Abbas that the brown bear had collapsed. Not Blind bear, not Wounded-Ass, not Luna Park bear; the other one. The big one that had allegedly killed looters. It had been on antibiotics for 48 hours for a shoulder wound. Small amounts of bloody froth oozed from its nose as it salivated dramatically. It was a caged area 200m from the lions. The bear looked as close to death as a living bear could be. The keepers had splashed some water on it to see if it would move. It lay immobile except for its slight, laboured breathing. We would ordinarily be too fearful of entering its enclosure yet there it lay, pitiful and helpless. The consensus was that it would likely die but that if blood samples could be drawn, that would be our only option to try to understand if there was any link with the lion situation. If it was distemper, how was the contagious virus spreading, what animals were already infected and how would the risk be managed to avoid it killing the nearby wolf, confined domestic dogs and the rest of the bears? We didn't have appropriate vaccines immediately available in the country. Would Dr Abbas be prepared to accept that there needed to be stricter controls in place for animal and contaminant movements? We needed to understand how the bear had encountered a carrier?

Dr Abbas and Waseem tried to raise a vein to draw blood, but in the bear's dehydrated and collapsed state it was nearly impossible to find a visible target. Despite the manipulations the bear continued to lay involuntarily immobile, unable to draw out the slightest instinct or energy to fight. It lay spread-eagled on its back as frothy white spit drained along its lip onto the floor tiles. Erin had arrived at the zoo with Lieutenant Lynge, a professional paramedic in William's unit. As a last resort, Dr Abbas agreed to let them try to bleed the bear. Adjustments of the Velcro tourniquet, attempts on limb-after-limb and multiple needle-stick locations was finally rewarded as the blood leaked slowly into the syringe. The bear was dead within half an hour. Dr Abbas, concerned that there may be a link to the lions' deaths, and at the risk of further contamination of the area, decided the bear would not be necropsied, but buried deeply to avoid stray dogs digging it up.

The following week the rescued pony collapsed and died. Although the consensus between Dr Abbas and the vets he consulted was that it was age-related, we openly wondered what would be next to die. It was another young lion. The same day. "Bloody hell!" Farah and Waseem necropsied the lioness. Jaffer, noticeably emotionally wounded, refused to watch. It was one of his favourite young lions that had been transferred by Lawrence from one of Uday's palaces in April. Despite Waseem's careful oversight of the feeding, it had grown increasingly emaciated, struggling for weeks with vomiting and then diarrhoea while most of the remaining lions appeared to maintain weight and activity levels. Internal haemorrhaging left another soupy mess among the organs. Despite the improvements, the surge of deaths was maddeningly frustrating and seemed beyond our control with the limited access to veterinary resources, both in equipment and appropriate knowledge of a diversity of exotic animals. "Hello! I am Salman. Lion, Tigers, Beers. Thirrrty two yirrss. Good! Very good!" Salman pronounced as he looked on with concern before going back to tend his lions.

It was a bittersweet relief when Erin arrived with the blood test results from Cornell. Finally. Canine Distemper! There was relief in the indisputable answer. Dr Hussam immediately objected. The results were wrong. Dr Abbas grudgingly accepted there might be merit in the results but remained adamant it was the lack of donkey meat in the diet that made the lions susceptible to infection. We could work with that. We had to. He would manage suggested actions. We could realistically only manage the symptoms and restrict potential contaminants. There was no response to develop a comprehensive battle plan. It felt ominously likely more animals would die. It was only a case of which ones. We had been in brief email contact with Dr Suzan Murray at Smithsonian National Zoo, Dr David Jones at the North Carolina Zoo and Nick Lindsay at Whipsnade Zoo, all of whom had issued advice for our challenging situation. We agreed on some simple, indisputable measures. There would be no animal movements from one enclosure to another within the zoo. Additional disinfection would be implemented for shoes, food buckets, water bowls, tools and compound holding areas. Waseem would continue to manage diets. Dr Hussam could continue to bestow his vitamin powder onto meals. Stray dogs roaming the zoo would need to be managed as a precaution. Dogs in the zoo grounds or on the periphery that Farah had become emotionally attached too (particularly those with puppies) would be vaccinated (we had recently received vaccines for domestic dogs through Farah's contacts in Jordan). When feasible they would be removed to isolated enclosure areas to be monitored for symptoms, and if clear, attempts would start to find them welcoming homes. That was in addition to the already quickly vaccinated 26 dogs being cared for in enclosures. The strays considered too feral to be handled safely were to be darted with an immobilising drug and euthanised. We recognised that other stray animals from the broader park area might fill the territorial void and so meat and bone food remains cleaned out of enclosures were to be burnt or removed from the zoo to minimise the temptation. We weren't in a position to manage the sporadic roving mongooses we believed could be another potential carrier of the virus.

To our growing relief, the deaths stopped. The combined effort of the staff had mobilised a response. Maybe we got lucky, but we wanted to believe the actions translating into results was obvious. Dr Abbas's confidence and engagement through the brilliant lamb dishes re-emerged.

CHAPTER 12

Saieda, the blind brown bear, was an ongoing source of concern. Although she was mobile when food was on offer and eating well, there was no release for her from the interminable boredom. She had no access to an outside area and wasn't the spunkiest soul after enduring 28 years of confinement and three sets of bombing in less than 12 years. There had been discussions about removing her to the similarly configured room in which the older bear had recently died. The difference was that enclosure linked to an outdoor swimming pool. Dr Abbas was concerned that her visual impairment and old age might somehow conspire to result in the old shaggy lady drowning. No move. The energetic dog temporarily occupying that housing could stay. Most of Saieda's day was spent either asleep or lying down listlessly and slowly, repetitively clawing at a growth on her chest.

Coincidentally, a veterinarian from an international animal welfare charity arrived at the zoo with a documentary film crew, a trivial donation of veterinary drugs, and the intention to perform surgery on a bear. The veterinarian had visited the zoo for a day six months earlier and recalled the blind bear. The intervention was an unsolicited attempt at self-promotion by the NGO. Their intention was to anaesthetise a bear, perform a health check, obtain the recorded footage and leave to promote their contribution. The unprincipled approach justifiably enraged Dr Abbas. That the crew had arrived at the zoo, made their way to the bear enclosure without so much as a courtesy stop at the director's office, and then told the puzzled keeper they were there to operate on the bear infuriated us too. It was a no go. Dr Abbas refused. Still not recognising their imposition, thinking the objection was about the specific bear, they moved to Wounded-Ass bear suggesting she would also suffice for the check-up and filming. After some heated debate, they were asked to leave the zoo premises.

The availability of Colonel Gants to supervise the surgery on Saeida's chronic chest wound had been what we had waited for. He was an experienced small animal surgeon, but his schedule had been relentless as he and Civil Affairs veterinary colleagues worked to restore and modernise wholly ransacked university veterinary facilities. We knew there was a risk that without knowing the bear's health history, and there being no appropriate diagnostic equipment, an anaesthetic and surgery could kill her. Dr Abbas agreed that he would feel comfortable with the procedure knowing the experienced support was close at hand. It was also an opportunity for Colonel Gants to give a keen young female Iraqi veterinary student experience at the zoo as she worked with Dr Abbas and Erin. Waseem, by then a proficient darter of bears due to his regular administration of antibiotics to an increasingly reluctant and agile Wounded-Ass, immobilised Saeida. Dr Abbas and Erin set about cleaning and slicing out the malignant tumour that had formed out of a sweat gland. To our relief, Saeida continued to breathe, and as the wound was being sutured closed, it was an opportunity for the bear to receive its first health check in 28 years. There was nothing we could do about the medieval condition of her teeth, but it was an opportunity to inspect the cataracts, clean the filth from her ears and crunch and saw our way through my Leatherman's first bear pedicure.

In stark contrast to the surrounding city, there was finally a palpable sense of dwindling drama and growing positive momentum at the zoo. The animals were surviving, and with each successful veterinary intervention, Dr Abbas began to trust the influence of the Army veterinarians. Waseem continued to monitor the lions' nutritional intake and Kadhim's donkey slaughtering. If Waseem couldn't get Kadhim or a keeper to clean the slaughter area, he would do it himself, or we would divide the duty. Waseem was also working to dart and vaccinate stray dogs once the zoo quietened down in the late afternoon. The zoo was seeing a steady stream of visitors, up to a few hundred a day on weekends. Both Farah and Waseem were taking on as much veterinary information as was available to them but, by their own admission, had been woefully underprepared by the educational system that was heavy on theory but light on practical experience. Their experience of small animal and exotic medicine was limited. Where would they learn about bears, monkeys, budgies, lions and tortoises? Farah had considered quitting veterinary medicine entirely after her embarrassed frustration boiled over when struggling to find a vein for blood sampling from a wild boar. She felt humiliated that she was a qualified veterinarian and was still struggling to navigate some of the basic techniques and procedures. She was practising suture patterns on slabs of buffalo meat. There was no doubt that both she and Waseem were capable and passionately willing, but hands-on mentorship simply did not previously exist for them.

Combining the U.S. Army veterinarians' ambitious generosity and Farah's exposure to the passionate Dr Ala Shehadeh at modern veterinary facilities in Jordan (whom Farah was liaising with regarding relocation logistics for the dogs at the zoo), there was the opportunity to cultivate skills. I was also starting to have occasional telephonic conversations with Dr David Jones at the North Carolina Zoo. He had been directing the American Zoo Association fundraising efforts to support the Baghdad Zoo. Importantly, he was a wealth of zoological knowledge, had many years' experience with animal welfare in the Middle East and had essential links to zoos in both the U.S. and the U.K. There was optimism. There was a genuine opportunity to plug Baghdad Zoo into the international zoo community. There was the talk of training opportunities, perhaps at wildlife facilities in Saudi Arabia or Bahrain. There was even talk of a skilled zoo architect being potentially available to visit Baghdad the following year to draft a new design based on modern zoological facilities.

Through Dr Abbas, there had been optimistic discussions with the engaging Dr Faris Al-Assam, the deputy mayor at the Baghdad Municipality, about potential zoo developments. Dr Faris had an undisclosed budget to fund renovations. Undisclosed budgets excited us. There was the even grander talk of a drive-through lion safari park on the outskirts of Baghdad where the palace lions could be relocated to. Our ambitions were more modest, just a new bear and a new tiger enclosure to start with. There were several empty large, well-treed paddocks at the rear of the zoo that could be renovated for the existing bears and remaining old tiger. That would then free up enclosure space for other small animals already at the zoo, to be moved into. How to move from talking to action without offending anyone was the perpetual challenge. I was a slow learner of the patient, fatalistic "Inshallah" (*God Willing*) approach. Dr Abbas had skilfully ensured Dr Faris remained a vital zoo ally within the stifling broader bureaucracy.

The 26th October 2003 was the first day of Ramadan, the Muslim holy month of fasting. Among some devotees, it is believed the sacrifice of fighting against foreign invaders during this month in particular, can have greater religious significance. What better target than the occupying forces of the imperialist United States, seemed to be on the minds of resistance forces during that period. Concern had been growing at the increasingly radicalised threat that was feared would erupt. Depending on whom one spoke to, there was fear Iraq was heading rapidly towards anarchy. *Al-Qaeda in Iraq* under Abu Musab Al-Zarqawi, professing to fight for a brand of radical Sunni Islam, were accused of launching violent and deadly attacks against U.S. military forces and Shiite Islam religious targets. Muqtada Al-Sadr was reported to be building and arming a violent Shiite militia, *Imam Mahdi's Army*, partly to protect against Sunni and U.S. attacks, but also in response to another ferocious competing Shiite militia, the *Badr Brigade*, the militant arm of a dominant political party. The period of religious introspection precipitated an onslaught.

Paul Wolfowitz arrived in the city. The US deputy secretary of defence was a hawk in the Bush administration. The ever-reliable beer-talk rumour mill was that he was one of the architects of the war. Cheney. Rumsfeld. Wolfowitz. Among the sceptics, those three often seemed to have the first name "Fuckin". "He's staying on the 12th floor – man this place is so easy to hit – stands tall". At least following the previous Al-Rasheed attack cute little breathing masks had been installed in each room in case of an attack. That little tick-box exercise must have delighted an officious Health & Safety superintendent.

The sledgehammer sounded at dawn. *Duf!* Brief pause. *Duf!* A quietly spoken U.S. Army administration officer had been temporarily assigned to the extra bed in my room. He opened his eyes, and from among the rumpled sheets and pillows. His face had that messy, confused expression of interrupted sleep. *Duf!-Duf!* We simultaneously shuffled off the beds and lay on the ground, the other guy between the two beds and myself in the coffin-width gap between the bed and bathroom wall. From the diffused sound, it was difficult to tell with certainty which side of the building was being hit by rockets. Lying next to the beds seemed a logical option in case something slammed into our room or a nearby wall. It was either that or lying like packed squid in the small bathroom, which seemed an unnecessarily intimate option. "How long does this last for?" he mumbled.
"No idea. Last time it finished up quickly."
Duf! Duf! Duf! It amazed me that 30 seconds earlier, we

had both been asleep. Then we were lying on the carpet, with brains acting like clicking counters. Every sound, every movement was registered with distinct clarity. I mentally worked through the room, pinpointing important items to take if we were evacuated again. Remember socks idiot! *Duf!* It seemed like eight thuds before the pause. Thoughts were pulsing. The attack felt noticeably prolonged compared to the first time. How long was long enough to wait? Was the pause to reload? Fuckin' Wolfowitz! Is this the precursor to a full assault on the hotel? Likely not more than a dragging minute or two passed and it seemed the sledgehammer had stopped. I opened the bedroom door slightly, enough to peer out into the corridor. A swirling grey haze of dust and smoke hung in the corridor air as if elves on speed had thrashed hundreds of dirty carpets while we slept. The ominous cloud was a startlingly odd sight in a hotel corridor. Through the murkiness, the door opposite looked like it had been gouged open at the lock by a crowbar. The splintered wood reflected the force that had torn through the room, door frame, hinges and lock. There was no other visible damage. A few human shapes moved in the gloomy distance, but there was no urgency. People standing nearer looked confused in their pyjamas, squinting to get a reference on their wakeup call. My roommate, small bag already repacked, left the room as I turned back into the room to gather possessions. An evacuation seemed likely given that was the response to the incident the previous month.

Work clothes on. Socks on. Passport. Laptop. I had stored the guns and ammunition belonging to Lawrence and me in the broken freezer compartment of the fridge. It had never worked, and the fridge barely cooled, but the additional compartment with its cover flap seemed to me to be the least likely place in an unsecured room any hotel staff who happened to gain access would look for something to steal. A firearm in the pocket. The two spare clips of ammunition into the backpack to make the zookeeper feel protected. The banging on the doors and calls of "evacuate" grew louder as soldiers moved along the corridor, hit my door and carried on past. As I reached the lift entryway, I looked to the right to room 720, the first room I had entered in the hotel, and where Mariette from IFAW had stayed. A South African security contractor had been staying in the room. Now it stood with the door blown open at the lock, and the large central window was partly smashed with cracks spider-webbed across the glass. Wires hung like entrails out of the corridor ceiling where panelling had fallen off or was dangling.

Entering the darkened stairwell was like joining an almost mute conga line of calm zombies in combinations of military fatigues, sleeping or work gear, or grey T-shirts with Army printed on them. The thickening haze settled in the air was choking as we worked our way slowly in the gridlock. Down another floor. As we passed each level's entrance, the shouting of soldiers in corridors increased. Calls for evacuations. Calls for assistance. From the fourth floor, blood was dripped and smeared on the handrail and stairs. The blood heightened the sense of bigger reality, and suddenly an experience that had been intensely surreal seemed visceral and threateningly real. The lower we descended in the dark stairwell, the deeper acrid smoke seemed to be reaching into each breath, forcing exaggerated inhalation to fill the lungs. I could feel the anxiety flicker slightly as I tried to suck breaths under my shirt collar I had pulled over my mouth and nose. I finally remembered the breathing mask installed in each room. Nobody appeared to have one with them. I didn't either. I made a quick mental apology to Health & Safety for being a cynic.

Stepping into the expansive foyer was a breath of relief. Lungs filled. A throng of personnel was gathering. Gym clothes, pyjamas and suits reflected what had been interrupted. I retrieved the envelope of zoo money from the safety deposit box. Working through the crowd, I aimed to find the South African security contractors. There would be comfort in the familiar association. I also assumed that the incident would be of minimal distress to them, and if we were genuinely still at risk, I wanted to be with people I believed could protect me. They were in good humour despite one not being able to hear anything. He was grinning, more concerned about not being able to smoke a cigarette in the lobby. He had been blown off his bed by the blast wave of a rocket that crashed through the window and detonated as it penetrated the wall behind him. It destroyed the bathroom with an explosive lashing of debris and shrapnel. A stretcher with a bleeding person was carried through the crowds, passed us and out the hotel entrance. From the distracted humour of the seconds before it suddenly seemed real again. I knew I needed to phone my parents back in South Africa. A burst of anxiety welled-up, leapt into my throat and like an elastic, dropped down again. For a second, I felt dismayed at the sensation. Michael Herr wrote in *Dispatches*, "Anxiety was a luxury, a joke you had no room for once you knew a variety of deaths and mutilations the war offered". Too true. I was in a comparatively luxurious, pampered scenario compared to what many conscripted Iraqi or coalition soldiers, and Iraqi civilians had faced until then.

The news of the attack was undoubtedly going to hit global headlines. I believed it would be better my parents heard from me rather than from the headlines of 'world news' when they got up. But then I knew they would be asleep in South Africa, and those sorts of phone calls are seldom considered cheerfully mistaken errors of time-zone management when groggily waking up to the loud ring. Maybe if I waited, they wouldn't see the news that day. It seemed a poor justification for not making the call. So instead I procrastinated. I phoned both William and Farah to eat up the minutes. I had never phoned my parents about any incidents before because of the unnecessary worry for them. The call home was quick and thankfully, to the point. A quick breakfast service had opened up in the chow hall (never miss a chance for a free breakfast!) before orderly evacuation and personnel counts across the road at the convention centre. The shock of the whole reality sank in for a few minutes. My hand shook as I started to consider whether it was worth getting killed for the zoo. That was essentially the equation at its barest. The option had never really struck me like that before. It should have, but it hadn't. I had time to mull it over as I drove to William's villa for a coffee. The lure of that novelty and reality was simply too powerful. Hell, I was driving past Saddam Hussein's palace to a U.S. Army commandeered villa that belonged to the Iraqi Republican Guard! The more I tried to justify the balance of the equation, the clearer it became that it was more than the zoo. It was the whole messy package of a perverse sense of joy and energy from the zoo, Baghdad, the novelty of palace lions, palaces, military hardware, Farah, William, Ahmed, Ali, Waseem and the freedom to make a plan where the only justification was "I think this will work". Selfishly, the opportunity to engage in a little subversive recklessness seemed like too much of a privileged position to give up on. The sense of autonomy was addictive. Most importantly, we saw obvious, tangible improvement in the physical condition of many animals. We were seeing positive steps in the daily zoo management and recognising opportunities to initiate significant changes. This sense of optimism was reinforced by knowing the deputy mayor was on our side. It was apparent that per unit of our effort sweated into Baghdad we got so much added reward and go-forward momentum than in the stifling bureaucracy of semi-organised countries.

I was very conscious there was something alluringly absurd about blasting out Linkin Park's *Meteora* album while driving past a missile-damaged Baath HQ in a free flashy car and having a silenced sterling sub-machine gun at an office in the Baghdad Zoo where an old man with lions couldn't help repeating "I am Salman. Lion, Tigers, Beers. Thirrrty two yirrss. Good! Very good!" The ridiculous novelty balanced out the downsides like shovelling desiccated lion poo, bland KBR olives, threat and the guilt of what I was quite sure I was putting my parents through. I knew if I left to escape the risk, I wouldn't return. I would regret abandoning friends and an unfinished job.

The zoo staff demonstrated a reassuringly touching show of empathy. "These attacks not Iraqis." They sounded like by trying to convince me they were also trying to convince themselves. Simply though, I was less concerned about the nationality of the rocket men and more concerned about their intent and vague attention to detailed targeting. Information regarding the attack was revealed as the day wore on. A van had pulled a trailer to within 400m of the hotel. On the trailer was a rocket launcher disguised as a generator, that was left within the grounds of Al-Zawra Park where a series of underpass road networks converged near the crossed swords recreational area. Much like the previous attack, a series of tubes had been connected to a timing device. Reports varied, but about 30 of the 40 rockets were fired. A U.S. Army Lieutenant Colonel was killed, and 15 further casualties were extracted. Apart from the exterior damage to the building, severed water pipes caused two floors to flood, and the electricity supply was cut in some sectors. By the afternoon, the decision had been made by the CPA to permanently evacuate the hotel. It was a sudden disconnection from what had become home. By my calculations, I was likely to be one of the longest squatting residents in the block; I no longer recognised anybody else from those early weeks with the 3rd ID as landlords. Residents were allowed a brief opportunity to clear their respective rooms; no diversions and no wandering the building! It was enough time to gauge some of the damage. Some bedrooms, like mine, were unharmed. In other rooms, doors hung open revealing smashed windows and ripped curtains. Masonry blown off walls lay sprayed on the beds and carpet. In some corridors, water dripped out the ceiling from among the dangling wires and cables. There was little to collect in my room other than the remaining backpack. I left Lawrence's gun in the fridge freezer thinking I wouldn't need it. I already had all the spare ammunition I felt I might need. By then us civilians had been issued a weapons permit by the CPA to carry a gun. If I was searched, I could explain one firearm, not two. In hindsight, it was a stupid error. Goodbye room 713, hello ex-Republican Guard villa.

I had no desire to be one of the many people hurriedly allocated a camping cot in public passageways or hastily converted dining and reception halls in the CPA palace. Empty halls were hastily converted to gigantic dormitories. It was an impressively quick response by the CPA, and plywood carpenters to the accommodation crisis thrust on them. William offered a camping stretcher in a passageway in the villa commandeered with his colleagues in the 354th Civil Affairs Brigade. The exclusive real estate option lifted my spirits immeasurably, and *hooch* hospitality immediately eased my nagging civilian sensation of imposition. A homemade Captain St. Laurent pizza generated from the assortments within care packages from the U.S. was a culinary revelation.

The decision to leave behind one gun came back to bite as "Dave" in charge of hotel security was looking for the "zoo guy" the next time I entered the Al-Rasheed. Despite the evacuation and access to the main foyer being blocked, the restaurants and dining hall on the ground floor remained functioning. So naturally, I returned for meals. I was led to the *school principal's* office by a Ghurkha for what turned out to be a fifteen-minute roasting about the weapons and quantities of ammunition stored in the room. It seemed a bit pedantic given the scale of war around us, but I was a minion, and worse, a civilian. What I had left behind had been found by the security contractors sweeping through the rooms after the evacuation. I naively thought that total honesty about my decision-making logic at the time would help my quick release back to the dining hall. From the brash attempts at intimidation, one would have thought I had been storing an arsenal of assault rifles in my fridge, but I knew I daren't joke that was at the zoo. After being offered some free advice from angry Dave, I was allowed to leave provided I understood I was being watched. "Yes, Dave." I went to the dining hall, making sure I approached my dinner more like a docile, skinny, lover of hedgehogs than a suspicious, ravenous Jihadi mercenary.

As I arrived at the zoo the following morning, Dr Abbas and a few other staff were standing gathered outside the office. The mood etched on their faces was hollow, drained of the usual morning cheer. "What's happened now?"

"Mr Faris has been shot dead," Dr Abbas said.

Dr Abbas had heard assassins walked into a tea house, shot the deputy mayor dead, walked out. Done. It was the penalty for collaboration with foreigners, with the Americans. Selfishly, it was a hammer blow to the zoo. All the promises of funding and development had only been verbal. Now he was dead. The plans were dead. I instantly regretted that was my first thought. A family had lost a father, and a wife had lost a husband. For what? For trying to help rebuild his city that foreigners had taken over.

Baghdad seemed to unravel at the seams. A wave of devastation was unleashed. Carnage and corpses threatened to sink the country. Unbridled fighting was gearing up, rooted in countless conflicting motivations. Multiple suicide bombers and a car bomb savagely struck the headquarters of the International Committee for the Red Cross (ICRC). The result was mass carnage. The ICRC began to withdraw staff from Iraq the following day. Suicide bombers crashed vehicles into police stations across the city resulting in slaughter and dismembered bodies being dragged from the rubble of collapsed buildings. An Iraqi newspaper editor working for The Times was assassinated. A mortar attack struck the University of Baghdad's College of Education (where the horse stables were located). The Green Zone received volleys of mortars and rockets. U.S. Army convoys were targeted across the country by ambushes and increasingly more powerful and sophisticated IEDs. Casualty tallies among civilians and military escalated daily. A U.S. Army Blackhawk helicopter was shot down with a rocket-propelled grenade. Prominent Shiite administrative figures and former Baathist officials were killed by unknown attackers. U.S. raids apprehended and killed militants and detained former government officials believed to be guiding elements of the emboldened insurgency. It was an opportune time to snitch on enemies or to settle personal grudges by informing to U.S. troops. Reports emerged of U.S. soldiers responding to tip-offs, kicking in house doors, barking orders, humiliating, threatening and detaining male family members en masse, confiscating family possessions or incriminating photos, weapons or money. Terrified wives, sisters or daughters would be left sobbing, begging for explanations, not knowing if they would see their detained family members again. There had been rumours of abuses by U.S. soldiers in prisons. As an outsider, there was no way to know what was truth or gossip or propaganda. Maybe those detained were violent insurgents, perhaps they weren't. Innocent shoppers in a marketplace were killed by reactive U.S. Army return-fire after they mistakenly believed they were under attack. It all fuelled loathing. Kidnappers increased their reach and activity, preying on victims, extorting ransoms from families. Terrified families would get no help. So desperate to raise the fees, anything from a few thousand to hundreds of thousands, they would sell their stored jewellery, cars, houses, anything; or beg for loans. Some of those abducted were tortured and released, others were killed and dumped. An improvised rocket launcher was found loaded near the Italian Embassy. Rockets were fired into the Palestine Hotel from a horse cart-mounted platform. A DHL A300 cargo plane was hit by a SAM-7 missile as it took off from Baghdad Airport but was, fortunately, able to land safely.

Daily life in the city continued as resilience and needs dictated it must. Traffic remained choked. Children went to school. Students went to university. Parents went to work; doctors, engineers, cleaners, professors, gardeners, clerics, teachers, bird sellers, butchers, profiteers, gangsters, mercenaries and bomb makers. Workers arrived at the zoo. If you were lucky enough to have a job, you had to arrive at work. Simple? Inside the Green Zone, concrete blast walls were planted and reshuffled by crane trucks according to presumed locations of a potential attack on the leafy fortress. The Red Zone, the rest of Baghdad, was managed by different rules with different ambitions. It was a free-for-all. Random checkpoints were set up to maintain a semblance of control. As much as international media headlines had earlier seemed to overplay the security risk when Baghdad was comparatively safe, at times of chaos it appeared the focus had shifted elsewhere internationally. The more attacks took place, the more it strangely seemed to blend into a prolonged spate of violence and became less newsworthy. That was probably reflected in some of our reactions too. The rumble of an explosion in the distance simply, callously meant it wasn't nearby.

Talk about the methods used to disguise IEDs ratcheted-up the everyday tension and refined concentration like I had never previously known possible when driving. Discarded Pepsi cans. Cardboard boxes. Dead dogs. New potholes. Filled potholes. A parked car under an overpass bridge. All of those items had already been reported as approaches discovered or exploded as IEDs at some point. On familiar driving routes, every visible object on or near the road was inadvertently, mentally catalogued to a level of precision and background memory flow that they were immediately recognised at a distance as new or from the previous day – even when you felt distracted by other thoughts. It wasn't like we believed every new item we saw was an IED, it was that your brain made a subjective judgement call on whether such an object appeared a likely threat. Imagine driving to your local supermarket but driving like you needed to observe all the details of the gutters and pavement to ensure you believed you were not going to get blown up. Whether it was rational or not, it became a normalised consideration. The problem was there weren't many routes available to the zoo. It was where it was. Drive fast when possible and hope for the best was still the general strategy. Avoid the obvious perceived threats when possible. I rarely diverted down a road because of such an object – usually overthinking the situation and wondering whether the intention would be to force a foreigner to drive down a side road.

The bleeding wounds in Sa'ad's head had been partly wiped and smeared in his dishevelled hair. He looked a forlorn and disorientated figure. His cousin helped him walk to the SUV where we eased his chubby frame into the seat. The taut seatbelt held him upright. Akram had first alerted Farah to the drama that had played out, and Sa'ad's cousin described additional shocking details. Sa'ad had been asleep in his bed when he woke in terrified response to two of his uncles trying to kill him by slamming a screwdriver into his head repeatedly. He scrambled and fought frantically and violently against the attackers, while desperately trying to survive. It was unclear how the assault had finally been stopped. Earlier, Sa'ad had refused to give them information on U.S. Army troop movements in and around the zoo and had reportedly refused to put a bomb in a Humvee. His mother's brothers had agreed to kill him for his pro-American treachery.

William had been making urgent phone calls to facilitate our access into the Green Zone with Sa'ad so he could be assessed at the *Cash* (Combat Support Hospital – CSH). Sa'ad as an Iraqi civilian could not ordinarily be admitted through the checkpoints and into the *Cash* but William, as always, delivered when it seemed desperately improbable. We were most concerned about the likely cracked skull among the caking blood, and potential brain damage. There was little chance an Iraqi hospital in Baghdad would be equipped to deal with such a critical case given their state after prolonged sanctions and then the looting rampage. William met us at the hospital near the CPA Palace, and

Sa'ad was rushed away by a small clinical team in combat fatigues and scrubs. We waited anxiously. Finally, the battered and frail Sa'ad, with a freshly bandaged head, was helped gingerly back through the doorway to the waiting area. To our enormous relief, none of the puncture wounds had penetrated his skull but instead sliced skin and flesh open. The rules had already been manipulated to help us that far, he wouldn't be allowed a night in the hospital. We loaded him into the SUV again and rushed back to the zoo. With Akram's help, we transferred Sa'ad into Farah's car, I collected zoo money from the laptop bag, and we rushed him to a nearby private hospital. We paid. Sa'ad could stay. The hospital was run down, rudimentary and far from as clean as the CSH, but it was a bed in a secure facility where doctors would oversee his immediate recovery. His family could not know where he was. Akram and Farah watched over Sa'ad.

It would be three days before Sa'ad was released from the hospital, bruised and weak. A small empty room joined to a concession stand selling refreshments, became his recovery room. It was when we were alone that he would ask if we knew people who could kill his uncles. When we questioned Dr Abbas for advice on how to secure accommodation for Sa'ad, his reply was blunt. Stay out of it. "You don't understand Iraq. You don't understand his family. For your safety, wash your hands of it." Beyond some token financial help, I heeded the warnings from Dr Abbas. Farah continued to help with food and money. Sa'ad recovered physically and regained most of his cheery demeanour, but the emotional toll of his dire situation festered below the projected surface.

Farah had become the Green Zone magnet for soldiers and CPA officials who had succumbed to the therapeutic charms of puppy eyes and wagging tails at checkpoints or commandeered villas. Soldiers would sheepishly confess their desperation to have their new friends join them back in the U.S. Others would arrive at the zoo for a visit, and thankfully surrender themselves to the manipulating joy of an excited puppy in one of the enclosures. With the number of pregnant dogs arriving there was no shortage of puppies, and after one demonstration surgery, Farah still didn't have the confidence to perform surgical spays. The puppy production dilemma extended to the stray dogs in Al-Zawra Park. One brownish generically dog-like looking stray with a wonderfully gentle demeanour became a favourite at the zoo entrance, particularly with the security guards who would feed her scraps. William quickly developed a soft spot for her, naming her *Dragon*, a complimentary twist on the intended name *Draggin'* in reference to her perpetually enormous, pendulous teats resulting from the many litters of pups she produced and fed (she would eventually be spayed).

Not everybody agreed with our improvised approach. One CPA official had developed an affinity for a particular puppy but had decided our free-spirited approach was unbearably cruel. We kept the puppy in the large aviary where it could roam through holes in the internal mesh fencing to socialise with pelicans in the makeshift pool, chase ducks or nibble on the tails of adult dogs at will. The spirited puppy thrived on the many inter-species recreational options at his disposal. It was like the bar in Star War's Tatooine, but without the alcohol or fights. The more intense the official's affection for the puppy developed with each visit, the increasingly condescending her tone became towards us, and vociferous she would be about leaving the puppy in its own secluded birdcage, "for its own safety." On its own, the puppy would slump down into a corner or paw up against the mesh while seeking affection. The debate was futile, a waste of our energy. We tolerated her reproaches because we knew she would adopt the puppy (which she did without ever thanking Farah for the extensive efforts at relocation). Each occasion, after she left the zoo grounds, we would return the puppy to the pelicans and ducks and dogs who would flap and chase and frolic with each other in Disneyesque pleasure.

Farah and I were called by a friend at the CPA. There was the talk of an injured dog amongst a row of trees between the edge of the main CPA parking lot and the area secured for landing helicopters. The sight was pitiful. The tan coloured dog had been struck by a vehicle. Its back was broken, and lower half paralysed. There was no telling the full extent of the internal injuries was, but the laboured breathing was ominous. The animal was meek and passive as it tried feebly to drag itself away from us. We had no access to an x-ray machine or stethoscope to check the animal further and knew that even if there was any chance the animal would survive, the prognosis of being able to care for it or find someone to do so in the circumstances was bleak to zero. Euthanasia seemed the most humane option, but until then, we had still not been able to source such drugs in Iraq. There was no chance I would get away with firing a gun in the Green Zone without causing a military response of sorts. The only option was the blade of my Leatherman. Farah walked away in tears. It felt like a depressingly barbaric morning as we headed back to the zoo, deflated. It felt like attempts to help out perpetually exposed us to animal death and killing, apparently much like the dark side of many veterinarian's days.

We needed an outlet for the dogs. The obvious option, the one that most soldiers who delivered dogs to the zoo advocated, was to send them to the soldiers' respective homes in the U.S. We had no money to do so, nor logistical precedent to replicate. There was certainly no possibility of sending them directly from Baghdad. The breakthrough came from the efforts of a wife of a soldier. She searched online for options and found the link for the Humane Center for Animal Welfare (HCAW) in Amman, Jordan, a charity established by Margaret and Peter Ledger in 2000. Margaret had already looked into the concept of moving four puppies from a military base in Iraq to Los Angeles. The opportune inquiry about the potential to vaccinate, spay and relocate the dog to the U.S. led to contact between Farah and Margaret via an animal welfare devotee, Marcy Christmas. The door had been ever-so-slightly nudged open.

The initial dialogue grew into a giant morphing beast, and before Farah even had a chance to visit Jordan to understand the logistics required, news spread quickly among soldiers that an initiative to relocate dogs to the U.S. had been established. Pressure mounted quickly. Airline approved travel boxes for dogs of different sizes were needed in Baghdad (understandably a rarity given the circumstances). Vaccination regimes and records needed to be set up. Spays and neutering needed to be part of the programme. Funding was needed urgently, but in Baghdad, the poorly kept secret needed to remain a poorly kept secret. Adopting animals in those circumstances violated the U.S. Army's General Order No. 1. The Army wasn't an avenue to source funding from. Soldiers funded what they could from their own pockets.

Farah took the 12-hour taxi journey from Baghdad to Amman for a logistical scouting trip. At the best of times, it was an arduous trip on seemingly endless desert highways, made more complicated by the suspicion of border officials of single young women crossing from Iraq to Jordan without a male family escort. The default assumption of *prostitute* usually needed quick-witted navigation. She finally made it to the welcoming sanctuary of the HCAW veterinary facilities on the limestone hills of Amman, overlooking terraced olive groves and exposed rocks that resembled crumbles of feta cheese. It was there, after so much contact through phone and emails she finally met Margaret and the energetic, skilled veterinarian Dr Ala Shehadeh.

The initiative quickly escalated beyond what initially seemed feasible as details were planned and contacts groomed for the first test-run shipment. The most significant concern while attempting to move an SUV taxi loaded with dogs (likely the first time that had happened) from Iraq into Jordan was still the *single woman = prostitute* equation. Over dinner, the voluntary assistance of two willing U.S.

Embassy officials, and later a helpful Jordanian Army Major based at the border post, was finalised to navigate a solution. The required vaccination protocols would be followed in Iraq, and the surgeries carried out by Ala in Jordan while training Farah. Keen interest in the potential moves among the welfare network in the U.S. resulted in additional crucial support being offered by the enthusiastic Marcy Christmas with her links to The Doris Day League. Soon after, Bonnie Buckley (who established Military Mascots) also joined the network to facilitate logistics for soldiers adopting dogs, source funding and find homes for those dogs and puppies at the zoo without secured destinations. Sarah Scarth, who had coordinated IFAW's earlier zoo intervention from South Africa, also became an essential sounding board for Farah to scale-up plans to develop a broader animal welfare campaign.

Back in Baghdad, the to-do list snowballed. As the war started, *JT* was adopted by soldiers as a puppy at the Iraqi-Kuwaiti border. He was raised in their tank through the battles to Baghdad. *Red* was a black dog named after his adoptee's army unit. *Leroy* was rescued from another private zoo in Baghdad and then adopted by a HEMMT truck driver who had been so willing and helpful. *Nicotine* was so named because she and her pups were integral in negotiations with Farah to quit smoking. *Dusty*, *BW*, *Wardena*, *Sapper*, *Snowflake*, *Rocky*, *Diesel*, *Ugliest Dog On The Planet* and the rest, all needed medical records, travel passports and secured, paid-for flight routes to their respective city destinations. Each dog needed a human receiver at a U.S. airport to facilitate transport, particularly if the pooch still required to be driven to another town. Travel crates arrived from Jordan. Letters were stamped and signed off from contacts in Jordan, and with a little military help, we ensured official-looking documents were generated from our Baghdad side. There was growing anticipation of the moves, and while logic dictated that the effort and money spent from the U.S. side may have been better used directly helping stray dogs in the U.S., the emotional bond between the Iraqi dogs and their American companions was too intense not to help where we could.

The excitement fizzed as the final crated dog was loaded into the SUV taxi at the zoo. It had been coincidental that a print media journalist had arrived at the zoo the day before, but once she heard of the plans afoot she was determined we give her the exclusive story on the move. Perhaps indicative of the competitive nature of her job, she spent much of the afternoon trying to get us to promise we wouldn't let any other media agencies know of the early-morning timing of the move. Dr Abbas seemed more relieved than all of us when the taxi and Farah finally departed the zoo with the first consignment of dogs. He could finally see he wouldn't have to explain to the municipality officials that we were turning the zoo into a dog hotel.

At the Iraqi border post, Farah turned on the persuasive charm she always seemed to radiate when in the company of handsome U.S. soldiers. It wasn't long before the long queue of cars was bypassed, and she was waiting to pass into Jordan. It was there her petite size enabled her to slip through a hole in the perimeter fence to make direct contact with the Jordanian Army Major to smooth the entry across the border. With the legalities complete, permits and health records checked, and passports stamped the SUV was allowed to bypass inspection, a grand turn of events when the vehicle is a load that no customs official at that border would want to touch. Within hours the dogs were offloaded at the HCAW. Less than two weeks later, reports and photos began to filter back from the U.S. of spirited animals unleashed on their new surrounds and thrilled families.

The subsequent journey to Jordan wasn't quite as smooth a ride, but it was a bigger consignment of dogs. Through a fantastic turn of events, Dr David Jones at North Carolina Zoo and Nick Lindsay at the Zoological Society of London (ZSL) secured an opportunity for an educational visit by Baghdad Zoo staff to zoological facilities in England. It was decided that Dr Abbas as the zoo director, Farah as the assistant director, and Ahmed as the person in charge of food supplies and diets would be the trio I would accompany as the facilitator. There was no visa application option in Iraq. It meant a journey to Jordan to apply for visas to the U.K. The two vehicles thundered down the desert highway, which was less busy than usual because of the fasting and heat of Ramadan. I was familiar with the somewhat optimistic risks drivers seemed to take as a matter of routine in Iraq, but as we sped towards the back of a truck, it looked an alarmingly unnecessary risk for a sexy overtake. I had been dozing in and out of concentration. Our speed had woken me, and from the passenger seat, I shot a quick glance across at the driver. He had fallen asleep with his forehead on the steering wheel. As I burst out a yell and slammed my hand on the dashboard (probably not the ideal response), he startled awake, swung the wheel wildly to miss the truck before regaining embarrassed composure with his eyes wide and white as bleached ping-pong balls. He declined both Farah and my polite suggestions that we could drive if he'd prefer to "fucking nap while leading us to our deaths". Several uneventful hours passed as the fasting driver delivered us to the border post. There Farah once again worked her charms with the U.S. troops to bypass sceptical Iraqi officials wondering why the single woman was travelling with three men in two taxis (thankfully they didn't notice the crates were full of dogs). It was the first time for both Dr Abbas and Ahmed to witness life beyond Iraq's borders. Several traffic diversions and mistaken navigations later by our taxi driver that we were becoming increasingly keen to discard, we finally arrived at the HCAW deep into the night. As seems to be the case in Iraq and Jordan, furiously hot summers can swiftly turn into brief autumn, and we shivered through the novelty of cold as we offloaded the dogs.

    A day later, with the visa formalities completed, Dr Abbas and Ahmed returned to Baghdad. Farah and I capitalised on Dr Ala's enticing offer to visit the archaeological gem of the imposing, ancient city of Petra. We organised to stay longer. The mammoth scale, detail and colours of the rock-carved buildings and amphitheatre in the vast canyon network were breath-taking and yet the oddest curiosity of the day was a piece of paper barely bigger than a passport photo.

As we walked along the expansive, worn, tracks of the main canyon, a tiny corner of paper protruding from the beige sand caught my eye where I placed my step. It was immediately recognisable by the colour combination as a portion of a small printed South African flag. I pulled it out in disbelief. Below the flag was a small typed Christian religious blessing. Farah and I stared at the tiny scrap of paper, mystified. The setting of a situation like Baghdad at that time frequently made me question the likelihood of being caught out, wounded, mutilated, killed or unharmed. An inch one direction. Another minute. Wrong bedroom. Wrong place wrong time. Mistaken identity. An apparently random act of kindness. A belligerent checkpoint soldier. Waking as a driver fell asleep. What determined the result of surviving or not? How much of the end result of surviving without incident was down to timing, chance, instinct, reflex, observation, hesitation, advice, some sort of deity or spiritual protection? I was a religious sceptic, and yet with each peculiar incident where others were hurt, or we weren't when we could have been, the nagging question of control over fate increased. It was inescapable. Yet given the anger, sadism, insanity, innocence and fear in the streets of parts of Baghdad, it seemed somewhat egotistical and selfish to assume that one's daily welfare was being micromanaged by a celestial being.

Back in Iraq, the logistics of managing the relocation of pets through Jordan to the U.S. was absorbing much of Farah's time, and it was becoming increasingly evident that the opportunity existed for a comprehensive welfare approach. Lawrence had suggested the idea of establishing an animal welfare society when Farah first met him, but until then there had been too many other urgent projects to prioritise. Farah's passion for the idea had grown with her confidence at organising successful relocations and her interactions with her active, motivated Jordanian partners. The increasingly unconditional support from Bonnie Buckley and her Military Mascots program in the U.S. was inspiring Farah to make a formal establishment a reality. William was confident he could source discretionary funds through the Civil Affairs units to renovate a building for a dedicated welfare facility. We set about planning the requirements, the vision, and what we envisaged would work in the circumstances of Baghdad. It was the birth of the Iraqi Society for Animal Welfare (ISAW).

While we plotted dog relocations, Lieutenant Colonel Lozada's determination to make a positive impact at the zoo had been unwavering. He finally delivered what he had worked on tirelessly; a veterinary surgical facility. Box after box of diagnostic and surgical equipment was carried by zoo staff staggering under the weights. It was a sophisticated, high-quality shipment to lead the advancement of veterinary training and animal care at the zoo. The $42 000 spent from the Commanders Emergency Response Fund of the 352nd Civil Affairs ensured an autoclave for sterilising the new surgical tools, a mobile x-ray machine and an anaesthetic machine. The next challenge was finding a zoo vet who knew how to use any of the equipment. Most of the equipment was so far advanced beyond what they recognised, that it was left in the boxes for days. Dr Abbas was overtly delighted and genuinely grateful, but taking the equipment out the boxes would embarrassingly expose the staff's dire dearth of skill and genuine surgical experience. The daily supplies were obviously more frequently used. Fortunately, it was only months before scenarios would manifest where the equipment would fulfil any surgical teaching potential, giving time for some familiarity with the tools.

Unexpectedly, Dr Hussam was dismissed, again, for his links to the former Baath regime! The rumour was that following a review of the previous review, which had overturned the initial decision to dismiss Dr Hussam, he was again considered as punishable. Although I had become frustrated with working with him, it seemed an outrage that anyone would be treated like that. Dismissed again without compensation. His livelihood was being manipulated cruelly on a bureaucratic whim, and his family were subjected to the crippling stresses of unemployment, as he was banned from a government office. It was easy to see how he would distrust or hate foreigners. He was guilty of something, or he wasn't. Again, in the absence of clarity, rumours of wicked but unconfirmed deeds previously committed, or complicity circulated in the fertile shadows of the zoo. When we raised the issue of transparency, consistency and pragmatism with the CPA authorities, we were again advised to mind our own business. If it was happening to him, it was likely happening to thousands of other Iraqis across the country.

Six months of regular treatment was aiding Wounded-Ass bear's physical recovery. The buttock area had mostly healed to scar tissue, but the pads on the underside of her feet stayed raw despite gradual wound closure. She walked without obvious discomfort, but that was likely a greater testament to her pain threshold than healing. Despite the wounds, she was active and healthy. Dr Abbas maintained compassionate sentiment for her, Ahmed always ensured she was fed extra treats and Waseem had taken on her veterinary care with unwavering consistency.

We had dreaded the day the animal trader would come calling for his bear. We hoped he would never arrive. When the swarthy, abrasive owner entered our office, it was clear whatever the exchange, we would not relinquish Wounded-Ass. We felt it would be deeply unjust for the bear. Farah translated as the opening discussions quickly soured.

The trader wanted $10 000 for the bear; that would be his price on the black market. $10 000 we didn't have. Not a chance. We offered $500. The trader looked like he may spit at the outrage. We argued that without the zoo's intervention, the bear would have died; he would have no animal to negotiate over. Dr Abbas arrived and appeared to have reverted to his calm, mildly hostile demeanour we by-then recognised when he was at his most stubborn. He was soon bristling, refusing to let the bear leave the zoo as it wasn't fully recovered (and because he knew it would be intolerably cruel). The half-hour discussion turned swiftly from pretend-polite tea-drinking conversation to a thunderous mood of gesticulating and trench-bound arguments. Dr Abbas seethed. The accusations about foreign manipulation were thrust angrily at me by the fuming trader, and I felt the rage boiling the more he waved his hands at me. He accused us of lying based on our initial discussions. He was right. But in our minds, we had nothing but swelling contempt for him. Between his attitude, actions and treatment of the bear, we all felt any fair dealings were no longer a necessary consideration. Farah unleashed her formidable brand of unsubtle. I considered the gun in the desk drawer as a simple means to end the argument. It seemed irrational. It was almost at that point. It was clear; there would be no resolution. Wounded-Ass would stay. We offered him an insulting $200 and played the final card we had; shift responsibility onto the infuriatingly unnavigable bureaucracy of lodging an arbitrary complaint with the U.S. Army. The trader could go rant at a checkpoint. It was officially an Army vehicle that had removed the bear from the veterinary facility. The irate trader seemed somewhat placated with the suggestion, believing his moral cause would receive the attention it deserved. I agreed to write a letter in English explaining the background of his complaint – "A bear in a severe state of neglect and physical trauma was removed from an unsuitably small rebar holding cage in this black market animal trader's possession. Without treatment, it would have certainly died given the severity of the buttock and feet wounds. It is now being held and treated at the Baghdad Zoo. It is making a slow recovery. We paid him $200. This man wants you to pay him $10 000."

"Good luck at the checkpoint" I muttered as I handed him the dollars and page of scrawled handwriting. With that settled, Dr Abbas organised that the zoo security escorts the trader from the zoo premises. The trader stormed out the office in a pall of indignation. The bear was going nowhere, and we could grin with relief. It was the last we ever saw of the trader. That was the end of that. Sour. Acrimonious. But the bear was safe.

CHAPTER 13

It was abruptly bitingly cold in Baghdad, and the coats on the bears, wolf and fox grew noticeably thicker and more luxuriant. In the subtle winter morning light, the sprinklers arching sprays of water out over the lush green lawns and colourfully filled flower beds was a beautiful sight. Combined with the range of morning bird calls and the bulbuls flittering between the date palm trees it all seemed quite serene, such an unlikely prognosis seven months earlier. The still air seemed to amplify the deep moaning call of lions. The frigid breezes didn't stop Samir, the bear relocated from Luna Park, splashing and diving after his wooden footballs he would slam dunk into the pool. Instead of avoiding heat as was the case for much of the year, most of the animals took any opportunity to warm themselves in the shards of sun we had spent many months trying to shelter them from. The cheetahs' arthritis was increasingly noticeable after they lay on the chilly floor tiles and then creaked and stretched their way with the moving rays.

Across the city, it was a case of occasional explosions being the new normal to the point that we didn't pay much attention to it. It was a rumble in the distance. If you didn't witness it, you became apathetic. It was someone else's pain and drama. The Green Zone was still subjected to sporadic mortar fire being lobbed into the supposedly secure area. Target whatever. Any destructive hit would suffice for the growing insurgency. Within the CPA palace, the sirens would sound to alert the hustling bureaucrats and soldiers in the maze of passages, marble halls and rapidly multiplying plywood offices to seek cover. At night short burps of all-slaughtering *justice* were familiar responses from somewhere up in the black skies. Over-watching C-130 Spectre gunship aircraft would unleash their arsenal of cannons and guns, raining down vindictive, concentrated barrages to obliterate launching sites for mortars targeting the Green Zone.

In December I committed to returning to South Africa for a friend's wedding. Farah and I decided it would be another opportunity to road-trip dogs to Amman given how smoothly the dog relocation logistics had shaped up. After goodbyes and promises to return, once again an SUV taxi stacked full of crates of sleeping dogs thundered west out of Baghdad. The familiar highway route skirted around the eastern and northern fringes of Fallujah, a fervently Saddam-loyalist town with more than 400 000 residents. It was seething with anti-American sentiment and would periodically flare up with insurgent resistance. Since the coalition invasion, there had been repeated violent instability in the *City of Mosques*. Our SUV driver assured us we needed to drive through Fallujah, partly because of safety concerns on the main highway, and then when pressed by an anxious Farah, he admitted he also need to collect a package to take to Jordan.

Neither of those reasons sat well with me, and I could feel the seed of fear growing. I had heard stories of Fallujah, and for pale foreigners, a serving of hostage-taking, torture and a merciless thrashing seemed much more likely than hot tea and welcoming dates. "Fuck! Honestly. Through the centre of Fallujah!" dominated my internal monologue. Who was this taxi driver really? It didn't escape my thoughts that we could easily be handed over to someone for a fee. It would be so easy, and Farah and I would have no choice but a concession. You force yourself into assuming you have mistakenly thought the worst, ugliest, most violent, unlikely option. I was sitting in the front passenger seat. Farah, gravely concerned at how conspicuous I was, suggested I shrink and contort myself into the footwell. A *yashmagh* was laid over me so pedestrians and passengers of vehicles in the choked traffic couldn't see me. Through a small gap between the cloth and the window, I could see portions of pedestrians walking alongside the car. We pushed on and on. After what felt like blood-pulsing endlessness we were on the road leaving the city, adjacent the idyllic, historically iconic Euphrates River. We passed a latticed, dominating iron bridge across the river. It would become infamous in March 2004 as the location where the beaten, dragged and charred corpses of four ambushed American security contractors were finally strung up by an enraged mob. I was temporarily captivated by the distraction that so many years after primary school history lessons, I finally saw the Euphrates River that led to the Fertile Crescent of Mesopotamia! Syrian and Turkish dams had withered its power and volume, but not diminished its romantic legend. We fed back onto the tedious desert highway.

Again Farah managed to navigate the border crossing, using her informal contacts and charm, as I attempted to navigate the merciless hell hole of the Jordanian border squat toilet. Desperation to use the facilities meant entering a toilet block with a stench and liberal scattering of turd, water and urine so alarming it was easy to imagine a fleet of raging Tasmanian Devils on a diet of laxatives had been unleashed. The human bustle inside was industrious. Feet were being washed in the basins. A jettisoned poo lay curled up in the wall-width, metal public urinal. The urinal! Ripples of foul water dispersed from around my boots as I stared at the faecal mounds protruding from the squat holes of each cubicle. I gagged as I took my place next to the brown smeared handprints on the wall. In the seeming eternity of my body still questioning my motives for baring my bum to such a beast, I had convinced myself cholera was inevitable unless I closed my eyes. Finally emerging from the building, relieved, with my boots and lower trousers only partially soaked from the floor, it felt like a supreme victory to inhale a fresh, dusty breath. Onwards.

We continued to speed along the rutted roads cut through the inhospitable landscape with its topping of thousands of black rocks cracked open on the endless flat, dry sands. Through small worn towns. Straight past the stop sign! Tyres fought with tarmac and brakes in a banshee howl as we ploughed into the side of the fruit and vegetable-laden pickup truck that had failed to stop moments before we failed to stop. In a reaction before crashing, I grabbed Farah, who was shocked awake by the sound and impact. The drivers stood arguing among the litter of smashed tomatoes as a small crowd gathered from nearby pavements to join in the remonstrations, and of course, choose sides in the allocation of blame. In the interests of not creating additional excitement, it seemed an inopportune time to be a ginger-pink foreigner standing next to a pretty young Iraqi woman next to an SUV full of dogs. People were staring at us, trying to gauge our connection to the incident before also gesticulating at the driver. To settle the matter, our driver paid a negotiated cash fee to the pickup driver, and we quickly left the chaotic scene of spectators. With the dogs finally delivered to the HCAW, we checked into the hotel. The following morning, I flew back to South Africa.

The first phone call I received back in South Africa was from Farah. She was sparking with excitement. "They've caught him! They found Saddam! Watch the news!" It was astonishing. Finally; and the day I had been en route home. So he wasn't hiding in a bunker under the zoo after all! We had discussed his speculative whereabouts almost every day for the previous seven months. The rumours of hiding places and escape strategies, and his influence in the insurgent resistance had filtered into so many conversations, been exaggerated, been elevated to the truth then faded as speculation. The insurgency would crumble with his capture! The insurgency would see him as a martyr and fight harder under the influence of loyalist generals! The insurgency was religiously based Jihad against Americans and far beyond Saddam's influence! Nobody appeared to really know. For days the undignified imagery of a stunned, dishevelled, wildly hairy Saddam being dragged out of a subterranean *spider hole* by U.S. forces on a farm near Tikrit (Saddam's hometown), was played out across the world's media. Whether Iraq would settle in response, or explode beyond recognition was the great unknown.

I chewed through the sinewy judgement of attempting to return to Iraq. I had survived unscathed, and that was a bonus. But among the comfort of home, there was already lurking guilt from temporarily abandoning Farah, William, Waseem, Ali and the palace lions. The job wasn't close to completion. Frustratingly the international news revealed almost nothing about daily life in Iraq. Over the phone Farah assured me all was normal; there were explosions, rumours, riots by former Iraqi soldiers and dismissed government employees, abductions and work was carrying on at the zoo as before. The palace lions were healthy and eating. I missed it intensely, but conflictingly I feared returning would be tempting fate, asking for a debilitating injury or worse.

Farah phoned again, in a mix of rage and tears. Extracts from her immediate follow-up email to anyone she knew may listen, set the tone.

"Dear people ...
I think it's my responsibility to let you the truth and the facts...

Yesterday around 2 p.m. a bunch of soldiers came to Baghdad Zoo. When they left they left a disaster behind their backs, just for having fun based on what one of them said. They drove inside the Zawra Park (the zoo is in the middle of the park), stopped their vehicles, gripped one of the puppies that wander around. She was 5 months old cute fluffy puppy, what we had in mind for her is that she's been adopted by American family and was supposed to fly to the states within the next 10 days. May be you will ask why is she wandering around??...

She was born in the zoo from a stray mom, a family of 3 pups and their mom. I told a lady in the States about them and she was more than happy to find them homes and she did. After a period of time when the pups stopped sucking milk & started eating well I decided to put them in an enclosure just to make sure that they are around but this little puppy she didn't let me touch her or pet her. She was so naughty, so cute. We decided to leave her around. She's everybody's friend, we kept feeding her same as all other animals in the zoo. She made new friends all around the park and the Iraqi force protection security guards were loving, caring and feeding her also. All of them knew that she's got a warm loving home waiting for her.
May be you think it's so much details but I need you to know the truth.

Back to the sad side of the story, they muzzled the pup, tied her hind limbs drawled her using a rope inside a lions enclosure. ????????????????????????????????? What do you feel right now??

Well unfortunately I know exactly your feeling because I had to go through this yesterday.
There was a keeper and one of the zoo veterinarians talked to the Iraqi Interpreter and told the soldiers don't do that but they said we are doing this for fun. He asked them do you do this back in the states, they said no. That wasn't enough for them; they took photos for what was going on. The veterinarian couldn't do anything because he was scared that he may follow the puppy. He came to report the incident; I rushed out with a Captain who've been helping the zoo and animals since April. We couldn't catch them. We reported this to the people in charge at the CPA and will keep looking for those soldiers. Now in the name of animal rights that you all defend for, I ask you to help me to get this poor animal's rights from those moron merciless soldiers. Do they think just because they are in Iraq? What will

happen to me if I throw one of the canine patrol dogs to the lions? What will happen to me if I through one of the soldiers to the lions just for having fun?

They came here to save the country ..... Save all the live creatures in Iraq from the cruelty of a bad ruler ....What did get instead??? Unfortunately, the tiger incident has been forgotten by everybody & we didn't even get a formal apology from any one in charge. From one side I'm helping American families to adopt dogs and sending them home for them and on the other side they are killing my pets and people's pets. I know you will do a lot that's why I wrote this to you.

I will keep following on this and I will not stop until I get revenge for the puppy, until I kick somebody's guts out for doing this.
I will need your help and support.

Thank you so much for giving time to read this sad story.
If you saw a soldier around you walk away, you may be the next meal for the lions."

In a fury, Farah drove to the CPA to enlist the assistance of the South African security contractors we knew from the Al-Rasheed days. Their operations base was in the CPA palace. Farah explained again how the puppy had been bound around the legs and thrown several meters to be torn apart by lions. The contractors' disgust at the actions of the soldiers led them to take Farah to Lieutenant Colonel Liz Kuh, already a friend and great supporter of the zoo efforts. The storm gathered momentum, and Farah with her hurricane attitude was soon unleashing an unbridled explanation of events at Brigadier General Kimmit (Deputy Director of Operations of Combined Joint Task Force 7 and the senior spokesman for the U.S. military in Iraq). Despite facing the tirade of an incensed young Iraqi veterinarian in his office, the response from the Brigadier General was remarkable, polite, swift and compassionate. A full, immediate investigation was ordered.

Another email followed.

"Dear friends.

Thank you very much for your response and again I didn't expect less than that. Also when I went to CPA to inform them about the incident I honestly didn't expect less than what they've done. Everybody was extremely cooperative and they were all mad starting from high rank generals ending up with soldiers at checkpoints. I've been in the CPA offices for the last 2 days & I met fascinating people whom assured me that they follow up with this till they find who did it. I took their word seriously, I knew they will do it and they did. Ambassador Bremer himself was personally informed and he asked his best soldiers to follow up with this. The generals and other rank soldiers whom I met yesterday were great people and they were the kind of people who I'm sure deserved to be call as soldiers. They were the type of people we expect to see in Iraq after the war.

This morning a Major and a Captain came to the zoo to take statements from the zoo staff and witnesses they were wonderful people, I'm sorry that I met them in these circumstances but I'm glad I met them. They've been great. In the same afternoon I received a phone call from the Major, he informed me that they found them. That was the best news ever. At the end of the day everybody was great, fantastic, cooperative, caring and loving for animals. It is my responsibility again to tell the world that not all the American Soldiers are bad as those soldiers. The U.S. Army has a lot of good well-mannered soldiers...

My special thanks to Ambassador Bremer, General Kimmit, Colonel Warren , Deputy Chief of Staff Lieutenant Colonel Stamps, Lieutenant Colonel Miklos, Lieutenant Colonel Kuh, Lieutenant Colonel Volmer, Ambassador ***** "Baghdad mayor", Colonel Pitchlynn, Captain Sumner (and everybody in Baghdad central office), Major Rago, Captain Cundy.

Thank you very much on behalf of Baghdad zoo director and staff.

I'm sorry if I forgot to mention anyone else but I met lots of people for the past two days and they were all great."

An official apology was given by U.S. Army officers, the soldiers responsible were demoted, and the unit was barred from entering the zoo without prior permission from the zoo management.

The mildly anxious anticipation of returning to the intensity of Baghdad was swept away on that dusty highway journey from the airport to the CPA. Any remaining palm trees that had lined the scrubby verges of the highway were bulldozed flat or scorched black from fires. Withered and dead fronds reflected a new, pummelled setting. What had been intended as a blunt elimination of hiding places for would-be attackers was a new matrix of toppled trees and churned sand tracks, that likely presented many added hiding options. To me, the shamelessly compelling enticement of military activity and unnecessary risk still seemed to outweigh the news reports that Baghdad's security and collective mental state was deteriorating. The speculation by the assortment of khaki-clad bureaucrats, media and contractors had moved from the previously familiar, "Where's Saddam?" to what retribution there would be from his supporters.

Hugging Farah in the CPA parking area, and then seeing William and his house crew, Waseem and the palace lions and being re-immersed into the zoo energy triggered a raft of sensations. Overwhelmingly that camaraderie made for an unlikely but seamless transition from a Cape Town Christmas. I quietly hoped the palace lions would have the same sensation, a flicker of recognition that one of their human companions had returned to care for them. If they did, they concealed it impeccably with dispassionate stares, a desire to tear apart donkey legs and ignoring any interaction beyond Brutus's attempt to scent mark a victim with a noxious liquid spray from his anal glands.

A few mornings later, as I sat on the loo before readying to head out to the zoo, the walls and window of the bathroom rocked as the deep rumble and concussion of the blast swept out from Assassins gate on the edge of the Green Zone. It was a sanitised announcement of the explosive carnage unleashed a few hundred metres down the road. A truck bomb tore through the rush-hour crowds and traffic choked at the gate while awaiting entry. Vehicles and road were scorched and tossed away in the furious, boiling wind. 24 people slaughtered. 63 to 120 reportedly injured; that all-encompassing term for broken bodies with anything from scratches to survivable mutilation, dismemberment and disfigurement. Limbs that weren't vaporised were dispersed in all directions.

Farah and William had over previous months, made enormous progress on the development of the Iraq Society for Animal Welfare (ISAW). It had gone as rapidly as expected, as was the norm; sporadic, interrupted, but inching forwards among the seemingly endless encroaching bureaucracy. The ISAW building had been a former restaurant, abandoned by the concession holder many months before the war. In re-allocations of the concession stand licences towards mid- and late 2003 by the CPA and Baghdad Municipality, that particular concession holder had been absent. It was presumed he had either run away, was dead or no longer wanted to engage in that business. A building contractor, with approximately $10 000 Civil Affairs funding William had sourced, had renovated the former restaurant, repaired water and electricity supplies, serviced air conditioners and fitted partitions for consultation rooms. A series of holding cage facilities were constructed for cases needing post-operative care, or for boarding animals in need of re-homing. Some of the veterinary equipment supplied by

Lozada was allocated to make a basic but functional surgery. The excitement was steadily building as ISAW was turning from a hazy, ambitious idea into a reality. The first animal welfare society in Iraq! Education. Advocacy. Direct pet care. Public health engagement. We were planning it all at pace, and in consultation with U.S. welfare agency policies. The ISAW was weeks from opening to the public.

Like a resilient yeast infection, the former concession holder returned, fuming. He was outraged that *his* restaurant, which he hadn't paid rent for since before the war started, was no longer *his* restaurant. He ranted at the zoo. He ranted at the park offices. He ranted at the municipality offices. He had no legal claims to the building, had been missing for nearly a year, and there was a new city administration. Such facts, when pointed out, only seemed to inflame his wounded pride. We had documented agreements supporting our stance. We had followed the tedious bureaucratic muddle to a point where we felt confident to spend the funding on the facility. Once again, William stepped in to pacify the dispute; a small token payment helped ease the irate concession holder's perception of his persecuted dignity. That age-old approach to papering over the cracks of conflict-solving, a payment, would be a perpetual bugbear we would encounter at almost every turn. That was the habitat. The problem was that we barely had any money, and to maintain any moral credibility we needed to ensure cash was always spent on a positive animal welfare outcome. The yeast infection was soothed; for a time.

On the 21st of January 2004 a cluster of nearly twenty municipality officials, military officers, media, opportunistic gardeners and an AK-47 toting Iraqi FPS (Facility Protection Service) recruit watched as Farah proudly cut the blue ribbon to inaugurate the ISAW building. Only Lawrence was missing, unable to make it across to see the fruition of the idea he had declared eight months earlier. Unlike the flamboyant attention-grabbing of politicians at the opening of the zoo, only Farah and William made brief introductory speeches. Farah nervously clutched her speech pages as all the attention focused on her outlining the society's ambitions. The air was cold and crisp. The optimism felt like simmering energy among us. We thought it was an opportunity to genuinely influence animal welfare policy in the city; whatever the myriad other concerns government officials may be prioritising. We knew we could lead change if we could ensure ISAW's persistence. Dr Abbas guided the guests into the building for the customary cursory nods and pointing before the attention focused on the cake and soft drinks. For Farah, William and me the relief of finally reaching that point was immense, an occasion we felt rather self-satisfied about.

The concept of an animal welfare charity was viewed as peculiar among the many Iraqi's we had engaged during the planning phase. "People don't have the dog for anything but only for the protection" was a typical response. Despite being a commonly held perception, it wasn't true. Some families in Baghdad did have pet dogs. The municipality response to stray dogs was to encourage the police to hone their marksmanship on the roving canids; to eliminate the evil disease-carrying public menace. The other option was to drop out meat laced with strychnine to poison whatever may eat it. The result was the same as it is in most countries with that inconsistent, reactionary, ill-informed approach; a variety of poisoned animals, some dead dogs, some brutally maimed dogs, and a continued problem with stray animals. So given that Baghdad was in a state of mildly functional chaos it was always encouraging to get the rare vote of support for our proposals of a long-term, spay-neuter campaign with a side-serving of adoptions. Even Dr Abbas, whose focus was strictly the Baghdad Zoo, had been helpful with municipality contacts and advice on which protocols to follow when navigating the bureaucracy. He had begun to show great interest in the financial aspect of the society, like how much we would be charging customers, how much donor funding we could source, and how much profit we could generate. The apparent growing curiosity in the ISAW was in how we had cunningly been able to build up an illusion through which we could harvest barrels-full of money.

It wasn't long after the opening that a bulky, dapper-suited but gruff-looking gentleman from a university in Baghdad visited Dr Abbas. It wasn't unusual to be introduced to Dr Abbas's many acquaintances that would arrive for a tea at the office, but on this occasion, Dr Abbas seemed especially eager to make the introduction. Dr Abbas politely introduced him to Farah and me as the new director of the ISAW. Slightly nonplussed, we asked him what he meant. Dr Abbas, (sensing their opportunity to step into the rain of money we were so obviously bathing in - my fashionably deconstructed sneakers and frayed trousers being the giveaway) informed us we would no longer have to concern ourselves with the daily running of ISAW. His associate, a veterinarian, would from then onwards run the ISAW while Farah and I ensured the donor funding continued to flow into a swelling account. It took me a few seconds of mental processing to work out if I was the delusional one, and had missed a cultural quirk or that there was actually a bizarre attempt in play to steal an NGO. "Thanks for that offer, but we aren't going to hand over this charity to someone we have never met and who has never had anything to do with animal welfare. A person cannot simply arrive and lay claim to an organisation." Once again, in what seemed a wholly surreal experience given that we were all educated adults, Farah had to explain what the concept of a charity was. Farah made it clear there would be no change. We walked out. It was the last we saw of the man. It was the last time Dr Abbas raised the matter directly to us. Yet as the months wore on, the unsubtly targeted questions (like "how much do you pay yourself from ISAW?") always seemed to leave the slightly aggravating impression that he suspected Farah and I were colluding to enrich ourselves. It didn't help that months later an international weekly news magazine published an article on U.S. administrative wastage, including a claim the CPA had paid a South African at the Baghdad Zoo more than $30 000 – a figure further exaggerated when an Iraqi daily newspaper published it. Explanations that I hadn't been able to secure any salary funding from the CPA to work at the zoo, so was volunteering again, was so inconceivable it seemed to generate the intrigue associated with me being a money-laundering genius, or a spy.

Despite this distraction, Farah's progress at ISAW was remarkable. In addition to the ongoing soldiers' pet adoption relocations and vaccination program, in the first six months, she had been able to secure donor funding to pay the salary of a full-time vet and assistant and rehome nearly forty sterilised dogs (and a few cats) to Iraqi families in Baghdad. Seeing the expressions of delight on parents and children's faces, that they had actually adopted an animal, entirely dismantled any scepticism I had about the potential success of a local adoption program Farah had been so adamant about implementing. Somehow though, it still seemed that most of the dogs arriving at the zoo were pregnant. It was impossible not to be both frustrated by the seemingly endless conveyor belt of new dogs and to melt into a compliant bleeding-heart at the prospect of being warmed in the cold office by cosy, sleeping puppies.

Somewhere in the distance, following the low rumble of an explosion beyond the dirt berm adjacent to the highway, a familiar grey plume rolled up towards the wispy clouds in the mostly clear blue sky. It was far enough away it didn't appear cause for much concern. The taxi drove on for hours and hours, through the seemingly endless sand and gravel plains, then finally beyond the choked up border, into frigidly cold Amman. Finally, Dr Abbas and Ahmed boarded their first-ever international flight – destination London – in soaking, freezing February. Nick Lindsay from the ZSL choreographed a whirlwind experience at facilities the Iraqis could only have dreamed of. The staggering assortments of creatures in their abundance of shapes, colours and created habitats seemed to defy belief. Tigers. Rhinos. Psychedelic coloured fish and frogs. Okapis. Penguins. Tapirs. Bandicoots. Cranes. Gazelles. Ferrets. Crocodiles. The husbandry, veterinary and conservation expertise of the many generously hospitable staff at the facilities kept Farah and I amazed, and once information was translated, sent Ahmed into feverish note scribbling on his A4 pad. We were genuinely taken by surprise that all the animals, from tiny fishes and geckos to giraffe seemed to be doted over with the same level of veterinary care. Diets and supplements, educational signage and crush pen designs were obsessively recorded in detail. Dr Abbas would observe quietly, dignified and often solemn. It always felt like a conscious concern for Nick, Farah and me that he recognised Baghdad Zoo would likely never match the facilities he was seeing, and as Director, rather than only being delighted at what he saw and the contacts he was making, would also be immensely frustrated. The difficulty was in navigating the vast chasm of knowledge, skills, equipment, budget, collection history, cultural expectations, and ambition to extract ideas and opportunities to pragmatically enhance or modify Baghdad Zoo. We needed to consider which observations were transferable to the Baghdad context. Yet, there was no denying the beaming smile escaping Dr Abbas's usually staid expression when seeing Whipsnade Zoo's elephants. A chance to feed ring-tailed lemurs on his shoulder melted any hesitation.

Before our leaving Baghdad, visitors had begun to engage in a peculiar game of using either their own limbs or their infant children to lure lions from resting points in the expansive enclosure. The high wall rising above the enclosure's shallow perimeter moat was lined with a row of vertically aligned, rebar fencing. Some visitors would wave a limb between the bars, or encourage their child to stand on the boundary wall to fit between the bars as an adult held them. Once the lions' curiosity was aroused and they walked towards the bait, visitors would be delighted by their personal cunning and the close quarters viewing of a "lazy lion". It was outrageously risky behaviour, and the keepers responsible for the lions would plead with the visitors to show better judgement. I thought the keepers had a watertight, rational argument against stupidity – despite Salman's tendency to occasionally walk among the lions with a stick like some diminutive wizard. Some visitors seemed to confuse their own ignorance with invincibility. The keepers' pleas were mostly ignored. That would incense Farah who would march to the enclosure and combust into expletive-laden educational tirades for the benefit of such visitors. On more than one occasion, Dr Abbas and Waseem were also called to resolve arguments about disrespect. In a city already filled with so much inherent risk, it baffled us that parents would be so irresponsible, and then defensive and argumentative. An armed security guard was posted at the lion enclosure to try to persuade visitors to behave rationally. While we were in London, our fears were realised. A father gave security the slip and held his infant child between the bars without realising lions were resting in the drying stone moat directly below his viewing point. A lion leapt up and bit off the top of the child's head. Gore and panic ensued as the child died. The emergency response was swift but essentially irrelevant. There was nobody at the zoo medically or logistically equipped to deal with such an outrageous scenario. The drama escalated rapidly once the horrified father recovered from the immediate shock, and began to threaten and then demand compensation from the zoo. Waseem, as the vet elevated to temporary zoo administrator in Dr Abbas's absence, had to navigate the situation with the municipality administrators. At a point of resolution, there were no winners; there could never have been. There was only unnecessary, avoidable death and trauma. The zoo staff had witnessed a tragic scenario, and the father had participated in the death of his child. For the lions, it was another day at the zoo.

We returned from London to a freezing, sludgy, snow-blanketed Amman, for the return drive from Jordan to Baghdad. It blew away any lingering, ignorantly clichéd impression of the Middle East as an exclusively hot, dusty, rocky, sandpit. Gracia Bennish, an American photographer, and close friend of Lawrence, was waiting to meet us. She was to make the drive to Baghdad with us, and over a series of days would build a photographic portfolio of scenes from our daily activities. We had no idea who she was and feared we would need to spend more time babysitting her than getting on with our work. The decrepit, seedy hotel we were restricted to staying in Amman (since access to our usual option was impossible in a sedan in the ice and snow) was her first test. Her cheery approach settled our scepticism. She was wonderfully friendly in that motherly American way, interested and interesting. It seemed Lawrence might have glossed over some of the details of what she should have expected to encounter. Once again we set off in an SUV taxi ride across the desert that was as alarming as usual; wild overtaking, high speed and a matter of waiting for a drama to unfold. We didn't have to wait long for escalation.

Once back in Iraq, our driver, sensing an overtaking opportunity where there was none, urged his SUV to outdo a vehicle ahead. We hollered untamed filth as the enormous, thundering oncoming truck was about to annihilate us! Our driver swerved into a gap back into our intended lane. Our left rear window exploded in a spray of glass as the truck clipped the finest of edges of the tail of our vehicle. The hurtling mass of cargo carrier careened into oversteer and off the highway, erupting plumes of dust and stones out from the desert gravel. Our vehicle jolted right and left from the blow and lashing air before the driver secured control. Fortune had favoured us again, and within a few hundred meters, we had pulled off the road to inspect our vehicle and compose our thoughts. Gracia screamed outrage at the driver, swearing we would abandon the vehicle, he wouldn't get paid, and we would get another driver to take us to Baghdad! We needed to highlight our location to her, the western desert of Al-Anbar Province (home to the agitated cities of Fallujah and Ramadi). We were exposed, isolated, it was freezing, and the province was reputed to be sparking with anti-American, insurgency sentiment. It was not the place for westerners to be wandering around outside a vehicle threatening the driver with impossible scenarios. Quite simply, there was no other option. The driver would have to continue to Baghdad. So would we. That would be best, safest and quickest for all of us. It was onwards into the flat, monotonous beige dust. The remaining seven hours of our journey was a sedate affair with the back window taped closed and overtaking relegated to memories of a former life.

We focused on our time with Gracia who snapped a barrage of photos of the palace lions, the bears, the Arabian horses being exercised outside the university stables, and school children visiting ISAW and the zoo with logistical support from a U.S. Army MP unit. The visit by the children was the first time a school had prompted and organised a tour, and it felt like a landmark occasion. It was far removed from the occasional, tasteless parading of orphans or school children through the zoo by U.S. Army or CPA officials trying to contrive positive public relations fodder. Media agencies would lap up the contrived feed but were conspicuous in their absence from the genuine, low-key visit. Most of the actual army assistance for the zoo went unnoticed by the outside world.

Gracia's visit also prompted an invitation from Waseem's mother to eat lunch at her house, resulting in us being whisked unobtrusively through back roads of neighbourhoods by Farah. There was an obvious risk for the family if Gracia and I as foreigners were seen entering the house, and we recognised the rare privilege they afforded us. The generous, vibrantly coloured spread of *kibbeh*, grilled *masgouf* fish, chicken, soups and *mezze* was spread out on a pink embroidered cloth on the lounge floor carpet, as we circled like starving foragers waiting for permission to land. Naturally, the conversation turned to the many perceptions of the invasion. Waseem's bespectacled elderly grandmother, sat quietly, watching, with her head and shoulders wrapped in a white, cotton, *Shayla*. It took all my restraint to not laugh when she did chirp up. She spoke with the unfiltered candour of the elderly. "Did the Americans invade us to bring the Jews back?" she asked between mouthfuls. I nearly reflexively snorted out my hummus in surprise. It was a candid, uncensored concern that served to highlight the rumours in the city. We didn't mention Gracia was Jewish. In Iraq, the Palestinian saga and views on Israel consumed many thoughts and tangled with prevailing theories of Weapons of Mass Destruction, liberation, revenge against Saddam, geographic hegemony and oil theft.

A litter of three lion cubs had been born at the zoo days before we left for London and by our return had become a point of fascination and concern for the young, new keepers. The combination of the cultural legacy of lions in the region, their raw power, their regal status and the cuteness of the cubs was captivating. The keepers would report daily on whether each cub had fed, how the mother was responding, and which cubs were still suckling. There was an opportunity, once the cubs had been temporarily separated from the mother for health checks, to enable the new keepers to feed their curiosity. Each wanted a photo with the cubs, and while we knew such actions would be frowned on in most reputable international facilities, we believed we needed to stimulate and encourage any interest we could. The lions weren't going anywhere, so we wanted keepers to be engaged. We wanted keepers to feel the enthusiasm and cultivate some level of empathy for the animals. We wanted keepers to share our passion. We wanted them to be curious. The keepers, many of whom were barely literate, were unlikely to get or respond to highly technical training, so we wished keepers to enjoy caring as a first priority. Some responded. The thrill of the opportunity meant the observations and reports never slowed in frequency or intensity.

Sawdust laid for insulation against the cold concrete floor of the inner holding section was replaced frequently, and there were regular requests about how the lions could be helped more. Given that the lion births had taken place in the enclosure that previously housed Malooh, the tiger shot by the soldier, we could only think that more space and a controlled sterilisation program to halt breeding would be the best next step. Including the palace cats, the zoo was caring for 19 lions. Neither of those management interventions was an option at the time. "We want many lions. 50. 100 lions!" explained one of the staff. It was partly in jest, partly not. The fertility of the lions gave the team an undeniable sense of pride. But I had fears that the lions could also be used as a bargaining chip to trade for other animals on the black market. Combined with the requirements of the zoos other carnivores and omnivores nearly 90 kilograms of meat was already required for daily feeding.

To our relief, Gracia left Baghdad contented, and without incident. We could again focus solely on our own safety. Soon after she left a keeper came rushing to Farah, Waseem and me at the zoo office, with news of a possible drowning in the canals. The police had already been phoned by a member of the public. We ran across towards the southern end of the zoo to find an animated crowd gathered in the road adjacent to the stone, sloped canal sidewall. There was panicked shouting and gesticulating as two men swam frantically in the murky green, frigid canal water. Threads of water weed swirled with each kick or splash of arms. The men could hardly swim but were desperately ducking under the surface trying to find a young woman that at first was thought to have slipped and fallen into the canal. Sa'ad and I helped to pull one of the men out of the water when it was clear he was too cold to support himself. He shivered violently as his sopping shirt and trousers clung to his scrawny frame. His light-brown face and arms had turned a ghoulish shade of grey-blue. A zoo vehicle was driven to the scene, and we used it to rush the man and his friend to the heated office. Unable to stand, the dripping man collapsed as we stripped off his wet clothes and wrapped and vigorously rubbed his nearly naked hypothermic body in towels and blankets. He slipped in and out of consciousness.

Waseem, Farah and several of the zoo staff had been managing the crowd as the police arrived to assist the man in the water retrieve the pale, weed-entangled, lifeless body of the woman from the canal. By the time the entourage arrived back at the office to meet the exhausted but talking, tea-drinking, towel-wrapped man, the true story of the incident had emerged. The police had arrested the drowned woman's husband. The young couple, recently married by arrangement, had visited the zoo and the husband had seized the opportunity to push his wife into the water, knowing she could not swim. We made another round of glasses of bitter Iraqi tea before leaving the zoo to feed to palace lions. Sa'ad, the keeper who had been stabbed in the head by his uncles, called Farah aside as she walked through the zoo on her morning inspection. Talking in hushed tones, he told her that he had overheard a plan by some of the older zoo staff; there would be an attempt to kidnap me if the opportunity presented itself. Sa'ad believed Farah would be discreet with the information. He didn't want to tell me directly and alarm me. I had suspected such an issue might arise at some point but imagined my lack of military worth would reduce my prospects of being bagged. If there was a chaotic distraction in the park or zoo, like an explosion or attack, that would be their opportunity to try to snatch me. If that was the case, from what Sa'ad had heard, I needed to get to a vehicle and leave, immediately. No fucking around. Leave. The suspects Sa'ad mentioned were no particular surprise as there had been rumours throughout our time at the zoo that several of them had been disgruntled by Saddam's removal. On the surface, there was always pleasant daily engagement, but some of us had suspected there was an increasingly political, religious and cultural bitterness simmering. I was foreign and represented a daily reminder of the U.S. invasion. I was fair game. It wasn't like we naively trusted everyone. We only told William and Waseem of Sa'ad's information. Most of the time in Baghdad, until then, had been about some attempt at risk avoidance. I had no intention of getting whacked or snatched on account of my own stupidity, despite being there for reasons that at times seemed challenging to articulate. Situational guidance from zoo staff I trusted implicitly, security contractors or U.S. military friends was what I relied on to reduce encountering potentially dangerous situations. My love of the conspicuous black SUV was the critical flaw in that strategy. I had started to make quick, discreet (likely only in my mind) searches under the car for obvious explosive devices before we left the zoo in the afternoons. We had heard more and more often about explosives being attached under cars of foreigners or "collaborators". When Farah relayed Sa'ad's news there was a mental shift to view everyone through the perspective of risk; were they a likely danger and what would a probable threat scenario entail? To those around us we projected a sense of normality; except I only ever walked through the zoo grounds with at least one of Farah, Ahmed, Waseem or Sa'ad, and always carried my concealed little 9mm gun. The carrying of a weapon was an unnatural, uncomfortable state of mind for me. It was a zoo. I didn't practise handling the gun regularly beyond dismantling and reassembly. I didn't have a military or law enforcement background, and training opportunities at the game reserve had been haphazard and with different weapons. I was acutely aware of that. And how does one project a sense that all is normal while trying to inconspicuously wear a t-shirt, no holster and a concealed weapon?

It wasn't particularly easy (or advisable) to hide the weapon in my baggy trouser pocket the morning we tried to catch five big, pink pigs and their little swarm of piglets for vaccination. The family of pigs had increased in size and number since their relocation from the awful Luna Park in

2003. As per the preventative medicine approach we had initiated, we needed to inoculate each pig. The concern was that they weren't exactly cooperative and had developed noticeably feral attitudes in their well-treed, paddock. There was no central holding facility to lure them into, and feeding had usually entailed scattering food throughout the paddock to encourage activity like sniffing, foraging and rooting. We tried the casual, friendly approach. The wily, suspicious pigs ran. We ran. The keepers ran. The weather had started to warm up again, quickly. We sweated copiously. The gun juggled up and down in my pocket. I knew how foolish and unsafe that was, but we eventually caught each pig by hand and rope and injected the vaccines. We lay there sweating, covered in mud, laughing, heaving phlegmy breaths. We basked in the surging sense of satisfaction and solidarity, having chased down the hogs and completed the job as a collective with the vets and keepers, rather than dictate duties from the office or through Dr Abbas. The keepers seemed energised, we felt strongly they would learn more with a hands-on approach with us; and it was obviously more entertaining for us than sitting around waiting. It was also those times that reinforced the enjoyment of working with Wasseem who compensated for his veterinary shortcomings by taking on more added responsibility than was fair and in a manner where he was almost apologetic for not shouldering extra burden. He never delegated any task he would not be prepared to do himself, and even when exhausted, and his blue overall was soaked through with sweat, he'd still manage an unassuming smile.

Among other competing financial and time needs, Farah and I were still visiting the Arabian horses at the university at least once a week. We had been able to drag out the *outrageous fee* versus *rent-free* stable negotiations with the administration to the point of amicable inertia. Farah was also working on the logistics of sending military-adopted pets out of Iraq and importing much-needed supplies like vaccines. Following the London trip, we had initiated a plan to renovate the paddock that had previously housed the gazelle, and then two goats. It was twice the size of an Olympic swimming pool but was indicative of the difficulty in changing mindsets. I felt it would be a fantastic area for the two cheetahs to live in and a striking highlight for the zoo. With some modifications to the fence, it would be secure, and once the water supply was repaired for irrigation, the area would undoubtedly become a lush, attractive area for both the cheetahs and viewing visitors. Two small buildings already in the paddock could be modified for storage, shade and warm shelter in winter. Three large shade trees remained, and another had fallen over to add a convenient raised viewing and territory mount for cheetahs. "But it is the gazelle area" was the initial response to the idea. When I pointed out there was no gazelle, the response was "yes, but there are two goats now until we get gazelle for breeding". The repeated suggestions that the goats could be moved to a smaller, but still substantial empty paddock were not immediately considered an option because it was not the goat paddock. But I suspect Dr Abbas grew tired of the requests for one large-scale experimental modification out of the original blueprint and conceded. Ali, the taxi driver, was quickly called to source a fencing contractor while the option was still on the table. Ali went a step further, and with a task at hand appointed himself the de facto project supervisor. Some keepers were invited to help with the renovations. In exchange they were offered additional money if they chose to work after-hours; much to the irritation of the lazier young keepers who had avoided any opportunity to work beyond the minimum effort.

  As was the customary way, the project progressed slowly, primarily since re-fencing the area took the contractor nearly four months. Once the moving day arrived, we were thrilled at how cooperation had created an area to be proud of. We predicted enthusiastic and energised cheetahs succumbing to curiosity rather than arthritis. They could scent mark their new territory, bask in the sunshine without any structure or bars above them, or enjoy the shade of trees or peer out over their new surrounds from the elevated option of the fallen trunk. There was a little smugness in the "this is more like what cheetahs do in the wilds" self-congratulations. We crated the two placid cheetahs, relocated them across the zoo and released them into our masterpiece. After a cursory patrolling inspection and sniff of their new world, they settled in the shade of a tree and for months hardly moved beyond that coveted corner other than to find food, drink water or enjoy an ear scratch from the staff.

Two keepers, Sa'ad and Faaiz, rushed over to the office to report one pelican had attacked the other during a feeding scuffle. Jaboory had thrown a fish to the one pelican, but in a launched attack of water, flapping wings and a lunge with its bill the other pelican had tried to steal the food. To us, it seemed an unlikely story. We didn't know pelicans would attack each other. It was a ghastly sight with the stretchy, yellow-skin throat pouch lacerated, blood oozing out where gaping holes had been torn. The lower bill was mangled into a disfigured twist like a highway guide rail after receiving a car. Jaboory, the gentle, ancient keeper was on the verge of tears, not able to comprehend why the assault had happened and worried about his pelican's future. Sa'ad and Faaiz covered the bloodied bird's head with a cloth to pacify it and carried the pelican to the office area. There Sa'ad sat in an office chair restraining the creature as Waseem and Farah set to work. The skin was debrided and cleaned, and attempts were made to suture the flaps closed. The bill remained contorted despite efforts to massage it into a more regular profile. Given the shape and location of the ripped strip of the elastic pouch, it wasn't possible to reattach skin directly to the bill. The pelican was left confined overnight until Dr Abbas arrived to help us think of a plan. All we could think of in addition to the previous afternoon's surgery was to attempt to brace the bill in the hope it would recover some of its original shape. We had no idea how and had no appropriate surgical materials. It was decided to try using two rigid plastic folder spines for holding A4 documents together. They were lightweight, inflexible and could be cut to almost fit the bill ridge. With help from Ali and Ali (keepers), Dr Abbas and Waseem sutured the disinfected braces to the manipulated bill. We didn't know how the blood circulation had been impacted by the attack or the follow-up surgeries, but the pouch and bill were cleaned again. The bird fed on fish passed into the pouch with surprisingly little difficulty. Unfortunately, through the week the blackening necrosis of the bill and pouch tissue became increasingly evident. The pelican continued to feed with assistance and was plied with antibiotics it was hoped would help fight any infection. Despite the withering bill, the bird unexpectedly maintained its health and became more comfortable to feed as it habituated to the daily human contact. As weeks progressed the broken portion of beak and torn areas of pouch wasted away to leave half of the lower bill fused closed with a healthy, but smaller bill pouch attached. It looked like a cartoon pelican with a severe overbite. A decision was made to return it to the zoo's one large pool aviary with the ducks and the avian assaulter, where it could bathe and sun itself. There was nowhere else we could contain it long-term that had both a steady water supply and a net structure to stop it flying away. We were tentative about how it would cope, and whether it would be attacked again, but it slipped back into its watery world with ease to Jaboory's beaming delight as he again tossed fish to both pelicans.

Al-Zawra Park and Baghdad Zoo (left) from the park's abandoned tower restaurant.

War-damage inspection of a lion enclosure. A detour from saving rare antiquities. (Photo: M Alleruzzo)

Abandoned pelican at Luna Park Zoo. (Photo: M Alleruzzo)

The Al-Rasheed Hotel valet parking service.

Every zoo needs a Surface-to-Air missile system truck. (Photo: W Sumner)

Saeida the "blind" bear.

Captain William Sumner looking suave at the zoo. (Photo: W Sumner)

Diehl's cafe: Lawrence (2nd left) fails to perpetuate the myth of my unrivalled ruggedness. Bradley Fighting Vehicle crews are stunned.

Ali (left) and Stefan (2nd left) meet the neighbours at the meat market.

Uday Hussein's abandoned palace lions.

Ali demonstrates his meat tossing prowess while dressed in appropriate olympic attire.

Athool ignoring the Bradley Fighting Vehicle and impromptu vice squad.

Farah explaining the nuances of cooperation versus temporary detention during the search for Saddam's stolen horses.

Samir demonstrates "Iraqi bears very strong" in Luna Park. (Photo: M. Alleruzzo)

Samir looking sceptically at the little wheels of Ali's hoisted transport cage.

Captain Little and his bear-recovery crew.

Pimping Uday Hussein's attention-craving cheetahs for friendship and protection.

Mariette Hopley hides among an Al-Zawra Park clean-up squad.

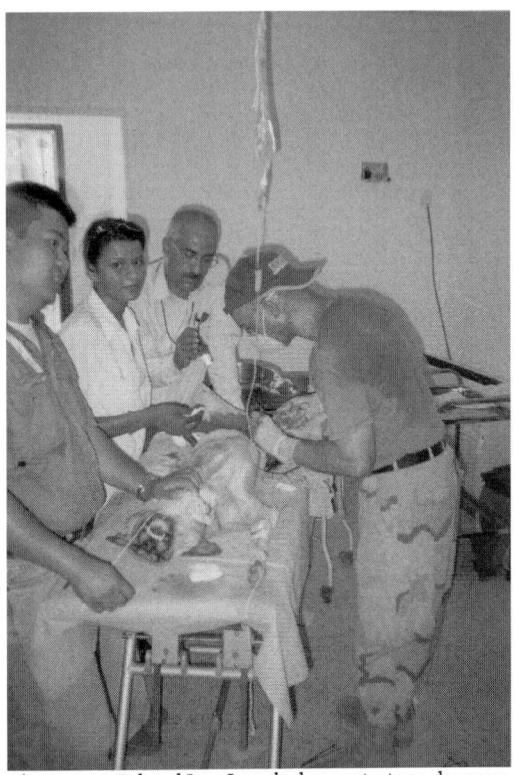

Lieutenant Colonel Jose Lozada demonstrates a dog spay surgery to Jackson Zee, Farah and the zoo director in the electricity-free office.

Ahmed (left), Akram and Saad (right) with the freshly groomed partner of "Ugliest Dog in the World".

The looted Iraqi Natural History Museum.

Jaboory demonstrates his mastery of pelican and geese feeding politics.

Another chilly day at the meat market.

Tiger. Shot dead.

Abandoned palace cheetahs feigning excitement in their new Baghdad Zoo enclosure. (insert: old enclosure)

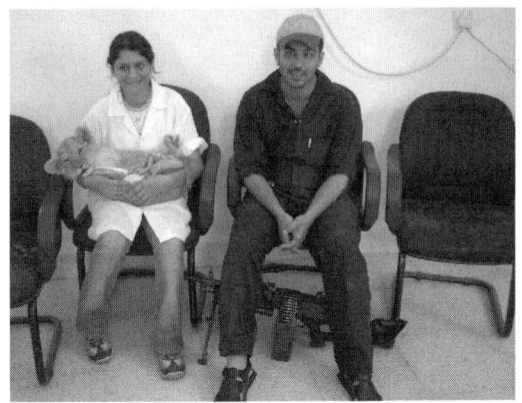

Farah and Wasseem establish protocols for post-operative care.

Author and Captain William Sumner wait eagerly for Ahmed's lunch delivery. Akram waits too. (Photo: W Sumner)

Farah and Dusty in Amman, Jordan. Dusty's flight to America set the trend.

The zoo director, Lieutenant Lynge and Specialist Erin McLoughlin miraculously draw blood from the dying bear.

Another day at the car wash

Baghdad's "I was there" landmark. (Photo: Sofa Salesman)

PART 3: FEAR, GUILT, HOPE AND DUCT-TAPING LIONS

CHAPTER 14

Across Baghdad, there was wholesale changing-of-the-guard in motion. While the civilian CPA staffing contingent seemed to be in a regular state of flux, the military employed less frequent, but divisional-scale change. The 1st Cavalry Division was arriving to relieve the 1st Armoured Division. That also meant a transition of Civil Affairs units, fortunately to the sustained benefit of the zoo. The dedicated veterinary support Lozada and Colonel Gants had provided to the zoo was transitioning to a reservist Public Health Team from the 425th Civil Affairs Battalion led by veterinarian Lieutenant Colonel Steve Watters. Within that team, a powerful driving force to help the zoo was the no-bullshit veterinarian, Major Sam Barringer. Barringer was unlike anyone we had encountered until that point. When Sam was around, you knew it. He was a square-jawed, physically imposing unit of outdoorsman. No T-shirt looked like it was having an easy day being stretched over his frame. He had extensive veterinary experience with livestock and large exotic cats - as one does. He talked directly and switched between uncompromisingly blunt speech and a sly grin. He never planned for maybe, only for clear steps to get from A to B. As far as he was concerned Farah and Waseem had unlimited potential and between Barringer and his band of colleagues, that potential would be realised if the Iraqi vets wanted the help. Within days of our introduction, the team had worked with Waseem to anaesthetise Wounded-Ass bear, to reassess and prescribe treatment for her chronically weeping, infected paw pads. Borton, Lee, the hulk-like Dickey and their team suddenly became regular visitors to the zoo in their column of Humvees. Their presence undeniably helped us wean ourselves off the 354th Civil Affairs team that William had engineered to be such a central force for the zoo restoration and establishment of ISAW.

For Farah and me, our friendship with William Sumner had evolved radically from our unlikely and serendipitous collective attraction to the mostly unknown zoo in Iraq. We had come to rely unerringly on each other to enable a bizarre range of missions, stay emotionally grounded, keep laughing and keep each other secure. Our time together was being forced to an end. His unit was deploying back to the U.S.

The impending redeployment of the 354th Civil Affairs meant homelessness was lurking on my horizon, again. William asked if another unit would take me in as their charitable stray, but the opportunities were shut. I approached the Baghdad Central office in the CPA. Their muted enthusiasm was underwhelming. I had no contract or formal permission to be in Baghdad, so nobody was responsible for providing me with accommodation. However, I did have that precious United States *Department of Defence Foreign National* ID card which guaranteed checkpoint entry and meals. I had also kept the GMC SUV through playing the vague game regarding who had given me permission to drive it. It was inspected and signed off through the contracted logistics company KBR on a monthly schedule, and fortunately, nobody pressed further on whether those that had given us zoo folk initial permissions, were still in Iraq. They had long since left. The vehicle was a sleeping option. The final approach option I had was going to a zoo-friendly Lieutenant Colonel through a former Al-Rasheed Hotel contact. To my relief, I was allocated a bed in the expansive blast-wall ringed, portacabin trailer park on the northern boundary of the CPA palace, adjacent to the Tigris River. The uniform rows of white, two bedrooms, air-conditioned, prefabricated cabins stretched out for hundreds of meters, with piles of sandbags stacked between. It was a heaving temporary suburb of contractor staff employed within the greater CPA machine. Combat boots crunched along on the freshly laid gravel as people crossed through the searing, enveloping heat between their beds and offices.

Peter was a fascinating, older and unfortunate soul allocated to share a bedroom with me. He was an architect and urban planner who had initially entered Baghdad as a Major in a reservist unit. He was one of the first in the initial invasion to investigate Saddam's abandoned Republican Palace (which became the CPA palace) as a possible headquarters for the coalition's incoming administration. He enjoyed the supposedly refined aspects of life like order, thick cigars and Frank Sinatra. My transient, squatter-like approach with hand-laundered underpants drying on the chair, no salary, no sense of clothing style, no formal protection, no medical cover and no Baghdad extraction plan exasperated him. Conversely, I thought he was suicidal for dressing in a dishdasha and driving his battered sedan outside of the Green Zone at night to socialise with Iraqi friends. His sense of humour could be dry, cutting and hilarious. The day I brought back a grass-filled shoebox with two tiny, pink hedgehog babies (that KBR contractors had passed on to Farah from a construction site), was the day he thought the zoo was encroaching a little too close. He seemed to look on with bemused, sympathetic novelty as I would wake up through the night to feed the helpless creatures their syringe of milk concoction and then give them a gentle, warm belly rub to aid digestion. When neither of the hedgehogs survived, I thought I saw a twinge of empathy emerge from his New Yorker gruffness.

He finally made his debut visit to the zoo for the transfer of Suker the lioness to the main lion enclosure. It felt like an opportunity to finally convince him of the rationality and ambition of seemingly nonsensical efforts and risk going into the zoo. I felt like I needed to show him what it was all about – likely partly to validate my sanity through his eyes. It was an opportunity to see Iraqi staff in full control of their logistics and animals. The logic behind the lion move was that there didn't appear to be any logic behind the lioness, a social cat, living in isolation. There was also a case for using available enclosed space more effectively; she rarely used her outside area that was mostly devoid of grass and contained a large but damaged and dry pool. In response, we had restricted her access to the outdoor exercise area as we repaired the pool, irrigated the planted grass and brought in logs for scratching posts. Her enclosure was adjacent to that of the old tiger (father of Malooh, the shot tiger). He had an awful, postage-stamp-sized outside area of cool mud and discarded scraps of metal fencing in the shade of an enormous palm tree. He spent little time outside, had lost his appetite and was increasingly emaciated in his old age. Through Dr Abbas, we planned to open his enclosure into the lioness's area once she was transferred. Each time we carried out a significant task it seemed we got a little added credit and leeway with which to try out another new idea, which sometimes explained why some obvious options took many months to activate.

Waseem sank Suker into sleep with a single immobilising dart. Five of the young keepers helped Waseem carry her on an extended wooden pallet onto the back of the waiting pickup. After a short drive and with some heavy lifting, she was carried into her new holding cell to recuperate. It felt risky hoping she would integrate into the existing, artificially constructed, pride of lions, but Dr Abbas assured us that in previous years she been living in the larger area with some of the same lions. They had removed her years before in an attempt to breed her with a tiger. Of course. Within days we had allowed her physical contact with the rest of lions; but with bars between. She quickly socially adjusted to a degree we enabled full contact. It worked seamlessly (anything working smoothly was by then a shockingly welcome surprise to us) and she slept amongst, and ate donkey meat with, the pride without any hint of antagonism.

We opened the inter-leading gate and used meat to encourage the old tiger to explore his newly refurbished area. The response was remarkable from an animal that had become so sedentary for years. He sauntered through into the grass, had a sniff of the logs and a bit of a token claw at them, territorially sprayed the wall and green rebar boundary and glided like a geriatric tiger down the stairs into the newly filled pool. The young keepers appeared genuinely amazed at the quick response of the cat. Usually, his only option was to lay on the tiled floor. His appetite revived. In response, so too did the gloss of his auburn and black coat as his flesh filled over the previously bony looking hips, spine and shoulders. It was that simple.

In early March 2004, William and his colleagues exited Baghdad, heading south towards Kuwait. It seemed like another routine logistical plan being executed. For Farah and me, beyond the standard awkward hugs, forced cheer and handshakes of seeing a friend leaving to head homeward to another continent, it was an emotionally deflating day. We had come to rely heavily on each other and William, and we knew that we had struck the jackpot in having experienced that ten-month bonding. Our perceived stability and comfort had been stabbed. William's gift to Farah of a modified version of Dr Suess's "If I ran the Zoo" remains one of her most sentimental treasures.

For some, the planning for redeployment home wasn't always an extended logistical operation. For Captain John Smathers, an Army colleague of William's from the 422nd Civil Affairs Battalion (coincidentally the same battalion from which the soldiers who shot the zoo tiger had come from), it was a rapid turnaround. I had met John several times during chow hall dinners at the Al-Rasheed Hotel. In his typically laconic style, the conversation would invariably return to Scout, a puppy John had rescued during initial actions to help secure Baghdad airport. John's bond with Scout was forged through months of caring for the puppy and watching him grow up in their unit's commandeered house. In early 2004 John and unit members were severely injured in an ambush of their SUV. The Iraqi translator supporting them was killed. John was transferred back to the U.S. for emergency medical treatment. Back in the U.S., between his numerous surgeries, John's attention turned to his forced abandonment of Scout. Farah knew of Scout when John was in Baghdad because she had made house visits to vaccinate and plan for Scout's relocation. When we heard that John had been injured and evacuated home, we initially assumed Scout had found a new home among military colleagues. Surprisingly, months later, we received a call that Scout had been found by a soldier John had been corresponding with. The soldier agreed to arrange that Scout be transferred to the ISAW until we could relocate the dog to John. Logistical planning constraints would eventually lead to further months of delays until finally, an attempt was made to move Scout across the Jordanian border, as had been the case with many soldier-adopted dogs until then. A paperwork drama meant the vehicle was barred from entering Jordan, turned around and Scout was returned to Baghdad. It would be added months, and increasingly frustrated attempts by all involved, including Farah, veterinarians, military personnel and several generous spirits in the U.S., to coordinate a route out of Iraq for Scout; through Kuwait. John and Scout were reunited in August 2004. In a twist of obscene tragedy, John collapsed and died a little over a year later while walking his dogs near his home.

Almost simultaneously, to unapologetically shoehorn in a pun, the cavalry rode in. How could they help Baghdad Zoo? We couldn't believe our good fortune. The cavalry leapt at the natural association with Saddam's rescued Arabian thoroughbreds. Farah's initial contact was with the quick-witted, industrious Texan, Staff Sergeant Robert Bussell at the cavalry's Camp Victory base at Baghdad airport. Bussell was the platoon sergeant and saddle maker for the Horse Cavalry Detachment in Fort Hood, Texas. In addition to the standard soldiering skills, troops from the equestrian and ceremonial military unit were skilled in horsemanship, herd management and equipment maintenance. Bussell's optimism and determination that the cavalry would prioritise our hopeful but flaky-on-the-detail vision for an equestrian legacy after the horse rescue was energising. The prospect of seeing the cavalry unit in full ceremonial regalia had also stuck in Farah's excited imagination after she saw the tack, swords and hanging uniforms.

We had run out of options to stall rent negotiations with the Baghdad University administration where the Cheval Equestrian Club stables were located. The novelty, for Farah and me, of regular trips across town to the Jadriyah campus had also started to wear thin as the potential risks mounted. On one occasion, heading back over the Tigris River, we weaved between the stumpy concrete road barriers of the checkpoint on the 14th of July Bridge, before having our identification checked as usual. We were waved through by a checkpoint soldier into the Green Zone. We passed a parked white sedan on the side of the bridge road, mid-bridge which seemed unusually located given it was the only parked car where there was no allocated parking. It was suspicious enough that Farah and I both pointed it out to each other at the same time. But it was on the inside of the Green Zone so we presumed there would be a rational explanation. We discussed nothing further of it until a lunch meal at the CPA, where we met a familiar face. She mentioned the bridge had been temporarily shut, apparently due to a white, explosives-filled car being defused.

After persistent encouragement, Dr Abbas consulted Abu Bakr and Abu Marwan, who had both been coordinating the daily management of the horses. That the 425th Civil Affairs veterinarians and the Cavalry Detachment were prepared to help at the zoo, was a strong influence in the decision. Within a week the horses, their food supplies, tack and grooms had been transferred to the elephant enclosure of the Baghdad Zoo. There was no elephant. Fortunately. The enclosure was improvised as a rudimentary, stable and yard complex. Through the collective efforts of the grooms, Abu Bakr, Waseem, Sam Barringer and his colleagues, and Bussell's team, the physical appearance of the horses quickly exceeded expectations. The horses were still petulant and high-spirited, and bite or kick wounds weren't unusual in the makeshift paddock. Stories and rumours began to emerge among whispers, and then as fact, that individuals in Baghdad were trying to claim ownership of the horses. The cultural and financial value of the horses was significant, nationally and internationally, and opportunists were waiting in the many shadows. The horses were also suddenly a substantial status symbol for the zoo. The most alarming story came to us through Dr Abbas who had been informed that the recently appointed mayor of Baghdad was donating all the horses to a Sheikh in a Gulf state (where the mayor was allegedly resident). The mayor had made the unilateral decision. The relocation of the horses was imminent. Dr Abbas raged and attempted to derail the plan through numerous meetings with Al-Zawra Park administration and municipality. He was shut down coldly. His status held no influence in the matter. The risks and effort taken to secure the horses were ignored by the decision-makers. It infuriated us. The appointed mayor, who had never seen the horses, was going to export them for his personal benefit and the bureaucratic system would simply trundle on without concern. We turned pleadingly to our last resort, the only *fuck you* scale power we knew, the 1st Cavalry. Through Bussell, a message was sent up the chain of command to Brigadier General Jeff Hammond, the 1st Cavalry Division assistant commander. He had visited the zoo. He had seen what had been achieved and appeared to wholeheartedly buy into the legacy of the horses. In a matter of days, the mayor's ambition for the horses was squashed. They would stay in Baghdad as an Iraqi state asset.

The fluctuating dysfunction, progress or security of Iraq and particularly Baghdad, was the subject of intense international media scrutiny. There was such a barrage of compelling political intrigue, explosive disaster, or blind optimism that fresh death needed to reach grotesque new levels of gore or body count to merit a headline. Print and television media were saturated with "exclusive access", and "eye-witness reports". Expert opinions ranged from the brazenly partisan to conspiratorial, cynical, warmongering or vapid. Just frequently enough to keep us addicted, some insubordinate mutineer like the BBC would defy mediocrity and deliver a compelling, insightful report, at which point we would self-indulgently pat ourselves on the back for viewing it the same way. For the first time in our lives, Farah and I could witness events and subjectively gauge whether news outlets fed out spoonfuls of fabrication or accounts reflecting general reality. We usually weren't encouraged by what we read or watched.

On the evening of the 7th of March 2004 the Welsh rugby team was pounding the defiant French defence in an attempt to secure a match-drawing, last-gasp Six Nations try. In the newly created sports bar set up in a secure basement room of the Al-Rasheed (after the rocket attacks of 2003 the velvet-chaired bump 'n grid nightclub had been shut, but those hormones still needed beery satisfaction) a crowd of us were wildly urging the red tide to break through the French. With three minutes left in the match, Wales dived under the posts to move within one converted try of the French score. American contractors, impervious to the surge of assumed rugby patriotism were knocking back beers while shooting pool on the new tables or clustered at the bar. The mood of those not watching the rugby changed quickly as a story spread of the Al-Rasheed being under attack. Again. With less than two minutes to go in the rugby match, with Wales surging forward, the televisions were switched to show CNN live feed. We were furious, desperate to see the end of the game. WTF America! There was a strange, quick, testosterone-fuelled standoff between those wanting to watch the rugby and those set on the grey Wolf of CNN, Mr Blitzer. He was live, with footage rolling of the characteristic, pyramid-shaped Council of Ministers building across the road from us, pouring out fire and smoke.

"BLITZER: We spoke with Ambassador Bremer just before these explosions that have been heard rocking the so-called green zone, the most secure area inside the Iraqi capital of Baghdad.

Our Ben Wedeman is there on the scene for us.

Ben, you're collecting some more information. What do we know about these series of explosions?

WEDEMAN: OK, Wolf, we have much better information at this point.

What we've been told by a senior coalition official is that an SUV Toyota was parked about 400 meters north of the Rasheed Hotel. That Toyota had some sort of homemade launching device. It fired seven rockets toward the green zone. Three of those rockets impacted on the Rasheed Hotel, resulting in a life-injuring of a civilian contractor.

Now, the vehicle has been found still with two rockets inside of it. Now, the rockets were described as small, somewhere between 68 and 81 millimeters. U.S. troops are searching the area for more impact zones.

This official said that, despite this incident, they believed that security is still sufficient in the area of the conference center, which of course, is right across the street from the Rasheed Hotel, to allow the signing of this interim constitution to go ahead -- Wolf." (CNN Transcript 2004)

The scene of the gigantic blocky pyramid on fire was dramatic, but we also knew that such attacks were increasingly common. Several of us, deflated by the sudden change of television, decided we would prefer to leave rather than be stuck in the basement watching Blitzer talk about what we would rather see live. The rockets had been fired. Based on recent experiences, the opportunistic, brief salvo was likely finished. The hotel was in lockdown. "Nobody leaves this room!" was the military response. We were annoyed but presumed it was a decision based on reason. The news broadcast continued, and the imagery remained dramatic. The pyramid poured out smoke. We wanted to see it for ourselves. If that was on fire, then it was unlikely the hotel had been damaged as extensively if only three rockets had struck it. It was likely the same crude, inaccurate firing into the Green Zone that had become familiar. There was no talk of the Al-Rasheed burning. We were in it and hadn't heard any explosions but assumed it was because of the bar and television noise. We also heard speculation that rockets had landed either in the hotel lawns or lawns across the road.

"BLITZER: The entire series of the attacks, the series of explosions, the timing, raises suspicions, Ben, as you well know, that it could be linked to tomorrow's scheduled signing of this interim constitution. All of the important Iraqis are supposedly going to gather at the conference center, which is in this green zone, not far from the Al-Rasheed Hotel. (CNN Transcript 2004)

Finally, over an hour later, we were released once the threat was considered to have gone. I took one last quick glance at the television. The building was still ablaze. A piece of me was excited to see live what the world was watching on the news. I expected to see carnage outside; a glow of the nearby fiery pyramid and to smell the lingering smoke cloaking our surrounds. What an anti-climax; fresh, still air, and a dark, starry sky. The roads were mostly empty of cars. All the things I would have normally been delighted by. I drove alongside the gigantic pyramid, scorched from fires from U.S. bombing in early 2003. There was no gratuitous building barbeque. It stood imposing, melancholy and silent as it did every night I saw it. I felt conned, almost offended and naive.

Driving back to the Green Zone from the zoo usually took less than ten minutes. It was a quick drive through the park, and then out onto a road that ran adjacent to the park boundary. It was all quite scenic when you weren't overly paranoid about exploding dead dogs or cardboard boxes. The densely treed park was on the left, high-walled houses of Al Kindi and Harithiya neighbourhoods on the right. Farah and I were advised by security contractor friends to occasionally mix up our routes and timing to the checkpoints to avoid being followed. If we felt we were being followed, we were to make at least three turns into new streets; if we were still being followed, then we hit the accelerator like a moonshine runner. Past the fringes of suburbia, the road would take a left turn under a large, concrete overpass bridge, the point where there was always an imposing Abrams tank on guard. It was unnerving, slightly bowel-dropping, to swing the car around the corner and be faced by the barrel of "Creeping Death" or "Death Deliverer". Few things felt more humbling than when it was directed at car windscreen level, and you drove around the corner to get a clear view looking straight into the ominously dark hole at the centre of the barrel. Yet, when it was directed upwards, only a little higher, it was oddly comforting, like a 60-ton pacifier.

One of those journeys home was particularly unnerving. I was about 600m along the initially straight road adjacent to the park boundary; about halfway before my first turn. I was speeding. In the back of the car were the large plastic containers with bloodied donkey parts for the lions. In my rearview mirror, I noticed a white sedan enter the road near the park entrance. It was rapidly gaining ground on me. To increase the distance between us, I would have had to drive top speed towards the onrushing turn. It raced through my mind that either it was somebody enjoying the freedom of being able to speed, or they were lining up an assault. Quicker and quicker, the white sedan grew larger in the mirror. Only a driver. No passenger. An isolated foreigner SUV was an easy target for an attack. I moved to the right lane to force the sedan to pull alongside or pass on the left. I raised my knees to hold the steering wheel in place as I quickly flicked off the safety catch on the gun and racked the slide across to load a bullet into the chamber. Pea-shooter time. Fuck. The weapon seemed smaller than ever. My driver's side window on my left was wound down. Decisions. As the sedan pulled alongside, I would slam the breaks, and fire rounds if it seemed warranted. Warranted? Weapon barrel aimed at me. Ok. That'll be the crossed line. Survive. Less than a 100m to go. The turn rushed nearer. Quicker. I glanced at the road ahead, then the mirror. WTF? Was it a drive-by shooting? Would he detonate? What the actual fuck? Would my tiny gun really help? The driver swung the sedan out from immediately behind to overtake on the left. I slammed on brakes and held the gun at shoulder height aimed at the car. The white car raced past and whipped around the corner. My heart thumped as I pulled hard around the corner and slowed to a gentle cruise, flicked the gun's safety back on, and drove on towards the calming relief of the tank's brutalist aura.

CHAPTER 15

Waseem frequently talked about their beautiful, small family property in Shaqlawa in the Kurdish north of Iraq. Farah and I had also often discussed the awful conditions Lawrence and I had seen at the zoo in Erbil, the Kurdish capital. A Lieutenant Colonel we socialised with was adamant that if we could secure the release of the animals, she and a few willing South African security contractors could facilitate the transport of the animals to Baghdad. Farah, Waseem and I decided to tick both boxes. A recce trip to the north seemed a great outlet for all our office plotting. Ali was the natural choice for taxi driver. We were uncertain about the exact security situation on the road north from Baghdad since news reports of insurgent activity was mixed. What did concern us were the numerous stories and news reports of rogue militias setting up their own roadblocks. Kidnapping was a lucrative entrepreneurial business enterprise requiring minimal start-up capital. The simmering religious sectarian pretext behind many of the reports appeared to add another layer of justification for abductions and torture. Distinguishing militias from legitimate government forces was apparently only guesswork.

Militiamen would dress in official police or new army outfits, or a combination of both with civilian additions. There were reports of police and army units doubling as sectarian agents of retribution. Ali assured us he could get us to the Kurdish north, and back, safely. We had trusted his judgement until then, and he had always been true to his word.

We also felt we could rationalise paying him for such a trip as long as we had the CPA funds and were going to investigate the option of clearing out Erbil Zoo.

Shortly after we left the urban fringes of Baghdad, we started to pass between small, lush farms and barren plots of carved up sandy wasteland with the occasional burnt-out military vehicle. It wasn't long before we encountered our first checkpoint. I could feel the tension building within the car and my body as we neared the dishevelled, makeshift shelter with at least three AK-47 armed men lounging in plastic chairs. Their handguns were resting in belt-tied holsters. Their trendy fashion sense combined equal parts of official police uniform and worn out civilian clothing. I immediately regretted not having accepted the AK-47 a Uruguayan civilian contractor in the adjoining portacabin room had offered me when he packed to leave Baghdad. At the time, I believed that accepting it would likely get me into more trouble than it would get me out of. As we slowed to the checkpoint, I wondered if having an assault rifle would have been a source of comfort or increased the likelihood of us getting scruffed and hauled out the vehicle.

My mind scrambled with assumptions of what might happen, then diverted through potential scenarios, responses and permutations. It flashed between unlikely Rambo-style bullshit and pragmatic self-preservation as I tried to rationalise appropriate responses for our survival. It was a bit late for planning. Who are these people? Do you show them official identification? What were the "correct" answers to who we were? Were there only three armed men? Will we suddenly be pulled out and shot? I felt for my handgun to know exactly where it was and mentally adjusted to perhaps needing to use it. I was more acutely aware then than at any other time in Baghdad at my lack of professionally-trained proficiency in the mechanics of firearms and dynamics of lethal force. I overthought it. Ali engaged in a quick-fire conversation with the quizzing armed man.

Ali dominated the conversation. The man looked over Ali at Waseem, glanced at Farah and me in the back seat, stepped back and waved us on. The mental and physical tension subsided as the car moved onwards up the highway.

Another checkpoint loomed. More armed men in mixed uniform. The emotions raced again. We had no gauge on their intent – malicious or innocent. We tried to observe all we could to know, at least on the surface, what we were driving towards. Again Ali talked us through. It would happen another nine times until we were sure we had entered Kurdish territory north of Kirkuk. Two additional checkpoints were operated by Kurdish Peshmerga soldiers. At that point, our concern was whether the Kurds would harbour, or act on, animosity towards Iraqi Arabs; Ali and Farah. The Kurds had suffered intense persecution, gassing and viciousness at the hands of Saddam's regime. Still, the release of tension at being in Kurdish Iraq was palpable. Suddenly, we felt we could talk and make jokes again. We stopped on the side of the road to enjoy the look and feel of soft, aromatic, lush green plains of grass and flowering weeds that extended to blocky mud-brick houses in the distance. Ali drew deeply on another cigarette. Beyond the carpets of colour, shallow green hills interrupted the horizon. Small red signs with white printed text and a skull and crossbones warned of landmines. Finally, we entered the *City of Hooting*, Erbil.

The zoo was as awful as I had remembered as it lay miserably below the sparkling new Sheraton Hotel. It felt like a minor relief that the gazelles and ostriches at least had fresh greens to eat and the flamingo and cormorant had access to a dirty pool. In addition to the depressing sight of the chained monkeys, there was still the assortment of hawks, eagles, pelicans, wolves, dogs, a bear, guinea pigs, peacocks and partridges confined as prisoners in little concoctions of cages. Pieces of brick, chicken wire, chainlink fence, rebar, rust and binding wire were mashed together to ensure captivity. There was a lion too. We met the owner; the real owner, Galeel Karwan. It wasn't the keeper Lawrence had mistakenly presumed to be the owner during our previous visit. We mentioned the conversation where a figure of $10 000 had been "agreed by Lawrence" to shut the facility. He laughed and sneered at our supposed ignorance. In case we didn't understand the reality, he kindly made sure to educate us - selling his lion and bear on the black market would earn him more than that. I'd been reluctant to raise that discussion of payment, but since there were no laws governing animal welfare and there was no way to enforce a shut-down to stop Mr Karwarn re-stocking his facility, we had no alternatives to work with. We had no authority. We tried sweet-talking, discussed the concerns of welfare and offered to help advise on improving conditions. He did not give two fucks about our concerns or the international perception of the animals' welfare. He knew his facilities were poor. Members of the public had told him all of this before. Local government was putting pressure on him to move or shut down and were likely to cut his utility access for unpaid bills. The Sheraton had apparently asked him to shut down or move. To him, the equation was simple; as long as animals were alive, people would pay to visit. Most visitors didn't care about animal welfare. They could feed and tease the monkeys, shout at the bear and lion, frighten the wolves and make the birds flap wildly in their cages. What wasn't there to enjoy? The less money he spent on the animals, the more he kept for himself. He had sold several animals since our previous visit, and that funded new animals to replace those sold or that had died. In truly ineffective, foreign-busybody style, we documented the list of animals and conditions by a series of photographs to use in a report we would later submit to the Interim Governing Council in Baghdad. We knew that would only be a token gesture to soothe our consciences. We left with our tails between our legs, intensely frustrated at what we knew we couldn't change until there was government willingness to enforce change. The ephemeral window of influence we had experienced in

Baghdad, to arrive with U.S. troops on the animal's behalf, was gone and would have been geographically irrelevant.

The time working with animals in Baghdad had taught us to partition our emotions, feel intense frustration or despair, stew intensely on it for a while, and then lock it away. That evening we enjoyed our modest, delicious meal in the humble, almost-wintery surrounds of Shaqlawa. At over 1 000m altitude, the chilly air, lush green fields, retaining walls and leafless trees lay between mountains and rocky hillslopes with exposed splits and erosions of terracotta-coloured soil. It was a visual and mental relief to see the variety of vivid colours and natural scenery after months of dilutions from beige dust.

Ali decided that based on information received, our return journey to Baghdad would be less likely to encounter checkpoints if we used the route heading west through Iraq's second-biggest city, Mosul. It seemed the penalty for that decision was a giant, wild cluster of gridlocked traffic that sparked wild gesticulations and abuse between drivers. Several drivers left their vehicles, swore and waved furiously like enraged traffic officers. Oddly enough, it was a technique which engineered the desired result of a reshuffling until we squeezed through and back to the highway. The driving was hazardous, even by Iraqi standards. We may have been on a two or three or four-lane highway. It was impossible to tell. I was confident we would die as we overtook a car overtaking a truck, at which point a car opportunistically passed us using the gravel roadside. We stared ahead in silence as we were transfixed by the oncoming vehicles in the distance. We breathed again as Ali whipped the car back between two transport trucks. We only encountered two checkpoints – that unexpectedly provided an opportunity to draw breath - before we reached the comparatively sedate, comforting streets of Baghdad.

Gentle, warm breezes returned to Baghdad. It was mid-morning when the zoo's FPS guards arrived at the office with an unkempt, blonde European backpacker they had seen walking through Al-Zawra Park. He spoke broken English, and the security guards spoke none. He was noticeably confused by the attention he had attracted. He thought he had been arrested, without reason. As Farah translated, the concerned expressions on the faces of the guards were visible. They hadn't arrested him but feared for his safety as he wandered alone. They had brought him to the office for us to understand and help him. They could not understand any of his explanations when they had approached him. It was cynically comical that the backpacker was entirely oblivious to any potential risk as he wandered through Baghdad. It seemed ridiculous to be trying to explain to him the city was still working itself out after an invasion and war. "Do you understand you are in a war zone?" I asked slowly. He genuinely had no idea what I was talking about. It was undeniable he was the most peacefully ignorant person I had met in Iraq, and I didn't know whether to slap him or give him a little pat on the head. He was about twenty years old and had hitchhiked a ride from Turkey to Baghdad with monks. All he was looking for was an ATM to draw money from and a supermarket to buy groceries. He had no accommodation organised, a situation that didn't seem to concern him. He was fixated on drawing money and finding a grocery store. I tried again to explain the security circumstances and how it would be better if he worked out how to leave the country. It was not penetrating his understanding. I gave up. The guards stared quizzically, at least content that the puzzling white foreigner was safe with another white foreigner.

Farah suggested he would likely find shops across the Tigris River in the Karrada neighbourhood. I agreed to try to get him through the Green Zone. The process rightly took interminable discussions, explanations and passport showing to finally convince the sceptical checkpoint soldiers I saw daily, to allow me to enter the Green Zone with the drifter. I drove him past the bombed-out Baath Party HQ and stretches of razor wire, across the 14th of July bridge, exited the checkpoint and left him on the pavement. Despite the checkpoints, the reality of where he was seemed to escape him. He tried to pay me for the lift. I urged him to use his money to find secure accommodation for the night and then leave the city before he got chewed up. I tried one final attempt to explain to him that he needed to be aware of his surrounds, that there was a risk.

Three days later we saw him again, with his unmistakable shock of blonde hair and backpack, walking through the park like a homing pigeon. The security guards watched in disbelief. I shrugged my shoulders. I could only hope the world treated his oblivious innocence with a gentle hand. We returned to our work.

Ayed had been an unsung hero of the zoo. His short, stiff frame was always dressed in a white, collared office shirt and dark trousers, his weathered face always partially shielded by his pale, equally weathered cap. He had worked tirelessly to irrigate, landscape and plant the zoo grounds with grass and flowers. The proof of his personal industry was in how he was transforming the zoo grounds from their battered, withered state with his scant resources. Throughout the grounds, grassy lawns reclaimed the bare mud patches. Flower beds became increasingly colourful and lush. Hedges had been shaved into blocky uniformity. He had been allocated reluctant parties of unskilled labourers during work-creation projects. Given their enthusiasm, you would have been forgiven for thinking they were paid in cactus thorns and beatings for every kilojoule exerted. The uninspired crews spent more of their limited energy reserves imitating trees with a shovel as a crutch, or actively melting into shadows to avoid work, than digging or planting. Despite this, Ayed made progress.

It fascinated me how much agonisingly deliberate effort went into not working. That it was a rare opportunity to earn a salary in Baghdad was apparently wholly irrelevant. The game compelled me to watch, mesmerised by the interminable intrigue. Some contractors would lean, motionless on a spade for longer than ten minutes, then lethargically twist some soil as a staff member walked past, before returning to the sedentary state. It was a masterful performance. Ayed would try to keep a check on all the staff dotted in work squads around the zoo, but couldn't. We would try to feed him some information when possible, but he never demonstrated even the slightest authoritative streak – he was too unassuming. Much of the burden he would take up himself without remonstration or asking for additional payment. He only knew one way, how to set the example of working hard and earnestly. When at his most demonstrative, in response to any thanks we offered him, his worn face creased into a bashful grin.

"Ayed is dead." The news from Dr Abbas stunned us in the office. Again a sombre Dr Abbas reported another death. There was the shock of the report, the shock of the injustice and then the associated guilt of feeling like an intruder at having heard the news so personal to the staff. The immediate account was that U.S. Marines assaulting a house had rolled a grenade into a room. The explosion killed Ayed. We didn't know the full story of why that house was raided or the details of what transpired. We didn't have facts. We would never get them. But to us, that wasn't the point. Ayed was dead. It was a cruel twist, and another of those moments of feeling distinctly foreign; culpability by association.

Ayed's family home was in gritty, tormented Fallujah. It had been a city plagued by violent uprisings, with speculation rampant whether the town was at the mercy of guerrilla forces or in full-blown, untameable rebellion against the foreign occupiers and Iraqi puppets. Chaos reigned over daily life. The prior months had seen explosions tear into mosques, rocket-propelled grenades launched into U.S. convoys, Iraqi security forces infiltrated by militias, and police stations assaulted by insurgents who slaughtered police officers and released prisoners. Provocative mobs openly cheered American deaths. Sectarian ideologues and factions stoked religious fervour in the explosive setting of raging frustration at collapsed amenities and heavy-handed American house raids, arrests and curfews. Resentment was fired up. Shootouts ensued. IEDs were planted and detonated.

At the end of March 2004, four American contractors from the private security company, Blackwater, were ambushed, killed, burnt to a contorted char and hung from a bridge in Fallujah. The 1st Marines Expeditionary Force had been recently deployed to the province (Al-Anbar) to change the blunt tactics; to implement foot patrols, surgical strikes and deploy humanitarian aid. They had recognised the counter-productive, inflammatory tactics leading up to their arrival. The Blackwater incident scrapped the playbook. A reactive, vengeful, enraged U.S. political establishment demanded a response. The Marines received orders to assault Fallujah. Their desired plan to wait, identify the culprits and extract them was scrapped. Shit was going to get fucked up – the rebellion squashed.

The city was besieged, surrounded and the roads blockaded. Residents were urged to leave. Many didn't. Where would they go? It was home. Those that remained were urged by radio broadcast to stay inside their homes and hand over those involved in the Blackwater incident. The First Battle of Fallujah started as sustained aerial bombardments and deadly sniper fire. Ground attacks were unleashed against ferocious resistance. Carnage ensued. U.S. forces clawed violently into militia territory before the politicians again reacted and called their beast to heel. A month later U.S. forces withdrew from Fallujah, handing over the remaining operations to another Iraqi militia (one from the correct side, of course) who struggled to impose dominance. Continuing skirmishes would lead U.S. forces to again be drawn into assaulting the city in November 2004.

The explosive prisoner abuse scandal at Abu Ghraib prison burst into the international media. The atrocious imagery and depraved stories emerging of torture and physical, sexual and psychological abuses committed by some U.S. soldiers on Iraqi prisoners flared local and international outrage and debate. It seemed shameful to look at the photos of enforced naked human pyramids. It was an utterly abnormal way to treat other people, like some weirdly merciless, pornographic initiation ritual. The creativity unleashed on ritualised humiliation was perverse. Even if some of the prisoners were guilty of barbarism before being detained, it was unlikely being stripped and choke-chained or fondled in a naked man-sandwich while an American took smiling photos was going to unlock valuable insurgent-related information and latent love for the Star-Spangled Banner. Buggery, electrocution, attack dogs, starvation, and forcing detainees to eat faeces was not going to win hearts and minds. The soldiers we knew, worked and socialised with were appalled, embarrassed and couldn't believe colleagues in their big machine could be so openly vile and intentionally stupid for so long without reproach. They would all be perceived as guilty by association of the uniform. None of us were fairy-worshipping, petulant uber-liberals but the interrogation, abuses, squalid conditions and grief-stricken families desperate for information reflected an obscene continuation of Saddam's days in charge.

Some of the zoo team struggled to reconcile that news with all the time they had enjoyed working with compassionate U.S. soldiers at the zoo. It made them think of the soldiers that shot the tiger and fed dogs to lions. It fitted a narrative of hatred, evil America and bigotry. What was really "Amrika's" intentions. Slavery of Iraqis? Who was good, who was bad? Who deserved what? Were those piles of naked humans bad people or the sons of families unjustly arrested? New master, a new regime, same shit, different day. It was a hot topic of debate at the zoo. Tea was brewed!

It appeared that for every positive outcome or well-intentioned reconstruction project of the American adventure, there was a debilitating scandal. Life on the ground, outside the Green Zone, was dysfunctional. Corruption was still entrenched. A new flag didn't make it a better country. Media briefings that outlined the Saddam-era neglect and demise of sewerage systems, infrastructure, national water supply or collapsing electricity supply while building extravagant palaces lost any gravity they may have had immediately post-invasion. People remembered that sanctions blockages caused their strife and openly began to mutter that life was better under Saddam. Volatility increased. Polarity increased. The line between liberation and occupation blurred. The social ecosystem grew increasingly toxic. Rationality faded. That left more Iraqis dead, insulted and enraged, reacting and detained, more politicians scrambling and bickering, more young American soldiers sucked into the bloodbath, more mangled bodies and minds and escalating war debt. The media was invariably filled with more ghastly images of partially roasted human corpses, sprays of blood and dollops of dismembered limbs. In other imagery, mothers, fathers and relatives would be wailing and howling in despair. It fuelled the imagination of potential horrors waiting for anybody, any time, any day. Within that terrifying mix, kidnappings and assassinations had reached epidemic proportions. Professors, scientists and doctors were being executed; nobody really knew why. We heard months later that one of the two female veterinary lecturers who helped demonstrate lion castrations to students at the zoo, was shot dead by unknown attackers.

Among the madness, we also knew it could be so much worse. Most daily lives carried on in the familiar reality, punctuated with sporadic bloodshed. In houses across Baghdad, beautiful Persian rugs would be going through the annual ritualistic cleaning, rolling and storage in time for the mid-summer heat. By May 2004 Joint Intelligence Committee security assessments estimated Coalition and Iraqi forces throughout Iraq were the targets of 500 attacks per week. A militant jihadist group posted a video online with the title "Abu Musab Al-Zarqawi slaughters an American". Abducted freelance American contractor, Nick Berg, is seen in an orange jumpsuit, bound and seated in front of five ski-masked militants, while a statement is read out explicitly calling on revenge for humiliations in Abu Ghraib. Berg is held to the ground as his head is sawn off with a knife. Abu Ghraib had become public relations gold for radical militias to recruit outraged citizens and foreign jihadists to unleash hell.

Simultaneously, as the Sunni insurgency grew in ferocity north and west of Baghdad, the Shiite militia, *Imam Mahdi's Army*, launched a fierce uprising offensive in Sadr City and the southern towns of Najaf, Karbala, Kut, and Kufa. Police stations and public buildings were stormed, and running battles ensued with U.S., Spanish, Polish and Salvadorian troops launching retaliatory attacks with helicopter and tank assistance. There were mass casualties on all sides. Rumours emerged that members of the rival Shiite militia, the *Badr Brigade*, had been paid to assist U.S. troops. Rumours also flourished that many in the new Iraqi armed forces, civil defence and police, actually belonged to militias too. Who did one trust if militiamen also wore official uniforms? Others, many of whom were untrained but had joined for a salary, had mutinied and fled the fighting.

Iraqis who could afford too bought massive generator units, large enough to power clusters of houses, and then charged neighbours to register for a daily allocation of power. The drone of generators and the sprawl of power cables became increasingly common. The problem was still the desperate fuel shortage. The CPA had estimated over half a million new and used cars had entered Iraq for sale in the first nine, post-invasion months. Fuel demand rose steeply. It was still an expensive, dirty, black market commodity despite the government threats to prosecute, fine or jail people selling or buying black market fuel. It had become another side-line business for contracted fuel tank drivers to syphon off quantities to sell on the black market for extra income. It made the context of some ignorant people inanely bitching about the toppings selection at the CPA salad bar that much clearer. I started to seriously consider what the future held.

Back into our parochial world, there was a growing focus among many of us on the palace lion situation. It seemed increasingly untenable that they could stay at the palace complex. Regardless of the city-wide carnage, some emotionally uptight military officers still found time to be distressed by an unwelcome garden feature. Some would politely confront Farah and me when we fed the lions to ask when we would be moving the pride. Others were less subtle about their lack of enthusiasm for a flaring mound of burning lion excrement. Despite the lions' novelty to us and many soldiers who would visit during the late afternoon, higher-ranking officers had become concerned that the lions were a distraction to soldiers. They were likely right. They feared a repeat of the zoo tiger incident. The increasingly belligerent officers would inform us at every opportunity that a military compound was no place for lions, as if we didn't understand their circumstances and our limitations. Our response would always be the same; if they knew of funding we could access to build new zoo facilities we would gratefully accept it and move the lions.

That changed the day Brigadier General Hammond from the 1st Cavalry Division made his first introductory visit to the zoo. The matter of the palace lions had not been formally raised to higher military levels because the focus was mostly on the rescued horses. Through Civil Affairs behind-the-scenes agitations, the lion predicament reached to the Brigadier General. The situation we had been trying to navigate for many months was changed by his simople command. It was hard not to develop a fleeting man-crush. Oh, the seductive power of money! We were instructed to secure three quotes with a complete design, materials required, and all-inclusive costs to deliver a new lion facility. Based on our recommendations from the zoo, the military would approve and financially manage construction which we would supervise. We were suddenly in a scramble to design a lion enclosure that walked the fine line between Iraq-practical, Iraq-affordable, Iraq-deliverable, safe, an opportunity for the lions to live the best possible captive life in Baghdad and being ever-so-sexy for the public. The daydreaming of earlier months versus actual planning were two very different streams of thought. Pragmatism tempered our Pepsi and tea-fuelled imagination. We knew that when word spread the U.S. Army was funding the enclosure, the bids would likely all be inflated.

It seemed more than half of the Iraqis we encountered were qualified engineers. Unsurprisingly, there was minimal technical design expertise to draw on in Baghdad to create an enticing, functional, modern lion enclosure at short notice. The reality was that construction material availability and quality in Iraq were also limited to such an extent that nothing except an overpriced boundary and basic holding building design could be constructed despite the generous budget. It was decided that the pig enclosure (about half the size of a rugby field), with its many mature trees, would be modified. There was to be a substantial double barrier fence (to avoid humans poking hands and babies through), a large plunge pool and wooden platforms for climbing, shade and basking. The prospect had us grinning like hipsters breaking the seal on a bottle of vintage beard oil.

Uday's palace lions were also still a source of great intrigue and distraction for people in the Green Zone who weren't allowed to leave the Green Zone to visit the zoo. On one occasion, a group from the CPA visited during feeding time. The atmospheric stench from burning lion poo and old bones ripening the hot air, combined with the sight of the dripping donkey blood was too much to handle for the weaker sensibilities of some office workers. The excitable fat red and yellow wasps that always descended with intent and danced and jostled with the flies on the leaked blood were not popular either. At that time the tangy reek of the area was undeniably offensive to most nasal cavities, but nine lions drop out bucket loads of meaty faeces in a short period and spray a considerable volume of urine. Waseem could testify to that volume from Brutus alone. On one occasion as Waseem was distracted, Brutus reversed to the fence, flicked his tail up and sprayed Waseem in the face and mouth with a volley of pungent urine. We were going to warn Waseem as we saw Brutus turn, but what are friends for? The whole moment had Farah and me howling in such childish hysterics it would have been a waste to miss out on that priceless visual. On the days I could lure the lions inside their holding cages I would clean out wheelbarrows full of old bones and faeces. It was the likely cause of more than one respiratory infection as the acrid dust would swirl around. The plunge pools needed to be emptied by hand bucket, scrubbed and refilled, at which point the lions would usually respond by dropping a fleshy donkey piece into the clean water. I couldn't prove they were vindictive even though I thought about it. The lions understood the game of attempting to lure them inside the holding building, and it was rare we could capture all nine inside together. Invariably one spirited lion would playfully push back through the swarming lions trying to enter, and burst back into the outside enclosure. That would block or jam the sliding door and spark a mass exodus, and they would chase each other through the plunge pools or up the shredded palm trees. If we couldn't get them all inside, we could not clean the outside.

During that particular CPA staff visit, an immaculately dressed lady was overly melodramatic, waving her arms in the air and animatedly fake-retching. Instead of merely leaving, she made a point of lecturing me on enclosure hygiene. She then walked animatedly around the cage perimeter, talking loudly about the "stupid lions" that were following her every step. I could feel myself seething with irritation at her attempted projection of superiority. It was moments like those when I boiled, in part because people like her were were getting a salary and I wasn't, that it was most difficult to remain diplomatic. I also knew it was my choice to be there and that we always needed to pander to whoever visited in CPA-chic office clothing, in the hope they may have influence beneficial for the zoo. She wanted a colleague to take a photo of her against the cage and stood against the sliding gate, the one part which didn't have additional chain-link mesh to prevent direct contact with the lions. The lions always responded to a turned back, or a child, by instinctively switching into a hunting behaviour. It was remarkable to witness and happened without fail. The lady turned her back to the younger, watching lions. As I put out my hand to warn her, for a second time, one of the yearling lions raised up onto its back paws and in a flash reached a stout front paw between the bars and swatted the lady on her back. The force of the swipe knocked her to the ground, tearing a strip at the back of her blouse. She sobbed as her colleagues led her away. She was physically undamaged, unhurt except for a bruised ego. I would be lying if I said I didn't enjoy that hint of retribution; an injection of schadenfreude to end the afternoon.

Another afternoon I was lying on the concrete border that fringed the enclosure fencing. It had become a habit to spend a few minutes lying next to the lions as they dozed against the adjacent bars and chain link fence. The younger lions would rest their chins on their paws pressed against the fence if Farah or I sat there and chatted to them. At times I would question our sanity – more that we talked to the lions than we lay where we did. It often felt like a peaceful moment to reflect on the day in the still surreal surrounds. As I lay there with the lions, a colonel walking 40m away on the asphalt road made a sharp turn to stride purposefully across the grass and dust towards me. The sour expression on his face stood out clearly beneath the desert camouflage, flat-top cap. It didn't look like a social chat was imminent. I stood up. "Who the fuck do you think you are when you are at home?" he barked at me assuming I was a soldier. For a brief moment, I tried to understand what the question was. "I'm the guy who looks after the lions" I replied. "Alright! Carry on with whatever the fuck you were doing!" he growled and stormed off as decisively as he had arrived.

We were becoming increasingly concerned about the health of the lions who were being visited throughout the day by soldiers, civilian contractors and imported labourers from the military compounds. In the afternoons, we would find discarded plastic water bottles, chip packets, sweet wrappers and MRE containers inside the lion enclosure. We found dog remains in the enclosure but could only speculate how they entered the lion area; it was unlikely to have been voluntary. During an afternoon visit, it became apparent that Xena, one of the palace lionesses, was ill. We suspected she might have ingested something that had blocked her digestive tract. It wouldn't have been the first time. The other consideration was that in earlier weeks Brutus had been aggressively mating both females when they were in heat. Her physical appearance didn't suggest pregnancy, but we were speculating at potential options. Whether pregnant or constipated, she seemed unimpressed with life. I passed the information on to the veterinarians.

I had made a habit of only usually leaving the portacabin car park after about 8.00 a.m. to head through checkpoints and onwards to the zoo. In my estimation, it had become apparent that most suicide bombers or car bombs struck checkpoints during the early morning congestion of traffic and pedestrian queues being searched before entry into the Green Zone. Another car bomb blast on the edge of the Green Zone at 7.26 a.m. on the 6th of May killed six Iraqis and a U.S. soldier and wounded 25 people. The checkpoint responses to the frequent detonations were to create increasingly elaborate and convoluted entry routes with concrete blast walls, to isolate and reduce the carnage of the blast force from an explosion. The by-product was slower processing of the queues. By 8.00 a.m. those choked up queues of people heading to work, home, or to argue administrative issues, had mostly been processed to a remaining steady trickle. I decided it was better to wait for the crowds to subside to reduce the chance of being caught out by a blast.

On the 17th May 2004, Xena's exaggeratedly deflated condition of the previous afternoon had been gnawing at my thoughts since I woke up. I imagined her lying in torturous discomfort. In one year we hadn't had one of the palace lions potentially ill enough to concern us to that degree. A kilometre from the Green Zone perimeter checkpoint that Farah and I navigated each day, my conscience nagged me incessantly. I drove on. "I'll check on Xena during a lunch break, I thought". At the last opportunity, I turned left to stop in at the palace enclosure. I needed to know if Xena had improved, or was dead. I phoned Farah to tell her. She would join me. It was another three minutes delay for the identification checks at the palace entrance and driving around the divider wall to the enclosure. I unlocked the door and entered the holding building to look at the dozing lions. The deep bass, explosive, rolling roar erupted. The ground and walls shuddered momentarily as the tremor pulsed through. Brutus, shocked at the sudden thunder, launched instinctively from a lying position in the holding building, into the outside enclosure. He wasn't easily distressed. He usually even ignored massive Chinook, tandem-rotor helicopters that would whip past above us at treetop level. He stood in the middle of the enclosure, unsure where to move next as the black plume in the distance rose its rolling conical way into the blue sky. A soldier ran from around the walled corner, holding his helmet on his head with one hand, his weapon and body-armour attachments with the other to stop them from bouncing. "There's been an explosion at the checkpoint. Everyone is on lockdown. Stay here!" He turned and ran off back towards the main entrance. I immediately phoned Farah. She had been diverted back towards the zoo.

An hour later, the all-clear was sounded. It was an hour I had to think about how close I had been to crossing that checkpoint at the time of the explosion. It was the only morning in 12 months that I had stopped in to see the lions. How long would it have taken me to drive those 700m and exit the security check? Maybe I would have missed it. It was an hour I had to consider that the chances I would die (or at least be injured) in Iraq seemed high enough to be inevitable the more months I stayed.

The scene shortly beyond the checkpoint was one of devastation. A massive crater metres wide and metres deep dominated the centre of the road. Charred shells of cars still stood where they had been scorched. A wall beyond the pavement was burnt black. Apocalyptic, black tree skeletons stood along the pavement. The massive car bomb, rigged using artillery shells, assassinated Ezzedine Salim, the head of Iraq's Governing Council. It killed nine additional people, including the bomber, and injured fourteen.

As I lay in my portacabin, it sounded as if the city had erupted. Gunfire was rattling, snapping and popping out in what sounded like every direction. Life rolled on between the jolts of political and sectarian reality. My thoughts turned immediately to whether it was the anti-American uprising that had so often been rumoured as impending. Was it the assault across the Tigris River that had been speculated was imminent? There had been rumours for weeks of Iraqi frogmen training to cross the river and assault the Green Zone. Dining halls loved a rumour. I walked out among the sandbagged walls to check the response of other people (like those scenes in a movie where you watch the character and think "that's a stupid idea"). Was there an evacuation? The gunfire was incessant, of different calibres and from different angles, but a little distant. Tracers arced into the sky. Other bewildered contractors were looking blankly at each other and shrugging shoulders. Nobody knew what was happening. Some contractors were in flak vests and helmets. Others like me didn't have that option. Plink. Plink. Plink. Bullets landed randomly on the portacabin roofs and the nearby gravel. "A bullet has come through my fucking roof" someone grouched. We didn't know if we should take our chances back inside the portacabins, stay among the sandbags (which wouldn't stop anything dropping onto us), or head across the open pathways and parking areas to a more secure area. We felt we at least had a tiny bit of protection and a few cold beers among the mix of flimsy cabins and sandbags. Farah was my default phone call to hear if there were Arabic news reports that may explain the *assault*. Iraq's u23 football team had beaten Saudi Arabia to qualify for the Olympic Games! Baghdadis were celebrating. Of course. The team had not participated in the Olympics for 16 years. Without the malicious intent attached, the randomly plinking bullets only seemed worthy of indignant tut-tutting, like irritated parents disappointed by a delinquent child.

It was mid-afternoon when Farah, Waseem and I were being childishly entertained by the hoarse gasping of the mating tortoise as he gripped the female below him with his muscular, scaly forearms. His dominant pose and the intensity of his gaze as he strained his wrinkly neck seemed to indicate a reptilian intent on enjoying his warm, amorous afternoon in Baghdad; as his mate preferred to search for fresh alfalfa stalks. Most weekday afternoons at the zoo had become sedate affairs of routine cleaning, feeding and veterinary treatment checks as small numbers of visitors ambled about. It felt peaceful enough to not carry the gun anymore. The heavier workloads were carried out through the morning, and most building contractor staff would leave shortly after a lunch break. The mornings were often manic affairs with management trying to get keeper staff to complete their tasks according to agreed protocols and routines. Given the fluctuating state of security within the city, and the personal circumstances, health and age of many of the staff, it was difficult to know who would arrive at work each day. It wasn't the most efficient system, but that was the system.

Another late afternoon Waseem, Farah and I had been sitting in the shade under a bridge arched across a canal in the zoo. We had completed the afternoon inspections, and Waseem decided to try catch fish with a makeshift stick, thread and hook. I had a small net tied onto the end of another stick. We sat there quietly chatting, passing the time as we broke off small pieces of stale bread and lethargically tossed them into the water. The sound of a small explosion in the distance, north of the zoo caught our attention. Surprisingly, we could see two dark specks, projectiles, arcing through the sky, beyond the open expanse of the park lakes, towards the Green Zone. Our view was mostly unobstructed as we watched the specks dip over the fringe of trees on the horizon. Small rising, curling clouds of beige dust drifted out from behind the tree line, followed by two almost simultaneous, distant sounds of explosions. We discussed how strange it seemed to be to see what we guessed were probably mortars, in mid-air. Waseem continued to bob the hook amongst the soggy floating bread.

Saeida, the blind brown bear, lay pathetically in the corner of her holding enclosure like a terminally ill patient. It was pitiful. At least she was mostly asleep behind those opaque eyes. She would periodically shuffle her hairy body across to the food bowl for her meals, slurp some water and then curl up again. The reality was that none of the bears had enclosures that we thought were even close to big enough or stimulating. Wounded-Ass was still recovering, and Samir was enjoying his pool, but space to roam didn't exist. Yet those two at least had access to an outside area with some soil to dig up, water to splash and direct sunshine to bask in. Saeida was merely alive. She was the bear Hilde had tried to relocate to a Greek sanctuary the previous year, but the fear was that Saeida might have been too frail to even survive a darting and relocation to an improved enclosure within the zoo. The zoo staff and management had a deep emotional affinity for her, but their protective sensitivities meant that any management suggestions were shrouded in fear she would die. At times I felt that would be her preferable way out of quasi-purgatory. So she lay there. Alive.

The cell adjacent to Saeida's was the same size but had a sliding door leading to a grassy, tree-shaded outside area of about twice the size of the indoor space. We had installed a fringe of shade cloth roofing along the upper fence perimeter to protect against most of the blazing sunshine the tree didn't pacify. There had previously been a dog staying in that enclosure, but it had since been adopted and relocated. My suggestion that we take a sledgehammer and knock a hole in the partition wall, and let Saeida use both areas, thereby giving her access to the outside, was met with the expected look that there was a reason not to try being hatched. It was becoming increasingly evident that unconventional suggestions were making Dr Abbas edgy. The wall was not meant to have a hole in it, and the municipality would not approve such a breach. Any ideas I felt weren't too outrageous I would discuss with Waseem and Farah first before they would gently float them into the conversation in the next-door office. It was to dilute the sense of a pushy foreigner over-staying his welcome and stepping over boundaries, although I'm not sure it always achieved that aim. I was happy to be the sledgehammer wielder and sweeper; no staff member would need to be held responsible if the idea went horribly wrong ("the wall will collapse"; "the roof will collapse"; "the bear will die"). As with most ideas, after days or weeks of cautious planting, the plan would seed, root and become an option to be explored. Approval was granted.

There was little concern Saeida would react aggressively to having a few humans in her enclosure. For many years staff had simply cleaned around her as she slept.

Wielding a sledgehammer against a wall felt undeniably macho, especially against a wall that crumbled with each blow. Saeida barely raised her head at the thudding. Curious visitors lined up on the outside of the enclosure to watch the spectacle, point and laugh at the sweating foreigner. Waseem and the keeper staff took turns to help wield blows until the escape hatch had been battered through the bricks. Some refined hammering tidied up the hole's edges, and we stood aside to admire our handiwork among the rubble, plaster and yellow paint chips. We cleaned up our mess, and with Ahmed carrying a bowl of leafy treats, we crouched through the hole and took the few steps to the grassy outside. Within five minutes, the "blind" bear found the hole and was tentatively bumbling around in the outside area; for the first time in over 20 years. It was that simple. It seemed that despite her cataracts, she wasn't as blind as we had all thought, and her nose still worked like a well-serviced forage detector. She spent the evenings wandering around or curled up, sleeping in the weeds and grass. Days passed before she made any attempt to return to the inside. Again we could feel the sheer, addictive upwelling of joy and smug satisfaction from such a modest action.

The ISAW was quickly establishing itself as a facility for primary veterinary health care and animal adoptions among a small portion of the educated, middle-class society in Baghdad. The most significant source of the dozens of animals being boarded was still departing U.S. soldiers leaving behind adopted companions hoping they could be relocated to their respective homes in the U.S. Farah didn't have the heart to turn anyone away. At the same time, she was still suffering through countless, inane phone calls with city officials trying to explain the purpose of the facility and society. There seemed to be a constant, lingering threat that the building would be shut down and reverted back to a concession restaurant in the park. The concept of an animal welfare society seemed genuinely culturally unconventional and thus suspicious.

Using funds left by the 354th Civil Affairs via William, and combined with funds from a World Society for Animal Welfare (WSPA) grant, Farah was able to hire additional staff. Two veterinarians and a cleaner were employed to manage daily veterinary cases while Farah worked at the zoo. As the ISAW developed, amazingly compassionate Iraqi volunteers would arrive unannounced to play with the animals. It was baffling. That wasn't the popular perception of Baghdad society so often portrayed as lacking empathy towards animals. We loved it. Some volunteers would go further, adopting dogs, or their puppies, that had been left by soldiers who didn't have the means to fund the relocation of a befriended furry companion to the U.S.

There were also personnel from the CPA, or western press agencies who were bringing their new pets, or strays, to the zoo because it was the only veterinary option available to them. Many CPA staff who had adopted animals around the palace complex were also trying to save their "loved ones" in the wake of a Halliburton campaign to kill all cats. Where staff hid animals in their rooms, contractors would be sent into the portacabins to kill the animals while the staff were at work.

One enthusiastic journalist arrived at the zoo with a small transport cage filled with a bristling, volatile, dirty-white, scarred tomcat. She had lured it from a nearby dumpster after multiple failed capture attempts. It was clearly unimpressed at being captured, swinging clawed paws as it hissed and spat filthy vitriol at any of our efforts to open the cage door. "I want it vaccinated" she insisted. It didn't seem a consensual declaration. Her unwavering commanding of our veterinary intervention seemed at odds with the feline venom directed at us. She whispered sweet nothings to the feral cat as it tried to maul her through the cage. We conceded, primarily because we didn't want a reputation of turning away animals assumed to be in need. It also seemed more straightforward than arguing the matter. There was clearly no way the cat would cooperate. Farah and I decided the safest option, to ensure the cat would not escape, was to give the injection in the confines of a nasty little, diamond-mesh fronted holding enclosure. We locked the door behind us. The low ceiling meant we were hunched over as we navigated the options. I wore a set of thick leather gloves with the definite intention that once I had scruffed the cat on the loose neck skin, and pulled it out the cage, Farah could deliver the injection. The hissing and spitting of *Buddy* the tomcat were punctured by his angry, wailing howls. If looks could have killed us! I opened the cage door and tried to grab the cat's scruff, which was surprisingly easy, given the acrimonious reception. "It's ok Buddy. We love you Buddy" the lady repeated peaceably.

As I pulled the hostile tom out of his cage, he turned in his skin and launched a bite through the glove, through my thumbnail, piercing into the flesh. As his rear claws shredded my arms like a revolving cheese grater, I let go of the supercharged, scarred berserker. He leapt over my shoulder, defied gravity and ran horizontal and vertical white swirls of fury along the walls, mesh and low ceiling. "It's ok Buddy. We love you Buddy" the lady repeated placidly to her cuddly ball of amorous fluff, obviously only enraged by our wicked demeanour. "For fuck's sake! This thing is bloody insane! Honestly, why didn't you just leave it where it was?" I blurted out. "Don't listen to the nasty man Buddy. We love you. It's ok boy." I finally managed a lunge and a scruffing with enough control Farah could quickly inject the vaccine before I plunged the cat back in its box. The blood leaked out my thumb, soaking into the leather as the slashed stripes on my arms dribbled more blood. "It's ok Buddy. We love you. It's all over now. He won't hurt you." She thanked Farah as they left, with the cat seething and hissing from inside the rocking cage.

The year that passed had been a remarkable, emotional high. Adrenaline had pulsed through moments of excitement, elation, fear and despair. For months it had been a case of getting to the next month and evaluating how much impact another month could make; and how long I could test the Iraqi hospitality. Yet I was starting to seriously evaluate a zoo exit strategy. The intense sense of personal belonging to a unique group and setting was undiminished, but progress was slowing, and the novelty was waning. There was a familiar rhythm about it all. It was still exciting to see a ridiculously cute, startled, rhesus macaque baby immediately after its birth or to watch the animated antics of tiny porcupine babies attempting to suckle under the armpit of their reluctant mother. But I knew that if I was getting my thrills through a disturbingly curious fascination at porcupine breastfeeding, I had too much spare time. There was still an incredible amount to do, to change, but without financial investment and investment in dedicated staff training, we were only maintaining.

There was a combination of factors that were also starting to eat at my thoughts. I was becoming increasingly stressed by an empty bank account, no income and no clear job prospects beyond Baghdad Zoo. Added to that it was growing progressively noticeable that the administration office was frequently the comfortable refuge of jovial tea drinkers as Farah, Waseem and I would make almost all the daily headway with the same few committed, enthusiastic keeper staff. With a little nudging, support and guidance, they were the unfailing heart of work completed daily. Critically, Waseem had a comfortable relationship with many of the younger staff and for a few extra dollars from his own pocket, and with him leading from the front by working harder than anyone else, it was guaranteed each day's routine work would be completed without fail. The drive to improve and change the zoo hit dragging inertia when we weren't pushing it, which wouldn't have been a critical concern if we had any real authority between us to change gear. We didn't. I could feel frustration welling. Fortunately, Waseem remained my bromantic sounding board. While I offered out severely questionable free advice on understanding western women (credentials = zero), he would reciprocate by trying his hardest to soothe my frequently frayed patience.

Added to those reflections was the small matter of growing safety concerns. The risk of living in Baghdad was undoubtedly increasing. I wasn't pretending I was a local citizen. That I had a route out and family back in South Africa meant I needed to seriously weigh up the risks versus rewards. My fears for Farah compounded the issues. We had spent over a year working together almost daily, in a pressurised, emotionally testing, quite outrageously odd setting. It had been superb, and her energy, bravery, sharpness and cutting banter had coloured the year in a way I could never have imagined. Looks added a little more allure. That was obvious. As compulsively protective as she and others had been over me, it was impossible not to feel the same for her. She had embraced the foreign influx and initiatives openly, worked with so many of us, and was indelibly tied to CPA/U.S. Army operations. She had become a crucial link between the zoo and the CPA and U.S. Army. Those organisations felt they had found an Iraqi that was intelligent, motivated and understood both American and Iraqi behaviour. She was always the one they contacted if there was a need to convey a message to the zoo administrators. It raised her profile among the U.S. and Iraqi administrators and at checkpoints. She moved in and out of the Green Zone with fluidity and operated with a brazen, confident approach to life in Baghdad. Her father had spoken to her bluntly about her options going forward. He believed it was only a matter of when, not if, she would be abducted and/or killed. I had reached the same conclusion and dreaded it. Kidnappings for ransom, settling of grudges, or executions were increasingly commonplace in Baghdad. It wasn't uncommon for notes, with or without a bullet to be left on a desk or doorway to terrorise innocent people for any reason a coward may choose. Gangland law crept into neighbourhoods. The only realistic option for her survival was outside Iraq.

The final consideration, the looming hatchet, was the political timing. The coalition authorities had set a timeline for formally handing over governance of Iraq to the Iraq Interim Government at the end of July 2004. The Iraqi Governing Council, the temporary governance body (supposedly set up to represent Iraqi interests in the U.S. administered Iraq) we had heard so often maligned by Iraqi citizens, was dissolved on 1 June. The change was inevitable and unpredictable. How it would shape up was the discussion that dominated many conversations in the Green Zone. Fear of the *outside* was making the foreign enclave increasingly insular. Trinket markets had been set up near the CPA palace to allow contractors to buy Iraqi souvenirs and pirated action and porn DVDs ("Hey meester you want porrno? Good porrno," the children would say as they ran next to you) without having to actually engage with Baghdad. The Green Zone even had its first Chinese restaurant, serving fresh wontons, cold Corona beer and, depending on who was talking, waitresses doubling as prostitutes. But those discussions would quickly return to the "what next" discussions. When, back in 2003, Iraqi Information Minister, Comical Ali, bombastically stated about the Americans that "They dropped their forces there and now they are in a trap, and we will turn the trap to full and continuous drainage" he had perhaps been more prophetic than he ever intended.

In reality, many reconstruction projects and plans had been stalled by the growing violence. The political jostling for power to draft a new Iraqi constitution was brazen, often in conflict with Bremer's decided path, and led to fury and apathy about the entrenched corruption and partisan manipulation. The processes were also increasingly at the mercy of powerful, influential religious leaders. Lawlessness dominated. Electricity supply was hopeless. Perpetual fuel shortages led to interminable queues, with the increased risk of suicide bombers. There was the gnawing pessimism that the country would plunge into unrestrained sectarian revenge. More house raids. More traffic blockages. More mutual resentment. More unscrupulous opportunists. More virulent resistance. More Iraqis on Valium to sleep at night.

The American's administrative presence was to change from an occupying entity to an embassy. The blast walls, imposing concrete entrance points and boom gates were being built at junctions in roads adjacent to the CPA roads. It was coming. The bureaucratic cracks I had slipped through in the system were closing. Once the CPA was dissolved, those cracks would too. I would no longer be able to live in the Green Zone. My transport would be reclaimed, and my ID card nullified. I had no contract with anybody. I had no paperwork to legitimately be where I was. I was relying on the generosity of individuals and the swampy muddle that was the CPA, and on my ID card. The writing was on the wall for me to go.

In a case of impeccably discerning timing, Major Barringer triggered the imagination. He suggested to Farah that he could facilitate an educational opportunity at Cheyenne Mountain Zoo in Colorado Springs in the U.S. He had seen she was a sponge for veterinary knowledge, had an affinity for the skills needed to progress and worked tirelessly with members of his team. He was adamant such an experience would be a professional boost. He lived in a town near to the zoo and set about investigating the externship opportunity. We discussed concerns that had been infiltrating my thoughts. To him, it was simple. He suggested that I also take the chance to spend time developing skills and experience. I could become a little verruca on her opportunity. Farah and I had gelled over the year; perhaps we would survive a little travel too. Funding it would be another matter, but the prospect of the adventure seemed foolish to ignore. We mulled over the logistics in our own quiet times. There was no need to spark up rumours of a secret relationship or nefarious U.S. military connections. Compounding the tension was trying to navigate the guilt that we would leave Waseem in Baghdad. He had been such a revelation as a forthright, humble, decent, generous person that the only way to think of it was that we were abandoning a close friend to a war zone. The memory of Waseem giving William his leather jacket off his back because William had innocently complimented Waseem on it (Waseem vociferously refused any other outcome) was only one example of his selflessness. The selfish consolation was knowing that as long as Waseem was at the zoo, he would undoubtedly fight to maintain the improving standards and hold the established protocols in place.

Checkpoint detonation.

Headless Saddam greets nobody the Baath Party HQ.

Hello. I am Salman. Lions. Tigers. Beers.

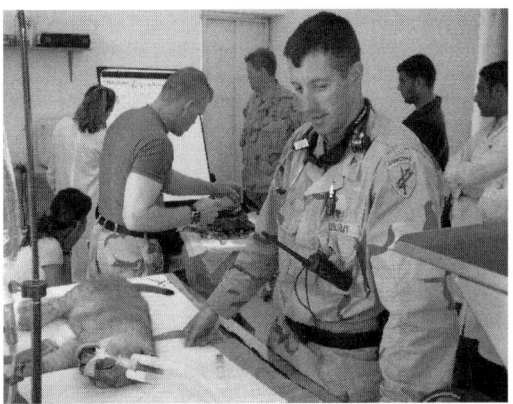

The exceptional public health team, from the 425th Civil Affairs Battalion, demonstrate surgical techniques. The lion cub is less impressed.

The US Army and Iraqi veterinarians cooperatively hunt for a sweat gland tumour. (Photo: US National Archives USAF)

(Photo: Sofa Salesman)

CHAPTER 16

It felt like the obsessive planning, sweating, cursing and heavy lifting had finally aligned to a single day; lion moving day! We had a new, enormous lion enclosure at Baghdad Zoo thanks to U.S. Army funding and the efforts of the contractor's team. We could have lions moaning out staccato, rasping demands simultaneously from either side of the zoo. The fencing was high and sturdy enough to stop a pride of pole vaulting lions escaping. Among the shade of Eucalyptus trees, a series of wooden platforms stood next to and above a small, door-less room. The new occupants could climb, scratch and retreat into hiding if they wanted too. A large plunge pool was filled with fresh, clear water which overflowed somewhat unintentionally into a muddy, weedy wallow. A large new, basic holding building was completed with sliding gates and several separation rooms to help keepers and veterinarians manage daily activities. Every aspect had been designed to be simple to operate and maintain, difficult to break, easy to clean and safe for keepers to work in. To remind us we couldn't win every debate - the floor was painted with a layer that was as slippery as ice when freshly mopped. The final product wasn't technically advanced, and it didn't all go exactly according to plan, but given the construction and finishing materials available in Baghdad, we knew it was functional. The lions could live out a healthy existence.

Early on the morning of the 25th July the small assorted convoy of modified Humvees rolled into the palace compound. On days when we felt our action was about moving animals into a better situations, irrespective of how quick it would be, there was always a palpable, stimulated camaraderie. There was an undeniable and addictive energy of constructive common purpose. The move had to start shortly after daybreak to ensure completion before the day's increasing heat made it physiologically unsafe for the cats to be drugged. The lions paced back and forth along the fence line as the doves cooed out the familiar gentle background tune. The rumble of fighter jets flying overhead was less subtle. Sergeant First Class Tommy Borton had arrived with his squad of familiar, ever-reliable faces. They had enthusiastically agreed to our request for help with the transfer. Major Sam Barringer remained on telephone standby in case we needed his veterinary advice. His instructions had been clear; we plan out the details, inform Borton, and the squad will execute the plan.

Soldiers started offloading the cargo of stretcher cots and rehydrating drips. Dickey and I used chunks of bloody meat to lure as many lions as possible into the holding cages while Waseem and Farah worked on mixing drugs and filling darts. The plan was quite simple. Dart the lions with immobilising drugs (Zoletil), vaccinate them, and then fit in an intravenous catheter for a drip. The lions would each have an empty, trimmed cloth sandbag pulled over their face as a makeshift blindfold (some animals do not close their eyes when chemically immobilised – the blindfold helps protect the eyes and reduces visual stimulation). The feet were to be wrapped together with duct tape as a precaution in case the lions woke up during transportation on the back of the Humvees. With that completed, each lion would be loaded onto a stretcher and heaved onto the load bin of a Humvee. Between the additional soldiers and Ali and Ali (keepers from the zoo), there were plenty of helping hands. Of course, given the location, a small cluster of soldiers from the resident Arkansas National Guard and labourers gathered to spectate and commentate. The soldiers wanted to get their last chance lions-in-Baghdad fix.

Except for a few darts bouncing out of the lions, and the last two lions, including Brutus, being wise enough to avoid entering the holding building, the first activities went like clockwork. That is except for the one confused lion whose tail Dickey needed to drag between the bars to get the lion close enough for Waseem to hand-inject a top-up Zoletil dosage. The lions were heavy enough to make carrying the stretchers at least a four-man job; sometimes with an extra pair of hands to stabilise a wobbling side. The initial batch of drugged lions was loaded into their allocated Humvees for a ride out the checkpoint, past the stretches of concrete blast walls, new fences and coils of razor wire. A shortcut accessible to soldiers led us past the crossed swords parade ground, out into the public road adjacent to Al-Zawra Park and back into the zoo grounds. The lions slept peacefully. It was a curious mix in the Humvees; mounted machine guns, young Iraqi veterinarians, soldiers with handguns available in case of a lion-related emergency, extra body armour and snoring, drooling lions. The precautions we had implemented to avoid some madness seemed a bit excessive, but the last thing we wanted was a waking lion somehow attacking someone or escaping and stumbling through suburban Baghdad. Batch one was offloaded under the excited watch of photojournalists and army reporting staff scurrying between the straining soldiers who carried the lion-laden stretchers. Drips were checked to see that the fluid was flowing and the lions were left in their new enclosure, with zoo staff, to begin recovery.

The morning activities and reconfigured plans rolled onwards until Brutus and his mistress of the day finally succumbed to their darts. They had refused to enter the holding building and made a concerted effort to outwit and frustrate Waseem by avoiding any positions he settled into for darting. Both animals were big enough to need six stretcher-bearers apiece. As enormous as Dickey was, even he paled into comparison with the weight of a sleeping adult male lion. It was also a chance for the veterinarians to fit in a quick close-up dental check; those pointy weapons that are humbling in their own rights. We cleaned up the debris from the morning and drove out from the palace compound for the last time – at the time it felt fitting it was on the back of U.S. Army Humvees with soldiers.

We couldn't quite believe we had finally pulled off the move. It was exhilarating and anti-climactic at the same time. The context felt bigger and wilder than us. But the task of the day was done. Finished. A CNN journalist enjoyed the novelty of the event, reporting on how much progress had taken place in the year since last visiting the zoo. To give an idea of the sentiment aimed towards the lions, Stars and Stripes newspaper reported -

'The move has drawn mixed feelings from soldiers at Forward Operating Base Warrior.
"Their home now is six times bigger than what they had here," said 1st Lieutenant Gorden Gregson of the 1-153rd's Headquarters and Headquarters Company. "It's cleaner, cooler and much nicer." But, he said, that doesn't take away a feeling of loss. "I look at our babies' empty room and get that sad feeling," Gregson said.

After more than a year of hoping, arguing and negotiating for a solution, we stood around shaking hands and grinning. It was so simple in the end. The lions would finally have what we felt was a reasonable space to roam and chase each other in. They had enough trees they could claw and attempt to climb, and a large enough pool they could all enjoy bathing and wrestling in, or fouling with food and crap. I was happy to no longer be the one to retrieve the chewed, anaemic donkey heads the lions seemed to enjoy storing in their palace pools. A conscious decision was initially made to not actively promote the history of the lions to the public through signage or generating publicity. It was agreed to avoid any potential retribution someone may have wanted to exact on the lions as vengeance against their former "boss", Uday Hussein. In Kabul Zoo, the iconic lion, Marjan, had suffered severe disfigurement from a grenade attack. The grenades were thrown at Marjan by an irate man in retribution for Marjan killing the man's brother days earlier when he had climbed into the enclosure to stroke Marjan's lioness companion.

The following day it almost seemed surreal to see those same lions, free of the chemical shackles of drugs, basking in the dappled sunlight on the wooden platforms. It was also the same day Brigadier General Hammond, in his role as assistant commander of the 1st Cavalry, visited the zoo to inspect the Division's contribution. Beyond the usual formalities of the physically imposing General and his entourage of body-armour laden staff sitting stiffly to meet Dr Abbas, it was suggested by soldiers familiar to us that he meet Farah, Waseem and me in the adjoining room. We had walked the zoo with him on previous occasions, but on this day we decided Farah should be the only one to accompany him. She was energetic, Iraqi, persuasive and had opinions to share. Hammond welcomed the opportunity. We wanted him to know what had been delivered and what was still envisaged. As they toured the zoo, Farah proudly showed off the progress made to the genuinely surprised General. He hadn't previously seen the new aviary, the new cheetah enclosure, the new lion enclosure, the blind bear's outdoor option or the old tiger's renewed enthusiasm for eating and bathing. He noted the horse husbandry advancements made by troops under his command, working with the Iraqi jockeys. All the while Farah explained the progress, the cooperation between Iraqis and foreigners and the new ambitions. A lack of funding was always a stumbling point for us. We wanted to create a new, large area for the two younger bears based on the basic template used for the new lion enclosure. It was always going to be step-by-step improvements rather than under the banner of a grand, master plan. We believed firmly that the appropriate progression for the cavalry involvement in the horse initiative would be an equestrian centre. The cavalry had the available expertise to oversee the project. Maybe they had the funds too? Farah also described the lingering bitterness around the shooting of the tiger in 2003 and lack of apology by the battalion concerned. Hammond was visibly frustrated at the tiger situation. It may have sounded trivial in the context of broader Baghdad, but he recognised it was about respect, dignity and an opportunity to be seen to be making amends for an unresolved mistake. He made it known he felt the lack of resolution by the U.S. Army was unacceptable and violated their commitment to build cooperation. Farah had laid out all the cards. The General picked them up. They returned to the office.

Hammond's response shocked us. Farah and I were leaving Iraq the next day. After so much protracted struggle and political navigation to make progress, the simplicity of his commitments took us by surprise. The 1st Cavalry would fund and ensure the completion of a new bear enclosure. The 1st Cavalry would replace the shot tiger with another tiger and ensure it had an area to live in positively comparable with the new lion enclosure. He also apologised to Dr Abbas for the U.S. Army's handling of the tiger shooting. His final pledge was that the 1st Cavalry would work with the horse staff to fund and build an equestrian centre in Al-Zawra Park. With that news still resonating among us, he and his body armour laden entourage mounted up in convoy. The roof turret gunners checked their weapons. The Humvees rolled on out of the zoo. Just another day. The atmosphere in the office was electric with excitement. Tea time!

The inevitable arrived. Handing back the keys to the black SUV that had served so reliably was deflating. I was a pavement-plodding pedestrian again. Gone was the false sense of grandeur I relished as I drove around the Green Zone with my bloodied boxes of lion food, three music CDs and a functioning air conditioner. I knew that soon the almighty lanyard and its lifesaving identification badge of the

Green Zone junkie would be meaningless except, like my deck of *Most-wanted Iraqis* playing cards as a token of "I was there". The palaces would be out of bounds. Checkpoints would be an impermeable barrier to entry, manned by unfortunate, faceless, visibly overheating Americans and Iraqis.

There was a curiously deep desire to absorb the final palace dinner in a ballroom surrounded by soldiers and bulky, moustachioed military contractors I didn't know. Suddenly it was a novelty again, like when I arrived. I felt disconnected. This time I knew it was all over. The excitement had run its course. Lawrence had been correct when he assured me I needed to enjoy the experience as long as it lasted because the outside world seemed comparatively regular and bland.

For Farah, it was a night of choked emotion and excitement at home. She was leaving her family behind in Baghdad. She was leaving her friends, dogs, ISAW, the zoo, her city, her history, the danger and her country behind. There was too much to contemplate. Her face was wet with tears. The familiar would be replaced by barrages of the unknown. We would leave to South Africa and then fly to the U.S. Two new countries for her. How would she be treated as an Iraqi? Would we see William again? We were leaving together. That brought relief and added fear of the unknown. And of course, that would fan more rumours.

The following morning, 27 July, Farah had organised for a close friend to drive us to the airport. They collected me at the palace, and we made our way to the zoo for the last time. The choking emotion of knowing we would not return, grew to an unanticipated visceral intensity. It was awful and nauseating. I felt overwhelming guilt that we were leaving Waseem behind. Dr Abbas was generous with gifts and goodbyes. Ahmed, our father figure and supplier of decadent quantities of food treats until the end, made claims he would resign and leave too, in an attempt to make us feel better. The staff gathered, and Farah joked with them as she fought, to the point of a pounding headache, to hold her visible emotions at bay.

"Hello! I am Salman. Lion, Tigers, Beers. Thirrrty two yirrss. Good! Very good!" Salman grinned as we shook hands. The *Ma'a salaamas* complete with cheek kisses and handshaking seemed to be on repeat. We knew we needed to get into the car to avoid melting into blubbering messes. It was like a mushy swell of stress and emotional investment and angst wanted to scupper any dignity at the exit by pouring out. Finally, we exited the zoo again and the self-indulgent moping mood hung in silence as we merged into the highway traffic. We were in a regular vehicle driving at a regular speed. When we drove close to the back of a slow-moving Humvee convoy, I felt the tensing up as a turret-mounted soldier gesticulated furiously and mouthed at us to "back the fuck away", helping us understand by directing his gun at us.

Baghdad International Airport was the end zone. No drama. No excitement. Just the anticlimactic lull of us people-watching baseball cap-wearing contractors and suited businessmen. Clunk went the exit stamp. Done. Nagging thoughts clung on. What would play out in the increasingly dangerous city we were leaving behind? What about Farah's family? What about the staff? Did we really help those animals or prolong gloom? Did we genuinely help anyone? It felt sickening to be leaving the fuel of our camaraderie behind. The questions contrasted with the precious distilled memories of almost compulsive generosity and hospitality, cutting black humour, dignity under duress and the unwavering resilience of many Iraqis we knew or had met.

The extreme heat snuck in a last assaulting scorch as we boarded the aircraft to Jordan. We had survived. Tea time!

EPILOGUE – BEYOND 2004

Sixteen years have passed since I was last driven out under the grand arch of Baghdad Zoo. Memories of that eccentric year still flicker into thoughts almost every day. It has been a mostly unwinnable challenge to match that combination of energy, thrill, anxiety, despair, pressurised camaraderie, perceived sense of relevance and utter bliss of life being lived by the hour in such a unique setting. Fortunately, as years accumulate and rogue ear hairs start to test conventional grooming, the cravings for chaos mellows. Slightly. Now there is still plenty of joy in quietly reminiscing rather than needing to chase that rush. It helps that seven years after we left, Farah and I married. So in hindsight and the absence of a romance gene, any excursion into memories of burning lion poo, stealing back Saddam's horses or Lawrence saying "you may like her" also evokes recollections of an unpredictable, unknown-at-the-time, unconventional, extended courtship.

The zoo survived the way Iraqis we encountered usually did, with a streetwise grit that is both admirable and unnerving to the uninitiated. Predatory government bureaucracy, conspiratorial politics and the creative infusion of a commission into every financial transaction were and are the norm. Yet stubborn individual resilience still found a way to advance the recovery. Any improvements were lubricated through the system with sugary tea, lamb fat and rice, and the type of streetwise social networking that is usually grounded on wit, a bold moustache and a well-placed friend of a relative. Daily functioning depended on government funding. That required hard-won signatures; and rubber stamping. Dr Abbas had his ways.

Daily animal welfare relied on a few compassionate veterinarians (some more eager than others), and earnest, animal-loving individuals that still covered the workload of those crafty municipality discards better skilled at work avoidance. The significance of these persevering individuals is best understood in context. Travel between work and home was dangerous, and the consequences potentially alarming. Between 2006 and 2008 freshly agitated sectarian fighting flared. The Iraq Body Count recorded 1 683 *violent* deaths in Baghdad in January 2007 (by comparison the official total at the Office of National Statistics of *all* registered deaths in inner London for the same period was 1 758).

Mid-summer temperatures touch 50°C. There is very little satisfaction in scraping and washing out poo, urine and food remains. Whether one did it well or not, the salary is the same. The motivation was either personal pride, a small salary, some fear of the boss, camaraderie or love and an emotional connection with the animals. For some, it was all of those combined. Many of those we knew left over the years and were replaced by new workers; some committed, some less so. Ahmed, who was until recently in charge of the food supply, enjoyed so much pride from his animals staying well fed. He has recently retired after decades of service. Jaboory, almost blind and seemingly ancient and fragile, continued to care for his pelicans until he finally retired. Other keepers, including Sa'ad and Akram endured for many more years despite chronic health problems. Another left the zoo, joined the police force where he was jailed for a year, before returning to the zoo. "Hello! I am Salman. Lion, Tigers, Beers. Thirrrty two yirrss. Good! Very good!" ceased forever when he was killed in a car bomb explosion.

Farah, through the help of the networks in Jordan

and the U.S., had relocated or rehomed more than 40 dogs, mostly to soldiers who had deployed home. Meticulous logistical planning and some generous goodwill meant the majority of the moves played out efficiently to smiling American owners with excitable Iraqi pets. When it became apparent Farah would be leaving to pursue the externship opportunity in the U.S., the transition to her family managing the ISAW was crucial to its survival. Farah's family started to become integral in the daily management of the ISAW. Their compassion for the animals was unwavering. Both her parents and her younger brothers took on the roles of liaising with soldiers, logistical facilitation and ensuring each animal received the appropriate veterinary treatments and vaccinations.

In the year beyond Farah's leaving Baghdad, her parents negotiated tirelessly with the municipality to sustain the efforts of the society. It was a relentless skirmish to endure the local political, financial and operational obstacles. As the security situation in the city deteriorated towards fractured factional wars, the day-to-day management of the society became increasingly difficult. The final animals had been rehomed (two more consignments of animals were rehomed by her family and the network to U.S. soldiers after Farah's departure) by the time the municipality dealt the headquarters its death blow. ISAW was run part-time from the family house until the security circumstances within Baghdad meant even that was untenable.

I have been fortunate to stay in periodic contact with veterinarian Wasseem who spent many more years in the cauldron. His unique brand of affable determination and industriousness seemed to enable him to navigate persistent misfortunes and trials. In 2010 he replaced Dr Abbas as director of the zoo until later leaving the country temporarily. Dr Abbas returned to the post. Some of the news was unexpectedly positive, at other times the gnawing cynicism about certain characters was well-founded. Our optimistic attempts at accountability at least enabled a temporary, structured buying system and momentum during the initial turnaround in the zoo's fortunes. There was allegedly some delight among administration individuals that Farah's and my pedantic ledger entries had finally been weathered. Our departure meant the financial management could resort to the longstanding natural ecology.

In the fleeting stability and political implosion, an unlikely, incredible transformation continued during periodic bursts of activity. Al-Zawra Park, where the zoo is located, was revived into a vibrant island of visitors, manicured lawns and flower beds, rejuvenated trees and lakes cluttered with psychedelically coloured paddle boats. The zoo looks noticeably better off than when we left, and it has grown in popularity with families. There have been striking face-lifts to some areas, and the lavish landscaping and reinvigorated gardens could be mistaken for those of a tropical hotel. Geese, ducks, pelicans and flamingos strut and flap in the refurbished ponds. An alligator house with a stark, large, clean, tiled pool was built. Grassy paddocks were renovated for gazelles and zebras. When compared with the zoo's prewar history, intervention in that little world changed the welfare trajectory for the positive.

Superficial changes are more accessible to implement than changing entrenched approaches. Like many zoos globally, there are undeniable, glaring shortcomings, particularly technical and philosophical. Its primary purpose is still amusement, not yet formal education or wildlife conservation. The scope for improvement remains immense, and the concerns understandable. It is still a zoo in Iraq, and long-term planning requires stability and vision beyond survival. Some prison-like cells and the tiny, standalone bird cages were unfortunately repopulated. In that respect, among others, we failed. It was much easier for the zoo management to resume informal supply sources than develop international exchange relationships. It wasn't the only unwelcome news. In 2007 a video posted on YouTube showed lions launching out of their holding building and killing two unsuspecting donkeys. The donkeys were released into the enclosure by zoo staff at the urging (and bribe) of visiting U.S. Army soldiers. It wasn't a surprising revelation given the number of times we had been urged (under the pretext of encouraging natural behaviour) and refused to satisfy that carnal bloodlust. There have also been some peculiar interviews posted online that have been creative with facts. One, with a staff veterinarian who didn't work at the zoo in 2003, claimed the zoo's tiger was shot "to get rid of him" because it displayed Iraqi characteristics and attacked Americans whenever it saw them. It was a similar time, roughly the peak of the 2006 sectarian cruelty, when an email arrived from a former acquaintance at the Coalition Provisional Authority palace – an invitation to a CPA reunion party in Washington D.C. It seemed so tone-deaf to what the CPA had left behind it was genuinely hard to fathom how they perceived their legacy. Back at the zoo, there was also the shipment in 2009 of surplus captive monkeys and a chimpanzee from Puerto Rico to Baghdad Zoo. The facilities in Baghdad were not appropriate, and the old-school zoo tragedy of taunting and feeding by visitors is a persistent concern.

Yet it wouldn't be Baghdad if there weren't also occasional flares of heart-warming redemption among the depressions, mini-successes, debris and inertia. Crucially for the zoo, there were intermittent injections of quality veterinary and husbandry expertise and financial aid, usually from that bizarrely improbable philanthropist, the U.S. Army. Some changes have been remarkable. After Farah's and my departure in 2004 the 1st Cavalry Division's Horse Cavalry Detachment continued to train and equip the small contingent of staff caring for the recovered presidential horses. After contact with Staff Sergeant Robert Bussell, who had become a mainstay in supporting the horses, a civilian in North Carolina, Ed Littlefox Copeland, set up a charitable website (Tack for Iraq) to source equipment and supplies for the horses. A small flurry of donations arrived from individuals and corporations. They were channelled through Dr Cynthia Baker of the University of Florida Racing Lab, to veterinarian Captain Katherine Knake who had taken over the team that replaced the Horse Cavalry Detachment. There was also still sustained support for the zoo from Major Barringer and his energetic team in the 425th Civil Affairs veterinary battalion. The palace lions continued to flourish in their new paddock, between long periods of sleep and meals of donkey meat they were chasing each other through shaded pools and around large trees. The plans of the improved bear and tiger areas we had endlessly discussed still simmered, but with military personnel rotating back home, action and funding stalled.

Then in 2007, a bout of investment by the 1st Cavalry Division reinforced the support they had demonstrated with the horses and palace lions. It was enough to leverage additional support from the Iraqi government. Through the 15th Brigade Support Battalion and with leadership from Captain Amy Cronin and Sergeant First Class Herbert Mowery, they focused on adapting the former giraffe enclosure into an area for the bears to roam and on building a horse stable complex. The two bears, Samir from Luna Park and Wounded-Ass, that had suffered intolerably before rescue to the Baghdad Zoo in 2003, were released into the enclosure to finally enjoy each other's company, grass, pools, shade and space. For those of us who saw those release photos from Wasseem and Ahmed after having first encountered the wounded bears in atrocious cages, there was a deep flush of satisfaction at the change in fortune. The following month a 23-stall stable complex with a training paddock was opened in Al-Zawra Park to serve as a permanent facility for the rescued horse collection. It was an incredible news report given what we had imagined the first time we heard the horses had been stolen. Even though from the last report it appears that lingering torpor may have overcome the initiative again, the risks taken by a small team in 2003 in defiance of the naysayers, remains one of my favourite memories.

In 2008 the progress continued as North Carolina Zoo sustained training support for Baghdad Zoo veterinary staff. There was another visit by Iraqi veterinarians to zoos in the UK, and then a sketchy, stuttering communication link was established via the internet to connect to North Carolina State University veterinary resources. When it worked and while it lasted this provided an opportunity for Baghdad Zoo veterinarians to source insight into treating a wide range of conditions. It was also in 2008 that the U.S. Army and State Department collaborated with an exotic wildlife centre in North Carolina (not North Carolina Zoo) to relocate two young, sterilised tigers to Baghdad Zoo as compensation for Malooh, the tiger shot dead in 2003. It was controversial in the U.S. The intention was sound, just not the understanding of Baghdad and its politicking. Army units had previously tried and been unsuccessful in navigating the bureaucracy and logistical timeline of such a tiger move. Through the team led by Lieutenant Colonel Robert Sindler and Major Freddie Zink, it was finally made a reality. Despite the ethical debates, it was remarkable that successive commanders in an army attempted and then followed through on their promise to replace a tiger; five years later. With additional tigers sourced by the zoo management within Baghdad, and of course subsequent breeding, the zoo now has enough tigers to create a lethal football team. Change can be fast and slow.

The zoo resurrection similarly extended to the aquarium hall. In 2003 looters battered the displays, leaving the room strewn with smashed glass. It proved a compelling enough story to have even featured in a February 2008 U.S. Embassy cable released in the 2011 WikiLeaks deluge. The folklore of alcoholic bears had grown somewhat while fish in the aquarium received a special mention for reportedly insensitively sporting laser tattoos of the old Iraqi flag.

Perhaps most crucially of all, irrespective of the easy criticisms that could be levelled at the administrators, animal sourcing or remaining poor enclosures, it is essential to recognise the trajectory from the pre-war dismay visitors reported, through the looting, to recent years. Primary provisions for the animals are reliably supplied. The animals are dependably well fed and watered in comparatively clean surroundings. It is a safe, re-energized, engaging space for citizens to disconnect from the city. The challenge continues. The U.S. Army reportedly ceased supporting the zoo after the controversy surrounding persistent embezzlement of funding by an Al-Zawra Park manager. Baghdad Zoo still falls short of the operational and ethical standards for inclusion into the World Association of Zoos and Aquariums. Regardless, it now has some spaces for animals that far exceed those at highly rated western zoos in first-world economies. It was principally Iraqis and small, motivated teams in the U.S. Army with support from North Carolina Zoo that enabled this beyond our exit, and who deserve much of the credit.

Lawrence Anthony was invigorated by his time in Iraq. It fired his ambitions to waste even less time on tedious administration and leave an expansive, inspirational conservation legacy. Besides re-engaging with Zulu communities to enlarge Thula Thula Private Game Reserve and initiate additional projects, the experience at Baghdad Zoo was the catalyst to founding The Earth Organization, a global non-profit focused on wildlife conservation. In recent years a chapter of the organisation has also been active in helping desperate captive animals in Ukraine. He didn't need that new platform to explore more outlandish outlets for his energy, but it did lead to almost incomprehensible remote forest dinners with the henchmen of the roving cult/rebel militia/war criminals, the Lord's Resistance Army, to discuss northern white rhino conservation. Before his upsetting death in 2012, at the age of 61, he co-authored three books with his brother-in-law Graham Spence. Babylon's Ark recounted Lawrence's time in Baghdad. The Elephant Whisperer has been a best-seller translated into twelve languages, and The Last Rhinos documented his experiences related to the northern white rhino.

William Sumner's irksome over-achieving continued. Slowly realising the futility of his attempts as an American to master the more exceptional motor and intellectual skills of cricket, he found distraction in academia and enlisting into the active-duty U.S. Army. He completed his M.A. in Archaeology and Heritage. Recognising that was insufficiently gruelling enough while serving in Europe, he accomplished the customary next step, an arduous PhD in Biodefense. Adding parenting duties, marriage and co-authoring Saving the Baghdad Zoo to these, it is remarkable he had time to dabble in his day job; nuclear disablement, counter-proliferation and response to incidents of Weapons of Mass Destruction. Never one to shy away from his grooming duties, his moustache remained impeccable despite Army-related travelling through much of Europe and Africa's snowy, arid and tropical climates. After returning to the U.S. to fulfil responsibilities for the planning, coordination, and management of the Chemical, Biological, Radiological and Nuclear Response Enterprise, the Lieutenant Colonel joined his local Community Animal Response Team. Despite his fondness for white sneakers and science fiction, Farah and I know how privileged we are to have encountered William in such outrageous circumstances as the zoo. The memories of working together daily are treasured. We stay in regular contact.

Stephan Bognar returned to Cambodia to continue his conservation initiatives with the NGO WildAid. True to form, before long he was the CEO of the Maddox Jolie-Pitt Foundation. He was the only one of us that would ever be able to combine refined Men's Health elegance with delivering conservation, agricultural and women's empowerment enterprises in rural Cambodia. He also combined that with guest lecturing at universities in Australia and the U.S. His role in South-East Asia evolved into an advisory one for the U.S. National Parks Service before the lure of home had him return to Canada and the coffee brewing cafés of New York. He now consults on social welfare and empowerment initiatives in vulnerable communities, and forest stewardship. He is a fan of the WhatsApp voice message.

Mariette Hopley remains a dominant organising force. Her positive, uncompromising character and booming laugh at the zoo energised us at a time when we were holding the line. Her ability to cut through the bullshit and coordinate cooperation from strangers remains a lesson learnt. Somewhere between tourism enterprises, running oil spill-related logistics, directing a welfare task team on dog trafficking, financial investments, entrepreneurial businesses and actively championing many conservation causes she's worked in being a passionate mother. And that is merely this week.

Jackson Zee's gentle, cherubic demeanour was always a disarming façade for his unquestionable determination and passion for the welfare of animals. Within China and the U.S., he worked for numerous conservation NGOs and remains an animal welfare advisor to the IUCN's SSC Bear Specialist Group. To add to his veterinary degree, he also completed a PhD in Behavioural Ecology. He is currently the Director of Disaster Relief at Vier Pfoten.

Sam Barringer remains a modern-day, veterinary version of Action Man. He leads. Now a full bird Colonel in the U.S. Air Force, he is the commander of the 932nd Medical Group overseeing the deployment of over 500 medical personnel. I imagine he does that with ease between being a welfare/breeding/feeding consulting guru to the beef and dairy industry. After we last saw him in 2005, he left the Army for the Air Force and was deployed to Afghanistan as the Deputy Command Surgeon for the Nato training mission. His influence on Farah and me stretched far beyond Baghdad. In 2004 he facilitated a veterinary internship for Farah at Cheyenne Mountain Zoo in Colorado Springs – a zoo relatively close to home for him. Recognising the opportunity to steer my potentially drifting ways he organised that I head there too. His wife Joanie is the generous mothership that helped us settle into life at 1839m altitude, 15 000km north-west of Cape Town.

David Jones became synonymous with generating and coordinating emergency funding for welfare work in zoos in war zones. It will be an injustice to try to capture his wide-ranging animal welfare legacy in a paragraph like this, but needless to say, he was a critical component of the recovery – unassumingly hidden in the heavily forested North Carolina Zoo. Before his links to Baghdad Zoo, he had been integral in coordinating international efforts to stabilise the welfare conditions in Kabul Zoo, exposed following the U.S. invasion of Afghanistan. If there were a genuine League of Extraordinary Gentlemen, he would fit the bill. It is rare to meet such an accomplished man with such unassuming poise and generosity. He retired as the Director of the North Carolina Zoo in 2015 but remains the Chairman of the U.S. arm of the equine welfare charity, Brooke, among his many other pursuits. Farah and I both experienced his generosity first hand as he facilitated a veterinary internship in 2005 for her at North Carolina Zoo. I was fortunate to join that fantastic team (through the North Carolina Zoo Society) to assist with stabilising Kabul Zoo.

One of David Jones's most enduring legacies will undoubtedly be Wild Welfare (*http://wildwelfare.org/*), an NGO he founded with outstanding zoo experts to alleviate the suffering of animals in sub-standard captive facilities around the world. It is a staggering task. The sagas at the zoos in Kabul and Baghdad were in part a catalyst to initiate Wild Welfare. Its vision is simple and yet incredibly complex, "to end the suffering of captive wild animals around the world, ensuring full and sustainable protection is given to all animals in human care". If you only ever supported one charity in your life, and you were passionate about improving the living conditions of captive animals, this would be an excellent choice.

Bonnie Buckley continued her incredible support for the efforts of Farah and her family, to enable U.S. soldiers to adopt dogs they had unexpectedly bonded with during deployment to Iraq. Based in Massachusetts, Military Mascots was her endeavour to facilitate the relocation of dogs from Iraq. In 2007, despite significant personal challenges, she established Alternative Dog Daycare and Learning Centre, a facility that continues today.

Farah always had the impatience to seize any opportunity to discover life and absorb knowledge and experiences. The daunting world outside of the home and controlled, temperamental, oppressive Iraq was a radical step, and it took time to recalibrate. Sam Barringer and David Jones facilitated life-changing opportunities in the snowy mountains and subtropics of America. In the U.S. she was embraced by exceptional veterinarians and vet nurses at the Cheyenne Mountain and North Carolina zoos. To many people, she was the first Iraqi they had ever met. When the sun set on our year in America, she volunteered and then worked for three years at a frenetic, highly-effective animal welfare charity, The Animal Anti-Cruelty League, in Cape Town, South Africa. Years learning to live and mature as a vet in South Africa, Oman and in the United Arab Emirates, have continued to refine her skills and keep the threat of a tactical neuter a reality for me.

I too dabbled in Colorado and North Carolina Zoo, with a minor diversion to Kabul Zoo. Seven subsequent years in the timelessly beautiful wilds of Hluhluwe-iMfolozi Park in Zululand, South Africa, re-engaged that spirit of camaraderie I had felt in Baghdad. I documented working for the Endangered Wildlife Trust's African wild dog conservation initiative in *African Wild Dogs: On the Front Line*. Again there were remarkable people, reinforced by dedication, beer and humour that sacrificed so much, then for the reward of securing wildlife and wild spaces. Marriage to Farah, a new life in Oman and a timely opportunity in the desert of Sharjah have all resulted in this book chapter finally coming to an end; almost.

Iraq continues to be a country severely challenged by political instability, social trauma and individuals ready to wreak havoc. Yet within that context, there are remarkable people who show incredible dedication and compassion for animal welfare. Our lives are almost all linked one way or another to animals, and we are better for it. If you want to support animal or zoo welfare charities directly linked to work in Iraq, or closer to your home, get out the device that connects you to the internet. Investigate the options. Support action over slick marketing. Act. Improve lives. Cherish them. You'll feel better for contributing.

Samir's transition from Luna Park depravity 2003 to Baghdad Zoo recovery - 2007. (Photo: Wasseem)

GRATITUDE

Self-publication feels like an interminable undertaking that enforces nothing. There is no deadline, only the temptations of distractions. Opportunities and reasons to quit dominate your thoughts year-after-year. Will your cat walking across your keyboard for the seventieth time be the breaking point? I cannot claim credit for the decision to self-publish. The fifty-three agents and publishers who rejected this work unintentionally made it better, compelling me into re-writes to sharpen the text and emboldening a greater focus on the raw, rude truth rather than a conventional, saleable narrative. They fuelled my competitive desire to finish this. Amazon provided the platform.

Without the support structure of traditional publishing, or any budget, one has to rely on friends, family and a network of unsuspecting cheerleaders (who often, by merely avoiding saying "that's a bad idea", are offering encouragement).

James Dick, a passionate English teacher and father, marked the original, hefty manuscript with dedication and speed while on a beach holiday with his family. I will always be grateful for his commitment and feedback. William Sumner and Graham Spence both dedicated time to review manuscripts for accuracy, and their ongoing comments and insights of incidents helped confirm what often seemed like bizarre truths. My brother, Gareth Whittington-Jones, helped immeasurably polish the final manuscript and validated my desire to leave in the abundance of contextual swear words. Blood is thicker than water. "Brummy" Bramwell was one of those cheerleaders whose optimism (even in the face of early-onset baldness) made completing this endeavour seem obviously doable. His entrepreneurial obsessions and passion for helping stray animals are examples of people with good-hearts that every society needs! He was also the crucial link to Robert Durrant (Graft Art & Design), who created the outstanding cover and navigated my countless queries and suggestions with the patience of a saint.

Farah, now my wife, has been a part of this story since we met in 2003. Much of what needs to be said, or implied, is already in the book. Most importantly, she enabled the space for me to get this completed over many years. She will know what that means to me. It has been about five years of me saying, "I think I just need another day or two." I hope this accurately characterises the remarkable start to our enduring friendship (and much more, of course).

Finally, but most significantly, are my parents. They have supported all of us four sons, perhaps more than they will ever realise. Their nurturing energy spent over many decades and ongoing support has made it possible for us to pursue our paths, despite the many grey hairs our decisions may have triggered. I am forever in their debt for that freedom.

REFERENCES

Baghdad lions to be relocated to South Africa; www.smh.co.au (Associated Press, 2003)

Baghdad's lions making a comeback in Africa; www.iol.co.za (Independent Online, 2003).

CNN Late Edition with Wolf Blitzer - Transcripts; CNN International (Cable News Network LP, 2004)

CRS Report for Congress; L. Elaine Halchin (Government and Finance Division, 2005)

Human Interest and Humane Governance in Iraq: Humanitarian War and the Baghdad Zoo; Alison Howell and Andrew W. Neal (Journal of Intervention and Statebuilding, 2012)

Humanitarian Operations Update – 05 May 2003 (Humanitarian Operations Centre, 2003)

IntelCenter Terrorism Incident Reference (TIR): Iraq 2000-2005; IntelCenter (Tempest Publishing, 2008)

Iraqi Arabians Rebound with Military and Civilian Aid; Stacey Reap (The Chronicle of the Horse, 2005)

JIC Assessment, 15 October 2003 (Joint Intelligence Committee, 2003)

JIC Assessment, 17 December 2003 (Joint Intelligence Committee, 2003)

JIC Assessment, 20 May 2004 (Joint Intelligence Committee, 2003)

JIC Assessment, 21 July 2004 (Joint Intelligence Committee, 2003)

JIC Assessment, 26 May 2004 (Joint Intelligence Committee, 2003)

JIC Assessment, 26 November 2003 (Joint Intelligence

Committee, 2003)
JIC Assessment, 28 April 2004 (Joint Intelligence Committee, 2003)
JIC Assessment, 30 June 2004 (Joint Intelligence Committee, 2003)
JIC Assessment, 31 March 2004 (Joint Intelligence Committee, 2003)
JIC Assessment, 7 January 2004 (Joint Intelligence Committee, 2003)
My Year in Iraq; L. Paul Bremer & Malcolm McConnell (The New York Times, 2006)
New Zoo Medical Equipment Updated; Chad D. Wilkerson (U.S. Department of Defense, 2003)
Refugee lions on their way 'home'; www.mg.co.za (Mail & Guardian, 2003)
Saddam lions head for Africa; www.bbc.co.uk (BBC, 2003)
Saving the Baghdad Zoo; Kelly Milner Halls & William Sumner (Greenwillow Books, 2010)
The Iraqi Marshlands: A Human and Environmental Study; Emma Nicholson and Peter Clark (Politico's Publishing, 2003)
The Mammals of Iraq; Robert T. Hatt (University of Michigan, 1959)
Tigers Return to Baghdad; Rob Nordland (Newsweek, 2008)
Uday Hussein's Lions Find Home in Africa; Reuters (The New York Times, 2003)
US Tank Shell Hits Media Hotel; Simon Jeffery and Jason Deans (The Guardian, 2003)
Welcome to the Green Zone; William Langewiesche (The Atlantic, 2004)